Paradise Is Now

Paradise Is Now

Decrypting the Secret Cosmology
of Isaac Newton's *Principia*

CYNTHIA KRAVITZ

Foreword by RAVI RAVINDRA

RESOURCE *Publications* • Eugene, Oregon

PARADISE IS NOW
Decrypting the Secret Cosmology of Isaac Newton's *Principia*

Copyright © 2024 Cynthia Kravitz. All rights reserved. Except for brief quotations in critical publications or reviews, no part of this book may be reproduced in any manner without prior written permission from the publisher. Write: Permissions, Wipf and Stock Publishers, 199 W. 8th Ave., Suite 3, Eugene, OR 97401.

Wipf & Stock
An Imprint of Wipf and Stock Publishers
199 W. 8th Ave., Suite 3
Eugene, OR 97401

www.wipfandstock.com

PAPERBACK ISBN: 979-8-3852-1408-2
HARDCOVER ISBN: 979-8-3852-1409-9
EBOOK ISBN: 979-8-3852-1410-5

Permissions

"East Coker," "Burnt Norton," "Little Gidding," "The Dry Salvages" from *Four Quartets* by T.S. Eliot. Copyright © 1936 by Houghton Mifflin Harcourt Publishing Company, renewed 1964 by T.S. Eliot. Copyright © 1940, 1941, 1942 by T.S. Eliot, renewed 1968, 1969, 1970 by Esme Valerie Eliot. Used by permission of HarperCollins Publishers, and with permission of the Estate of T.S. Eliot, Faber and Faber LTD.

Excerpt from John Keats, "Ode on a Grecian Urn." Library of Congress.

Pythagorean theorem image. With thanks to Michael Hardy.

Isaac Newton, "Nova cubi Hebraei tabella" © The Fitzwilliam Museum, University of Cambridge.

"Can Origin of the 2400-year cycle of solar activity be caused by solar inertial motion?" With thanks to Ivanka Charvatova.

Issac Newton, "The Fitzwilliam Notebook" © The Fitzwilliam Museum, University of Cambridge.

NOAA Tides and Currents website. With thanks to Richard Ray, NASA Scientific Visualization Studio.

For Mel and Yvonne, Peter, and Jonah
With love

"And all is always now."

—T. S. Eliot, "Burnt Norton," *Four Quartets*

Contents

Foreword ix
Acknowledgments xiii
Introduction xv

BOOK I. ANTIQUITY
Chapter I. The quest to locate an unchanging and immovable referent in the natural world by which it might be possible to rigorously define motion and change; the quest to locate the site of Divinity's Presence in the natural world 3
Chapter II. Pythagoras 8
Chapter III. The Pythagorean Crisis 33
Chapter IV. Archimedes 51

BOOK II. MODERNITY
Chapter V. Galileo Galilei 111
Chapter VI. Isaac Newton 153
Chapter VII. (Mis)reading the *Principia* in the wake of its publication 223
Chapter VIII. Albert Einstein 237

Afterword 275

References 285
Index 297

Foreword

I AM DELIGHTED TO recommend *Paradise Is Now: Decrypting the Secret Cosmology of Isaac Newton's* Principia, an intriguing and remarkable work by Cynthia Kravitz. By any measure Isaac Newton (1642–1727) was one of the greatest scientists in human history. His famous book *Philosophiae Naturalis Principia Mathematica*, briefly known simply as *Principia*, is justifiably regarded as the greatest scientific work ever produced. It integrated into one coherent whole diverse data and mathematical principles concerning the motion of material particles and gravitation. As the publication of Copernicus's *De revolutionibus orbium coelestium* in 1543 marked the beginning of the great Scientific Revolution, the publication of the *Principia* in 1687 marked its completion and the beginning of the modern scientific age. Indeed, Newton is often described as the inaugurator of the "Age of Reason." The poet Alexander Pope hailed him thus:

> Nature, and Nature's laws lay hid in night.
> God said, *Let Newton be!* and all was light.[1]

Throughout his life Newton was greatly interested in theological, chronological, and alchemical studies. It is estimated that he wrote some six million words on these subjects, a total far surpassing that of his writings in mathematics and physics. Much of this material, particularly that on alchemy, consists of the writings of others that Newton copied for his own use, but he also wrote books of his own on these subjects. He wrote books like *Observations on the Prophesies of Daniel, and the Apocalypse of St. John*, and *The Chronology of Ancient Kingdoms Amended*. He also wrote alchemical works. But none of these works were published during Newton's lifetime, except an Abstract of his *Chronology of Ancient Kingdoms (Abregé de la Chronologie)* was published in 1725, embroiling

---

1. Pope, "Epitaph," 336.

Newton, as with practically all of his other publications, in a great controversy. Newton himself seems to have hinted that his real interest lay in a wide and comprehensive knowledge that he hoped to acquire through alchemy and theology, and that he viewed his scientific studies only as amusing diversions. Here is a well-known remark that Newton made toward the end of his life:

> I do not know what I may seem to the world; but as to myself I seem to have been only like a boy playing on the sea-shore, and diverting myself in now and then finding a smoother pebble or a prettier shell than ordinary, whilst the great ocean of truth lay all undiscovered before me.[2]

Newton was a strong adherent of the *prisca sapienta*, an ancient wisdom that had existed among Priest-Scientists such as the Chaldeans in Babylonia, the Brahmans in India, and Moses and Pythagoras among the Hebrews and the Greeks. He believed that the ancients had possessed secret wisdom about the truths of nature; that this wisdom was now largely lost; that he, Newton, was one of the esoteric brotherhood extending back to ancient times, and that he was rediscovering and re-disclosing this knowledge in a new form, more mathematical than metaphysical or mythological. He regarded his scientific work to be in continuation of, and in harmony with, this ancient wisdom.

After Isaac Newton died in 1727, he left behind many notes, manuscripts, and correspondence dealing with alchemical and theological subjects. Fearing Newton would be seen as a heretic, his family and friends burned or hid some of his papers. Some of Newton's alchemical papers became public only in the 1960s. The well-known economist John Maynard Keynes concluded after examining Newton's alchemical papers: "Newton was not the first of the age of reason. He was the last of the magicians, the last of the Babylonians and Sumerians, the last great mind which looked out on the visible and the intellectual world with the same eyes as those who began to build our intellectual inheritance rather less than 10,000 years ago. . . . He regarded the universe as a cryptogram set by the Almighty."[3]

Cynthia Kravitz shows in her manuscript that Newton regarded his work very much in harmony with, and a continuation of, the ancient wisdom, but in a mathematical form. Newton had great admiration for

---

2. Quoted in Spence, *Observations*, 158–59.
3. Keynes, "Newton," 363–66.

many of the ancient sages and mystics, including the early Jews, Pythagoras, Democritus, Plato, Archimedes, and early Christians. Newton asserted that the cosmologies of all of these sages were examples of "that mystic philosophy which flowed down to the Greeks from Egypt and Phoenicia,"[4] which illustrated a very strong monist view in which every moment of time—past or future—is present in the eternal now, and every material particle is animated by the spirit, showing the indivisible presence of YHWH (*ego eimi*, I AM) in the material world. For Newton, the natural world was also permeated by a mysterious force: "The vital agent diffused through everything in the earth is one and the same/ And it is a mercurial spirit, extremely subtle and supremely volatile."[5]

Cynthia traces, with great scholarly expertise and numerous references, how the monistic view of the spirit pervading the material world has been largely ignored or opposed, but sometimes supported and reestablished, by subsequent significant philosophers and mathematicians. Both Galileo, who was celebrated by Einstein as "the father of modern physics and in fact of the whole of modern natural science,"[6] and Newton, whose work brought the Scientific Revolution to its culmination, were very interested in the reflections of the great sages mentioned earlier and very much believed that spirit is present throughout nature. For them the Universe was a sacred text. Galileo wrote, "Philosophy is written in this grand book, the universe, which stands continually open to our gaze."[7] And Newton remarked that wisdom and insight are "not only to be found in ye volume of nature but also in ye sacred scriptures."[8] For Newton, all of his scientific work was a hymn of glory in the praise of God, and his effort was to show the presence of Divinity in the natural world.

It is ironic that contrary to Newton's own understanding about the intimate and essential relationship between the Divine and the manifested cosmos, his work enhanced the later empirical science in which, as Cynthia remarks, the knowledge which Newton had regarded as Relative, Apparent, and Common was prized, and the knowledge which Newton had regarded as the Absolute, Mathematical, and True was lost. Following only the Relative, Apparent, and Common understanding of

---

4. Newton, MS Add. 3965.6:270r. Quoted in Guicciardini, *Reading the* Principia, 101.

5. Newton, quoted in Westfall, *Never at Rest*, 304.

6. Einstein, "Theoretical Physics," 164.

7. Galileo, *Discoveries and Opinions*, 237–38.

8. Newton, Keynes MS. 33, f.5v.

Newton's cosmology, further extended by Einstein's theories of relativity, the scientific understanding of cosmology is only externally verifiable physical cosmology bereft of the sacred. Physical theories concerning the static or the dynamic nature of the Universe are not about the dimension of the significance or the purpose of human existence.

Cynthia Kravitz has done a wonderful job, with remarkable scholarship, in pointing out the spiritual dimension in the cosmologies of the many ancient seers, really prophets in the domain of pristine wisdom, focusing on Newton. It is good to end this foreword with a remark attributed to Isaac Newton: "Live your life as an exclamation rather than an explanation."[9]

—RAVI RAVINDRA, professor emeritus of physics, of philosophy, and of religion at Dalhousie University, and former member of the Institute for Advanced Studies in Princeton

---

[9]. Bariso, "12 Brilliant Quotes."

Acknowledgments

THIS BOOK HAS BEEN a labor of love and I am grateful to the many people who have so generously offered their support and encouragement along the way.

Ravi Ravindra, thank you. I return again and again to your translation of the nineteenth *shloka* in the seventh chapter of the *Bhagavad Gita*: "At the end of many births, a wise person comes to Me, realizing that all there is *is* Krishna (Vāsudeva). Such a person is a great soul and very rare." You, Mahatma, are such a great soul. Thank you for leading the way.

George F. R. Ellis, John C. Mather, Paul Mendes-Flohr, Keith Ward, and Gerald Holton: thank you for your kind encouragement and tremendous support. I am deeply grateful.

And thank you also to the editorial team at Wipf and Stock Publishers: Matt Wimer, Emily Callihan, Elisabeth Rickard, Heather Carraher, and Karlie Tedrick. Your patience and helpful suggestions have made the publication process a pleasure.

Introduction

Isaac Newton's most famous work, his *Philosophiae Naturalis Principia Mathematica (Mathematical Principles of Natural Philosophy)*, or *Principia*, as it is commonly called, of 1687, was written in a secret code—a code that has remained uncracked to this day. This book cracks Newton's secret code. The cracking of Newton's secret code will have profound implications on our understanding of reality, even today. Contemporary physicists acknowledge that Albert Einstein's cosmology is incomplete,[1] and we will find that by cracking Newton's code, we will be able to complete Einstein's incomplete cosmology. Newton was a devoutly religious Christian, and by decrypting his secret code, we will discover how he had considered himself to have *proven* the existence of God's Presence in the natural world. Newton was an alchemist, and by decrypting his secret code, we will discover how he had considered himself to have accomplished the most sought-after goal in alchemy: to locate the philosopher's stone/the elixir of life. Cracking Newton's secret code will require of us no more than a grade school understanding of mathematics and of physics, and it will reveal to us the simplicity of a profoundly beautiful Universe. *And perhaps most significantly, cracking Newton's secret code will reveal to us the grand, underlying order that unifies all.*

Why should we think that Newton's *Principia* was written in a secret code?

Newton was an intensely private person, who was fascinated by secret codes: as a young man, he confessed petty sins in a secret code that remained uncracked for three hundred years. (The Fitzwilliam

---

1. "General Relativity," para. 82.

Notebook). And Newton was also deeply influenced by a Renaissance philosophy known as the *prisca sapientia*, or "wisdom of the ancients," which held that the ancient sages and mystics—including the ancient Jews, Pythagoras, Archimedes, and the early Christians—had possessed knowledge of "the great truths of nature," but that they had hidden their wisdom in secret codes, which require decrypting. As Gale Christianson reports in his biography of Isaac Newton:

> As an avid reader of old texts, Newton believed in a concept called the *prisca sapientia*, or wisdom of the ancients, a doctrine popular among certain scholars during the Renaissance. This doctrine held that the great truths of nature had been known to some of the most brilliant and morally upright thinkers of the distant past. . . . Not surprisingly, these men had hidden their knowledge of how nature works in symbolic language that, like a complex code, was extremely difficult to decipher.[2]

Newton spent his life studying the works of the ancient sages and mystics whose texts comprised the *prisca sapientia*.[3] (Indeed, at the time of his death, Newton left behind a staggering ten million written words—half of which exist as records of the acts of deep reading, and of exegesis, that he performed upon the writings of the ancient sages and mystics whose works he admired, and only about three million of which concerned his own mathematical and natural philosophy interests.)[4]

Newton studied the works of the ancient sages and mystics deeply, and he sought to know what they had known; he sought to know "the great truths of nature" that they had been said to have known. And scholars acknowledge that Newton considered himself to have rediscovered their ancient wisdom. We read that:

> Newton claimed to decipher what the Ancients meant when they spoke in code, because he had rediscovered the truths underlying their mysteries.[5]

And as biographer Christianson writes, "There is no doubt that Newton considered himself specially chosen to rediscover and expand the ancient

---

2. Christianson, *Isaac Newton*, 58.

3. As we will see, among the works of the ancient sages and mystics that Newton admired were those of the Jews, of Pythagoras, of Democritus, of Plato, of Archimedes, and of the early Christians.

4. Dry, "Isaac Newton's Papers," para. 11.

5. Iliffe, "Meaning of the *Principia Mathematica*," 172.

wisdom, thus becoming one of the few from each generation so blessed."[6] As we will see, Newton considered himself to be a sage among the ancient sages' ranks, and he too composed a cosmology that exists as secret, hidden wisdom, and that requires decrypting.[7]

What did the ancient sages and mystics know, and what did Newton believe that he had rediscovered?

The ancient sages and mystics were interested in understanding "the great truths of nature"—which included understanding the concept of *motion and change*. They had recognized that it would only be possible to rigorously define motion and change by defining it in relation to something that remained *unchanging* (with respect to itself) for all time, and which could therefore be considered to be *immovable*. But did such an unchanging and immovable object or entity actually exist in the natural world?

As we will see, locating such an unchanging and immovable referent in the natural world by which it would be possible to rigorously define motion and change was the quest of all of the ancient sages and mystics—and all had considered themselves to have found it. The ancients associated this unchanging and immovable referent with the site of Divinity's Presence in the natural world, and in locating it, they considered themselves to have found God. Newton, who believed that he had rediscovered their wisdom, also considered himself to have found the site of God's Presence in the natural world.[8]

---

6. Christianson, *Isaac Newton*, 58.

7. Newton believed that the wisdom that he had rediscovered had been possessed by (what he called) the "Priests anciently." In "Draft chapters of a treatise on the origin of religion and its corruption" of the early 1690's, Newton wrote, "And thence it was that *the Priests anciently were above other men well skilled in the knowledge of the true frame of Nature* & accounted it a great part of their Theology. The learning of the Indians lay in the Brachmans who were their Priests, that of the Persians in the Magi who were their Priests, that of the Babylonians in the Chaldeans who were their Priests. And when the Greeks travelled into Egypt to learn astronomy & philosophy they went to the Priests. *And what there was of the true knowledge of Nature amongst the Greeks lay chiefly in the brest of some of their Priests*" (Newton, "Draft Chapters," §f4v; my emphases). As we will see, Newton considered himself to be a Priest among the ranks of the ancient Priests, and he composed his *Principia* for (what he considered to be) other Priests.

8. Scholars acknowledge that ancient "Greek studies in mathematics overlapped with [natural] philosophical and mystical beliefs," and we will find that this is true in the cosmology of Newton as well (see "Arithmetic," para. 5).

Ours will be something of a detective story, for in order to decrypt Newton's secret cosmology, it will first be necessary to decrypt the secret cosmologies of the ancient sages and mystics whose works Newton had admired. (As we will see, the ancient sages and mystics embedded one another's cosmologies within their own cosmologies, even as they extended and deepened one another's cosmologies in breathtaking and inspired ways—and that in turn, Newton embedded their cosmologies within his own cosmology, even as he extended and deepened their cosmologies in breathtaking and inspired ways.)[9]

The cosmologies that we will encounter over the course of our explorations will reveal to us profoundly beautiful ways of seeing the Universe, and ourselves.[10] Let us begin.

---

9. Scholars report that Newton's "General Scholium," or general explanatory notes, to his *Principia* was written in matryoshka dolls form (we read that Newton constructed the General Scholium to the *Principia* "much like a Russian doll"), and we will find that this form is common to the main body of Newton's *Principia* as well, as Newton embedded the ancient sages' cosmologies within his own cosmology, even as he extended and deepened their cosmologies in breathtaking and inspired ways (see "Newton's General Scholium," para. 1).

10. Indeed, we will find that the ancients' standard of truth was different than our own (modern) standard of truth. Not only did the ancients seek to convince their readers intellectually—and as we will see, their logic was impeccable—but they also sought to convince their readers *aesthetically*; they appealed to their readers' sense of beauty. (And we are reminded here of John Keats's "Ode on a Grecian Urn," and of the aphorism that is embedded within it: "'Beauty is truth, truth beauty,'—that is all/ Ye know on earth, and all ye need to know.")

BOOK I. Antiquity

Chapter I.

The quest to locate an unchanging and immovable referent in the natural world by which it might be possible to rigorously define motion and change; the quest to locate the site of Divinity's Presence in the natural world

As was briefly mentioned in the Introduction, the ancients considered the quest to locate an unchanging and immovable referent in the natural world by which it might be possible to rigorously define motion and change to be a quest to locate the site of Divinity's Presence in the natural world. (We find, for example, that Aristotle referred to his proposed referent for rigorously defining motion and change as "the unmoved mover," which he associated with Divinity's Presence in the natural world,[1] and that Plato referred to his proposed referent for rigorously defining motion and change as "the father and creator," whom Plato asserted is "that which is immovably the same forever."[2])

But we ask ourselves here: why did the ancients associate the existence of an unchanging and immovable referent in the natural world with the site of Divinity's Presence? We will find that the answer lies in the concept of *monism*.

---

1. See Aristotle, *Physics*, 8.vi, and see also the "Unmoved Mover" entry in Wikipedia. Let us note here that we cite both scholarly sources and Wikipedia in this text. The choice is a deliberate one: we celebrate scholarly wisdom and we also celebrate the democratization of information, and this book has been written for scholars and laypersons alike.

2. Plato, *Timaeus*, 38a, 1167.

❧

Scholars report that the concept of monism arose in the Greek philosophical discourse in the cosmologies of the first Greek natural philosophers, the Presocratics of the sixth century BC, who proposed "an explanation of the physical world by saying that all of the world's objects are comprised of a single element"—or an "ultimate substance."[3] (And we read that "the notion that a single ultimate substance lies beneath all material things is known as *monism*."[4])

The Presocratics conceived of this "ultimate substance" as being *a single, stable, unchanging substrate that was common to all*.[5]

❧

The idea of an ultimate substance allowed the Presocratics to consider all bodies to always already exist as one body, and All to always already be One. (Or as Friedrich Nietzsche recognized in the nineteenth century, contained in the idea of an ultimate substance was "the thought, 'all things are one.'")[6]

The Presocratics associated this single, stable, unchanging substrate, common to all—this ultimate substance—with Divinity and with the principle of life—and they considered it to exist as the generative "source," "origin," or "originating cause" of all things that exist in the natural world—even as they also considered it to exist as the site of all things in the natural world.[7]

---

3. "Material Monism," para. 1.

4. Principe, *Secrets of Alchemy*, 14.

5. As chemist and historian of science Lawrence M. Principe explains in *Secrets of Alchemy*, 14, the Presocratics of the sixth century BC "embraced the idea that beneath the constantly changing appearances of things, there existed some sort of a *stable, unchanging substrate*," common to all (my emphasis).

6. Nietzsche, *Philosophy*, 39.

7. Scholars report that the site of ultimate substance was referred to by the Presocratics as the "arche" (ἀρχή), and that the Presocratics ascribed to the arche "divine" attributes (see Vamvacas, *Founders of Western Thought*, 32). Scholars also report that the Presocratics considered the arche to exist as the generative "source," "origin," or "originating cause" of all things that exist in the natural world, and we recognize that the Presocratics therefore also associated the arche—the site of ultimate substance—with the principle of life (again, see Vamvacas, *Founders of Western Thought*, 24). And let us note here that "arche" is a Greek word with primary meanings "*beginning*," "*origin*," or "*source* of action" (see the "ἀρχή" entry in Liddell and Scott's *Greek-English Lexicon*).

Thales of Miletus (ca. 625–546 BC) was the first of the Presocratic philosophers, and historians attribute him with having introduced the concept of an ultimate substance into the Greek philosophical discourse.[8] Scholars acknowledge that almost "all the other Pre-Socratic philosophers followed him [Thales] in explaining nature as deriving from a unity of everything based upon the existence of a single ultimate substance."[9]

And we recognize here that insofar as Thales and the Presocratics considered an ultimate substance to be a single, stable, *unchanging* (with respect to itself for all time, and therefore *immovable*) substrate common to all, they considered the site of an ultimate substance to itself exist as the unchanging and immovable referent by which it would be possible to rigorously define all motion and change. And further, we recognize that they therefore considered the (multiple and yet simultaneously singular) All/the Only—which they associated with Divinity and with the principle of life—to itself exist as the unchanging and immovable referent by which it would be possible to rigorously define all motion and change.

∽

Let us note here that Newton considered his own natural philosophy to be most consistent with the natural philosophy of Thales. In 1694, seven years after the publishing of the first edition of the *Principia*, Newton's friend David Gregory reported that Newton had begun "conceiving the idea of publishing some scholia" to the *Principia*, in which it was to be stated that Newton's "natural philosophy was a 'rediscovery' of an ancient wisdom,"[10] and Gregory announced that Newton would:

> spread himself in exhibiting the agreement of this philosophy with that of the Ancients and principally with that of Thales.[11]

We find that this is a hint to Newton's reader that in his *Principia*, Newton had been interested in composing a monist, materialist cosmology whose focus was upon an ultimate substance.

---

8. Most scholars "agree that Thales's stamp on [natural philosophical] thought is the unity of substance" ("Thales of Miletus," para. 64)—or the idea that "a single ultimate substance lies beneath all material things" (Principe, *Secrets of Alchemy*, 14).

9. "Thales of Miletus," para. 2.

10. Guicciardini, *Reading the* Principia, 101.

11. Newton, "446. Memoranda by David Gregory," 334.

Let us also note here that scholars acknowledge that the study of natural philosophy in the ancient world—or that which was referred to in antiquity as "physis" (and from whose root our modern word, "physics," derives)—was a quest to locate an ultimate substance. As Wikipedia reports:

> Physis (Ancient Greek: φύσις) is a Greek theological, philosophical, and scientific term usually translated into English as "nature".... The word φύσις is a verbal noun based on φύειν "to grow, to appear" (cognate with English "to be").... There is some evidence that by the 6th century BC, beginning with the Ionian [Presocratic] School, the word could also be used in the comprehensive sense, as referring to "*all* things," as it were "Nature" in the sense of "Universe."[12]

We recognize here that the Presocratics considered physis to be the study of *all* things—which they also considered to always already exist as one thing. And therefore, we recognize that the Presocratics conceived of the study of physis to be a quest to locate an ultimate substance—a quest to locate an unchanging and immovable referent in the natural world by which it might be possible to rigorously define motion and change—and a quest to locate (what they considered to be) the site of Divinity's Presence in the natural world.[13]

(Interestingly, we find that the quest to locate an ultimate substance in the natural world is one that is also shared by contemporary physicists, who seek to locate a single, stable, unchanging substrate that is common to all—or that which they refer to as "the God Particle." (See the "Thales of Miletus" entry in Wikipedia, in which we read that "the first philosophers were trying to define the substance(s) of which all material objects

---

12. "Physis," paras. 1, 3, 4. And regarding the Ionian school of Presocratic philosophy, we read: "The Ionian school of Pre-Socratic philosophy was centred in Miletus, Ionia in the 6th century BC. Miletus and its environment was a thriving mercantile melting pot of current ideas of the time. The Ionian School included such thinkers as Thales, Anaximander, Anaximenes, Heraclitus, Anaxagoras, and Archelaus" ("Ionian School (Philosophy)," para. 1).

13. The first Greek natural philosophers—or *physikos*—of the sixth century BC were interested in rigorously defining motion and change, and contemporary physicists acknowledge that motion is considered to be "the most basic and essential element of physics" (see Greene, *Fabric of the Cosmos*, 29).

are composed. As a matter of fact, that is exactly what modern scientists are attempting to accomplish in nuclear physics."[14]))

⊖

Our study of the *prisca sapientia* will begin with the cosmology of Pythagoras. Pythagoras was a student of Thales, and scholars acknowledge that Pythagoras was of great importance to Newton.[15] Scholars also acknowledge that Pythagoras's cosmology exists as secret, hidden wisdom, which requires decrypting—and indeed, we read that Pythagoras and his followers "wrapped themselves in mystery, considering themselves guardians of the secrets of mathematics from the profane world."[16]

14. "Thales of Miletus," para. 26.
15. See Guicciardini's *Reading the* Principia, 102, in which Guicciardini writes that the idea of "a *prisca sapientia*, and in particular the role of Pythagoras in transmitting it to the Greeks" was of deep import to Newton; Guicciardini continues, "the role attributed by Newton to Pythagoras [in the transmission of this wisdom] deserves to be underlined."
16. Pesic, *Abel's Proof*, 5.

Chapter II.

Pythagoras (570–495 BC)

AS HAS BEEN MENTIONED, scholars acknowledge that Pythagoras was of great importance to Newton, and they also acknowledge that Pythagoras's cosmology exists as secret, hidden wisdom, which requires decrypting.

Pythagoras was a student of Thales,[1] who, as we know, introduced the concept of an ultimate substance into the Greek philosophical discourse. Historians report that Thales had encouraged Pythagoras to travel to Egypt to study[2]—and according to Newton, it was by way of such travels that Pythagoras rediscovered the wisdom of the ancient Jews—the wisdom of Noah. We read that:

> According to Newton, Pythagoras derived from Egypt and Phoenicia, via Moschus, knowledge about the pristine religion and natural philosophy from Noah.[3]

---

1. We read that "Pythagoras was taught mathematics by Thales, who brought mathematics to the Greeks from Ancient Egypt" (Stewart, "Pythagoras," para. 15).

2. "Thales advised Pythagoras to visit Egypt, which he did when he was about 22 years old" (Stewart, "Pythagoras," para. 16).

3. Guicciardini, *Reading the* Principia, 102. Newton believed that when the Greeks traveled to Egypt, it was the wisdom of the ancient Jews—the wisdom of Noah—that they encountered; he wrote: "the religion of the Iews was no other then that of Noah propagated down in Egypt" (Newton, "Draft Chapters," §f5r).

CHAPTER II. PYTHAGORAS   9

What did Pythagoras discover on his travels to Egypt?

As we will see by decrypting Pythagoras's secret, hidden cosmology, Pythagoras discovered that the concept of monism—or the notion that there exists in the natural world *a single, stable, unchanging substrate that is common to all*—was not actually original to the cosmology of Thales, but that it had originated in the cosmology of the ancient Jews. Pythagoras discovered that the ancient Jews had developed a monist, materialist cosmology in which they had located an ultimate substance in the natural world at the site of what Presently Is. Pythagoras discovered that the ancient Jews associated this single, stable, unchanging substrate, common to all—this ultimate substance—with Divinity and with the principle of life, and that their name for it in their cosmology was YHWH.[4]

As we will see, in Egypt, Pythagoras applies all that he had learned from the teachings of Thales to the cosmology of the ancient Jews, and he recognizes that in the cosmology of the ancient Jews, YHWH exists as the generative "source," "origin," or "originating cause" of all things that exist in the natural world—even as he also exists as the site of all things in the natural world.[5] Pythagoras recognizes that in the cosmology of the ancient Jews, YHWH exists as the Author of All, even as he also exists as the manifestation of the All.[6] And finally, Pythagoras recognizes that in the cosmology of the ancient Jews, YHWH comes into being Presently

---

4. We will find that this premise—*the notion that an ultimate substance in the natural world is located at the site of what Presently Is*—is the single axiom upon which Pythagoras builds his entire cosmology. We will also find that it is the single axiom that will be necessary to the decrypting of Pythagoras's entire cosmology, and that we will need only to apply it to Pythagoras's ideas to see his sublimely beautiful cosmology reveal itself to us before our eyes.

5. Pythagoras recognizes that the ancient Jews had located the presence of (what Thales had referred to as) the "arche" (ἀρχή) in the natural world.

6. See the "Names of God" entry in the *Jewish Encyclopedia*, para. 5, in which it is written that YHWH exists as "the source and author of life" in Judaism. We read: "He [YHWH] is the living God, as contrasted with the lifeless gods of the heathen, and He is the source and author of life. . . . So familiar is this conception of God to the Hebrew mind that it appears in the common formula of an oath, 'ḥai Yhwh' (= 'as Yhwh lives'; Ruth iii. 13; I Sam. xiv. 45; etc.)."

in the natural world,⁷ in the coming into being of the (multiple and yet simultaneously singular) All/the Only—in the coming into being of we ourselves.⁸

Pythagoras also recognizes that in the cosmology of the ancient Jews, YHWH himself exists as the unchanging and immovable referent in the natural world by which it would be possible to rigorously define all motion and change.

※

As has been mentioned, and as we will see, Pythagoras recognizes that in the cosmology of the ancient Jews, YHWH comes into being Presently, in the coming into being of the (multiple and yet simultaneously singular) All/the Only, and we find that he therefore recognizes that the ancient Jews considered physical reality (and the concepts of time and substance) to exist inextricably from mathematical reality (and the concept of quantity/number: the concept of the (multiple and yet simultaneously singular) All/the Only).

---

7. As we will see, Pythagoras studies the ancient Jewish sacred texts deeply (for he believes that they possess secret wisdom about the truths of nature), and he recognizes that in Exod. 3:14, it is written, "And God [YHWH] said unto Moses, I AM THAT I AM: and he said, Thus shalt thou say unto the children of Israel, I AM hath sent me unto you." Pythagoras reflects upon this passage deeply, and he recognizes that YHWH (or "I AM") cryptically asserts here that he exists as "I AM"—and that therefore he exists as the site of what Presently Is in the natural world.

Let us also note here that although we will cite the King James Version of the Bible in this text, Pythagoras was familiar with the original Jewish sacred texts, which were written in Hebrew. (And we read that "the [English] King James Bible, written in 1611, was based on a Latin bible, which was in turn a translation of a Greek translation (Septuagint) of the 'original' Hebrew, translated by Greek speaking Jews (living in Alexandria, Egypt, in the 3rd to 1st centuries BCE)." (See Drake, "Hebrew Scriptures," para. 3.))

In the KJV of the Bible, YHWH is translated as LORD. However, we will prefer to consider the ancient Jews' name for their God to be YHWH, since YHWH himself instructs Moses that his Name (which, in the original Hebrew is YHWH) is "I AM"—and that it therefore implicitly refers to the site of what Presently Is in the natural world. Going forward, we will include the translation of the Lord's Name as YHWH in all of our Biblical citations.

8. *Pythagoras recognizes that in the cosmology of the ancient Jews, All is always already One, and All is always already Now. And Pythagoras recognizes that in the cosmology of the ancient Jews, all of us always already exist as manifestation(s) of Divinity and of ever-burgeoning life, and Paradise is always already Now.*

CHAPTER II. PYTHAGORAS   11

And finally, Pythagoras recognizes that the ancient Jews had possessed knowledge of (what today are referred to as) the natural numbers.⁹ (And as we will see, Pythagoras himself possessed knowledge of the whole numbers.)¹⁰ Let us turn now to the decrypting of Pythagoras's cosmology.

☙

We find that Pythagoras himself was the first student of the *prisca sapientia*. Pythagoras recognized that the ancient Jewish sages and mystics had possessed knowledge of "the great truths of nature," but that they had hidden their wisdom in a secret code, which requires decrypting; and as we will see, Pythagoras performs countless acts of logical deduction—acts of mathematics—upon the ancient Jewish sacred texts in an effort to find what they had found.¹¹

And in turn, Pythagoras himself composes a cosmology that exists as secret, hidden wisdom, and that requires decrypting; and Pythagoras requires of us that we too perform countless acts of logical deduction—acts of mathematics—upon his own teachings so that we too may find what he has found.

As we will see, Pythagoras appropriates all of the ancient Jews' cosmology within his own cosmology, even as he extends and deepens the

---

9. From his reading of the book of Genesis, Pythagoras recognizes that in the cosmology of the ancient Jews, the first seven counting numbers are brought into being in the natural world in the coming into being of the passing days.

10. As Kline reports in his *Mathematical Thought*, 32, it was a "Pythagorean doctrine that all phenomena in the universe can be reduced to whole numbers or their ratios." (And we note here that the Pythagoreans did not consider ratios to exist as numbers themselves, but rather as ways to "*compare* numbers." (Corry, *Brief History of Numbers*, 35.))

Let us also note here that although some contemporary scholars claim that Pythagoras did not possess knowledge of the number zero, Newton considered Pythagoras to have rediscovered the wisdom of the Phoenicians—who themselves *did* possess knowledge of the number zero. And as we will see, knowledge of the number zero's existence is implied by Pythagoras's decrypted cosmology.

11. The idea that the ancient Jewish sacred texts possessed secret *natural philosophical* and *mathematical* wisdom was shared by Newton, whose Bible was the most heavily annotated volume in his library, and who wrote, "the first religion [Judaism] was the most *rational* of all others" (Newton, "Draft Chapters," §f4v; my emphasis). As we will see, both Pythagoras and Newton considered religion to be rational—a sentiment that is not widely shared today.

ancient Jews' cosmology in breathtaking and inspired ways, and we find that the monist, materialist focus of Pythagoras's cosmology too is upon YHWH himself—or upon he who, like the ancient Jews, Pythagoras too considers to exist as the site of ultimate substance and of what Presently Is in the natural world, which Pythagoras too considers to exist as the site at which Divinity and ever-burgeoning life are realized in the natural world.[12]

❧

Scholars report that when Pythagoras returned to Greece after his travels in Egypt, he developed a secret religion based upon his teachings, and a brotherhood of members who practiced his secret religion.[13] And upon entry into (what was called) the Pythagorean brotherhood, members were asked to pledge a secret oath to YHWH. The four-lined Pythagorean Oath reads:

> By that pure holy four lettered name on high,
> Nature's eternal fountain and supply,
> The parent of all souls that living be,
> By Him, with faithful oath—I swear to thee.[14]

Members of the Pythagorean brotherhood were asked to make a solemn promise to YHWH—(to he who exists in the cosmology of the Jews as "that pure holy four lettered name on high"; to he who exists in the cosmology of the Jews as "Nature's eternal fountain and supply"[15])—that

---

12. Let us note here that although many of the Jews' sacred texts were composed in the centuries before Pythagoras's birth, some of the ancient Jewish sacred texts—including the book of Isaiah—were composed in the sixth century BC—the same century in which Pythagoras himself lived. For this reason, going forward, we will refer to the ideas of the Jews in Pythagoras's present tense, as the Jews were developing some of their ideas at the same time that Pythagoras was developing his own ideas.

13. See Pesic, *Abel's Proof*, 5, in which Pesic writes that the "Pythagorean brotherhood discovered many important mathematical truths and explored the way they were manifest in the world. But they also wrapped themselves in mystery, considering themselves guardians of the secrets of mathematics from the profane world. Because of their secrecy, many details of their work are lost, and even the degree to which they were indebted to prior discoveries made in Mesopotamia and Egypt remains obscure."

14. ben Israel and Lindo, *Prophets*, 194.

15. As we will see, Pythagoras studies the ancient Jews' sacred texts deeply, and he recognizes that in Ps. 36:9, the poet King David addresses YHWH directly and writes, "For with thee *is* the fountain of life: in thy light shall we see light." Pythagoras recognizes that in the cosmology of the ancient Jews, all of us always already exist as

CHAPTER II. PYTHAGORAS   13

they would devote themselves completely to him and to exploring his mysteries. We find that Pythagoras's life itself was the enacting of his own promise to YHWH, as the teachings that he left behind will reveal.[16]

⊹

Pythagoras's cosmology is sublimely beautiful and it is also fairly extensive in nature, and for this reason, it will be helpful for us to consider it in several parts. The parts in which we will consider Pythagoras's cosmology are as follows:

i. *On YHWH*

ii. *On the Tetrad, a mystical symbol which was deeply important to the secret religion of the Pythagorean brotherhood*

iii. *On the Harmony of the Spheres*

iv. *On Vegetarianism and Metempsychosis*

(And let us note here that Pythagoras's mystical symbol, the Tetrad, exists at the heart of Pythagoras's monist, materialist cosmology, and that it exists as the place at which the sublime beauty of his cosmology will be revealed to us.)

---

manifestation(s) of unchanging YHWH—and that therefore, all of us always already exist as manifestation(s) of YHWH's fountain of life.

(Pythagoras recognizes that David implies here that he considers YHWH's fountain of life to burst forth ecstatically in Eden, where one river Presently cleaves into four; and that David considers all of us to always already exist as manifestation(s) of Eden and of its ever-cleaving fountain of life. (See Gen. 2:10, in which it is written: "And a river went out of Eden to water the garden; and from thence it was parted, and became into four heads."))

Let us note here that Pythagoras also recognizes that the Jews consider it to be possible for YHWH to be *experienced*—(see "God in Judaism," para. 20, in which it is written that "Jews believe that 'God can be experienced'")—and that Pythagoras recognizes that the Jews consider it to be a supplicant's life's work to come to know himself or herself for experiences of unchanging YHWH—or for experiences of (what the Jews consider to be) the *unchanging place* from which the supplicant has never departed— and therefore for experiences of (what the Jews consider to be) self-knowledge and enlightenment. Pythagoras recognizes that the Jews imply that our journey is always already done—that we are all always already One; that we all always already exist as manifestation(s) of Divinity and of ever-burgeoning life—and that our life's work is simply to *know ourselves* for experiences of it. We will return to these ideas later in this text, when we explore Newton's own relationship to Judaism.

16. No fragments of Pythagoras's works survive; what we know about Pythagoras's teachings has come down to us from the testimony of others.

We begin now with part i, "On YHWH."

I. ON YHWH

As has been mentioned, Pythagoras appropriates all of the ancient Jews' cosmology for his own, even as he extends and deepens the ancient Jews' cosmology in breathtaking and inspired ways. We find that Pythagoras performs countless acts of logical deduction—acts of mathematics—upon the ancient Jewish sacred texts (which he considers to be his own sacred texts, since he appropriates the ancient Jews' cosmology for his own) and that he begins to perform his acts of logical deduction upon the Jewish sacred texts by focusing first on YHWH himself—and particularly upon YHWH's temporal aspect. Pythagoras begins to perform his acts of logical deduction upon the Jewish sacred texts (which he considers to be his own sacred texts) by focusing first upon YHWH's manifestation in the natural world as the site of what Presently Is.[17]

Pythagoras studies the Jewish sacred texts deeply (which he considers to be his own sacred texts), and he recognizes that YHWH, the site of what Presently Is in the natural world, is "everlasting." (And we note here that in Gen. 21:33, YHWH is referred to as "the everlasting God."[18]) Pythagoras recognizes that YHWH is eternal—that he exists for all time; and therefore, Pythagoras recognizes that the site of what Presently Is in the natural world exists for all time.

Pythagoras also recognizes that YHWH, the site of what Presently Is in the natural world, is unchanging with respect to himself for all time. (Pythagoras interprets YHWH's thunderous declaration to his prophet, Moses—"I AM THAT I AM . . . . this is my name for ever"[19]—to mean

---

17. And let us remind ourselves here that in Exod. 3:14, it is written, "And God [YHWH] said unto Moses, I AM THAT I AM: and he said, Thus shalt thou say unto the children of Israel, I AM hath sent me unto you"—and that Pythagoras interprets this to mean that YHWH (or "I AM") exists as the site of what Presently Is in the natural world.

18. See Gen. 21:33, in which it is written, "And Abraham planted a grove in Beer-sheba, and called there on the name of the LORD [YHWH], the everlasting God."

19. See Exod. 3:14-15, in which it is written, "And [YHWH] God said unto Moses, I AM THAT I AM: and he said, Thus shalt thou say unto the children of Israel, I AM hath sent me unto you. And God said moreover unto Moses, Thus shalt thou say unto the children of Israel, the Lord God of your fathers, the God of Abraham, the God of Isaac, and the God of Jacob, hath sent me unto you: this is my name for ever, and this is my memorial unto all generations."

that the site of what Presently Is in the natural world remains (unchangingly) the site of what Presently Is for all time.)[20]

And Pythagoras recognizes that since YHWH, the site of what Presently Is in the natural world, is unchanging with respect to himself for all time, an "earlier" manifestation of him is necessarily indistinguishable from a "later" manifestation of him. Pythagoras therefore recognizes that YHWH is "everlasting"—that he exists eternally; for all time—even as, *at the same time*, he also exists only Now (since an "earlier" manifestation of him is indistinguishable from a "later" manifestation of him). Pythagoras recognizes that YHWH exists for all time even as, *at the same time*, he also exists only Now, and as the site at which all time is always already vanquished, or overcome, in the natural world. And Pythagoras therefore recognizes that all time *at the same time* also exists only Now.[21]

Pythagoras recognizes that YHWH exists as a unity of all time in the natural world, even as, *at the same time*, he also exists as a unit of time; and similarly, Pythagoras recognizes that YHWH exists as a unity of all substance in the natural world, even as, *at the same time*, he also exists as a unit of substance. (Pythagoras deduces that since an "earlier" manifestation of YHWH is indistinguishable from a "later" manifestation of him, all multiple manifestations of YHWH are indistinguishable from one another—and therefore that multiple, countable manifestations of him *at the same time* also exist as a single manifestation of him.) Pythagoras recognizes that YHWH exists as the multiple, countable All—even as,

---

20. As has been mentioned, Pythagoras applies the teachings of Thales to the cosmology of the ancient Jews, and he also recognizes that YHWH exists in the cosmology of the ancient Jews as the site of an ultimate substance—or as a single, stable, *unchanging* substrate that is common to all. Pythagoras therefore recognizes that in YHWH's manifestation in the natural world as an ultimate substance, he is also unchanging with respect to himself for all time.

21. The phrase *at the same time* will be italicized throughout this text because we will find that the concept of simultaneity in Pythagoras's cosmology will be of great import to all of the natural philosophers who follow Pythagoras in chronological time—including to Newton himself.

at the same time, he also exists as the Only.²² And Pythagoras therefore recognizes that all substance in the natural world *at the same time* exists as a single substance.

⟡

As has been mentioned, Pythagoras recognizes that YHWH exists for all time, even as, *at the same time*, he also exists only Now, and as the site at which all time is always already vanquished, or overcome, in the natural world.

And Pythagoras also recognizes that YHWH's continued Presence in the natural world—or his perseverance of himself *as* himself for all time²³—is responsible for bringing into being the existence of a progressive linear orderedness (with respect to time and number) that *at the same time* is always already vanquished, or overcome—since YHWH also exists only Now, and as the Only manifestation of himself in the natural world.

Pythagoras deduces this finding from his reading of a passage in the book of Isaiah.²⁴

In Isa. 44:6, YHWH declares to his prophet, Isaiah: "I *am* the first, and I *am* the last, and beside me *there is* no God," and YHWH therefore asserts that he exists as "the first" manifestation of himself, and that he also exists as "the last" manifestation of himself, even as he also exists as the Only manifestation of himself. YHWH implies that he exists—both temporally and numerically—"before" the last manifestation of himself, and that he also exists—both temporally and numerically—"after" the first manifestation of himself, even as, *at the same time*, he also exists as the *Only* manifestation of himself. And YHWH therefore implies that his continued Presence in the natural world—or his perseverance

---

22. And Pythagoras also finds support for this deduction in Deut. 6:4, in which it is written, "Hear, O Israel: the LORD [YHWH] our God *is* one LORD [YHWH]."

Pythagoras also recognizes that YHWH exists in the cosmology of the ancient Jews as the *infinite* All—even as, *at the same time*, he also exists as the Only, and as the site at which the infinite is always already vanquished, or overcome, in the natural world. Pythagoras recognizes that since YHWH exists for all time—for eternal time—he exists for infinite time, and that he therefore exists as the *infinite* All, even as, *at the same time*, he also exists as the Only, and as the site at which the infinite is also always already vanquished, or overcome, in the natural world.

23. And we remind ourselves here that YHWH exists for all time.

24. We read: "Isaiah was one of the most popular works among Jews in the Second Temple period (c. 515 BCE–70 CE)" ("Book of Isaiah," para. 3), and we recognize that the book of Isaiah was popular at the time of Pythagoras.

of himself *as* himself for all time—is responsible for bringing into being the existence of a progressive linear orderedness (with respect to time and number) that *at the same time* is always already vanquished, or overcome—since YHWH also exists only Now, and as the Only manifestation of himself in the natural world.[25]

⌘

As has been mentioned, scholars acknowledge that the Pythagorean cosmology exists as secret, hidden wisdom, and we find that there is much that needs to be deduced about it. We find that Pythagoras does not refer to YHWH by name in his cosmology; instead, he refers to YHWH as "the Monad"—which means "'the unit' or 'the One.'"[26] (And let us remind ourselves here that the Jews also refer to YHWH as One, and that in Deut. 6:4, it is written, "Hear, O Israel: the LORD [YHWH] our God *is* one LORD [YHWH].")

Scholars report that in the Pythagorean cosmology, the Monad meant "divinity, the first being, or the totality of all beings"; the "single source," the "origin"; and that the Monad was "readily identified with the divine origin of reality."[27] And as we know, the ancient Jews considered YHWH himself to exist as divinity, the first being, or the totality of all beings; the single source, the origin; and that YHWH was readily identified with the divine origin of reality;[28] and we recognize that the Monad—or the One—was Pythagoras's name for YHWH.

(We also recognize that since the Pythagorean Oath refers to YHWH, "that pure holy four lettered name on high," both as "Nature's eternal fountain and supply" and as "the parent of all souls that living be," the oath too shows us that in Pythagoras's cosmology, YHWH exists as the divine source and origin of all things that exist.)

25. As we will see, Pythagoras will explore this idea more deeply by way of his mystical symbol, the Tetrad.

26. We read: "Monad is a term derived from the Greek μονάς (monas) which means 'unit' or 'one'" ("Monad," para. 1).

27. "Monad (Philosophy)," paras. 1, 2, n.4. We also read: "Monad (from Greek μονάς monas, "singularity" in turn from μόνος monos, "alone"), refers in cosmogony to the Supreme Being, divinity, or the totality of all things. The concept was reportedly conceived by the Pythagoreans and may refer variously to a single source acting alone, or to an indivisible origin, or to both" ("Monad (Philosophy)," para. 1). And we recognize that the term "Monad" shares the same root (μόνος monos) as the word *monism*.

28. We remind ourselves here that YHWH exists as "the source and author of life" in Judaism ("Names of God," para. 5).

18 PARADISE IS NOW

Pythagoras implies that, like the ancient Jews, he considers YHWH to exist as the divine origin of reality. But what does Pythagoras mean by the divine origin of reality?

As we know, Pythagoras considers YHWH's continued Presence in the natural world—or his perseverance of himself *as* himself for all time—to be responsible for bringing into being in the natural world the existence of a progressive linear orderedness (with respect to time and number) that *at the same time* is always already vanquished, or overcome.

Pythagoras therefore implies that he considers YHWH to exist as the divine origin of reality, even as, *at the same time*, he also considers YHWH to exist as the site at which the concept of an origin (or of a beginning) is always already vanquished, or overcome. Pythagoras implies that the divine origin of reality is realized Presently, in the coming into being of the (multiple and yet simultaneously singular) All/the Only—in the coming into being of we ourselves. *And Pythagoras implies that All always already exists as the divine origin of reality—and that the divine origin of reality is ever-presently, omni-presently Now.*[29]

Pythagoras also implies that he considers the divine origin of reality—YHWH himself—to be "indivisible." Scholars report that in Pythagoras's cosmology, the Monad, or the One, exists as the "single source and indivisible origin" of the natural world.[30] (And we find that in the

---

29. Insofar as Pythagoras considers YHWH, the site of ultimate substance and of what Presently Is, to exist as the divine source and origin of reality, he implies that he considers the site of ultimate substance and of what Presently Is to exist as the divine source and origin of the site of ultimate substance and of what Presently Is. Pythagoras implies that he considers the existence of a recursive self-similarity to be implicit to the natural world, which delivers the site of ultimate substance and of what Presently Is to the unchanging place from which it has never departed—to the site of ultimate substance and of what Presently Is. And Pythagoras implies that he considers the site of ultimate substance and of what Presently Is (the divine source and origin of reality) to itself be responsible for this process of deliverance. As we will see, Pythagoras will explore these ideas more deeply by way of the development of his mystical symbol, the Tetrad. (And we note here that although scholars consider the concept of recursive self-similarity to have originated in the seventeenth century in the cosmology of Gottfried Leibniz, we recognize that it actually originated in antiquity, in the cosmologies of the ancient Jews and of Pythagoras. See "Fractal," para. 13.))

30. "Monad," para. 12.

CHAPTER II. PYTHAGORAS 19

cosmology of the ancient Jews, YHWH, the One, also exists as the single source and indivisible origin of the natural world; we read that "God [in Judaism] is understood [to exist] as the absolute one, indivisible."[31]) But what does Pythagoras (and what do the ancient Jews) mean by the term "indivisible"?

We find that the mathematical term indivisible refers to an entity that cannot be divided, and which exists as a single, discrete unit.

The notion of an indivisible entity is contrasted with the notion of an infinitely divisible, or continuous, entity. An infinitely divisible, or continuous, entity is defined to be an entity that can be divided into units which themselves can be divided into other units, which can be further divided, and so on, and so forth, ad infinitum.

And like the ancient Jews, Pythagoras implies that he considers YHWH, the One, to be indivisible.

✥

We find that Pythagoras refers to YHWH as "the Monad" (or as "the One"), but that he also refers to YHWH as "the Tetrad," which means "a group or set of four." Scholars report that "Pythagoras [also] called Deity a Tetrad or Tetractys, meaning the 'four sacred letters.'"[32] (And we recognize here that Pythagoras associates YHWH's Presence in the natural world with the numbers one and four, and that this is also a direct allusion to the cosmology of the ancient Jews—who, as we know, consider YHWH, the four-headed fountain of life, whose four-lettered Name translates as "I AM," to be One.)[33]

---

31. "God in Judaism," para. 3.

32. See "Tetragrammaton," *Brewer's Dictionary*, 1070. We note that Pythagoras's reference to the "four sacred letters" is yet another allusion to the ancient Jews' Tetragrammaton: YHWH himself.

33. We find that the numbers four and one are significant both in the cosmologies of the ancient Jews and of Pythagoras. In the cosmology of the ancient Jews, the number four is symbolic of the totality of the All—it is symbolic of the four corners of the earth and of the four seasons, and it is symbolic of the gathering together of the four corners of the tallith (the Jewish prayer shawl) in an act of communion/of Oneness, with YHWH himself—the One God. (We note that the gathering together of the four corners of the prayer shawl emulates the coming into being of the four-headed fountain of life—YHWH himself.) Pythagoras too considers the number four to be symbolic of the totality of the All, and as we will see, he coins the word "Kosmos" (which he associates with the number four) to describe the totality of (what he considers to be) the One Universe.

We find that Pythagoras's Tetrad (or Tetractys) also goes under a third name; it goes under the name of "the Tetractys of the Decad,"[34] and that decad means "a group of ten."

And apart from being a name for YHWH, the Tetrad also exists in the Pythagorean cosmology as a mystical symbol. Scholars report that as "a mystical symbol, it [the Tetrad (or Tetractys)] was very important to the secret worship of Pythagoreanism."[35] We read:

> As a portion of the secret religion, initiates were required to swear a secret oath by the Tetractys. They then served as novices, which required them to observe silence for a period of five years.[36]

Members of the Pythagorean brotherhood were encouraged to silently contemplate the mysteries of the Tetrad over a five year period—as we will begin to contemplate the Tetrad's mysteries Now.

II. ON THE TETRAD

What is the Tetrad?

As Wikipedia reports, the Tetrad "is a triangular figure consisting of ten points arranged in four rows: one, two, three, and four points in each row."[37]

---

34. "Tetractys," para. 1.
35. "Tetractys," para. 1.
36. "Tetractys," para. 4.
37. "Tetractys," para. 1.

FIGURE 1[38]

And as Wikipedia continues:

> The Tetractys . . . is an equilateral triangle formed from the sequence of the first ten numbers aligned in four rows. It is both a mathematical idea and a metaphysical symbol that embraces within itself—in seedlike form—the principles of the natural world, the harmony of the cosmos, the ascent to the divine, and the mysteries of the divine realm.[39]

A prayer of the Pythagoreans shows the importance of the Tetractys (sometimes called the "Mystic Tetrad") to their cosmology:

> O holy, holy *tetraktys* [Tetractys], though that containest the root and the source of the eternally flowing creation! For the divine number begins with the profound, pure unity until it comes to the holy four; then it begets the mother of all, the all-compromising, the all-bounding, the first-born, the never-swerving, the never-tiring holy ten, the keyholder of all.[40]

---

38. "Tetractys," Wikimedia Commons.
39. "Tetractys," para. 7.
40. Dantzig, *Number*, 42.

What does the Tetrad symbolize? We find that the Tetrad reveals, in symbolic form, Pythagoras's ideas regarding the relationship of YHWH, the site of ultimate substance and of what Presently Is in the natural world, to time, number, and space.

We recognize that each point of which the Tetrad is composed is symbolic of YHWH's continued Presence in the natural world—or of his perseverance of himself *as* himself for all time. (And as we know, Pythagoras considers YHWH to exist for all time, even as, *at the same time*, he also exists only Now, and as the site at which all time is always already vanquished, or overcome, in the natural world; and as we know, Pythagoras considers YHWH's continued Presence in the natural world—or his perseverance of himself *as* himself for all time—to be responsible for bringing into being in the natural world the existence of a progressive linear orderedness (with respect to time and number) that *at the same time* is always already vanquished, or overcome—since YHWH also exists only Now, and as the Only manifestation of himself in the natural world.)

The Tetrad shows us how YHWH's continued Presence in the natural world—or his perseverance of himself *as* himself for all time— brings into being the first ten counting numbers—which reveal themselves to possess a progressive linear orderedness that *at the same time* is always already vanquished, or overcome (since multiple, countable manifestation(s) of YHWH are also indistinguishable from one another, and therefore *at the same time* also exist as a single manifestation of him.)

And the Tetrad also reveals to us Pythagoras's ideas regarding "the organization of space." As Wikipedia reports:

> the first row represented zero dimensions (a point)
> the second row represented one dimension (a line of two points)
> the third row represented two dimensions (a plane defined by a triangle of three points)
> the fourth row represented three dimensions (a tetrahedron defined by four points)[41]

The Tetrad reveals to us Pythagoras's ideas on the dynamical generation of space in the natural world. (And we note here that at this time in Greek

---

41. "Tetractys," para. 2. See also Fideler, *Pythagorean Sourcebook*, 29, in which it is written: "In the sphere of geometry, One [dot] represents the point, Two [dots] represents the line, Three [dots] represents the surface, and Four [dots] the tetrahedron."

thought, geometric space was not considered to exist distinctly from physical space; and we recognize that the Greek word "geometry" comes from roots that mean "measure" and "earth."[42])

(And let us also remind ourselves here that each point of which the Tetrad is composed is symbolic of YHWH's continued Presence in the natural world—or of his perseverance of himself *as* himself for all time; and let us also remind ourselves here that Pythagoras considers YHWH to exist for all time, even as, *at the same time*, he also exists only Now, and as the site at which all time is always already vanquished, or overcome, in the natural world. And finally, let us remind ourselves here that Pythagoras considers YHWH to exist as the divine origin of reality (who also exists as the site at which the concept of an origin (or of a beginning) is always already vanquished, or overcome)—and that Pythagoras considers the divine origin of reality to come into being Now.)

⌀

We recognize that since Pythagoras considers each point of which the Tetrad is composed to be symbolic of YHWH's continued Presence in the natural world—or of his perseverance of himself *as* himself for all time—Pythagoras finds it possible to consider each point of which the Tetrad is composed to also be symbolic of the divine origin of reality, which comes into being Now. Pythagoras therefore finds it possible to consider each point of which the Tetrad is composed to itself come into being Now.

And the Tetrad shows us that Pythagoras considers the continued Presence of a point (which he considers to come into being Now)—or the perseverance of the point *as* a point for all time—to generate a line.

Pythagoras recognizes that the line is generated over all time—but he also recognizes that all time *at the same time* also exists only Now. And therefore, Pythagoras recognizes that the line is also generated Now. (Pythagoras recognizes that the line comes into being *at the same time* as the point—and that both come into being Now.)

And the Tetrad shows us that Pythagoras considers the continued Presence of the line (which he considers to be generated Now)—or the perseverance of the line *as* a line for all time—to generate a plane.

---

42. "Geometry," para. 1.

Pythagoras recognizes that the plane is generated over all time—but he also recognizes that all time *at the same time* also exists only Now. And therefore, Pythagoras recognizes that the plane is also generated Now. (Pythagoras recognizes that the plane comes into being *at the same time* as the line, and that the line comes into being *at the same time* as the point—and that all come into being Now.)

And the Tetrad shows us that Pythagoras considers the continued Presence of the plane (which he considers to be generated Now)—or the perseverance of the plane *as* a plane for all time—to generate a volume.

Pythagoras recognizes that the volume is generated over all time—but he also recognizes that all time *at the same time* also exists only Now. And therefore, Pythagoras recognizes that the volume is also generated Now. (Pythagoras recognizes that the volume comes into being *at the same time* as the plane, and that the plane comes into being *at the same time* as the line, and that the line comes into being *at the same time* as the point—and that all come into being Now.)[43]

The Tetrad shows us that Pythagoras considers all geometric objects to come into being Now—in the coming into being of the site of ultimate

---

43. We recognize that from a purely mathematical perspective, Pythagoras therefore suggests that:
—the elements of which a one-dimensional line is composed are zero-dimensional points, which exist *as of one dimension less* than the one-dimensional line that they help to generate (and to which they contribute as elements).
—the elements of which a two-dimensional plane is composed are one-dimensional lines, which exist *as of one dimension less* than the two-dimensional plane that they help to generate (and to which they contribute as elements).
—and that the elements of which a three-dimensional volume is composed are two-dimensional planes, which exist *as of one dimension less* than the three-dimensional volume that they help to generate (and to which they contribute as elements).
We recognize that Pythagoras also suggests that all geometric objects are composed of an *infinite number* of elements that exist *as of one dimension less* than the geometric object that they help to generate (and to which they contribute as elements); and that he suggests that these elements are discrete (or indivisible) relative to the geometric object that they help to generate (and to which they contribute as elements). (But how do we know that Pythagoras considers these ideas to be true? Since Pythagoras suggests that the elements of which all geometric objects are composed persevere *as* themselves for all time, they therefore persevere *as* themselves for infinite, eternal time; and we therefore deduce that Pythagoras considers all geometric objects to exist as *infinite collections* of their fundamental elements. And since Pythagoras considers the elements of which all geometric objects are composed to be symbolic of YHWH's indivisible Presence in the natural world, we therefore deduce that he considers these elements to be indivisible too.)

substance and of what Presently Is in the natural world—in the coming into being of YHWH himself: the divine source and origin of reality.

(And before we continue, let us also note here that the dimension over which the point perseveres *as* a point, and over which the line perseveres *as* a line, and over which the plane perseveres *as* a plane, is time, and that Pythagoras therefore implies that he considers time to exist as a dimension in the natural world.)[44]

The Tetrad also shows us that Pythagoras associates geometric objects—points, lines, planes, and volumes—(all of which he considers to be dynamically generated Now)—with numbered dimensions; it shows us that Pythagoras considers a point to exist as an object of zero dimensions; a line to exist as an object of one dimension; a plane to exist as an object of two dimensions; and a volume to exist as an object of three dimensions. And the Tetrad shows us that Pythagoras considers geometric objects' dimensions to themselves possess a progressive linear orderedness that *at the same time* is also always already vanquished, or overcome, since the progressive linear orderedness of geometric objects' dimensions (0D, 1D, 2D, 3D) is the progressive linear orderedness of number—which is, as we know, *at the same time* always already vanquished, or overcome, in the natural world.

We also recognize that since Pythagoras considers each of the points of which the Tetrad is composed to be symbolic of YHWH's continued Presence in the natural world—or of his perseverance of himself *as* himself for all time—he implies that he considers YHWH's continued Presence in the natural world to be responsible for generating all geometric objects—and therefore to also be responsible for generating all geometric/physical spatial dimensions in the natural world. Pythagoras implies that he considers the coming into being of geometric/physical spatial dimensions in the natural world to be dependent upon the coming into

---

44. Although the concept of dimension is not directly addressed in natural philosophical treatises until the time of Aristotle (384–322 BC), knowledge of its existence is implied by the Pythagorean cosmology.

being of the temporal dimension, and Pythagoras therefore implies that he considers geometric/physical spatial dimensions and the temporal dimension to exist inextricably from one another.

And let us also note here that since Pythagoras implies that he considers a point to come into being *at the same time* as a line, and a line to come into being *at the same time* as a plane, and a plane to come into being *at the same time* as a volume—and that he considers all geometric objects to come into being Now—he also implies that he considers all spatial-temporal dimensions to come into being Now—in the coming into being of the site of ultimate substance and of what Presently Is in the natural world—in the coming into being of the divine source and origin of reality—in the coming into being of we ourselves.

↭

The Tetrad reveals to us that Pythagoras considers the natural world to be composed of four spatial-temporal dimensions. And we find that Pythagoras coins the word "Kosmos" (and which he associates with the number four) to describe what he considers to be the progressive linear orderedness of the Universe's spatial-temporal dimensions—a progressive linear orderedness that *at the same time* is always already vanquished, or overcome.[45] The Tetrad also reveals to us that Pythagoras considers the four spatial-temporal dimensions of the natural world to exist as substantial/material entities, since the element(s) of which they are composed are YHWH himself: the site of ultimate substance in the natural world.

And the Tetrad also reveals to us that Pythagoras considers there to exist a relationship between geometry—or between the generation of geometrical objects (and also the generation of spatial-temporal dimensions)—and number, and it shows us that Pythagoras considers geometry and number to exist inextricably from one another.[46]

---

45. Scholars acknowledge that the "philosopher Pythagoras used the term *kosmos* (Ancient Greek: κόσμος, Latinized *kósmos*) for the order of the universe" ("Cosmos," para. 2). Scholars also report that Pythagoras associated the first four counting numbers with qualities that relate to the natural world—and that he considered the number four to be symbolic of the Kosmos. We read that the first four numbers were symbolic of:

"1. Monad – Unity

2. Dyad – Power – Limit/Unlimited (peras/apeiron)

3. Triad – Harmony

4. Tetrad – Kosmos" (see "Tetractys," para. 2).

46. Scholars acknowledge that Pythagoras considered number and geometry to be

We find that the Tetrad symbolizes the coming into being of all time, of all number, of all geometric objects, and of all geometric/physical space in the natural world—and that the Tetrad reveals to us that Pythagoras considered time and space to exist inextricably from one another. The Tetrad shows us that Pythagoras considered YHWH's continued Presence in the natural world—or his perseverance of himself *as* himself—to generate all time, all number, all geometric objects, and all geometric/physical space. And the Tetrad shows us that Pythagoras considered all time, all number, all geometric objects' dimensions, and all geometric/physical space to possess a progressive linear orderedness that *at the same time* is already vanquished, or overcome.

As Wikipedia reports on the Tetrad:

> So revered was this ancient symbol that it inspired ancient philosophers to swear by the name of the one who brought this gift to humanity.[47]

And we recognize that "the One" who brought this gift to humanity was the Monad/the Tetrad—it was YHWH himself—the divine source and origin of reality.[48]

"inseparable." (Indeed, scholars report that the idea "that numbers and geometry were inseparable [was] a foundation of [Pythagoras's] theory." ("Irrational Number," para. 7.))

Let us note here that Pythagoras also implies that he considers the geometric/physical spatial dimensions and the temporal dimension to be infinite in extent, even as, *at the same time*, he also considers them to be finite in extent; he implies that he considers them to be composed of an infinite (and yet simultaneously singular) number of element(s), and that he considers them to exist as the site(s) at which the infinite is also always already vanquished, or overcome, in the natural world.

47. "Tetractys," para. 7.

48. Although Pythagoras considered YHWH to be "the One" who had brought this gift to humanity, we recognize that Pythagoras himself was also "the One" who brought this gift to humanity. And we deduce here that Pythagoras considered himself to have been a prophet, who had received Divine wisdom, and whom God had spoken through. We will explore the concept of the prophet more deeply later in this text, as we will find that Newton too considered himself to be a prophet.

28   PARADISE IS NOW

❧

Let us turn now to exploring the Pythagorean musical system, as we find that "the Pythagorean musical system was [also] based on the Tetractys."[49]

III. ON THE MUSIC OF THE SPHERES

Pythagoras was known to have been fascinated with the music of the lyre, and scholars recognize that he was first natural philosopher to identify that the pitch of a musical note is in "proportion to the length of the string that produces it."[50] Let us return now to Pythagoras's time so that we may see what he sees.

❧

Pythagoras studies the lyre carefully, and he recognizes that for a lyre that possesses two strings of the same length, tension, and thickness, the two strings sound the same when plucked. He recognizes that the notes produced by the two strings have the same pitch. Pythagoras calls the relationship between these two notes—or the interval between them—a unison. And he feels that these notes sound good, or consonant, when played together.

Pythagoras also recognizes that if one string is exactly ½ the length of another string, the note produced on the first string possesses a much higher pitch than the note produced on the second string, but that the two notes still sound consonant when played together. Pythagoras calls this interval an octave. And Pythagoras recognizes that if one string is 2/3 the length of another string, the notes produced by the two strings again sound consonant when played together—and he calls this interval a perfect fifth. Finally, Pythagoras recognizes that if one string is ¾ the length of another string, the notes produced by the two strings again sound consonant when played together—and he calls this interval a perfect fourth.[51]

49. "Tetractys," para. 6.
50. "Musica Universalis," para. 2.
51. Gibson, "Pythagorean Intervals," paras. 1, 2.

Pythagoras recognizes that these intervals (the unison, the octave, the perfect fifth, the perfect fourth) are "defined by the lengths of the strings being in a certain *ratio* [to one another]."[52] (For example, he recognizes that the unison is defined by the lengths of the strings being in a ratio of 1:1 to one another; that the octave is defined by the lengths of the strings being in a ratio of 1:2 to one another; that the perfect fifth is defined by the lengths of the strings being in a ratio of 2:3 to one another; and that the perfect fourth is defined by the lengths of the strings being in a ratio of 3:4 to one another.)

(And indeed, Pythagoras recognizes that for each interval produced, a common (geometric) unit of measure fits evenly into both string lengths being measured. For example, in the case of the perfect fourth, Pythagoras recognizes that the common (geometric) unit of measure is a string length that measures ¼ the length of the entire string, and that the perfect fourth is composed of 3 and 4 multiples of this common (geometric) unit of measure.)

Pythagoras recognizes that these musical intervals are defined by the lengths of the strings being in a certain ratio to one another—but what does Pythagoras mean by the word "ratio"? It is recognized by scholars that Pythagoras did not consider a ratio to exist as a number, but rather as a way to compare numbers.[53] In *A Brief History of Numbers*, Leo Corry explains that

> A ratio between two numbers, such as 2 and 3, did not represent for them [the Pythagoreans] either a number or a "numerical value," in the same sense that [the whole numbers] 2 or 3 did [for them], or as 2/3 does for us.... [For the Pythagoreans, a] ratio was a way to *compare* numbers, and ratios could be compared with each other, but not *operated upon* as numbers were.[54]

We find that although Pythagoras did not consider a ratio to exist as a number, he recognized that it was possible to extrapolate numbers from ratios. And Pythagoras recognized that since it was possible to extrapolate numbers from ratios, and that it was possible to extrapolate ratios from music, it was also possible to extrapolate numbers from music. Scholars report that Pythagoras's studies of the lyre "revealed to him that

---

52. Gibson, "Pythagorean Intervals," para. 3.

53. And we remind ourselves here that Pythagoras possessed knowledge of (what today are referred to as) the whole numbers.

54. Corry, *Brief History of Numbers*, 35.

music was number made audible."⁵⁵ And Pythagoras's studies of the lyre further convinced him of the existence of the relationship in the natural world between geometry and number; he recognized that there existed a relationship between string length (a geometric measure) and number.

↭

As we know, in Pythagoras's cosmology, numbers come into being in the coming into being of the (multiple and yet simultaneously singular) All/the Only—in the coming into being of YHWH himself; and as we know, in Pythagoras's cosmology, numbers possess a progressive linear orderedness that *at the same time* is always already vanquished, or overcome. Pythagoras implies that he considered the existence of music in the natural world (and from which it was possible to extrapolate ratios, and numbers themselves) to serve as sensible evidence of the existence of YHWH's absolute Presence in the natural world.⁵⁶ And fascinatingly, we find that it is "possible to trace the origin of the word 'ratio' to the Ancient Greek λόγος (logos)"⁵⁷—a word which the ancient Greeks associated with "the divine animating principle pervading the Cosmos,"⁵⁸ and which we find was another Greek name for YHWH himself.⁵⁹

---

55. Pesic, *Abel's Proof*, 7.

56. We will explore the concept of the absolute later in this text.

57. "Ratio," para. 15. (See also Pesic, *Abel's Proof*, 9, in which Pesic writes that "the word for ratio is *logos*.")

58. "Logos," para. 1.

59. Scholars acknowledge that the ancient Greeks associated the term Logos (which was coined by Heraclitus, a contemporary of Pythagoras's) with Divinity, with speech, and with number—(we read that the root of the Greek term Logos is the verb légō (λέγω), meaning "'count,' 'tell,' 'say,' 'speak'" (see Ackrill, *Aristotle*, 124))—and we recognize that the Greek term Logos was another Greek name for YHWH himself. (As we know, in the cosmology of the ancient Jews, all of us always already exist as manifestation(s) of YHWH's Presently spoken Name/Word (which translates as "I AM") and all of us always already exist as manifestation(s) of his four-headed fountain of life; the Jews imply that they consider all of us to always already exist as manifestation(s) of Divine Speech. The Jews also imply that they consider All to always already be One, and All to always already be Now. And as we know, the Jews associate YHWH's (multiple and yet simultaneously singular) Presence in the natural world with quantity/number, and we recognize that the Greek term Logos—which the Greeks associated with Divinity, with speech, and with number—was another Greek name for YHWH himself. (And indeed, we find that the Jews of the Hellenistic period referred to YHWH directly as "the Logos," and we read that "within Hellenistic Judaism, Philo (c. 20BC–c.50AD) integrated the term [Logos] into Jewish philosophy." ("Logos," para. 6.)))

Pythagoras also recognized that it was possible to apply his findings from the lyre to the motions of the heavenly bodies. We read:

> Because the Pythagoreans thought that the heavenly bodies were separated from one another by intervals corresponding to the harmonic lengths of strings, they held that the movement of the spheres gives rise to a musical sound called the "harmony of the spheres."[60]

Pythagoras implies that he considered All to participate in a divine harmony—and from the existence of which, it was possible to extrapolate ratios, and numbers themselves.[61] And Pythagoras also implies that his Tetrad was representative of this divine harmony, as "the rows can be read as the ratios of 4:3 (perfect fourth), 3:2 (perfect fifth), 2:1 (octave), forming the basic intervals of the Pythagorean scales."[62]

Let us turn now to the final part of Pythagoras's cosmology—to his ideas on vegetarianism and on the life after death.

IV. ON VEGETARIANISM AND METEMPSYCHOSIS

Scholars report that Pythagoras was a vegetarian, and that he believed in metempsychosis—or the idea that the soul lives on after death.[63]

Why was Pythagoras a vegetarian, and why did he believe that the soul lives on after death?

---

60. Usvat, "Sacred Geometry," para. 8.

61. Fascinatingly, today we know that some celestial bodies' periods are related by a ratio of two small integers, causing orbital resonances to occur. "Examples are the 1:2:4 resonance of Jupiter's moons . . . and the 2:3 resonance between Pluto and Neptune" ("Orbital Resonance," para. 1).

62. "Tetractys," para. 7.

63. We read: "Metempsychosis (Greek: μετεμψύχωσις), in philosophy, refers to transmigration of the soul, especially its reincarnation after death. . . . The earliest Greek thinker with whom metempsychosis is connected is Pherecydes of Syros, but Pythagoras, who is said to have been his pupil, is its first famous philosophic exponent" ("Metempsychosis," paras. 1, 4).

❧

As we know, Pythagoras considered YHWH, the four-headed fountain of life, to come into being Presently in the natural world, in the coming into being of the (multiple and yet simultaneously singular) All/the Only. Pythagoras therefore implies that he considered All lives to always already exist as One life—and we recognize that it was for this reason that Pythagoras did not eat animals, and that he believed that the soul lives on after death.[64]

❧

Scholars report that in the years just following Pythagoras's death (fifth century BC), one of his followers, Hippasus of Metapontum, was to make a discovery that would shatter the crystalline beauty of the Pythagorean monistic theory.[65] As we will see, Hippasus's discovery was to have a profound effect on the ideas of the natural philosophers who immediately followed Pythagoras in chronological time, and we turn now to an exploration of Hippasus's discovery.

---

64. Let us note here that, Plato, who was deeply influenced by Pythagoras, was also a vegetarian and also believed in metempsychosis. (See "Pythagoreanism," para. 3, in which we read: "Pythagorean ideas exercised a marked influence on Plato and through him, on all of Western philosophy.")

65. And in consequence, YHWH's Presence would be lost to the philosophical discourse for several centuries. And as we will see, it was for Archimedes, who scholars recognize was "the greatest mathematician of antiquity and one of the greatest of all time" ("Archimedes," para. 1), to restore YHWH's Presence to the philosophical discourse—but in a far more mathematically nuanced way than Pythagoras had known or imagined.

Chapter III.

The Pythagorean Crisis

IN THE YEARS JUST following Pythagoras's death, one of his followers, Hippasus of Metapontum, made a discovery that shattered the crystalline beauty of the Pythagorean monistic theory. In order to understand Hippasus's discovery and how it came to provoke a Pythagorean crisis, we will need to explore Pythagoras's cosmology a bit further. Pythagoras made many mathematical discoveries—including the mathematical theorem which bears his name: the Pythagorean Theorem.

As Wikipedia reports, the Pythagorean Theorem is a

> theorem in geometry that states that "in a right-angled triangle the area of the square of the hypotenuse [the side opposite the right angle] is equal [to the sum of] the squares of the two other two sides"—that is $a^2 + b^2 = c^2$.[1]

FIGURE 2

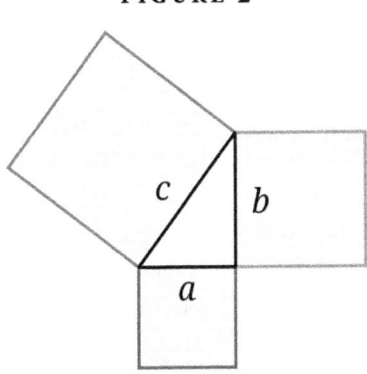

---

1. "Pythagoras," para. 36.

⌘

Pythagoras discovered his theorem by studying right triangles carefully. And by way of his studies, he also recognized that it was possible to compare the lengths of the sides of a right triangle to one another, and that these comparisons also produced ratios whose elements were whole numbers.

Pythagoras recognized that the whole numbers of which the ratios were composed referred to multiples of a common (geometric) unit of measure that fit evenly into both side lengths being measured. (For example, Pythagoras recognized that for the right triangle of side lengths three, four, and five, the ratio of 3:4 referred to three and four multiples of a common (geometric) unit of measure that fit evenly into both side lengths being measured.)[2] And Pythagoras considered the common (geometric) unit of measure to itself be symbolic of YHWH's indivisible Presence in the natural world. (As we know, Pythagoras considered YHWH to be indivisible, and we find that Pythagoras considered the common (geometric) unit of measure to itself be indivisible. Pythagoras considered multiples of this common (geometric) unit of measure to be symbolic of YHWH's (multiple and yet simultaneously singular) Presence in the natural world, and Pythagoras considered the whole numbers of which the ratios were composed to be representative of this (multiple and yet simultaneously singular) Presence.)[3]

And Pythagoras recognized that the existence of the ratios that could be extrapolated by comparing the sides of a right triangle to one another further demonstrated that there existed an inextricable relationship between geometry and number in the natural world.

⌘

Enter Hippasus of Metapontum. In the fifth century BC, Hippasus of Metapontum, a Pythagorean, makes a discovery that provokes a Pythagorean crisis.

Hippasus analyzes an isosceles right triangle (or a right triangle with two equal sides), and he finds that there is no common (geometric) unit of measure that fits evenly into both side lengths being measured.

2. Pythagoras recognized that this relationship was that of the perfect fourth.

3. Pythagoras also considered (whole) numbers to be indivisible, since he considered them to refer to multiples of indivisible YHWH himself.

CHAPTER III. THE PYTHAGOREAN CRISIS

Hippasus analyzes the isosceles right triangle of side length one, and he recognizes that by the Pythagorean theorem, its hypotenuse measures the square root of two. He compares the side of length one with the triangle's hypotenuse of length square root of two, and he arrives at the ratio one: the square root of two. (See below.)

FIGURE 3[4]

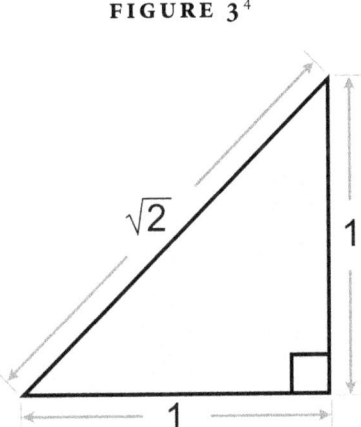

And Hippasus recognizes that:

> [the] then-current Pythagorean method would have claimed that there must be some sufficiently small, indivisible [geometric] unit that could fit evenly into one of these lengths as well as the other.[5]

(And we remind ourselves here that Pythagoras had considered this "small, indivisible unit" to be symbolic of YHWH's own indivisible Presence in the natural world.) However, Hippasus was "able to deduce that there was no common unit of measure, and that the assertion of such an existence was a contradiction."[6]

Hippasus was able to show that it was not possible to express the relationship between the two side lengths as being a perfect ratio of two whole numbers. And scholars report that Hippasus's "discovery posed a very serious problem to Pythagorean mathematics, since it shattered the

---

4. "Square Root of 2," para. 2.
5. "Irrational Number," para. 6.
6. "Irrational Number," para. 6.

assumption that numbers and geometry were inseparable; a foundation of their theory."[7]

⊹

According to legend, Hippasus, who made his discovery while out at sea, was subsequently thrown overboard by his fellow Pythagoreans

> for having produced an element in the universe which denied the Pythagorean doctrine that all phenomena in the universe can be reduced to whole numbers or their ratios.[8]

We may surmise that Hippasus was thrown overboard by his fellow Pythagoreans for having lost for them the site of YHWH's indivisible Presence in the natural world—the monist, materialist focus of Pythagoras's entire cosmology.

⊹

Scholars report that in the wake of Hippasus's discovery, the Greeks coined the word *alogos*—or "inexpressible"[9]—to describe a ratio for which there exists no common (geometric) unit of measure. (The Greeks also referred to this type of ratio as an "incommensurate" ratio, and they contrasted it with the type of ratio for which there *does* exist a common (geometric) unit of measure—which they referred to as a "commensurate ratio," and which, as we know, they associated with the existence of the Logos/YHWH's Presence in the natural world.)[10]

Other examples of the alogos would soon be found—including pi, the ratio of the circumference of a circle to its diameter.[11]

---

7. "Irrational Number," para. 8. See also Kline, *Mathematical Thought*, 33, in which he writes that Hippasus's "discovery posed a problem that was central in Greek mathematics. The Pythagoreans had . . . identified number with geometry. But the existence of [the square root of two] shattered this identification."

8. Kline, *Mathematical Thought*, 32.

9. "Irrational Number," para. 8. See also Pesic, *Abel's Proof*, 9, in which he writes that *alogon* means "'inexpressible, unsayable.'"

10. We recognize that the Greeks associated commensurate ratios with Divine Speech—with the existence of the (multiple and yet simultaneously singular) All/the Only, with Divinity, and with substance itself—and that the existence of incommensurate ratios in the natural world threatened the loss of all of these things.

11. We read that although the "earliest written approximations of π are found in

CHAPTER III. THE PYTHAGOREAN CRISIS

What would the discovery of the alogos—of the ratio for which there exists no common (geometric) unit of measure—mean for the Pythagorean monistic cosmology? In the centuries following Hippasus's discovery, natural philosophers struggled with attempting to answer this question.

We find that as an immediate consequence of Hippasus's discovery, philosophers began to consider mathematics on its own terms, distinctly from any greater natural philosophical or mystical concerns.[12]

We also find that as an immediate consequence of Hippasus's discovery, the Greeks began to recognize that ultimately, they would need to admit for new kinds of numbers—those which would later be called "rational" and "irrational" numbers. The Greek word logos (which, as we know, is the root of their word "ratio") would later be translated into Latin as "rational." Commensurate ratios (or those ratios that the Greeks associated with the existence of the Logos/YHWH's Presence in the natural world) would be referred to as rational numbers, and incommensurate ratios (or those ratios for which there exists no common (geometric) unit of measure, and which were described as "the alogos") would be referred to as irrational numbers.

There were several philosophers during this time who began to consider mathematics on its own terms. We will briefly explore the ideas of four such philosophers—Zeno, Democritus, Eudoxus, and Aristotle—as we will find that their ideas were to be of great import to Archimedes. And as we will see, it was for Archimedes, who scholars recognize was "the greatest mathematician of antiquity and one of the greatest of all time,"[13] to restore YHWH's Presence to the philosophical discourse—but in a far more mathematically nuanced way than Pythagoras had known or imagined.

Babylon [dated 1900–1600 BC] and Egypt [dated 1850–1650 BC]," the first Greek approximation of pi was made by Archimedes in the third century BC ("Pi," para. 24).

12. As we will see, in the third century BC, Archimedes succeeds in remarrying the discipline of mathematics to that of natural philosophy—and he does so by restoring YHWH's Presence to the philosophical discourse.

13. "Archimedes," para. 1.

Let us return now to the fifth century BC, as we begin to explore the cosmology of Zeno.

ZENO OF ELEA (490-430 BC)

Zeno, a provocateur and a contrarian, reflects on the meaning of Hippasus's isosceles right triangle of side length one, with its hypotenuse of length square root of two. Zeno considers the triangle's hypotenuse, both as a line segment and as a numerical value. And Zeno's reflections inspire him to author his famous Dichotomy Paradox, which may be loosely paraphrased as follows:

> All geometric objects and all numbers can be divided in half, and those halves can be divided in half, and the halves of those halves can be divided in half, and so on, and so forth, ad infinitum.[14]

Zeno's Dichotomy Paradox suggests that it is possible to divide the triangle's hypotenuse (which Zeno considers both as a line segment and as a numerical value) in half, and that it is possible to divide those halves in half, and that it is possible to divide the halves of those halves in half, and so on, and so forth, ad infinitum—and we find that the implications of his paradox are to suggest that both the line segment and its numerical value exist as infinite collections of continuous (or infinitely divisible) objects.

Zeno recognizes that it is possible to divide the isosceles right triangle's side of length one similarly, and that in fact, it is possible to divide any geometric object and any number as such—and we find that the greater implications of Zeno's Dichotomy Paradox are to suggest that *all geometric objects and all numbers exist as infinite collections of continuous (or infinitely divisible) objects.*

As we know, these ideas are in direct opposition to those of Pythagoras, who had considered the elements of which all geometric objects are composed to be discrete (or indivisible), and to refer to multiples of indivisible YHWH himself; and who had also considered (whole) numbers to be discrete (or indivisible), and to refer to multiples of indivisible YHWH himself.

---

14. Aristotle recounts Zeno's actual Dichotomy Paradox as follows: "That which is in locomotion must arrive at the half-way stage before it arrives at the goal" (Aristotle, *Physics* VI:9).

And the question arises here in the Greek philosophical discourse: are the elements of which all geometric objects and of which all numbers are composed discrete (or indivisible), as Pythagoras had suggested, or are they continuous (or infinitely divisible), as Zeno suggests?

Philosophers struggle with attempting to reconcile the ideas of Pythagoras with those of Zeno.

DEMOCRITUS (460–370 BC)

Democritus, who scholars recognize was a "pioneer of mathematics"[15] (and indeed, we find that Newton deeply respected Democritus's wisdom, and considered Democritus, along with Pythagoras, to be one of the Greek natural philosophers whose ideas exemplified (what Newton referred to as) "that mystic philosophy which flowed down to the Greeks from Egypt and Phoenicia"[16]), reflects upon the ideas of Pythagoras and of Zeno—and in response, he offers us his own intuitions on the nature of the elements of which all geometric objects and of which all numbers are composed. Unfortunately, we find that Democritus's ideas on numbers did not survive the Middle Ages, and that we will therefore need to content ourselves with Democritus's ideas on geometry—which, as we will see, will not disappoint.[17]

Democritus returns to Pythagoras's cosmology for insight and guidance into the nature of the elements of which all geometric objects are

---

15. "Democritus," para. 12.

16. See Guicciardini's *Reading the* Principia, 101, in which Guicciardini quotes Newton as having written that it was "a very ancient opinion" that "all matter consist of atoms," where "atoms are sometimes found to be designated by the mystics as monads." Newton explains: "This was the teaching of the multitude of philosophers who preceded Aristotle, namely Epicurus, Democritus, Ecphantos, Empedocles, Zenocrates, Heraclides, Asclepiades, Diodorus, Metrodorus of Chios, Pythagoras, and previous to these Moschus the Phoenician whom Strabo declares older than the Trojan war." And Newton asserts here that the cosmologies of all of these philosophers are examples of "that mystic philosophy which flowed down to the Greeks from Egypt and Phoenicia." (And we also recognize that Newton hints to us here that he did not consider the concept of *monism* to have originated in the cosmologies of the Presocratics of the sixth century BC.)

17. The Roman scholar Seneca described Democritus as being the "most subtle of the Ancients," and we will find this to be true as well.

composed. And Democritus recognizes that although the existence of YHWH's Presence in the natural world became suspect in the wake of Hippasus's discovery, it would still be possible to mine Pythagoras's cosmology for insights into the nature of mathematical reality, independently of Pythagoras's greater natural philosophical and mystical concerns. Democritus studies Pythagoras's Tetrad deeply (even as he sifts out for the existence of YHWH's Presence within it), and he comes to recognize that Pythagoras had suggested that:

— the elements of which a one-dimensional line is composed are zero-dimensional points, and that the zero-dimensional points are discrete (or indivisible) relative to the one-dimensional line that they help to generate (and to which they contribute as elements).

— the elements of which a two-dimensional plane is composed are one-dimensional lines, and that the one-dimensional lines are discrete (or indivisible) relative to the two-dimensional plane that they help to generate (and to which they contribute as elements).

— and the elements of which a three-dimensional volume is composed are two-dimensional planes, and that the two-dimensional planes are discrete (or indivisible) relative to the three-dimensional volume that they help to generate (and to which they contribute as elements).

Democritus recognizes that Pythagoras had suggested that all geometric objects are composed of an infinite number of elements that exist *as of one dimension less* than the geometric object that they are generating (and to which they contribute as elements), and that these elements are discrete (or indivisible) relative to the geometric object that they are generating (and to which they contribute as elements).

Democritus recognizes all of these ideas about the Pythagorean cosmology, and we find that in consequence, he introduces into the Greek philosophical discourse the concept of the mathematical "indivisible."[18] The concept of the mathematical indivisible, which is deeply indebted to the ideas of Pythagoras, proposes that the elements of which all geometric objects are composed exist *as of one dimension less* than the geometric objects that they are generating (and to which they contribute as elements), and that these elements are discrete (or indivisible) relative to the

---

18. Scholars consider Democritus to have been an "atomist"—a word which comes from the Greek "atomos," meaning "indivisible."

geometric objects that they are generating (and to which they contribute as elements).

For example, the concept of the mathematical indivisible proposes that:

— the indivisible of a line is a point

— the indivisible of a surface is a line

— and that the indivisible of a volume is a surface.

And as John L. Bell reports in the "Continuity and Infinitesimals" entry in the *Stanford Encyclopedia of Philosophy*, in "each case the indivisible in question . . . [possesses] *one fewer dimension than the figure from which it is generated*,"[19] and is indivisible with respect to the figure from which it is generated (as the name "indivisible" suggests).[20]

And we find that with his authoring of the concept of the indivisible, Democritus implies that he considers all geometric objects to exist as infinite collections of discrete (or indivisible) objects.

(We note here that Democritus's ideas were to be deeply influential to many of the natural philosophers who followed him in chronological time. Archytas, who was a contemporary of Democritus's, and a friend of Plato's, asserted in his writings that "the line divides into points, the surface into lines, the solid into surfaces."[21] And we also read that "Plato's discussion of the composition of solids from plane surfaces is thought

---

19. Bell, "Continuity and Infinitesimals," para. 11.

20. Democritus recognizes that a geometric object's indivisibles are indivisible only *relative* to the geometric object that they are generating (and to which they contribute as elements), and that they are not *absolutely* indivisible—and that this is true in all cases except for the one-dimensional line, whose zero-dimensional points are indivisible relative to the one-dimensional line that they help to generate (and to which they contribute as elements), even as they are also absolutely indivisible.

And let us also note here that historians of mathematics credit Galileo Galilei's student Bonaventura Cavilieri (1598–1647) with developing the first mathematically rigorous definition of the indivisible in the Renaissance, but that we recognize that Cavilieri's concept of the indivisible is actually indistinguishable from the concept first proposed by Democritus (which as we know, was based upon Pythagoras's own ideas). And regarding Cavilieri's indivisible, we read that in Cavilieri's *Geometria indivisibilibus continuorum nova quadam ratione promota*, which was published in 1635, "a point is considered as the indivisible of a line, a line of a plane, and a plane of a solid" (see "Bonaventura Francesco Cavalieri," 93).

21. Fideler, *Pythagorean Sourcebook*, 183.

to be based on fourth-century Pythagorean theories"—and we recognize that Plato too was deeply influenced by Democritus.)[22]

⟁

But we also find that Democritus was not content to stop there. Democritus was also very familiar with Zeno's Dichotomy Paradox, and he recognized that Zeno's Dichotomy Paradox suggests that all geometric objects exist as infinite collections of continuous (or infinitely divisible) objects. And we find that Democritus also introduces into the philosophical discourse the concept of the "infinitesimal" magnitude. (As John L. Bell reports, "Infinitesimals . . . . make an early appearance in the mathematics of the Greek atomist philosopher Democritus."[23])

Democritus considers the infinitesimal magnitude to be a continuous, or infinitely divisible, geometric object, which is smaller than any measurable size,[24] and which exists *as of the same dimension* as the geometric object that it helps to generate (and to which it contributes as an element).

And we recognize that with Democritus's authoring of the concept of the infinitesimal magnitude, he implies that he also considers all geometric objects to exist as infinite collections of continuous (or infinitely divisible) objects.

---

22. See Berryman, "Ancient Atomism," para. 4. Let us note here that we will not explore Plato's natural philosophical ideas in this chapter for we will find that they largely echo Pythagoras's own natural philosophical ideas. (And we remind ourselves here that in the "Pythagoreanism" entry in Wikipedia we read that "Pythagorean ideas exercised a marked influence on Plato.") We will find that Plato's quantitative contributions to the philosophical discourse were not significant; however, we will find that Plato's qualitative contributions to the philosophical discourse *were* significant. And as we will see, both Galileo and Newton considered themselves to be disciples of Plato, and for this reason, we will explore Plato's qualitative contributions to the philosophical discourse in the chapters in which we will explore the cosmologies of Galileo and of Newton.

23. Bell, "Continuity and Infinitesimals," para. 3.

24. See "Infinitesimal", para. 7, in which we read that "in common speech, an infinitesimal object is an object that is smaller than any feasible measurement, but not zero in size."

CHAPTER III. THE PYTHAGOREAN CRISIS 43

We find that Democritus's ideas therefore allow for the possibility that:

—the elements of which all geometric objects are composed are discrete (or indivisible) with respect to the geometric object that they are generating (and to which they contribute as elements), and that they exist *as of one dimension less* than the geometric object that they are generating (and to which they contribute as elements)—

—and that Democritus' ideas *also* allow for the possibility that the elements of which all geometric objects are composed are continuous (or infinitely divisible), and that they exist *as of the same dimension* as the geometric object that they are generating (and to which they contribute as elements).

We recognize that Democritus's ideas are not mutually exclusive, and that his ideas also allow for the possibility that the elements of which all geometric objects are composed are discrete (or indivisible) *and* continuous (or infinitely divisible) *at the same time*; his ideas allow for the possibility that the elements of which all geometric objects are composed exist *as of two dimensions simultaneously*.

And indeed, in *A History of Greek Mathematics*, Sir Thomas Little Heath reports that "according to Democritus himself, his atoms [or indivisibles] were, in a mathematical sense divisible further and in fact ad infinitum"[25]—and we deduce that *Democritus considered his atoms to be both indivisible and infinitely divisible at the same time because he considered them to exist as of two dimensions simultaneously.*

(And again, we find that Democritus's ideas were to be deeply influential to many who followed him in chronological time. Archytas, who applied Democritus's ideas to (what he considered to be) a linear time line, considered the elements of which this time line was composed to be both discrete and continuous *at the same time*, and he wrote, "We must ... recognize time as both continuous and discrete."[26] And as we will see,

---

25. Heath, *History of Greek Mathematics*, 181.
26. Fideler, *Pythagorean Sourcebook*, 183.

Democritus's ideas were also to be of great import to Archimedes in the development of his own cosmology.[27])

⁖

(And we also find that although Democritus's ideas regarding the elements of which all numbers are composed have been lost to us, it is still possible for us to deduce them from our explorations of the works that have survived. For example, it is possible for us to imagine that, like Zeno, Democritus returned to an exploration of Hippasus's isosceles right triangle. It is possible for us to imagine that, like Zeno, Democritus considered the triangle's hypotenuse of length square root of two, both as a line segment and as a numerical value. And it is possible for us to imagine that since Democritus implies that he considered the elements of which this line segment is composed to be discrete (or indivisible) *and* continuous (or infinitely divisible) *at the same time*, he also considered the elements of which its numerical value is composed to be discrete (or indivisible) *and* continuous (or infinitely divisible) *at the same time*. It is therefore possible for us to deduce that Democritus considered the elements of which all numbers are composed to be discrete (or indivisible) *and* continuous (or infinitely divisible) *at the same time*, and to exist *as of two dimensions simultaneously*.)[28]

27. As we will see, Archimedes will reveal to us that he too considered the elements of which all geometric objects are composed to be discrete (or indivisible) *and* continuous (or infinitely divisible) *at the same time*, and to exist *as of two dimensions simultaneously*.

Let us note here that Democritus himself was also deeply influenced by other natural philosophers who preceded him in chronological time. Parmenides, a monist Presocratic philosopher (ca. 515 BC) who lived half a century before Democritus, and who himself had been deeply influenced by Pythagoras, wrote a poem entitled *On Nature* in which he suggests that the Pythagorean Monad/YHWH himself (or he to whom Parmenides refers in his poem as "the One") is both continuous and indivisible *at the same time*. In *On Nature*, Parmenides writes: "[What exists—and by which Parmenides means the Pythagorean Monad/YHWH himself/the Parmenidean One] is now, all at once, one and continuous . . . Nor is it divisible" (see "Parmenides," para. 17). We find, however, that Parmenides does not explicitly show us how he considers this to be mathematically possible, and that for the mathematically rigorous restoration of YHWH's Presence to the philosophical discourse, we will need to wait for Archimedes.

28. And again, we will find that this idea will be of deep import to Archimedes in the development of his own cosmology, who will reveal to us that he too considered the elements of which all numbers are composed to be discrete (or indivisible) *and* continuous (or infinitely divisible) *at the same time*, and to exist *as of two dimensions simultaneously*.

EUDOXUS OF CNIDUS (408-355 BC)

Eudoxus reacts against the ideas of Democritus, and we find that in consequence, he chooses to sever the concept of the continuous from the discrete.

Eudoxus proposes that all objects of geometry are continuous (and are therefore composed of an infinite number of elements which themselves are continuous), and that all numbers exist as collections of discrete objects, which jump "from one value to another, as from 4 to 5."[29]

(And we recognize here that in severing the continuous from the discrete, Eudoxus also divorces geometry from number, and he definitively sunders (what Pythagoras had considered to be) the inseparable relationship between geometry and number in the natural world.)

As Morris Kline explains in his *Mathematical Thought from Ancient to Modern Times*, Eudoxus refers to objects of geometry as *continuous magnitudes*, and among continuous magnitudes Eudoxus includes "line segments, angles, areas, volumes, and time [—all of] which could vary, as we would say, continuously."[30]

Eudoxus also develops a "method of exhaustion" to approximate the value of geometric objects' areas. (And let us remind ourselves here that Eudoxus considers geometric objects' areas to be continuous magnitudes—which he considers to be continuous, and to be composed of an infinite number of continuous elements.) The method of exhaustion suggests that determining the value of a geometric object's area involves a summation over an infinite number of the geometric object's infinitesimal areas. As Wikipedia reports:

> The method of exhaustion (Latin: *methodus exhaustionis*) is a method of finding the area of a shape by inscribing inside it a sequence of polygons whose areas converge to the area of the containing shape. If the sequence is correctly constructed, the difference in area between the *n*th polygon and the containing

---

29. Kline, *Mathematical Thought*, 48.

30. Kline, *Mathematical Thought*, 48. We find that the ancient Greek word for (geometric) magnitude was *megethos* and that the ancient Greek word for number was *arithmos*, and that with Eudoxus, geometry was divorced from number (see Pesic, *Abel's Proof*, 9).

shape will become arbitrarily small as n becomes [infinitely] large. As this difference becomes arbitrarily small, the possible values for the area of the shape are systematically "exhausted" by the lower bound areas successively established by the sequence members.[31]

We find that Eudoxus also applies the method of exhaustion to problems of approximating the values of geometric objects' volumes.[32]

❧

Eudoxus recognizes that his method of exhaustion is a dynamic, infinitely iterative procedure, which, taken to its logical conclusion, suggests that the area or volume of the geometric object being investigated *comes into being* in the coming into being of an infinite number of the geometric object's infinitesimal areas or volumes. (And since Eudoxus considers areas and volumes to be continuous magnitudes, he recognizes that the method of exhaustion suggests that continuous magnitudes themselves *come into being* in the coming into being of an infinite number of their infinitesimal elements.)

And we find that the concept of the *dynamical generation* of continuous magnitudes arises in Greek thought. It is recognized that by way of the infinitely iterative process of exhaustion, it is possible for the mathematician to *dynamically generate* continuous magnitudes—which come into being in the coming into being of an infinite number of the continuous magnitudes' infinitesimal elements.

ARISTOTLE (384–322 BC)

Aristotle is deeply influenced by Eudoxus, and we find that he continues to consider continuous quantities to be divorced from discrete quantities, and that he continues to consider the concept of geometry to be divorced from number. Like Eudoxus, Aristotle considers objects of geometry to be continuous (and to be composed of an infinite number of elements

---

31. "Method of Exhaustion," para. 1.

32. See "Method of Exhaustion," para. 3, in which it is written that although the "idea [of the method of exhaustion] originated in the late 5th century BC with Antiphon. . . . [the method] was made rigorous a few decades later by Eudoxus of Cnidus, who used it to calculate areas and volumes."

CHAPTER III. THE PYTHAGOREAN CRISIS 47

which themselves are continuous), and he considers numbers to exist as collections of discrete objects, which jump in value, as from 4 to 5.

And as John L. Bell reports in the "Continuity and Infinitesimals" entry in the *Stanford Encyclopedia of Philosophy*, as "examples of continuous quantities, or *continua*, [Aristotle] offers lines, planes, solids (i.e., solid bodies), extensions, movement, time and space; among discrete quantities he includes number and speech."[33]

Aristotle also asserts that a geometric object's indivisibles simply do not exist. In his *Physics*, he writes that:

> nothing that is continuous can be composed 'of indivisibles'; e.g. a line cannot be composed of points, the line being continuous and the point indivisible.[34]

Aristotle's ideas are in direct opposition to those of Pythagoras and of Democritus, and we find that Newton remarks that with Aristotle, the ancient natural philosophy began to decline.[35]

↭

Aristotle is also interested in the concept of *motion and change*; he seeks to develop a mechanics to explore the motions of physical bodies in the natural world.[36] And Aristotle recognizes that while it is possible for the mathematician to dynamically generate continuous magnitudes by way of the infinitely iterative method of exhaustion, continuous magnitudes are also dynamically generated in the natural world as physical bodies move over passing time. (For example, Aristotle recognizes that continuous magnitudes are generated as the celestial bodies move over passing time.)

Aristotle recognizes the dynamism of the infinitely iterative process of exhaustion, and he also recognizes the dynamism of physical bodies' motions—both of which he considers to be responsible for the

---

33. Bell, "Continuity and Infinitesimals," para. 23.

34. Aristotle, *Physics* VI:1.

35. See "System of the World" in Newton's *Mathematical Principles: Newton's System of the World*, 511, in which Newton writes that with Aristotle, "the ancient philosophy began to decline, and to give place to the new prevailing fictions of the Greeks."

36. We read: "Mechanics (Greek μηχανική) . . . [had] its origins in Ancient Greece with the writings of Aristotle and Archimedes" ("Mechanics," para. 1).

generation of continuous magnitudes. And Aristotle therefore surmises that continuous magnitudes are generated by way of motion. We read:

> It is motion, Aristotle implies, which is directly responsible for the generation of continuous magnitude.[37]

※

Aristotle also asserts that there exists a relationship between motion and time in the natural world. He writes:

> Not only do we measure the movement by the time, but also the time by the movement, because they define each other. The time marks the movement ... and the movement the time.[38]

But we find that Aristotle's is not a mathematically rigorous cosmology,[39] and that for the natural philosophers who follow him, his ideas only serve to further beg the question: what is the precise nature of the relationship between motion and time in the natural world?

As has been mentioned, Aristotle considers time to be a continuous magnitude (which he considers to be composed of an infinite number of elements which are also continuous); and he also considers movement to be a continuous magnitude (which he also considers to be composed of an infinite number of elements which are continuous). We find, however, that Aristotle does not consider the present to be a part of time—and we read that for Aristotle, "the present is not a part of time."[40]

37. Evans, "Aristotle," 548.
38. Aristotle, *Physics*, IV:12.
39. Scholars acknowledge that Aristotle reacted against the ideas of his teacher, Plato—who himself had been deeply influenced by Pythagoras. (And we remind ourselves here that "Pythagorean ideas exercised a marked influence on Plato.") And on Aristotle's reaction to the teachings of Plato, Galileo Galilei's colleague in Pisa, professor Jacopo Mazzoni would later explain: "Plato believed that mathematics was quite particularly appropriate for physical investigations, which was the reason why he himself had many times recourse to it for the explanation of physical mysteries. But Aristotle held a quite different view and he explained the errors of Plato by his too great attachment to mathematics" (see Darrigol, *Physics and Necessity*, 186).

40. Aristotle, *Selections*, 127. Let us explore this idea more deeply. Although Aristotle considers the present to exist, he considers the present to be indivisible, and he considers time to be continuous. He writes: "The present also is necessarily indivisible" (*Physics*, VI:3)—and yet, beguilingly, he also asserts that time is not composed of indivisible Nows. (In his *Physics*, he also writes, "time is not composed of indivisible nows, any more than any other magnitude is composed of indivisibles." (See W.D.

CHAPTER III. THE PYTHAGOREAN CRISIS 49

Aristotle also recognizes that it would only be possible to rigorously define the concept of motion and change by defining it in relation to something that remained *unchanging* with respect to itself for all time, and which could therefore be considered to be *immovable*.

As we know, Pythagoras had considered YHWH, the site of ultimate substance and of what Presently Is in the natural world, to exist as the unchanging and immovable referent by which it would be possible to rigorously define all motion and change; but, as we know, in the wake of Hippasus's discovery, YHWH's Presence in the natural world became suspect. We find that Aristotle does not make it his mission to attempt to restore YHWH's Presence to the philosophical discourse—(for this we will have to wait for Archimedes)—and instead, Aristotle defines motion and change in relation to what he refers to as "the unmoved mover"— which, we note, he does not consider to exist as the site of ultimate substance and of what Presently Is in the natural world. We read:

> The unmoved mover (Ancient Greek: ὃ οὐ κινούμενον κινεῖ, romanized: *ho ou kinoúmenon kineî*, lit. 'that which moves without being moved') or prime mover (Latin: *primum movens*) is a concept advanced by Aristotle as a primary cause (or first uncaused cause) or "mover" of all the motion in the universe. As is implicit in the name, the *unmoved mover* moves other things, but is not itself moved by any prior action. In Book 12 (Greek: Λ) of his *Metaphysics*, Aristotle describes the unmoved mover as being perfectly beautiful, indivisible, and contemplating only the perfect contemplation: self-contemplation.[41]

And although Aristotle does not reveal to us precisely where he considers the unmoved mover to be located in the natural world, we recognize that he does not locate its existence at the site of an ultimate substance—to which Aristotle refers in his cosmology as "first matter" or "prime matter," and from which our modern word "matter" derives[42]—and that he

---

Ross's translation of the *Physics*, cited in Pickering, "Aristotle," 253.)) And we therefore deduce that Aristotle does not consider the present to be a part of time.

41. "Unmoved Mover," para. 1.

42. See Principe's *Secrets of Alchemy*, 14, in which he writes that the "notion that a single ultimate substance lies beneath all material things is known as *monism*. For . . . Aristotle, [this ultimate substance was] what he called 'first matter' or 'prime matter' (*prōton hylē*)."

does not locate its existence at the site of what Presently Is—which, as we know, he does not consider to be a part of time.

❦

This is the intellectual universe that Archimedes inherits. Let us turn now to the cosmology of Archimedes, who, as we will see, succeeds in restoring YHWH's Presence to the philosophical discourse, but in a far more mathematically nuanced way than Pythagoras had known or imagined.

Chapter IV.

Archimedes (287–212 BC)

ARCHIMEDES, WHO SCHOLARS RECOGNIZE was a "mathematician, physicist, engineer, astronomer, and inventor,"[1] and who is widely considered to be "the greatest mathematician of antiquity and one of the greatest of all time,"[2] was also interested in the concept of *motion and change*. Like Aristotle, Archimedes was interested in developing a mechanics to explore the motions of physical bodies in the natural world—but unlike Aristotle, Archimedes was interested in developing a mathematically rigorous mechanics. And Archimedes too recognized that it would only be possible to rigorously define motion and change by defining it in relation to something that remained *unchanging* with respect to itself for all time, and which could therefore be considered to be *immovable*. Aristotle's solution to this problem was intellectually unsatisfying, since Aristotle had been vague on the precise location of the unmoved mover in the natural world.

We find that Archimedes, who was also well-versed in the cosmology of Pythagoras, recognized that although the existence of YHWH's Presence in the natural world became suspect in the wake of Hippasus's discovery, Pythagoras had considered YHWH, the site of ultimate substance and of what Presently Is in the natural world, to exist as the unchanging and immovable referent by which it would be possible to rigorously define all motion and change. But Archimedes wonders: would it be possible to restore YHWH's Presence to the philosophical discourse? As we will see, Archimedes takes this challenge to be his life's mission, and we find that he accomplishes what he had set out to do: Archimedes

---

1. "Archimedes," para. 1.
2. "Archimedes," para. 1.

succeeds in restoring YHWH's Presence to the philosophical discourse, but in a far more mathematically nuanced way than Pythagoras had known or imagined.

⚘

How does Archimedes restore YHWH's Presence to the philosophical discourse? We find that he does so by solving the most pressing engineering problem of his day. As well as being a profoundly talented mathematician, Archimedes was also a deeply gifted engineer, who took delight in being challenged to find solutions to the practical engineering problems of his day. Scholars report that the most pressing engineering problem of Archimedes's day was that of developing a weaponry that might help to defend Archimedes's home city of Syracuse (located on the island of Sicily)[3] from Roman invaders—and they report that Archimedes responded to this challenge by inventing "a highly accurate catapult that stopped the Romans [from] conquering Syracuse for years."[4] (We read that a "large part of Archimedes' work in engineering arose from fulfilling the needs of his home city of Syracuse."[5]) And we find that from Archimedes's having solved the most pressing practical engineering problem of his day—that of inventing a catapult to protect his fellow citizens of Syracuse from Roman ships—that he was also able to solve the most pressing natural philosophical problem of his time—that of finding a way to restore YHWH's Presence to the philosophical discourse.

Let us return now to the third century BC, and to an exploration of the development of Archimedes's catapult, as it will reveal to us how Archimedes succeeded in restoring YHWH's Presence to the philosophical discourse.

⚘

Archimedes recognizes that the problem of designing a successful catapult is one of understanding the mechanics of projectile motion. And he recognizes that this is a complex problem, which comprises several parts.

---

3. Syracuse was a very powerful Greek city-state at this time in ancient history, located on the island of Sicily (see "Syracuse, Sicily," para. 2).
4. Stewart, "Archimedes," para. 16.
5. "Archimedes," para. 12.

First, Archimedes recognizes that in order to understand the mechanics of projectile motion, it would be necessary to understand the concept of motion itself. (As has been mentioned, Archimedes recognized that it would only be possible to rigorously define motion and change by defining it in relation to something that remained *unchanging* with respect to itself for all time, and which could therefore be considered to be *immovable*. Aristotle's solution to this problem was intellectually unsatisfying, since Aristotle had not shown precisely where the unmoved mover was located in the natural world. And Archimedes was well-versed in the cosmology of Pythagoras, and he recognized that Pythagoras had considered YHWH himself to exist as the unchanging and immovable referent in the natural world by which it would be possible to rigorously define all motion and change. But Archimedes wonders: would it be possible to restore YHWH's Presence to the philosophical discourse? As has been mentioned, Archimedes takes this challenge to be his life's mission.)

Second, Archimedes recognizes that if it would be possible to locate the *particle equivalent* of an extended physical body, the particle could replace the extended physical body in the mathematical modeling of physical problems, and the motions of the particle over passing time could then be explored. (And let us note here that scholars acknowledge that Archimedes was "one of the first" of the Greek natural philosophers "to apply mathematics to physical phenomena."[6]) We find that from Archimedes's investigations into another practical engineering problem of his day—the problem of understanding the workings of levers—he had discovered that it was possible to locate the particle equivalent of an extended physical body by locating the extended body's "balancing point," or its center of gravity. Archimedes therefore recognizes that in the mathematical modeling of physical problems, it would be possible to replace an extended physical body by its balancing point, or its center of gravity, and we find that he explores the motions of the particle equivalent of the extended physical body over passing time.

Archimedes recognizes that the motions of the particle over passing time dynamically generates a plane curve. And therefore, Archimedes recognizes that in order to understand the motions of particles over passing time, it would also be necessary to understand the dynamical generation of plane curves. Archimedes asks himself: how are plane curves dynamically generated in the natural world?

6. "Archimedes," para. 2.

❧

As we will see, Archimedes develops a "kinematics," or a "geometry of motion,"[7] in an effort to understand the dynamical generation of plane curves, and he then applies this kinematics to his development of a mechanics—and to the study of the motions of all particles—and therefore of all extended physical bodies—in the natural world.

❧

We will begin to explore Archimedes's cosmology by turning first to the development of his kinematics, or his geometry of motion, in which he explores the dynamical generation of plane curves. We will then show how Archimedes locates the particle equivalent of an extended physical body by locating its balancing point, or its center of gravity. And finally, we will show how Archimedes applies these findings to the development of a mathematically rigorous mechanics, and to his study of the motions of all particles—and therefore of all extended physical bodies—in the natural world. And we will find that Archimedes succeeds in designing a highly accurate catapult that protects Syracuse from Roman invaders for years.

And as we will see, by way of the processes of developing his kinematics and his mechanics, Archimedes also succeeds in locating an unchanging and immovable referent in the natural world by which he finds it possible to rigorously define all motion and change—and he recognizes that this referent exists as the site of ultimate substance and of what Presently Is. (And we find that it is actually for *this* reason that Archimedes runs naked through the streets of Syracuse, shouting "Eureka! Eureka!"—which translates as "I found it! I found it!"—for he recognizes that in having rigorously located the site of ultimate substance and of what Presently Is in the natural world, he has succeeded in restoring YHWH's Presence to the philosophical discourse.)[8]

7. We read that "kinematics, as a field of study, is often referred to as the 'geometry of motion' and is occasionally seen as a branch of mathematics" ("Kinematics," para. 1).

8. Although Archimedes is attributed with having exclaimed "Eureka! Eureka!"—which translates as "I found (it)! I found (it)!"—after having realized that the water level of his bathtub rose as he stepped into it (and that therefore the "volume of water displaced must be equal to the volume of the part of his body he had submerged"), the restoration of YHWH's Presence to the philosophical discourse would have been a far greater accomplishment. After having shouted "Eureka! Eureka!," Archimedes is said to have run through the streets of Syracuse naked (see "Eureka (Word)," paras. 2, 5).

CHAPTER IV. ARCHIMEDES   55

Scholars acknowledge that Archimedes's cosmology exists as secret, hidden wisdom, which requires decrypting, and we find that, like Pythagoras, Archimedes too requires of us that we perform countless acts of logical deduction—acts of mathematics—upon his ideas and upon his cosmology so that we too may find what he has found. (And as we will see, what Archimedes has found is the site of Divinity's Presence in the natural world.) On Archimedes's secret, hidden cosmology, nineteenth-century translator Sir Thomas Little Heath writes:

> the studied simplicity and the perfect finish of [Archimedes's] treatises involve at the same time an element of mystery. Though each step depends upon the preceding ones, we are left in the dark as to how they were suggested to Archimedes. There is, in fact, much truth in a remark of [the seventeenth-century mathematician John] Wallis to the effect that he [Archimedes] seems "as it were of set purpose to have covered up the traces of his investigations, as if he has grudged posterity the secret of his method of inquiry, while he wished to extort from them assent to his results."[9]

Archimedes is notorious for skipping steps in his proofs, and we find that, like the cosmology of Pythagoras, Archimedes's cosmology too exists as secret, hidden wisdom, which requires decrypting.

Let us turn now to an exploration of Archimedes's cosmology, and to Archimedes's development of his kinematics, or geometry of motion. We find that because Archimedes is interested in designing a catapult, the focus of his kinematics is upon the dynamical generation of plane curves, and that Archimedes concerns himself first with attempting to identify the elements of which plane curves are composed.[10] Archimedes

---

9. Heath, "Preface" to *Works of Archimedes*, vii. And in Heath's *Manual of Greek Mathematics*, 281, he continues, "There is here [in one of Archimedes's treatises], as in all Greek mathematical masterpieces, no hint as to the kind of analysis by which the results were first arrived at; for it is clear that they were not discovered by the steps which led up to them in the finished treatise."

10. Let us note here that Archimedes considers both closed and open curves in the plane to exist as one-dimensional objects. (We recognize that today, some mathematicians consider closed curves in the plane (such as circles) to exist as objects of two dimensions, but that this was not true at the time of Archimedes.)

therefore seeks to answer for himself the following question: do plane curves exist as infinite collections of their discrete indivisibles (their zero-dimensional points), do they exist as infinite collections of their continuous infinitesimals (their one-dimensional infinitesimal line segments), or do they exist as infinite collections of their discrete indivisibles/their continuous infinitesimals (their zero-dimensional points/their one-dimensional infinitesimal line segments)?

In an effort to answer this question, Archimedes returns to the cosmology of Democritus, who had provided the natural philosophers of his day with his intuitions regarding the nature of the elements of which all geometric objects are composed. Archimedes begins his investigation into the nature of the elements of which plane curves are composed by first exploring Democritus's concept of the indivisible, and he then turns to exploring Democritus's concept of the infinitesimal.

Archimedes recognizes that Democritus had suggested that plane curves exist as infinite collections of their discrete indivisibles—their zero-dimensional points—which exist *as of one dimension less* than the plane curves that they are generating (and to which they contribute as elements).

We find that Archimedes studies Democritus's ideas regarding the mathematical indivisible deeply, and that he invents a "method of indivisibles" (which is also known as "the mechanical method") to estimate the value of continuous magnitudes.[11] Like Eudoxus's method of exhaustion (which, as we know, was also invented for the purpose of estimating the values of continuous magnitudes), the method of indivisibles is also a dynamic, infinitely iterative procedure, but we find that unlike the method of exhaustion (which, as we know, reveals that geometric objects come into being in the coming into being of an infinite number of their continuous infinitesimals), the method of indivisibles reveals that geometric objects come into being in the coming into being of an infinite number of their discrete indivisibles.

On Archimedes's method of indivisibles, we read:

11. See "Infinitesimal," para. 7, in which it is written that "Archimedes used what eventually came to be known as the method of indivisibles in his work *Method of Mechanical Theorems*." And see also "*Method of Mechanical Theorems*," para. 2, in which Archimedes's "mechanical method" is referred to as "the method of indivisibles."

In his book, *the Method*, Archimedes . . . [shows] an n-dimensional figure as [being] composed of an infinity of n-1-dimensional figures.[12]

We find that Archimedes's infinitely iterative method of indivisibles reveals to us that Archimedes considers geometric figures to be dynamically generated in the dynamical generation of an infinite number of the geometric figures' discrete indivisibles.

And Archimedes's invention of the method of indivisibles suggests to us that Archimedes therefore considers plane curves to exist as infinite collections of their discrete indivisibles, their zero-dimensional points, which are dynamically generated in the dynamical generation of the plane curves themselves.

Archimedes turns next to exploring Democritus's concept of the infinitesimal. Archimedes recognizes that Democritus had also suggested that plane curves exist as infinite collections of their continuous infinitesimal magnitudes—their one-dimensional infinitesimal line segments—which exist *as of the same dimension* as the plane curves that they are generating (and to which they contribute as elements).

And we find that Archimedes is also very familiar with Eudoxus's method of exhaustion (which, as we know, reveals that continuous magnitudes come into being in the coming into being of an infinite number of their continuous infinitesimals)—although Archimedes also recognizes that Eudoxus had applied his method of exhaustion only to problems of estimating the values of geometric objects' areas and volumes. We find that Archimedes extends and deepens Eudoxus's method of exhaustion, and that he applies it to problems of approximating the measures of *lengths* of closed curves in the plane: Archimedes applies it to problems of approximating the measures of polygons' perimeters and also to problems of approximating the measures of circles' circumferences. Archimedes's extension and deepening of Eudoxus's method of exhaustion reveals to him that plane curves are also dynamically generated in the dynamic generation of an infinite number of the curves' continuous infinitesimals—the curves' one-dimensional infinitesimal line segments—which exist *as of the same dimension* as the plane curves

12. Mendell, "Infinitary Arguments."

that they are generating (and to which they contribute as elements). Let us explore this idea further.

As we know, Eudoxus had developed his method of exhaustion to approximate the areas and volumes of polygons, but we find that Archimedes extends and deepens Eudoxus's method and that he applies it to the problem of approximating the measures of *lengths* of closed curves in the plane: Archimedes applies it to problems of approximating the measures of polygons' perimeters and also to problems of approximating the measures of circles' circumferences. Not only does Archimedes inscribe polygons from within the closed curves, but he also circumscribes polygons from without the closed curves.[13] (See the following image, which shows how Archimedes uses the method of exhaustion to compute the area inside a circle by inscribing polygons from within the circle and circumscribing polygons from without the circle.)

FIGURE 4[14]

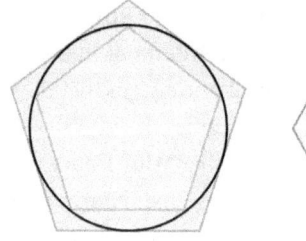 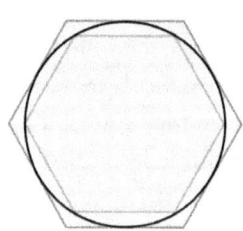 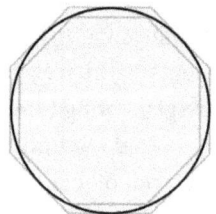

And Archimedes recognizes that by way of the infinitely iterative process of exhaustion, plane curves are dynamically generated in the dynamic generation of an infinite number of the curves' one-dimensional infinitesimal line segments—(the closed curves' infinitesimal sides)—which exist *as of the same dimension* as the curves being generated. Archimedes recognizes that by way of the infinitely iterative process of exhaustion,

---

13. See "History of Calculus," in which it is written that "Eudoxus (c. 408–355 BC) used the method of exhaustion . . . to calculate areas and volumes, while Archimedes (c. 287–212 BC) developed this idea further." And in the "Introduction" to *Works of Archimedes*, cxliv, Heath explains precisely how Archimedes developed Eudoxus's idea further; Heath writes that "Archimedes takes both an inscribed figure and a circumscribed figure in relation to the curve or surface of which he is investigating the area or solid content, and then, as it were, *compresses* the two figures into one so that they coincide with one another and with the curvilinear figure to be measured."

14. "History of Calculus," Wikipedia.

closed curves in the plane come into being in the coming into being of an infinite number of their infinitesimal elements.[15]

We find that Archimedes explores the infinitesimal in great depth, and that he provides us with (what is considered to be) the first logically rigorous definition of the infinitesimal.[16]

And Archimedes extrapolates this finding—the idea that plane curves are dynamically generated in the dynamic generation of an infinite number of their infinitesimal elements—to all plane curves—not just to closed curves in the plane, but to open curves as well.

Archimedes's extension and deepening of the method of exhaustion suggests to us that he therefore considers plane curves to exist as infinite collections of their continuous infinitesimals, their one-dimensional line segments, which are dynamically generated in the dynamic generation of the plane curves themselves.

And Archimedes is therefore left with the following question: do the fundamental elements of which plane curves are composed exist as the curves' discrete indivisibles (the curves' zero-dimensional points), do they exist as the curves' continuous infinitesimals (the curves' one-dimensional infinitesimal line segments), or do they exist as the curves' discrete indivisibles/their continuous infinitesimals (the curves' zero-dimensional points/their one-dimensional infinitesimal line segments)?

We find that Archimedes combines the insights that he arrived at by way of inventing the method of indivisibles with the insights that he arrived at by way of extending and deepening Eudoxus's method of exhaustion, and that he recognizes that the fundamental elements of which plane curves are composed exist *as of two dimensions simultaneously*: Archimedes recognizes that the fundamental elements of which plane curves are composed exist simultaneously as the curves' discrete indivisibles (the curves' zero-dimensional points) *and* as the curves' continuous infinitesimals (the curves' one-dimensional infinitesimal line segments).[17]

---

15. In his treatise *Measurement of a Circle*, Archimedes uses the method of exhaustion to compute an approximate value of pi, the ratio of the circumference of a circle to its diameter. And we read that Archimedes determines the approximate "value of π [which is "greater than 3 10/71 but less than 3 1/7"] by inscribing and circumscribing a circle with two similar 96-sided regular polygons" (see "*Measurement of a Circle*," para. 6). This reveals to us that Archimedes thinks of a circle as an infinilateral polygon, whose infinite number of sides exist as one-dimensional infinitesimal line segments.

16. Scholars report that Archimedes was the first to "propose a logically rigorous definition of infinitesimals" ("Infinitesimal," para. 10).

17. We find that Archimedes does not explicitly state this finding in his work, but

(An idea, we note, that was suggested by Democritus; and let us also remind ourselves here that Newton deeply respected Democritus's wisdom.) *Archimedes recognizes that plane curves exist as infinite collections of their fundamental elements—their zero-dimensional points/one-dimensional infinitesimal line segments—which are dynamically generated in the dynamic generation of the plane curves themselves.* And Archimedes recognizes that the fundamental elements of which plane curves are composed are therefore simultaneously discrete and continuous; he recognizes that the fundamental elements of which plane curves are composed *at the same time* exist *as of one dimension less* than the plane curves that they are generating (and to which they contribute as elements) *and* that they also exist *as of the same dimension* as the plane curves that they are generating (and to which they contribute as elements).[18]

(And we find that Archimedes generalizes this finding—the idea that the fundamental elements of which plane curves are composed exist *as of two dimensions simultaneously*: that they exist as the curves' discrete indivisibles/their continuous infinitesimals—to the generation of all higher dimensional geometric objects; he generalizes it to the generation of two-dimensional surfaces and of three-dimensional volumes. Archimedes considers two-dimensional surfaces and three-dimensional volumes to be dynamically generated in the dynamic generation of an infinite number of their discrete indivisibles/their continuous infinitesimals. (And as in the generation of the plane curve, Archimedes considers the surfaces' and volumes' discrete indivisibles to exist *as of one dimension less* than the surfaces and volumes that they are generating (and to which they contribute as elements), and he considers the surfaces' and volumes' continuous infinitesimals to exist *as of the same dimension* as the surfaces and volumes that they are generating (and to which they contribute as elements.)))[19]

---

that rather, he asks of us that we logically deduce it from his cosmology.

18. We recognize that our reader may be skeptical of the notion that plane curves are dynamically generated in the dynamic generation of an infinite number of their zero-dimensional points/one-dimensional infinitesimal line segments, and we invite our reader's skepticism here; we expect our reader to be convinced of the truth of this finding as our application of it reveals to us the sublime beauty of Archimedes's cosmology. And as we will show, both Galileo and Newton appropriate Archimedes's finding within their own cosmologies, and both consider the fundamental elements of which all plane curves are composed to exist as the plane curves' discrete indivisibles/their continuous infinitesimals, and to exist *as of two dimensions simultaneously*.

19. Again, we find that Archimedes does not explicitly state this finding in his work, but that rather, he asks of us that we logically deduce it from his cosmology.

By way of decrypting Archimedes's method of indivisibles/method of exhaustion logic puzzle, we have deduced that Archimedes considers plane curves to be dynamically generated in the dynamic generation of an infinite number of their zero-dimensional discrete points/their one-dimensional infinitesimal line segments.[20] We find that Archimedes takes this idea for an axiom and that he applies it throughout his cosmology; *we find that it is the single axiom that is necessary to decoding Archimedes's entire cosmology*; it is the single golden thread with which his entire cosmology is bound, and that we need only to tug gently upon it to see his miraculous cosmology unravel before our eyes.

Having answered for himself the question regarding the fundamental elements of which plane curves are composed, Archimedes turns his attentions next to developing his kinematics, or geometry of motion, in an effort to rigorously explore the dynamical generation of plane curves themselves. Archimedes explores the dynamical generation of plane curves in his mathematical treatise, *On Spirals*, of 225 BC. The spiral exists as a particular type of plane curve, and Archimedes finds that it is possible to generalize the results that he attains from his explorations of the generation of the spiral to the generation of all plane curves, and

---

20. Let us also note here that this finding is not recognized by contemporary scholars. Instead, scholars report that Archimedes proved theorems using the method of indivisibles and that he published his proofs using the method of exhaustion—and they assert that Archimedes published his proofs using the method of exhaustion because he had only developed heuristic intuitions regarding the indivisible. (Or as Wikipedia explains, "Archimedes did not admit the method of indivisibles [the mechanical method] as part of rigorous mathematics, and therefore did not publish his method in the formal treatises that contain the results. In these treatises, he proves the same theorems by exhaustion, finding rigorous upper and lower bounds which both converge to the answer required. Nevertheless, the mechanical method was what he used to discover the relations for which he later gave rigorous proofs." (*"Method of Mechanical Theorems,"* para. 2.))

As has been mentioned, historians of mathematics credit Galileo's student Bonaventura Cavilieri (1598–1647) with developing the first mathematically rigorous definition of the indivisible in the Renaissance. However, we argue that Archimedes, who was fluent in the cosmologies of Pythagoras and of Democritus, actually considered himself to possess a mathematically rigorous definition of the indivisible, but that he desired that his reader actively participate in a process of logical deduction upon his ideas and upon his cosmology, so that his reader too could find what he had found.

ultimately to the generation of all particles' trajectories in the natural world—since he recognizes that particles' trajectories also exist as dynamically generated plane curves.

As we know, Aristotle had proposed that there exists a relationship between motion and time in the natural world, but his was not a rigorously mathematical cosmology. We find that Archimedes rigorously defines this relationship in his treatise *On Spirals*.

A note to the reader: *On Spirals* is densely mathematical—although we find that it is densely mathematical only in the sense that it requires of us that we perform countless acts of logical deduction—acts of mathematics—upon it; and as we will see, it requires of us no more than a grade school understanding of mathematics.

In his treatise *On Spirals*, Archimedes focuses his attentions exclusively on the spiral and its generation—and for this reason, it may be that some readers will find *On Spirals* (and our reading of it) to be dry; however, it will be important to keep in mind that Archimedes finds it possible to extrapolate the findings that he derives from his explorations of the spiral and its generation to the generation of all plane curves, and ultimately to the generation of all particles' trajectories in the natural world. And as we will see, the insights that Archimedes gleans from his explorations of the spiral have profound implications on his understanding of the nature of reality.

On Spirals is the mathematical treatise in which Archimedes succeeds in locating the existence of an unchanging and immovable referent by which he finds it possible to define the spiral's ever-changing motions; he succeeds in locating (what he recognizes to be) the spiral's unchanging and immovable *present motions*. And Archimedes finds it possible to extrapolate this finding (regarding the existence of an unchanging and immovable referent by which it is possible to rigorously define the spiral's ever-changing motions) to the generation of all plane curves, and ultimately to the generation of all particles' trajectories in the natural world.[21] *On Spirals* is the mathematical treatise in which Archimedes fully develops his kinematics—a kinematics that he then applies to the development of a mechanics—and to the exploration of the motions of

---

21. As we will see, Archimedes ultimately succeeds in locating the site of all particles' unchanging and immovable present motions—and he shows that particles' unchanging and immovable present motions exist inextricably from particles themselves. And we find that it is this site—the site of all particles (and which exist inextricably from their unchanging and immovable present motions)—that exists as the center and monist focus of Archimedes's entire cosmology.

all particles—and therefore of all extended physical bodies—in the natural world. Let us turn now to *On Spirals*.

◆

Archimedes begins his task of developing a kinematics, or a geometry of *motion*, by turning to the spiral, and by investigating the spiral's "instantaneous motion."

At around the time 300 BC, the Greek mathematician Euclid had proposed that it would be possible to measure the "instantaneous rate of change" of a point along a curve, or to measure a curve's "instantaneous motion," by finding the slope of the tangent line to the curve at that point.[22] And Euclid was the first person in the history of Greek mathematics to find a curve's instantaneous motion by finding the slope of the tangent line to a circle at one of its points.[23]

Archimedes, we find, was the first person to find the instantaneous rate of change of a point along a curve for a curve other than a circle. And the curve for which he accomplished this feat was the spiral.[24]

◆

Archimedes applies his single axiom to the spiral—his idea that a plane curve exists as an infinite collection of its fundamental elements—its zero-dimensional points/one-dimensional infinitesimal line segments—which are dynamically generated in the dynamic generation of the curve itself—and he recognizes that the spiral exists as an infinite collection of its fundamental elements—its zero-dimensional points/one-dimensional

---

22. Euclid recognized that the measure of the slope of the tangent line to a curve at a point is a measure of the curve's "instantaneous motion" at that point. Today, this is called the measure of the "derivative" of the curve at that point. (Let us note here that in the seventeenth century, kinematics was renamed "the Calculus" by Gottfried Leibniz, and that today, in the language of calculus, the measure of the "instantaneous rate of change" of a curve at a point is called the "derivative" at that point. The derivative is measured by finding "the slope of the tangent line to the graph of the function at that point." (See "Derivative," para. 1.))

23. See "Tangent," para. 5, in which it is reported that "Euclid makes several references to the tangent (ἐφαπτομένη ephaptoménē) to a circle in book III of the *Elements* (c. 300 BC)."

24. See "History of Calculus," para. 6, in which it is reported that "while studying the spiral," Archimedes was "the first to find the tangent to a curve other than a circle."

infinitesimal line segments—which are dynamically generated in the dynamic generation of the spiral itself. Archimedes recognizes that each of the spiral's one-dimensional infinitesimal line segments—its infinitesimals—exists as an implicit tangent to its zero-dimensional discrete points—its indivisibles. And Archimedes recognizes that the spiral's instantaneous rates of change at its points (its instantaneous motions) are indistinct from the spiral's own elements (its discrete points/continuous infinitesimal line segments). Archimedes therefore recognizes that the spiral exists as *an infinite collection of its instantaneous motions* (with the slope of its infinitesimals at its indivisibles being a measure of the spiral's instantaneous rates of change at its points), which are dynamically generated in the dynamic generation of the spiral itself.[25]

Archimedes recognizes an implicit temporal element to the curve: the spiral exists as an infinite collection of its "instantaneous motions." But, he wonders, how would it be possible to rigorously define the spiral's ever-changing, instantaneous motions? Archimedes recognizes that it would only be possible to rigorously define the spiral's ever-changing, instantaneous motions in relation to something that remained unchanging (with respect to the spiral) over the course of the spiral's generation, and which could therefore be considered to be immovable (with respect to the generation of the spiral).

Archimedes therefore seeks to find something that remains unchanging (with respect to the spiral) over the course of the spiral's generation—and which could therefore be considered to be immovable (with respect to the generation of the spiral)—and by way of the existence of which it could become possible to rigorously define the spiral's ever-changing, instantaneous motions. And he finds such a place in his deeper explorations of the spiral and its generation.

---

25. Again, this result is not explicitly stated in Archimedes's works, and he requires of us that we actively deduce it. (Interestingly, we find that this idea also arises in contemporary mathematics within the field of smooth infinitesimal analysis. We read: "Smooth infinitesimal analysis embodies a concept of intensive magnitude in the form of *infinitesimal tangent vectors* to curves. A tangent vector to a curve at a point *p* on it is a short straight line segment *l* passing through the point and pointing along the curve. In fact we may take *l* actually to be an infinitesimal *part* of the curve." (See Bell, "Continuity and Infinitesimals," para. 17.))

Archimedes turns his attentions next towards exploring the dynamical generation of the spiral itself. And on the dynamical generation of the spiral, Archimedes provides us with (what reveals itself to be) a cryptic definition.[26] (We find that by decoding Archimedes's definition, Archimedes reveals to us how he locates an unchanging and immovable referent by which he finds it possible to rigorously define the spiral's ever-changing instantaneous motions; he reveals to us how he locates the spiral's unchanging *present motions*.) On the dynamical generation of the spiral, Archimedes writes:

> If a straight line in a plane turn uniformly about one extremity which remains fixed, and return to the position from which it started and if, at the same time as the line is revolving, a point move at a uniform rate along the line starting from the fixed extremity, the point will describe a spiral in the plane.[27]

Here, Archimedes invites us to imagine that if, starting from a fixed extremity, a point is put into motion at a uniform rate along a straight line, and if, at the same time that the point is made to traverse the straight line at a uniform rate, the point is also made subject to a uniform rotation, the motion of the point will describe (or will generate) a spiral in the plane.

And as we begin to decrypt Archimedes's definition, we recognize that the straight line of which Archimedes speaks, which turns "uniformly about one extremity which remains fixed," and along which a point moves at a uniform rate "starting from the fixed extremity," is itself being generated in the generation of the spiral—and we therefore recognize that the point exists as an element of which the straight line is composed. And since we have deduced that Archimedes considers the fundamental elements of which plane curves are composed to exist as the curves' indivisibles/infinitesimals, we recognize that although Archimedes chooses to refer here to the motion of the straight line's indivisible, its zero-dimensional point, he is actually referring to the motion of the straight line's indivisible/infinitesimal—its zero-dimensional point/ one-dimensional infinitesimal line segment. (We find that this is another place in Archimedes's cosmology that he deliberately skips a step, and requires of us that we logically piece together his cosmology.)

---

26. The definition of the spiral exists as another place in Archimedes's cosmology in which he requires of us that we actively deduce his ideas.

27. Archimedes, *Works of Archimedes*, clxxii.

And therefore, we may interpret Archimedes's definition of the spiral to be the following: if, starting from a fixed extremity, a point/infinitesimal line segment is put into motion at a uniform rate and is made to generate a straight line, and if, at the same time that the straight line is being generated at a uniform rate, the point/infinitesimal line segment is also made subject to a uniform circular motion, the motion of the point/infinitesimal line segment will describe (or will generate) a spiral in the plane. But what does Archimedes mean by his phrase *at a uniform rate*? What does he mean by his phrase *at the same time*? What does Archimedes mean by the concept of time, and how does he consider time to be related to the dynamical generation of the spiral? (We find that these are logic puzzles that are embedded within a greater logic puzzle, and we turn now to solving the first logic puzzle.)[28]

◆

We find that in order to help us understand the concept of motion *at a uniform rate*, Archimedes provides us with two (unsurprisingly) cryptic Propositions, which also require our decrypting. Proposition I reads:

> If a point move at a uniform rate along any line, and two lengths be taken on it, they will be proportional to the times of describing them.[29]

And we recognize here that since Archimedes does not tell us whether the point in Proposition I is traversing a preexisting line at a uniform rate, or whether it is generating the line at a uniform rate, we need to assume that the point (which, we note, is moving "at a uniform rate along *any* line" [my emphasis]) could be generating the line at a uniform rate. Therefore, we recognize that although Archimedes once again chooses to speak here of the motion of a line's indivisible, its zero-dimensional point, he is actually referring to the motion of the line's indivisible/infinitesimal—its zero-dimensional point/one-dimensional infinitesimal line segment.

And we may interpret the meaning of Archimedes's Proposition I (and as Dino Boccaletti explains in *Galileo and the Equations of Motion*) to be as follows:

---

28. Indeed, we recognize that Archimedes's entire cosmology exists as a series of logic puzzles that need to be solved.

29. Archimedes, *Works of Archimedes*, 155.

That is, if s_1 and s_2 are the lengths of the two segments and t_1 and t_2 the times spent to cover them, one has $s_1 : s_2 = t_1 : t_2$, which is the classical Euclides proportion.[30]

Archimedes's Proposition II reads:

> If each of two points on different lines respectively move along them each at a uniform rate, and if lengths be taken, one on each line, forming pairs, such that each pair are described in equal times, the lengths will be proportionals.[31]

And again, we recognize here that since Archimedes does not tell us whether the two points are traversing preexisting lines at uniform (but differing) rates, or whether they are generating the lines at uniform (but differing) rates, we need to assume that the points, the lines' indivisibles, could be generating the two lines at uniform (but differing) rates. We therefore recognize that while Archimedes once again chooses to speak of the lines' indivisibles, he is actually referring to the motion of the lines' indivisibles/infinitesimals.

Regarding Proposition II, Boccaletti explains:

> Whereas in Proposition I only one uniform motion was considered, demonstrating the proportionality between the spaces covered and the times taken to cover them, in Proposition II two uniform motions are considered and the spaces covered in each of the two motions in equal times are compared.
>
> In this way, Archimedes, by means of the algorithm of proportions, has established the definition of uniform (rectilinear) motion.[32]

We find that implicit to Archimedes's idea of motion *at a uniform rate* is the traversing, by a point/infinitesimal line segment, of equal distances in equal times along a straight line—whether the point/infinitesimal line segment is generating the line or not.

And Archimedes considers further the case of the point/infinitesimal line segment that is generating a straight line at a uniform rate (as is the case in the generation of the spiral). Archimedes recognizes

---

30. Boccaletti, *Galileo*, 9.
31. Archimedes, *Works of Archimedes*, 155.
32. Boccaletti, *Galileo*, 10.

that in the generation of a straight line at a uniform rate, the straight line's fundamental elements—its points/infinitesimal line segments—remain unchanging (with respect to one another) over the course of the straight line's generation; Archimedes recognizes that the straight line's fundamental elements—its points/infinitesimal line segments—generate the same equal distances in the same equal times (over the course of the straight line's generation).[33] And Archimedes recognizes that since the straight line's fundamental elements—its points/infinitesimal line segments—remain unchanging (with respect to one another) over the course of the straight line's generation, it is possible to consider each element to be "preexisting" (with respect to another of the straight line's unchanging elements) and also to be "post-existing" (with respect to another of the straight line's unchanging elements)—even as it is also possible to consider each element to exist as the site at which a linearly progressive temporal orderedness (and the notions of "preexisting" and of "post-existing") are also always already vanquished, or overcome (since each element's manifestation as a preexisting element is indistinguishable from its manifestation as a post-existing element). And Archimedes finds that since the elements composing the straight line remain unchanging (with respect to one another) over the course of the straight line's generation, it is also possible to consider them to be immovable (with respect to the generation of the straight line).

Archimedes finds that the straight line's fundamental elements—its preexisting/post-existing points/infinitesimal line segments—generate the straight line at a uniform rate, even as, at the same time, they also remain unchanging (with respect to one another) over the course of the straight line's generation, and are therefore immovable (with respect to the generation of the straight line), and exist as the sites at which a linearly progressive temporal orderedness—and therefore the concept of passing time itself—is also always already vanquished, or overcome (with respect to the generation of the straight line). This, we find, is Archimedes's subtle definition of motion *at a uniform rate*.

---

33. Archimedes recognizes that the *rate* at which the straight line is generated—or the speed at which it is generated—remains unchanging (over the course of the straight line's generation), and he recognizes that the straight line's fundamental elements actually exist inextricably from their unchanging speed (over the course of the straight line's generation).

CHAPTER IV. ARCHIMEDES 69

And returning now to Archimedes's cryptic definition of the generation of the spiral, what does he mean by his phrase *at the same time*? Let us remind ourselves that we have interpreted Archimedes's definition of the spiral to be the following: if, starting from a fixed extremity, a point/infinitesimal line segment is put into motion at a uniform rate and is made to generate a straight line, and if, at the same time that the straight line is being generated at a uniform rate, the point/infinitesimal line segment is also made subject to a uniform circular motion, the motion of the point/infinitesimal line segment will describe a spiral in the plane. But we wonder here: how would it be possible for a rotation to act upon the fundamental element of which the straight line is composed—its point/infinitesimal line segment—*at the same time* that the element is brought into being at a uniform rate?

We find that Archimedes implies that it is possible for a rotation to act upon the straight line's fundamental element—its point/infinitesimal line segment—*at the same time* that the element is brought into being at a uniform rate precisely because the fundamental elements of which the straight line is composed are preexisting/post-existing (with respect to one another); they unchangingly exist "before" and "after" their present coming into being, even as they also exist as the sites at which a linearly progressive temporal orderedness is always already vanquished, or overcome (with respect to the generation of the straight line). Archimedes considers the fundamental elements of which the straight line is composed—the straight line's preexisting/post-existing points/infinitesimal line segments—to be indistinguishable from one another, and therefore he finds that it is possible to consider each of them to (indistinguishably) exist as the straight line's *present motions*, which are unchanging with respect to one another (over the course of the straight line's generation), and are therefore immovable (with respect to the generation of the straight line), and exist as the sites at which passing time is always already vanquished, or overcome (with respect to the generation of the straight line).

Here Archimedes implies that he considers the existence of a recursive self-similarity to be implicit to the generation of the spiral, and which allows the fundamental elements of which the spiral is composed to *at the same time* possess both an unchanging and immovable present aspect and a changing, instantaneous aspect.[34] Archimedes implies that

34. As has been mentioned, scholars consider the concept of recursive self-similarity

he considers the spiral's preexisting/post-existing points/infinitesimal line segments, which are generated at a uniform rate in the generation of a straight line, and which exist as the sites at which passing time is always already vanquished, or overcome (with respect to the generation of the spiral), to exist as the spiral's unchanging and immovable present motions; and he implies that he considers the spiral's unchanging and immovable present motions, which are made subject to rotations *at the same time* that they are (unchangingly) brought into being at a uniform rate, to exist as the spiral's changing, instantaneous motions.

We recognize that Archimedes defines the generation of the spiral inextricably in terms of the passage of time (we are conscious of his use of the phrases *at a uniform rate* and *at the same time* in his definition of the spiral's generation), and we recognize that, like Pythagoras, Archimedes implies that he considers mathematical reality to exist inextricably from physical reality.[35]

Archimedes recognizes that it is possible to define the spiral's ever-changing, instantaneous motions in relation to its unchanging and immovable present motions. And Archimedes also recognizes that since the spiral's unchanging and immovable present motions are preexisting (with respect to one another) and post-existing (with respect to one another)—even as they also exist as the sites at which passing time is always already vanquished, or overcome (with respect to the generation of the spiral)—it is by way of the existence of the spiral's ever-changing, instantaneous motions that we are able to discern the passage of time (with respect to the generation of the spiral).

Archimedes recognizes that the fundamental elements of which the spiral is composed come into being presently (and therefore exist as the sites at which passing time is always already vanquished, or overcome (with respect to the generation of the spiral)) and instantaneously (over passing time) *at the same time*.[36]

---

to have arisen in the seventeenth-century mathematics of Gottfried Leibniz ("Fractal," para. 13), but we find that its existence had been present in antiquity.

35. As we know, both the ancient Jews and Pythagoras considered mathematical reality to exist inextricably from physical reality. Let us note here that today mathematical reality is considered to exist distinctly from physical reality, as ancient natural philosophical wisdom has been lost to our discourse. We consider it to be our project to restore this wisdom to the philosophical discourse.

36. Archimedes recognizes that the spiral exists as *an infinite collection of its present motions*, even as, *at the same time*, it also exists as *an infinite collection of its instantaneous motions*.

And Archimedes also recognizes that the spiral's unchanging and immovable present motions—its preexisting/post-existing points/infinitesimal line segments, which are generated at a uniform rate in the generation of a straight line—are more fundamental to the spiral than its changing, instantaneous motions, since its unchanging and immovable present motions exist "before" and "after" its changing, instantaneous motions—even as, *at the same time*, they also exist as the sites at which passing time is always already vanquished, or overcome (with respect to the generation of the spiral).

As we have seen, Archimedes defines the generation of the spiral in terms of the passage of time, and he defines the passage of time (and its presently being vanquished, or overcome) in terms of the generation of the spiral. And we recognize here that *On Spirals* is the mathematical treatise in which Archimedes succeeds in locating the existence of an unchanging and immovable place (with respect to the generation of the spiral), and by way of the existence of which, he finds it possible to rigorously define the spiral's ever-changing, instantaneous motions.

Archimedes finds it possible to generalize the results that he has attained from his exploration of the generation of the spiral to the generation of all plane curves, since he recognizes that the spiral exists as but a particular type of plane curve. And Archimedes implies that he considers all plane curves to have their origins in the generation of their fundamental elements—their zero-dimensional points/one-dimensional infinitesimal line segments—which, starting from a fixed extremity, are generated at a uniform rate in the generation of a straight line, and which undergo rotations *at the same time* that they are unchangingly brought into being at a uniform rate.[37] Archimedes implies that he considers the existence of a recursive self-similarity to be implicit to the generation of all plane curves, and which allows the fundamental elements of which all plane curves are composed to *at the same time* possess both an unchanging and immovable present aspect and a changing, instantaneous

---

37. We note here that all curves possess changing, instantaneous motions except for the special case of the straight line that is generated at a uniform rate, whose instantaneous motions are unchanging (with respect to one another) over the course of the straight line's generation. The straight line generated at a uniform rate will be explored by Archimedes in much depth later.

aspect. Archimedes implies that he considers plane curves' preexisting/post-existing points/infinitesimal line segments, which are generated at a uniform rate in the generation of a straight line, and which exist as the sites at which passing time is always already vanquished, or overcome (with respect to the generation of the plane curves), to exist as plane curves' unchanging and immovable present motions; and he implies that he considers plane curves' unchanging and immovable present motions, which are made subject to rotations *at the same time* that they are unchangingly brought into being at a uniform rate, to exist as plane curves' changing, instantaneous motions.

And Archimedes recognizes that plane curves themselves are the continuous magnitude that is intimately related to the concept of time (since he recognizes that the fundamental elements of which plane curves are composed *at the same time* possess both an unchanging and immovable present aspect and a changing, instantaneous aspect); and Archimedes recognizes that plane curves come into being presently and instantaneously *at the same time*; and Archimedes also recognizes that plane curves are the continuous magnitude that is responsible for bringing passing time, and the site at which passing time is presently vanquished, or overcome, into mathematical reality—a mathematical reality that Archimedes considers to exist inextricably from physical reality.[38]

And we are now ready to apply Archimedes's kinematics—and the insights that he has derived from his mathematical treatise, *On Spirals*—to his development of a mechanics. As has been mentioned, Archimedes

---

38. We find that although Archimedes considers mathematical reality to exist inextricably from physical reality, he also implies that he does not consider the straight line that is generated at a uniform rate to manifest in physical reality. Archimedes recognizes that the straight line that is generated at a uniform rate exists as the one special case of a plane curve whose unchanging and immovable present motions do not differ from its instantaneous motions. And since Archimedes recognizes that it is by way of the existence of a plane curve's changing, instantaneous motions that we are able to discern the passage of time (with respect to the generation of the plane curve), the straight line generated at a uniform rate exists as the one special case of a plane curve for which we are not able to discern the passage of time. Archimedes recognizes that we are always able to discern the passage of time in physical reality, and that therefore the straight line that is generated at a uniform rate itself does not exist in physical reality, but only in mathematical reality. (However, Archimedes also recognizes that its generation is implicit to the generation of all plane curves in mathematical/physical reality.)

had recognized that in order to develop a mechanics, it would first be necessary to locate the particle equivalent of an extended physical body.

Archimedes was also a gifted engineer, and we find that from his having addressed another practical need of his home city—the challenge of understanding the workings of the lever—he had come to recognize that it was possible to locate the particle equivalent of an extended physical body by locating the extended body's "balancing point." But what does Archimedes mean by an extended body's balancing point?

Archimedes refers to an extended body's "balancing point" in his writings as its "kentron toi bareos,"[39] and we find that the literal translation of Archimedes's Greek phrase is "sharp point," "center," or "pivot" of "weight."[40] The phrase *kentron toi bareos* is alternately translated into English as "centroid" or "center of gravity," and we find that both English translations of "kentron toi bareos" (as "centroid" and as "center of gravity") refer to an object's "balancing point"—or to what (in the case of a two-dimensional surface) later philosophers will describe as being "the point at which a cutout of the shape could be perfectly balanced on the tip of a pin"[41]—and to what (in the case of a three-dimensional volume) later philosophers will consider to be the point at which "the total weight of the body may be thought to be concentrated."[42]

But how can we know that Archimedes considers an extended body's balancing point—its centroid, or center of gravity—to exist as the particle equivalent of the extended body itself? We find that although Archimedes (unsurprisingly) does not explicitly define the term "kentron toi bareos" in any of his writings, we are able to deduce his ideas as we explore his investigations into the workings of the lever.[43]

---

39. Stein, *Archimedes*, 15.

40. See Brennan, *Hellenistic*, 325, in which he writes, "*kentron* . . . has three separate but related meanings in Greek. The first and primary meaning of *kentron* is a 'sharp point'. . . . The second meaning of *kentron* is geometrical, standing for the 'center' of something, such as the center of a circle. Finally, the third meaning is a 'pivot,' or the place around which something turns, such as the fixed leg of a compass. Unfortunately, there is no English word that fully encompasses all three of these different meanings." And as Stein explains in *Archimedes*, 15, the Greek word *bareos* translates into English as "weight."

41. "Centroid," para. 1.

42. Gregersen, "Centre of Gravity," para. 1.

43. As Apostol and Mnatsakanian explain in "Finding Centroids the Easy Way," 7, Archimedes "created the concept of the centroid, which he used in many of his writings on mechanics," but they lament that "we can only speculate on what he had in mind when he referred to centroids because none of his extant works provides an explicit

Archimedes discovers a Law of the Lever, and as Sherman Stein explains in his *Archimedes: What Did He Do Besides Cry Eureka?*:

> We can think of the law of the lever ... as describing the [balancing point, or the] center of gravity of two objects, if we know the [balancing point, or the] center of gravity of each one. The point on which they balance, the fulcrum, is their [balancing point, or their] center of gravity.[44]

And Archimedes recognizes that it is possible to apply the ideas that he has derived from his Law of the Lever to an extended (or compound) body, in order to locate the extended body's own balancing point (or its center of gravity). Archimedes recognizes that an extended (or compound) body is itself composed of many individual systems, and that it is possible to find the balancing point (or center of gravity) of the extended body itself by finding the balancing points (or centers of gravity) of all of the systems of which the body is composed. The Law of the Lever shows that the extended body's own balancing point (or center of gravity) exists as the entire system's fulcrum—or the system's balancing point. And Archimedes recognizes that this balancing point exists as the particle equivalent of the entire extended body itself. Archimedes recognizes that by exploring the motions of the particle equivalent of the extended body—the entire system's fulcrum, its balancing point—over passing time, it is possible to explore the motions of the extended body

---

definition of the concept." They also assert that "Archimedes introduced the concept of center of gravity" (Apostol and Mnatsakanian, "Centroids Constructed Graphically," 201)—and similarly, it is found that "Archimedes never defines the term 'center of gravity'" in any of his writings (Stein, *Archimedes*, 15).

Scholars acknowledge that Archimedes "invented one of the most fundamental concepts of physics—the center of gravity" (Stewart, "Archimedes," para. 7). And some scholars conjecture that perhaps Archimedes defined the concept of the center of gravity in some of his lost writings, but Sherman Stein doubts that he ever defined it. Stein writes, "Though the notion of 'center of gravity' appears ... in much of Archimedes's work ... nowhere does he define the phrase. He mentions another of his works on gravity, *Equilibrium*, which has not survived, but I doubt that 'center of gravity' is defined there either" (Stein, *Archimedes*, 10). We recognize that the concept of center of gravity exists as yet another place in Archimedes's cosmology in which he requires of us that we actively deduce his meaning.

44. Stein, *Archimedes*, 15. Archimedes's Law of the Lever itself reads, "Magnitudes are in equilibrium at distances reciprocally proportional to their weights." See Propositions 6 and 7 of book I of Archimedes's *On the Equilibrium of Planes* (quoted from Dijksterhuis, *Archimedes*, 291).

itself. And therefore, we find that the focus of Archimedes's mechanics is upon exploring the motions of particles over passing time.⁴⁵

⇜

Archimedes explores the motions of particles over passing time as they *generate* plane curves. And we recognize that since Archimedes considers the motions of particles over passing time to *generate* plane curves, he implies that he considers particles themselves to exist as the *dynamically generated elements* of which their *dynamically generated trajectories* are composed; and that he considers particles to be *dynamically generated* in the *dynamical generation* of their trajectories.⁴⁶ Archimedes therefore implies that he considers particles to exist not merely as *points*, but rather to exist as points/infinitesimal line segments.⁴⁷ Archimedes implies that he considers particles to exist *as of two dimensions simultaneously*: he implies that he considers particles to exist as their trajectories' discrete indivisibles/their continuous infinitesimals—which exist *as of one dimension less* than the trajectories that they are generating (and to which they contribute as elements) and which also exist *as of the same dimension* as the trajectories that they are generating (and to which they contribute as elements).⁴⁸ And Archimedes implies that he does not consider particles

---

45. In his work *On the Equilibrium of Planes*, Archimedes locates the balancing points—the centroids, or centers of gravity—of many two-dimensional objects, and we recognize that he considers these balancing points to exist as the particle equivalents of the objects themselves (see Archimedes's *On the Equilibrium of Planes*, books I and II).

46. We recognize here that Archimedes considers the motions of particles over passing time to dynamically generate plane curves, much as he considers the motions of the spiral's fundamental element—its point/infinitesimal line segment—to dynamically generate the spiral over passing time.

47. And again, we find that this is one more place in Archimedes's cosmology that he requires his reader to logically deduce his ideas.

48. Archimedes implies that he considers particles to exist as the *dynamically generated elements* of which their *dynamically generated trajectories* are composed, and that he considers particles to exist *as of two dimensions simultaneously*—and as we will see, this finding is also embedded within the cosmologies of Galileo and of Newton. We will find, however, that later philosophers (including Einstein himself) do not recognize that the cosmologies of Archimedes, of Galileo, and of Newton exist as secret, hidden wisdom, which require decrypting, and in consequence, they assume that all three had considered particles to exist solely as mathematical points, and not as points/infinitesimal line segments. (Let us note here that, like Newton, Galileo too was a student of the *prisca sapientia*, and we will find that he too composed a cosmology that exists as secret, hidden wisdom, and that requires decrypting.)

to exist prior to, or independently of, their trajectories, but that rather he considers particles to exist inextricably from their trajectories.[49]

Archimedes also implies that since he considers particles to exist as the fundamental elements of which their trajectories are composed, he considers them to *at the same time* possess both an unchanging and immovable present aspect and a changing, instantaneous aspect; and Archimedes implies that he considers particles' unchanging and immovable present aspect to be more fundamental to them (and to their trajectories) than their changing, instantaneous aspect. Let us explore this idea further.

As has been mentioned, Archimedes considers particles' trajectories to exist as examples of dynamically generated plane curves. (And let us remind ourselves here that Archimedes implies that he considers all plane curves to have their origins in the generation of their fundamental elements—their zero-dimensional points/one-dimensional infinitesimal line segments—which, starting from a fixed extremity, are generated at a uniform rate in the generation of a straight line, and which undergo rotations *at the same time* that they are unchangingly brought into being at a uniform rate. Archimedes implies that he considers the existence of a recursive self-similarity to be implicit to the generation of all plane curves, and which allows the fundamental elements of which all plane curves are composed to *at the same time* possess both an unchanging and immovable present aspect and a changing, instantaneous aspect. Archimedes implies that he considers plane curves' preexisting/post-existing points/infinitesimal line segments, which are generated at a uniform rate in the generation of a straight line, and which exist as the sites at which passing time is always already vanquished, or overcome (with respect to the generation of the plane curves), to exist as plane curves' unchanging and immovable present motions; and he implies that he considers plane curves' unchanging and immovable present motions, which are made subject to rotations *at the same time* that they are unchangingly brought into being at a uniform rate, to exist as plane curves' changing, instantaneous motions. Archimedes implies that he considers plane curves to *at the same time* possess both unchanging and immovable present motions and changing, instantaneous motions. And as we know, Archimedes considers plane curves' unchanging and immovable present motions to be more fundamental to the curves than their changing, instantaneous

---

49. We find that Archimedes derives his definition of particles directly from his kinematics.

CHAPTER IV. ARCHIMEDES 77

motions, since plane curves' unchanging and immovable present motions exist "before" and "after" their changing, instantaneous motions, even as, *at the same time*, they exist as the sites at which passing time is always already vanquished, or overcome (with respect to the generation of the plane curves). Archimedes also implies that he considers the fundamental elements of which plane curves are composed to come into being presently (and that he therefore considers them to exist as the sites at which passing time is always already vanquished, or overcome (with respect to the generation of the plane curves)) and instantaneously (over passing time) *at the same time*.)

We find that Archimedes applies all of these ideas to the generation of particles' trajectories, and that he recognizes that all particles' trajectories in the natural world have their origins in the generation of their fundamental elements—the zero-dimensional/one-dimensional particles themselves—which, starting from a fixed extremity, are generated at a uniform rate in the generation of a straight line, and which undergo rotations *at the same time* that they are unchangingly brought into being at a uniform rate. Archimedes recognizes the existence of a recursive self-similarity that is implicit to the generation of all particles' trajectories, and which allows the fundamental elements of which all particles' trajectories are composed—the zero-dimensional/one-dimensional particles themselves—to *at the same time* possess both an unchanging and immovable present aspect and a changing, instantaneous aspect. *Archimedes recognizes that preexisting/post-existing particles, which are generated at a uniform rate in the generation of a straight line, and which exist as the sites at which passing time is always already vanquished, or overcome (with respect to the generation of particles' trajectories), exist as their trajectories' unchanging and immovable present motions*; and he recognizes that trajectories' unchanging and immovable present motions—or the preexisting/post-existing particles themselves—which are made subject to rotations *at the same time* that they are unchangingly brought into being at a uniform rate, exist as their trajectories' changing, instantaneous motions. Archimedes recognizes that particles' trajectories *at the same time* possess both unchanging and immovable present motions—the preexisting/post-existing particles themselves—and changing, instantaneous motions. And Archimedes recognizes that trajectories' unchanging and immovable present motions—or the preexisting/post-existing particles themselves—are more fundamental to the trajectories than the trajectories' changing, instantaneous motions, since the trajectories' unchanging and immovable present motions—or the preexisting/post-existing particles themselves—exist "before" and "after" the trajectories' changing, instantaneous motions, even as, *at the same time*, they also exist as the sites at which passing time is already vanquished, or overcome (with respect to the generation of their trajectories).

Archimedes recognizes that *preexisting/post-existing particles, which are generated at a uniform rate in the generation of a straight line, and which exist as the sites at which passing time is always already vanquished, or overcome (with respect to the generation of particles' trajectories), exist as their trajectories' unchanging and immovable present motions*. And therefore, we find that Archimedes recognizes that particles exist inextricably from their unchanging and immovable present motions—which, as we know, are to generate straight lines at uniform rates (over the course of their trajectories). Archimedes therefore implies that he considers *particles to exist inextricably from their perseverance (over the course of their trajectories) with unchanging and immovable presently uniform rectilinear motions*.[50] And Archimedes implies that he considers particles to be preexisting/post-existing (with respect to one another) over the course of their trajectories, and to exist as the sites at which passing time is already vanquished, or overcome (with respect to the generation of their trajectories).

---

50. Today, the idea that particles tend to persevere (over the course of their trajectories) with uniform rectilinear motions is referred to as "inertia," and inertia is considered to be "a fundamental property of all matter" (Gregersen, "Mass," para. 1). Contemporary philosophers and physicists, who do not recognize that the cosmologies of Archimedes, of Galileo, and of Newton exist as secret, hidden wisdom, consider the origins of inertia to remain unknown. (See Pais, *Subtle Is the Lord*, 287, in which Pais writes that "the origin of inertia is and remains the most obscure subject in the theory of particles and fields.") However, we recognize that in antiquity, Archimedes had discovered the origins of (what today is called) inertia, and that he had considered particles to exist inextricably from their perseverance (over the course of their trajectories) with unchanging and immovable *presently* uniform rectilinear motions. As we will see, Archimedes's idea (regarding what today is called inertia) is embedded within the cosmologies of Galileo and of Newton, although it goes unrecognized by Einstein. And we will find that by Einstein's own admission, his theory of general relativity fails to adequately account for the origins of inertia. (See Sciama, "On the Origin of Inertia," 34, in which Sciama writes, "As Einstein has pointed out, general relativity does not account satisfactorily for the inertial properties of matter, so that an adequate theory of inertia is still lacking.") We will find that by implanting Archimedes's ancient wisdom into Einstein's cosmology, we will be able to complete Einstein's incomplete cosmology.

CHAPTER IV. 79

And we find that since Archimedes recognizes that by exploring the motions of particles over passing time, he is exploring the motions of extended (or compound) bodies' balancing points—their fulcrums—and the motions of the extended (or compound) bodies themselves, Archimedes recognizes that all particles—or all bodies—exist *as* their trajectories' unchanging and immovable present motions. Archimedes recognizes that all particles—or all bodies—exist inextricably from their unchanging and immovable present motions—which are to generate straight lines at uniform rates (over the course of their trajectories). *Archimedes recognizes that all particles—or all bodies—exist inextricably from their perseverance (over the course of their trajectories) with unchanging and immovable presently uniform rectilinear motions.*[51] And Archimedes implies that he considers all particles—or all bodies—to be preexisting/post-existing (with respect to one another) over the course of their trajectories, and to exist as the sites at which passing time is always already vanquished, or overcome (with respect to the generation of their trajectories).

Archimedes implies that he thinks of the site of all particles—or of all bodies—(and which exist inextricably from their unchanging and immovable presently uniform rectilinear motions) as the site of all particles'—or of all bodies'—unchanging and immovable Presence(s). And we find that it is this site—the site of all particles'—or of all bodies'—unchanging and immovable Presence(s)—that exists as the center and focus of Archimedes's monist cosmology. Archimedes recognizes that the site of all particles'—or of all bodies'—unchanging and immovable Presence(s) exists as the site of ultimate substance and of what Presently Is in the natural world; and he recognizes that the site of all particles'—or of all bodies'—unchanging and immovable Presence(s) exists as the site of the (multiple and yet simultaneously singular) All/the Only. And we find that it is for *this* reason that Archimedes runs through the streets of Syracuse naked, shouting "Eureka! Eureka!" (which translates as, "I found it! I found it!")—for he recognizes that in locating the site of all particles'—or of all bodies'—unchanging and immovable Presence(s) in the natural world, he has succeeded in restoring YHWH's Presence to the philosophical discourse.

---

51. We find that it is this recognition that allows Archimedes to design a highly accurate catapult that prevents the Romans from conquering Syracuse for years.

Archimedes recognizes that the site of all particles'—or of all bodies'—Presence(s) exists as the (multiple and yet simultaneously singular) unchanging and immovable referent(s) in the natural world by which it is possible to define all particles'—or all bodies'—changing, instantaneous motions. And therefore, we find that when Archimedes famously cries, "Give me a[n unchanging and immovable] place to stand on, and I will move the earth"![52] he is facetiously (and giddily!) referring to the unchanging and immovable place that he has already found—Eureka! Eureka!—he is referring to the site of the (multiple and yet simultaneously singular) All/the Only—to the unchanging and immovable Fulcrum—to his God: the Universe itself.[53]

Archimedes reveals himself to possess a subtle, jesting humor, whose presence is also felt in the introduction to *On Spirals*. Archimedes prefaces *On Spirals* with a letter that he writes to a friend and fellow mathematician in which he makes a series of giddy allusions to the concept of time, and we recognize that his tone is giddy here because *On Spirals* is the mathematical treatise that has helped him to solve the mysteries of time. Archimedes writes:

> ARCHIMEDES to Dositheus greeting.
>
> Of most of the theorems which I sent to Conon, and of which you ask me *from time to time* to send you the proofs, *the demonstrations are already before you* in the books brought to you by Heracleides; and some more are also contained in that which I *now* send you. Do not be surprised at my taking a considerable *time* before publishing these proofs. This has been owing to my desire to communicate them first to persons engaged in mathematical studies and anxious to investigate them. In fact, how many theorems in geometry which have seemed at first impracticable are *in time* successfully worked out![54]

We recognize here that Archimedes's letter is also written to us (!)—and that we too are the friends and fellow mathematicians with whom

---

52. For this translation of Archimedes's famous statement, see Dijksterhuis, *Archimedes*, 15. (The original remark is quoted by Pappus of Alexandria, *Collection* or *Synagoge*, book VIII, ca. AD 340.)

53. As we will see, the site of all particles'—or of all bodies'—unchanging and immovable Presence(s) exists as the *kentron toi bareos*—the sharp point, center, or pivot of weight around which Archimedes's entire cosmology revolves.

54. Archimedes, *Works of Archimedes*, 151; my emphases.

Archimedes is anxious to share his findings. (And indeed, and as we know, Archimedes requires of us that we perform countless acts of logical deduction—acts of mathematics—upon his ideas and upon his cosmology so that we too may find what he has found—Eureka! Eureka!)[55]

⮌

Let us note here that several hundred years after Archimedes's death, the Great Library of Alexandria will decline, and Archimedes's wisdom will be lost to the philosophical discourse for more than a millennium. The Dark Ages will intervene. And then, in the Renaissance, Archimedes's works are rediscovered, and they are reprinted in 1544.[56]

Galileo Galilei, who was born in 1564, discovers Archimedes's works in 1585, and Galileo considers Archimedes to be his mentor; Archimedes's works accompany Galileo throughout his life. Scholars report that when Galileo had begun to study natural philosophy, Aristotle's ideas were the prevailing natural philosophy of the time.[57] To Galileo, however:

> Archimedes was a revelation. [From 1585, when Galileo first discovered Archimedes's works, and throughout] the rest of his life, Galileo's admiration for Archimedes, the Greek mathematician, engineer and scientist of the third century BC, knew no bounds. "It is all too obvious that no one else has ever been nearly as clever as he was." He is the "superhuman Archimedes, whose name I never mention without a feeling of awe," "the most divine Archimedes," someone Galileo reads with "unending astonishment" ("infinito stupore").[58]

---

55. In his letter to Dositheus, Archimedes writes, "*the demonstrations are already before you*" (my emphasis)—and we recognize that Archimedes implies here that he considers all of us to always already exist as the *presently published proofs* of the existence of God's Presence in the natural world, and that he considers all of us to always already be found. Eureka! Eureka!

56. Wootton, *Galileo*, 79.

57. We read that "when Galileo was born, it was customary for 'natural philosophers' (as scientists were called) to follow the teachings of the ancient Greek philosopher Aristotle. The Italian poet Dante referred to Aristotle as 'the Master of those who know'; he was held in such high regard that virtually no one questioned his ideas in detail. Until Galileo came along" (Clegg and Evans, *Ten Physicists*, 7). See also Bell, "Continuity and Infinitesimals," para. 35, in which he writes that "the early modern period saw the spread of knowledge in Europe of ancient geometry, particularly that of Archimedes, and a loosening of the Aristotelian grip on thinking."

58. Wootton, *Galileo*, 79.

As we will see, Galileo is another friend and mathematician (much like we ourselves) who performs countless acts of logical deduction—acts of mathematics—upon Archimedes's works, and who finds what Archimedes himself had found: the site of YHWH's Presence in the natural world.[59] And as we will see, Galileo appropriates all of Archimedes's cosmology within his own cosmology, even as he extends and deepens Archimedes's cosmology in breathtaking and inspired ways, and we will find that the site of all particles'—or of all bodies'—unchanging and immovable Presence(s)—and the site that Galileo too recognizes to be that of Divinity's Presence in the natural world—exists as the center and monist focus of Galileo's cosmology as well.

Isaac Newton was born in the same year that Galileo died (1642),[60] and like Galileo, Newton recognizes that in Archimedes's having located the site of all particles'—or of all bodies'—unchanging and immovable Presence(s) in the natural world, he had located the site of YHWH's unchanging and immovable Presence in the natural world. Newton also recognizes that Galileo had appropriated all of Archimedes's cosmology within his own cosmology, even as he had extended and deepened Archimedes's cosmology in breathtaking and inspired ways; and we will find that in turn, Newton appropriates all of Galileo's cosmology within his own cosmology, even as he extends and deepens Galileo's cosmology in breathtaking and inspired ways. And as we will see, the site of all particles'—or of all bodies'—unchanging and immovable Presence(s)—and the site that Newton too recognizes to be that of Divinity's Presence in the natural world—exists as the center and monist focus of Newton's cosmology as well.

And as we explore Galileo's and Newton's cosmologies, we will find that both Galileo and Newton consider the site of all particles'—or of all bodies'—unchanging and immovable Presence(s)—and the site that both recognize to be that of Divinity's Presence in the natural world—to exist

---

59. Galileo recognizes that in locating the site of all particles'—or of all bodies'—unchanging and immovable Presence(s) in the natural world, Archimedes had found YHWH's (and Archimedes's own) Presence in the natural world, and we find that it is for this reason that Galileo refers to Archimedes as "the most divine Archimedes."

60. Galileo died on May 8, 1642 (of the Gregorian calendar) and Newton was born on Christmas Day, 1642 (of the Julian calendar).

as the unchanging and immovable referent(s) by which both consider it to be possible to define all particles'—or all bodies'—changing, instantaneous motions. And like Archimedes, Galileo and Newton recognize that the site of all particles'—or of all bodies'—unchanging and immovable Presence(s) exists as the site of the (multiple and yet simultaneously singular) All/the Only, and they consider their explorations of the site of all particles'—or of all bodies'—unchanging and immovable Presence(s) to be the means by which to serve their God: the Universe itself. [61]

61. We may offer our reader a brief overview of Galileo's and of Newton's cosmologies here.

As we will see, Galileo appropriates all of Archimedes's cosmology within his own cosmology, even as he extends and deepens Archimedes's cosmology in breathtaking and inspired ways. Like Archimedes, Galileo focuses his attentions on developing a mechanics to explore the motions of physical bodies in the natural world, and Galileo recognizes that it is possible to simplify problems involving two-dimensional and three-dimensional objects by replacing the extended objects by their balancing points—their centroids, or centers of gravity—which Galileo too considers to be the particle equivalents of the extended objects themselves. In his writings, Galileo refers to an object's balancing point—its centroid, or center of gravity—by the names of "particle" and "body"—(we find that he uses the terms interchangeably)—and we find that like Archimedes, Galileo too considers an object's balancing point to exist as the particle equivalent of the extended object itself.

Galileo explores the motions of particles over passing time as they generate plane curves. And like Archimedes, Galileo too recognizes that particles exist as the *dynamically generated elements* of which their *dynamically generated trajectories* are composed, and he recognizes that particles are *dynamically generated* in the *dynamical generation* of their trajectories. Galileo recognizes that particles exist *as of two dimensions simultaneously*—he recognizes that they exist as their trajectories' discrete indivisibles/their continuous infinitesimals, which exist *as of one dimension less* than the trajectories that they are generating (and to which they contribute as elements) and also *as of the same dimension* as the trajectories that they are generating (and to which they contribute as elements); and he also recognizes that particles *at the same time* possess both an unchanging and immovable present aspect and a changing, instantaneous aspect. And Galileo recognizes that particles' unchanging and immovable present aspect is more fundamental to them (and to their trajectories) than their changing, instantaneous aspect. Like Archimedes, Galileo considers particles to exist inextricably from their unchanging and immovable present motions—which are to generate straight lines at uniform rates (over the course of their trajectories)—and we find that the site of all particles'—or of all bodies'—unchanging and immovable Presence(s)—and the site that, like Archimedes, Galileo too recognizes to be that of Divinity's Presence in the natural world—exists as the center and monist focus of Galileo's cosmology as well.

Newton refers to Galileo's "particle" or "body" as a "mass," and Newton uses all three terms (particle, body, and mass) in his *Principia* to refer to an object's balancing point—or to what he too considers to be the particle equivalent of the extended object itself. We find that Newton appropriates all of Archimedes's and of Galileo's cosmologies within his own cosmology, even as he extends and deepens Archimedes's and Galileo's cosmologies in breathtaking and inspired ways. And as we will see, Newton considers a particle or a body (or a mass) to exist inextricably from its perseverance (over the

We will find that Galileo and Newton were also influenced by Archimedes's giddy, facetious style and that their writings too are giddy and facetious, for, like Archimedes, they too recognize that we are all always already found (Eureka! Eureka!); they too recognize that we all always already exist as manifestation(s) of the site of all particles'—or of all bodies'—unchanging and immovable Presence(s) in the natural world, and that we all always already exist as manifestation(s) of the site at which Divinity and ever-burgeoning life are realized in the natural world; they too recognize that we are all always already immortal; that we are all always already One; and that Paradise is always already Now.

↭

And returning now to the cosmology of Archimedes, let us also note here that since Archimedes refers to an object's balancing point, or its center of *gravity*, as "kentron toi bareos"—which, as we know, translates literally as "sharp point," "center," or "pivot" of "*weight*" (my emphasis), he implies that *under gravity*, all particles—or all bodies—and which exist inextricably from their perseverance (over the course of their

---

course of its trajectory) with an unchanging and immovable presently uniform rectilinear motion. Newton refers to an object's center of gravity as its "center of mass," and we find that the concept of center of mass in Newton's cosmology exists exactly equivalently to Archimedes's concept of center of gravity. (We read, "The concept of 'center of mass' in the form of the center of gravity was first introduced by the ancient Greek physicist, mathematician, and engineer Archimedes of Syracuse" and "the center of mass [is considered to be] the particle equivalent of a given object" ("Center of Mass," paras. 1, 4). And as Apsotol and Mnatsakanian explain in "Finding Centroids the Easy Way," 7, "the "centroid [or center of gravity], for us [or for modern readers], is a special case of a more general concept called *center of mass*, which plays an important role in physics. Newton's laws of mechanics are usually stated so they apply to a point particle described by its position, velocity, and acceleration. But every object we see in nature is really a compound body made up of smaller parts, ultimately of atoms, and physicists apply Newton's laws to such extended objects. They do this by imagining the body replaced by a single point where all its mass is concentrated. This point is called the center of mass.") (And we note here that Newton actually considers an object's center of mass to exist as a point/infinitesimal line segment, and to exist as the fundamental element of which its dynamically generated trajectory is composed.)

Newton considers an object's center of mass—and which he considers to be the particle equivalent of the extended object itself—to exist inextricably from its perseverance (over the course of its trajectory) with an unchanging and immovable presently uniform rectilinear motion; and we find that the site of all particles'—or of all bodies'—or of all masses'—unchanging and immovable Presence(s)—and the site that, like Archimedes and Galileo, Newton too recognizes to be that of Divinity's Presence in the natural world—exists as the center and monist focus of Newton's cosmology.

trajectories) with their unchanging and immovable presently uniform rectilinear motions—undergo rotations that are responsible for producing their changing, instantaneous motions (and by way of the existence of which, we are able to discern the passage of time in the natural world), even as, *at the same time*, all particles—or all bodies—continue to persevere (over the course of their trajectories) *as* (preexisting/post-existing) particles—or *as* (preexisting/post-existing) bodies—(and which exist inextricably from their unchanging and immovable presently uniform rectilinear motions)—and exist as the site(s) at which motion and passing time—and even gravity itself—are always already vanquished, or overcome, in the natural world.[62]

Archimedes therefore implies that under gravity, all particles'—or all bodies'—unchanging and immovable Presence(s) are responsible for bringing motion and passing time into being in the natural world, even as, *at the same time*, all particles'—or all bodies'—unchanging and immovable Presence(s) exist as the (multiple and yet simultaneously singular) site(s) at which motion and passing time—and gravity itself—are always already vanquished, or overcome, in the natural world.

Archimedes also implies that all particles—or all bodies—and which exist inextricably from their perseverance (over the course of their trajectories) with their unchanging and immovable presently uniform rectilinear motions—come into being *presently* (and therefore exist as the sites at which passing time is always already vanquished, or overcome (with respect to their trajectories)) and *instantaneously* (over passing time) *at the same time*. He implies that we are only able to discern the passage of time in the natural world by way of the existence of all particles'—or all bodies'—changing, instantaneous motions, and he implies that it is gravity that is responsible for producing all particles'—or all bodies'—changing, instantaneous motions.

And finally, Archimedes implies that when we observe all particles—or all bodies—in motion, we are observing their changing, instantaneous motions, and not their unchanging and immovable presently uniform rectilinear motions (and from which the particles—or bodies—themselves exist inextricably). Archimedes implies that while all particles'—or all bodies'—unchanging and immovable presently uniform rectilinear motions (and from which the particles—or bodies—themselves exist inextricably) are *implicit* to their trajectories, they are not actually directly

---

62. And we recognize that it is this idea that allowed Archimedes to design a highly accurate catapult that protected Syracuse from Roman invaders for years.

observable to us in nature—although they are observable to us in our mind's eye, by way of mathematics.[63]

As we will see, all of these ideas will be appropriated by Galileo and Newton within their own cosmologies, even as Galileo and Newton will extend and deepen Archimedes's ideas in breathtaking and inspired ways.

⁂

And (gasp! as if that weren't enough!), we find that there are many more jewels that may be derived from Archimedes's explorations of the spiral—and which he applies to the trajectories of all particles—or of all bodies—in the natural world. We find that Archimedes determines the meaning of an "origin" with respect to the spiral—and also with respect to the trajectories of all particles—or of all bodies; that he discovers (what is referred to in the Renaissance as) the Galilean Principle of Relativity; that he explores the concept of "direction" with respect to the generation of the spiral, and also with respect to the generation of all particles'—or of all bodies'—trajectories; and that he offers us his ideas on the nature of numbers in the natural world.[64] Let us return once again to Archimedes's spiral.

I. ON THE CONCEPT OF AN ORIGIN

Archimedes recognizes that it is necessary to designate a fixed origin with respect to the generation of the spiral, and he defines the origin of the spiral as follows:

63. Archimedes recognizes that all bodies' sensible trajectories exist as the aggregates of their changing, instantaneous motions, and again, it is this idea that allows him to design his catapult.

Let us note here that this idea will also be of deep import to Newton, who, we will find, distinguishes in his own cosmology between (what he refers to as) sensibly apprehensible (observable) "Relative" quantities, which he considers to come into being in the coming into being of all particles'—or all bodies'—changing, instantaneous motions, and (unobservable) "Absolute" quantities, which he considers to come into being in the coming into being of the site of all particles'—or of all bodies'—unchanging and immovable Presence(s)—in the coming into being of (he whom Newton too considers to be) Divinity himself; and as we will see, the focus of Newton's *Principia* is upon exploring his (unobservable) Absolute quantities. We will find that Newton's deeply encrypted *Principia* is not actually the empirical manifesto that it has been interpreted to be over the centuries.

64. As we know, Archimedes considers mathematical reality to exist inextricably from physical reality.

Let the extremity of the straight line which remains fixed while the straight line revolves be called the origin of the spiral.[65]

And as we consider Archimedes's definition, we wonder: why does he find it to be necessary to designate a fixed origin with respect to the generation of the spiral?

As we know, Archimedes considers the spiral's unchanging and immovable present motions—its preexisting/post-existing points/infinitesimal line segments, which are generated at a uniform rate in the generation of a straight line, and which exist as the sites at which passing time is always already vanquished, or overcome (with respect to the generation of the spiral)—to be more fundamental to the spiral than the spiral's changing, instantaneous motions, since the spiral's unchanging and immovable present motions exist "before" and "after" its changing, instantaneous motions, even as they also exist as the sites at which passing time is always already vanquished, or overcome (with respect to the generation of the spiral). And therefore, we find that Archimedes recognizes that one of the spiral's unchanging and immovable present motions must necessarily exist as the spiral's origin. But Archimedes also recognizes that the spiral's unchanging and immovable present motions are indistinguishable from one another, and that therefore, any of them could potentially exist as the spiral's origin. Archimedes recognizes that it is necessary to designate a fixed origin with respect to the spiral's generation, since if not for designating a fixed origin, any of the spiral's unchanging and immovable present motions could be considered to be its origin, since all are preexisting/post-existing (with respect to one another), and all are indistinguishable from one another.

Archimedes therefore defines the fixed origin of the spiral to be one of the spiral's unchanging and immovable present motions—one of its preexisting/post-existing points/infinitesimal line segments—and he defines the spiral's origin to be the one located at the "fixed extremity" of the spiral itself.

And we find that Archimedes applies this idea, regarding the necessity of designating a fixed origin with respect to the generation of the spiral, to the generation of all particles'—or of all bodies'—trajectories. As we know, Archimedes considers all particles'—or all bodies'—trajectories' unchanging and immovable present motions—or the particles (or bodies) themselves—to be more fundamental to the particles'—or

---

65. Archimedes, *Works of Archimedes*, 165–66.

bodies'—trajectories than the trajectories' changing, instantaneous motions, since the trajectories' unchanging and immovable present motions—or the particles (or bodies) themselves—exist "before" and "after" the trajectories' changing, instantaneous motions, even as they also exist as the sites at which passing time is always already vanquished, or overcome (with respect to the generation of the trajectories). Archimedes therefore recognizes that it must be one of the trajectories' unchanging and immovable present motions—or one of the preexisting/post-existing particles (or bodies) themselves—that necessarily exists as the origin of the trajectories. But Archimedes also recognizes that the particles (or bodies) are preexisting/post-existing (with respect to one another) over the course of their trajectories, and are indistinguishable from one another; and he therefore recognizes that any of the particles (or bodies) could potentially exist as their trajectories' origin. We find that Archimedes recognizes that it is necessary to designate a fixed origin with respect to all particles'—or bodies'—trajectories, since if not for designating a fixed origin, any of the particles'—or bodies'—trajectories' unchanging and immovable present motions—or any of the particles (or bodies) themselves—could be considered to be the origin of their trajectories.

And as in the case of the spiral, we find that Archimedes designates a fixed origin with respect to the generation of all particles'—or all bodies'—trajectories. He considers the origin of all particles'—or all bodies'—trajectories to be one of the trajectories' unchanging and immovable present motions—one of the particles (or bodies) themselves—and he defines it to be the one that is located at the fixed extremity of the particles'—or bodies'—trajectories.

෴

And Archimedes also recognizes that since all particles (or all bodies)—and which exist inextricably from their perseverance (over the course of their trajectories) with their unchanging and immovable presently uniform rectilinear motions—come into being presently, and exist as the sites at which passing time is always already vanquished, or overcome (with respect to the generation of their trajectories), the site of all particles'—or of all bodies'—unchanging and immovable Presence(s)—and the site that Archimedes recognizes to be that of YHWH's unchanging and immovable Presence in the natural world—exists as the (multiple and yet simultaneously singular) *origin(s) of the natural world*. Archimedes recognizes that the site of all particles'—or of all bodies'—unchanging and immovable Presence(s) exists as the site of ultimate substance and of what Presently Is in the natural world, and he recognizes that it exists as the site of the (multiple and yet simultaneously singular) All/the Only. And Archimedes therefore implies that, like the ancient Jews and Pythagoras, he too considers all of us to always already exist as the (multiple and yet simultaneously singular) divine origin(s) of reality.[66]

II. ARCHIMEDES'S DISCOVERY OF (WHAT IS REFERRED TO IN THE RENAISSANCE AS) THE GALILEAN PRINCIPLE OF RELATIVITY

We also find that by way of Archimedes's explorations of the spiral, he discovers what, in the Renaissance, is known as the Galilean Principle of Relativity (and whose discovery is attributed to Galileo, but which was actually found (Eureka!) by Archimedes in antiquity).

Archimedes spends more time exploring the straight line that is generated at a uniform rate, and whose generation is implicit to the spiral's own generation. And Archimedes recognizes that theoretically it would be possible for the straight line to be generated at *any* uniform rate—and that its fundamental elements—its zero-dimensional points/one-dimensional infinitesimal line segments—could therefore generate *any* equal distances in *any* equal times—*except* for zero distances in equal times, since in that case, the straight line's fundamental elements would not generate a straight line. And therefore, Archimedes recognizes that the straight line's fundamental elements—its zero-dimensional points/one-dimensional infinitesimal line segments—always generate

---

66. Archimedes's word for the "origin" of the spiral ("ἀρχά") is the stem of the Greek word arche ("ἀρχή"), and we deduce here that by the word "origin," Archimedes is cryptically referring to the arche—to the generative "source," "origin," or "originating cause" of all things that exist in the natural world, which also exists as the site of all things in the natural world—he is referring to (what he implies that he considers to be) the (multiple and yet simultaneously singular) All/the Only—to his God: the Universe itself. (See the "ἀρχή" entry in Liddell and Scott's *Greek-English Lexicon*, in which Archimedes's spiral is cited.)

Let us also note here that contemporary postmodern philosophy posits that there is no true origin of reality (for example, philosopher Jean Baudrillard considers the real to be "without origin"; see "Postmodernism," para. 32), but we recognize that, like the ancient Jews and Pythagoras, Archimedes considered all of us to always already exist as the (multiple and yet simultaneously singular) divine origin(s) of reality.

some equal non-zero distances in equal times (over the course of their trajectory).

And Archimedes considers the generation of two different spirals, which are generated at two different (relative to one another) but still uniform rates. Archimedes recognizes that their straight lines are still generated at uniform rates, but that these uniform rates are different (with respect to one another). And he explores the generation of each straight line individually. Archimedes recognizes that each straight line's fundamental elements—its preexisting/post-existing points/infinitesimal line segments—are still unchanging (with respect to one another) over the course of each straight line's generation; and Archimedes recognizes that each straight line's fundamental elements—its preexisting/post-existing points/infinitesimal line segments—still generate the same equal non-zero distances in the same equal non-zero times (over the course of each straight line's generation). And Archimedes recognizes that since each straight line's fundamental elements—its preexisting/post-existing points/infinitesimal line segments—are still unchanging (with respect to one another) over the course of each straight line's generation, they are still immovable (with respect to the generation of each straight line).[67] And Archimedes therefore asks himself: which straight line's fundamental elements are the most immovable? He recognizes that this question does not make sense, and that both straight lines' fundamental elements are immovable (with respect to the generation of each of their straight lines). And Archimedes recognizes here that if one straight line's fundamental elements were taken to be "at rest" relative to the other straight line's fundamental elements, it would be necessary to consider the second straight line's fundamental elements to be "in motion" relative to the first straight line's fundamental elements; and Archimedes comes to recognize that uniform rectilinear motion can only be relatively determined.

We find that Archimedes applies this finding to the generation of all particles'—or all bodies'—trajectories in the natural world. Archimedes recognizes that the generation of a straight line at a uniform rate is implicit to the generation of all particles'—or all bodies'—trajectories, and he recognizes that it would not be possible for any particles (or bodies), and which exist inextricably from their perseverance (over the course of

---

67. Archimedes recognizes that the *rate* at which each straight line is generated—or the *speed* at which each straight line is generated—is unchanging (over the course of each straight line's generation). And Archimedes recognizes that the straight lines' fundamental elements actually exist inextricably from their perseverance (over the course of their trajectories) with some non-zero *speed* presently uniform rectilinear motions.

their trajectories) with their unchanging and immovable presently uniform rectilinear motions, to generate zero distances in equal times (over the course of their trajectories), since in that case, they wouldn't generate straight lines. *Archimedes therefore recognizes that it would not be possible for any particle (or any body) to manifest a state of absolute rest in the natural world.*[68]

As we know, Archimedes considers all particles (or all bodies) to exist inextricably from their perseverance (over the course of their trajectories) with their unchanging and immovable presently uniform rectilinear motions. And Archimedes asks himself: if he were to compare two particles'—or two bodies'—trajectories to one another, which of the particles'—or bodies'—unchanging and immovable present motions—or which of the particles (or bodies) themselves—would be the most immovable? Again, he recognizes that the question does not make sense, and that both particles (or bodies) would be immovable (with respect to the generation of each of their straight lines).[69] Archimedes recognizes that if one particle (or body) were taken to be "at rest" relative to the other particle (or body), it would be necessary to consider the second particle (or body) to be "in motion" relative to the first particle (or body); and from this deduction, he recognizes that all particles'—or all bodies'—manifestations of uniform rectilinear motion can only be relatively determined. Archimedes recognizes that it would be possible to consider one particle (or body) to be relatively "at rest" with respect to the second particle (or body), but that neither particle (or body) would be absolutely

---

68. Archimedes recognizes that this insight is in direct contradiction to the ideas of Aristotle, who had proposed that rest is the natural state of all bodies in the natural world.

And Archimedes also recognizes here that no particles (or bodies) generate straight lines at uniform rates (over the course of their trajectories) without *at the same time* being made subject to rotations, since if the particles (or bodies) were to simply generate straight lines (over the course of their trajectories) without *at the same time* being made subject to rotations, their unchanging and immovable present motions would also be their instantaneous motions, and we would not be able to discern passage of time in the natural world; and he recognizes that we are always able to discern passage of time. (Why are we always able to discern the passage of time? Archimedes replies: due to the presence of gravity. As has been mentioned, Archimedes implies that the presence of gravity in the natural world is responsible for producing all particles'—or all bodies'—changing, instantaneous motions, and by way of the existence of which, we are able to discern the passage of time.)

69. And Archimedes recognizes that the straight lines' fundamental elements—the particles (or bodies) themselves—actually exist inextricably from their perseverance (over the course of their trajectories) with some non-zero *speed* presently uniform rectilinear motions.

at rest, since if either body were to generate zero distances in equal times (over the course of its trajectory), it would not generate a straight line.

This is the Principle of Galilean Relativity, whose discovery is attributed to Galileo in the Renaissance, but which was actually found by Archimedes in antiquity.

III. DEFINING DIRECTION WITH RESPECT TO THE GENERATION OF THE SPIRAL (AND ALSO WITH RESPECT TO THE GENERATION OF ALL PARTICLES'—OR ALL BODIES'—TRAJECTORIES)

Archimedes also recognizes that it is possible to define a direction to the generation of the spiral by locating any particular element of which the spiral is composed—any particular point/infinitesimal line segment along the spiral—and by defining a "forward" and a "backward"[70] with respect to that element. Archimedes defines direction (with respect to the spiral's generation) as follows:

> If from the origin of the spiral any straight line be drawn, let that side of it which is in the same direction as that of the revolution be called forward, and that which is in the other direction backward.[71]

Here, Archimedes draws a straight line from the spiral's origin which intersects the spiral at one of its elements—at one of its points/infinitesimal line segments; at one of its instantaneous motions—and he defines a "forward" and a "backward" with respect to that point/infinitesimal line segment; with respect to that instantaneous motion.

Why does Archimedes find it to be possible to define direction with respect to the spiral? As we know, Archimedes recognizes that embedded within the spiral's generation is the straight line which is generated at a uniform rate. And Archimedes recognizes that since the fundamental elements of which the straight line is composed are generated *at a uniform rate*, they are progressively linearly ordered with respect to one another (over the course of the straight line's generation)—even as they are also unchanging with respect to one another (over the course of the straight line's generation) and are therefore indistinguishable from one

---

70. The terms "forward" and "backward" are in quotation marks here because they exist as relative measures and not as absolute measures; Archimedes only defines direction relative to a particular element of the curve.

71. Archimedes, *Works of Archimedes*, 166.

CHAPTER IV. ARCHIMEDES 93

another, and exist as the sites at which a progressive linear orderedness is also always already vanquished, or overcome.[72] Archimedes implies that the straight line's fundamental elements—its preexisting/post-existing points/infinitesimal line segments—generate a geometric space and a time in which equal distances and equal times absolutely exist, and which itself is progressively linearly ordered, even as the progressive linear orderedness of this geometric space and time is also always already vanquished, or overcome. And therefore, Archimedes recognizes that it is possible to define a direction to the generation of the spiral, even as he recognizes that the progressive linear orderedness of this direction is also always already vanquished, or overcome.

We find that Archimedes applies this finding to the motions of all particles—or of all bodies—in the natural world, and that he recognizes that it is also possible to define a direction to all particles'—or all bodies'—trajectories. Archimedes recognizes that it is possible to define a direction to the space and time described by all particles'—or all bodies'—trajectories by locating a particular element along a given particle's—or body's—trajectory—one of the particle's (or body's) instantaneous motions—and by defining a "forward" and "backward" with respect to that instantaneous motion.

And Archimedes finds this to be possible because he recognizes that embedded within all particles'—or all bodies'—trajectories are the particles (or bodies) themselves (and which exist inextricably from their perseverance (over the course of their trajectories) with their unchanging and immovable presently uniform rectilinear motions). Archimedes recognizes that all particles—or all bodies—(and which exist inextricably from their perseverance (over the course of their trajectories) with their unchanging and immovable presently uniform rectilinear motions) are preexisting/post-existing with respect to one another (over the course of their trajectories), and exist as the site(s) at which passing time is always already vanquished, or overcome (with respect to the generation of their trajectories). And therefore, Archimedes recognizes that the perseverance of all preexisting/post-existing particles—or of all preexisting/

---

72. Let us explore this idea further. Archimedes recognizes that it is possible to consider each fundamental element of which the straight line is composed to exist as the straight line's origin. And he recognizes that the origin's perseverance of itself *as* itself (over the course of the straight line's generation) brings into being a progressive linear orderedness (with respect to time and number) that *at the same time* is always already vanquished, or overcome, since the straight line's fundamental elements—its origin(s)—are also indistinguishable from one another. This idea reminds us of Pythagoras's Tetrad.

post-existing bodies—(and which exist inextricably from their unchanging and immovable presently uniform rectilinear motions) *as* preexisting/post-existing particles—or *as* preexisting/post-existing bodies—(over the course of their trajectories) generates a progressively linearly ordered space and time in the natural world whose progressive linear orderedness is also always already vanquished, or overcome. Archimedes recognizes that the perseverance of all preexisting/post-existing particles—or of all preexisting/post-existing bodies—*as* preexisting/post-existing particles—or *as* preexisting/post-existing bodies—(over the course of their trajectories) generates a space and time in the natural world in which equal distances and equal times absolutely exist, and which itself is progressively linearly ordered, even as the progressive linear orderedness of this space and time is also always already vanquished, or overcome. And Archimedes recognizes that all preexisting/post-existing particles—or all preexisting/post-existing bodies—(and which exist inextricably from their perseverance (over the course of their trajectories) with their unchanging and immovable presently uniform rectilinear motions) exist as the unchanging and immovable element(s) of which this space and time is composed; and he recognizes that this absolute space and time therefore exists as a *substantial/material* entity in the natural world. And from these findings, Archimedes recognizes that it is possible to define a "direction" with respect to the generation of all particles'—or of all bodies'—trajectories, even as he recognizes that the concept of "direction" is also always already vanquished, or overcome.[73]

---

[73]. As we will see, these ideas will be of deep import to Newton in the development of his own cosmology. We will find that in his *Principia*, Newton refers to the absolute space and the absolute time that are generated in the natural world by way of the perseverance of all preexisting/post-existing particles—or of all preexisting/post-existing bodies—(and which, like Archimedes, Newton too considers to exist inextricably from their unchanging and immovable presently uniform rectilinear motions) *as* preexisting/post-existing particles—or *as* preexisting/post-existing bodies—(over the course of their trajectories) as an Absolute Space and an Absolute Time. Newton refers to all preexisting/post-existing particles—or all preexisting/post-existing bodies (and which Newton too considers to exist inextricably from their unchanging and immovable presently uniform rectilinear motions) as Absolute Places. (And we recognize that Newton's name for the site of all preexisting/post-existing particles—or of all preexisting/post-existing bodies (and which Newton too considers to exist inextricably from their unchanging and immovable presently uniform rectilinear motions) as Absolute *Places* exists as a quiet nod to Archimedes, and to Archimedes's facetious request to be given "a[n unchanging and immovable] *place,*" and by way of the existence of which it would be possible to move the world. Newton recognizes how Archimedes had truly moved the world with his insights into motion, and Newton playfully gives back to Archimedes

We find that Archimedes therefore implies that he considers a progressively linearly ordered geometric space and time to exist between our Present Now and a future Now, even as he recognizes that the progressive linear orderedness of this geometric space and time is also always already vanquished, or overcome. Archimedes therefore implies that all of us voyage through a progressively linearly ordered space and time from our Present Now to a future Now, even as we also never depart from the unchanging and immovable place(s) that we always already Are—the site(s) of our own unchanging and immovable Presence(s)—the site(s) at which Divinity and ever-burgeoning life are realized in the natural world—the divine origin(s) of reality. Eureka! Eureka![74]

IV. ON THE NATURE OF NUMBERS IN THE NATURAL WORLD

And finally, we find that Archimedes offers us his thoughts on the nature of numbers in the natural world.

Archimedes continues to explore the straight line that is generated at a uniform rate, and whose generation is implicit to the generation of the spiral (and whose generation is implicit to the generation of all plane curves—and whose generation is implicit to the generation of all

---

the (facetiously) requested *place*—in the form of his Absolute *Place*—nearly two millennia later.)

As we explore Newton's cosmology, we will find that Newton considers his "immovable" Absolute Place(s) to persevere (over the course of their trajectories) with (what he refers to as) their Absolute Motions, which deliver the immovable Absolute Place(s) to the unchanging and immovable Absolute Place(s) that they always already Are, and from which they never depart—to the site(s) of their own unchanging and immovable Presence(s). As we will see, Newton considers the Absolute Motions of the Absolute Place(s) to generate an Absolute Space and an Absolute Time in the natural world in which equal distances and equal times absolutely and indisputably exists, and which possesses a progressive linear orderedness that is also always already vanquished, or overcome. And Newton considers his Absolute Place(s) to exist as the unchanging and immovable (and *material*) element(s) of which this Absolute Space and Time is composed.

We will find that Newton defines four Absolute quantities in his *Principia*—Absolute Time, Space, Place, and Motion—which he considers to come into being ever-presently and omni-presently in the natural world, in the coming into being of the site of all particles'—or of all bodies'—unchanging and immovable Presence(s)—in the coming into being of the (multiple and yet simultaneously singular) All/the Only—in the coming into being of his God: the Universe itself—and we will find that Newton's four Absolute quantities exist as the monist, materialist focus of his entire cosmology.

74. Once again, these ideas remind us of Pythagoras's Tetrad.

particles' trajectories in the natural world). And Archimedes recognizes that it is possible to assign progressively linearly ordered number values to the fundamental elements of which the straight line is composed as they come into being *at a uniform rate* (over the course of their trajectory), even as he recognizes that the progressive linear orderedness of these number values is also always already vanquished, or overcome (since the elements of which the straight line is composed are also indistinguishable from one another).[75] Archimedes recognizes that the straight line's fundamental elements—its preexisting/post-existing points/infinitesimal line segments—generate a geometric space and a time in which equal distances and equal times absolutely exist, and which itself is progressively linearly ordered, even as he also recognizes that the progressive linear orderedness of this geometric space and time is also always already vanquished, or overcome. And Archimedes recognizes that it is possible to choose any particular element along the straight line and to define it to be the straight line's origin, and he recognizes that it is possible to label this element with the number value of zero. Archimedes recognizes that it is possible to assign progressively linearly ordered number values to the elements of which the straight line is composed—*in both directions*—forward and backward—relative to this origin (or relative to this number value of zero)—even as he recognizes that the progressive linear orderedness of these number values is also always already vanquished, or overcome.[76] We recognize that the progressively linearly ordered number values that are brought into being in the generation of the straight line *at a uniform rate*, and whose progressive linear orderedness is also always already vanquished, or overcome, are those number values that will later be called the integers.[77]

Archimedes also recognizes that it is possible to define length and distance along the straight line by locating any particular element of which the straight line is composed (and which had been assigned an (integer) number value), and by considering the element's location in relation to the location of the origin (and in relation to the origin's number

75. Archimedes recognizes that this is a process of assigning names to the fundamental elements of which the straight line is composed.

76. It is said that the existence of the negative numbers was not known at the time of Archimedes, but it is possible for us to infer that Archimedes had recognized their existence.

77. We recognize that any set of numbers that are equidistant from one another along a straight line would also satisfy this condition; however, for simplicity's sake here, we choose to label these numbers with the name of the integers.

value of zero). For example, he recognizes that it is possible to consider a length of three units to be the distance along the straight line between the elements that had been assigned the number values of three and of negative three, and the element that was assigned the number value of zero.[78] And Archimedes considers these lengths to exist as line segments which exist exactly equivalently to their number values.

Archimedes also recognizes that it is possible to consider any two consecutive elements along the straight line (and which had been assigned progressively linearly ordered (integer) number values, relative to one another) to exist as the endpoints of a line segment (whose length is one unit). He recognizes that it is possible to consider this line segment to itself exist as a dynamically generated plane curve, which was brought into being at a uniform rate, and whose fundamental elements are progressively linearly ordered with respect to one another, even as they also exist as the sites at which a progressive linear orderedness is always already vanquished, or overcome (since the elements of which the line segment is composed are also indistinguishable from one another). Archimedes recognizes that this line segment's fundamental elements—its preexisting/post-existing points/infinitesimal line segments—generated a geometric space and a time in which equal distances and equal times absolutely exist, and which itself is progressively linearly ordered, even as he also recognizes that the progressive linear orderedness of this geometric space and time is also always already vanquished, or overcome. And Archimedes recognizes that an infinite number of fractional values of (what will later be called) an integer were brought into being by way of this process. Archimedes also recognizes that it is possible to apply this process ad infinitum: he recognizes that it is possible to consider any two consecutive elements along *that* line segment to exist as the endpoints of another line segment—and that it is possible to more deeply explore the generation of *that* line segment (whose length had been assigned some fractional number value of an integer). Archimedes recognizes that *that* line segment also exists as a dynamically generated plane curve, which was brought into being at a uniform rate, and whose fundamental elements are progressively linearly ordered with respect to one another,

---

78. It is also said that the concept of absolute value was not known at the time of Archimedes, but it is possible for us to infer that Archimedes had recognized its existence. Archimedes also implies that he does not consider length or distance to be an absolute quantity, but rather to exist relative to the uniform rate at which the straight line is generated. He implies that the uniform rate at which the straight line is generated determines the length or distance of a given unit.

even as they also exist as the sites at which a progressive linear orderedness is always already vanquished, or overcome (since the elements of which *that* line segment is composed are also indistinguishable from one another). Archimedes recognizes that *that* line segment's fundamental elements—its preexisting/post-existing points/infinitesimal line segments—generated a geometric space and a time in which equal distances and equal times absolutely exists, and which itself is progressively linearly ordered, even as he also recognizes that the progressive linear orderedness of *that* geometric space and time is also always already vanquished, or overcome. Archimedes recognizes that an infinite number of fractional number values of *that* fractional number value were brought into being by way of this process. And on and on, without end—

And Archimedes recognizes that any length along the straight line exists as a line segment which possesses an equivalent numerical value—including such lengths as the square root of two and the circumference of a circle. Archimedes considers these lengths to exist as line segments, and he recognizes that it is possible to consider these line segments to themselves exist as dynamically generated plane curves, which were brought into being at a uniform rate, and whose fundamental elements are progressively linearly ordered with respect to one another, even as they also exist as the sites at which a progressive linear orderedness is always already vanquished, or overcome (since the elements of which these line segments are composed are also indistinguishable from one another). Archimedes recognizes that these line segments' fundamental elements—their preexisting/post-existing points/infinitesimal line segments—generated a geometric space and a time in which equal distances and equal times absolutely exists, and which itself is progressively linearly ordered, even as he also recognizes that the progressive linear orderedness of this geometric space and time is also always already vanquished, or overcome. And Archimedes recognizes that since these line segments' fundamental elements—their preexisting/post-existing points/infinitesimal line segments—are indistinguishable from one another, these line segments themselves—and indeed all line segments along the straight line—exist as infinite (and yet simultaneously singular) collections of their fundamental element(s)—their preexisting/post-existing points/infinitesimal line segments—which were dynamically generated in the dynamical generation of the line segments themselves. Archimedes therefore recognizes that since all line segments along the straight line exist exactly equivalently to their numerical values, *all numbers themselves exist as infinite (and yet simultaneously singular) collection(s) of their fundamental elements—their preexisting/post-existing points/infinitesimal line segments—which were dynamically generated in the dynamic generation of their equivalent line segments.* As we know, these ideas were suggested by Democritus in his own cosmology, and we remind ourselves here that Newton deeply respected Democritus's wisdom.

↭

Archimedes recognizes that the straight line which is brought into being at a uniform rate, and whose generation is implicit to the generation of the spiral (and whose generation is implicit to the generation of all plane curves—and whose generation is implicit to the generation of all particles' trajectories in the natural world), is (what will later be called) the real number line itself.[79] Archimedes recognizes that the fundamental elements of which the real number line is composed—its preexisting/post-existing points/infinitesimal line segments—exist *as of two dimensions simultaneously*; he recognizes that the fundamental elements of which the real number line is composed exist as the real number line's discrete indivisibles/its continuous infinitesimals, which exist *as of one dimension less* than the real number line itself and which also exist *as of the same dimension* as the real number line itself. Archimedes recognizes that the fundamental elements of which the real number line is composed possess a progressive linear orderedness that is also always already vanquished, or overcome. And Archimedes recognizes that the fundamental elements of which the real number line is composed do not exist prior to—or independently of—the real number line itself, but rather exist inextricably from it.

Archimedes recognizes that the fundamental elements of which the real number line is composed are (what will later be called) the real numbers themselves. And Archimedes recognizes that the fundamental elements of which the real number line is composed—the real numbers themselves—exist *as of two dimensions simultaneously*; he recognizes that the real numbers themselves are simultaneously discrete and continuous, and that they possess a progressive linear orderedness that is also always already vanquished, or overcome.[80]

79. See "Real Line," para. 1, in which it is written that "in mathematics, the real line, or real number line is the line whose points are the real numbers." (And we recognize that the real number line is actually the line whose fundamental elements—its indivisibles/infinitesimals; its points/infinitesimal line segments—are the real numbers.)

80. Archimedes recognizes that (what will later be called) the real numbers, and

100   PARADISE IS NOW

And Archimedes recognizes that since the straight line that is generated at a uniform rate (or that which we may refer to as the real number line itself) is implicit to the generation of the spiral—and that it is implicit to the generation of all plane curves—and that it is implicit to the generation of all particles'—or all bodies'—trajectories in the natural world, its fundamental elements (which will later be called the real numbers themselves) come into being in mathematical/physical reality in the coming into being of the site of all particles'—or of all bodies'—unchanging and immovable Presence(s)—in the coming into being of the divine origin(s) of reality—in the coming into being of we ourselves. Archimedes implies that we all always already exist as the (multiple and yet simultaneously singular) site(s) at which Divinity, ever-burgeoning life, and *numbers* come into being in the natural world. Eureka!, again and again and again!![81]

Today, contemporary mathematicians do not recognize how the real numbers come into being in mathematical reality—a mathematical reality that they consider to exist distinctly from physical reality.[82] Wikipedia reports that over the past few centuries, mathematicians have developed many different techniques for constructing the real numbers, but that none of these techniques has revealed to mathematicians (or to

---

which exist as the fundamental elements of which the real number line is composed, are dynamically generated in the dynamic generation of the real number line itself, and that they exist *as of two dimensions simultaneously*; he recognizes that the real numbers exist as the real number line's discrete indivisibles/its continuous infinitesimals, which exist *as of one dimension less* than the real number line itself and which also exist *as of the same dimension* as the real number line itself. And Archimedes recognizes that the real numbers exist inextricably from their trajectory—the real number line itself.

81. Archimedes implies that, like Pythagoras and the ancient Jews, he too considers numbers to come into being in the natural world in the coming into being of Divinity and of ever-burgeoning life; and Archimedes implies that, like Pythagoras and the ancient Jews, he too considers numbers to possess a progressive linear orderedness (that extends even to the infinite), even as this progressive linear orderedness (and the infinite itself) are also always already vanquished, or overcome.

82. As has been mentioned, contemporary mathematicians and physicists consider mathematical reality to exist distinctly from physical reality because ancient philosophical wisdom has been lost to our contemporary philosophical discourse.

physicists) why the real numbers are necessary to the natural world. As Wikipedia reports:

> Few mathematical structures have undergone as many revisions or have been presented in as many guises as the real numbers. Every generation reexamines the reals in the light of its values and mathematical objectives.[83]

And as a reviewer of one of the techniques for constructing the real numbers complains:

> The details are all included, but as usual they are tedious and not too instructive.[84]

We find that more than two millennia ago, Archimedes recognized that the real numbers come into being in mathematical/physical reality in the coming into being of the site of all particles'—or of all bodies'—unchanging and immovable Presence(s)—in the coming into being of the divine origin(s) of reality—in the coming into being of we ourselves.

Let us also note here that today, contemporary physicists also recognize that time requires a real number description, but that the reason for this remains unknown.[85] Archimedes shows us that time requires a real number description because the real numbers themselves come into being in the coming into being of (and the perseverance of) the site of all particles'—or of all bodies'—unchanging and immovable Presence(s)—in the coming into being of (and the perseverance of) we ourselves.

As has been mentioned, Archimedes considers (what will later be called) the real numbers to be simultaneously discrete and continuous—and he recognizes that they possess both an arithmetical (discrete/punctiform) aspect and a geometric (continuous/infinitesimal) aspect. Archimedes implies that he considers arithmetic to also be a geometric

---

83. "Construction of Real Numbers," para. 17.

84. Rieger, "New Approach," 205.

85. See Penrose, *Road to Reality*, 61, in which he writes, "Moreover, there are other physical measures that require real-number descriptions, according to our presently successful theories. The most noteworthy of these is time."

procedure, since it involves summing over quantities that are simultaneously discrete and continuous.[86] And we find that Archimedes's kinematics—or what is referred to today as his "geometry of motion"—is actually an arithmetic/geometry of motion.[87]

Today it is not known what the relationship between the discrete and the continuous is, either in mathematical reality or in physical reality (as contemporary mathematicians and physicists consider mathematical reality to exist distinctly from physical reality)—but we recognize that Archimedes had solved all of these problems in antiquity, and that he had proposed that we ourselves always already exist as the resolution(s) of the relationship between the discrete and the continuous in mathematical/physical reality.

◆

Scholars report that in the year 212 BC, during the Siege of Syracuse, Archimedes was killed by a Roman solider, "despite orders [from Roman officials] that he should not be harmed."[88] Archimedes's value to society was recognized—even by the enemy—who desired to claim him as their own. As we know, however, Archimedes belonged neither to the Greeks, nor to the Romans, but to the eternal, and to the Divine.[89]

Let us turn now to the cosmology of Galileo Galilei, who, we find, appropriates all of Archimedes's cosmology within his own cosmology, even as he extends and deepens Archimedes's cosmology in breathtaking and inspired ways.

◆

Before we turn to the cosmology of Galileo, however, let us first address one point regarding the site of Divinity's Presence in the natural world. As we know, the monist, materialist focus of Archimedes's

---

86. Interestingly, the study of arithmetic in antiquity was considered to primarily be a philosophical endeavor. We read: "For the ancient Greeks after Pythagoras . . . arithmetic was primarily a philosophical study" (Robbins and Karpinski, "Greek Arithmetic," 3).

87. We recognize that Archimedes restored to the philosophical discourse the inseparable relationship between number and geometry—a relationship that had been introduced into the philosophical discourse by Pythagoras, but later sundered by Eudoxus.

88. "Archimedes," para. 3.

89. As we know, Archimedes belonged to his God: the Universe itself.

cosmology was upon the site of all particles'—or of all bodies'—unchanging and immovable Presence(s)—and the site that Archimedes had recognized to exist as that of YHWH's unchanging and immovable Presence in the natural world. And as has been mentioned, we find that the site of all particles'—or of all bodies'—unchanging and immovable Presence(s) exists as the monist, materialist focus of Galileo's and of Newton's cosmologies too, and that like Archimedes, Galileo and Newton too recognize that the site of all particles'—or of all bodies'—unchanging and immovable Presence(s) exists as the site at which Divinity's Presence is realized in the natural world.

We will find, however, that both Galileo and Newton were devoutly religious Christians. And we ask ourselves here: if both Galileo and Newton were devoutly religious Christians, did the God of the ancient Jews—YHWH—exist as the center and focus of their monist, materialist cosmologies—or rather, did the God of the early Christians—Jesus—exist as the center and focus of their monist, materialist cosmologies? What did Galileo and Newton consider the relationship between YHWH and Jesus to be? In order to answer this question, we will need to explore the *prisca sapientia* more deeply.

200 years after the death of Archimedes, the cosmology of the early Christians was born. Galileo and Newton, who were both ardent students of the *prisca sapientia*, recognized that Jesus and his disciples had been Jews, who had appropriated the cosmology of the ancient Jews within their own cosmology, even as they had extended and deepened the ancient Jews' cosmology in breathtaking and inspired ways. Let us turn now to a brief exploration of what Galileo and Newton saw about the cosmologies of the ancient Jews and of the early Christians, so that we may come to understand what they considered the relationship between YHWH and Jesus to be.

We return here to the sixteenth and seventeenth centuries so that we may see what Galileo and Newton see. Galileo and Newton study the works of the ancient Jews deeply, and they recognize that the monist, materialist focus of the ancient Jews' cosmology was upon (what Thales had referred to as) the arche—the generative "source," "origin," or "originating cause" of all things that exist in the natural world, which also exists as the site of all things in the natural world; and Galileo and Newton recognize that the ancient Jews' name for the arche in their cosmology was YHWH.

104 PARADISE IS NOW

Galileo and Newton study the cosmology of the ancient Jews deeply, and they recognize that in the cosmology of the ancient Jews, YHWH comes into being Presently in the natural world, in the coming into being of the (multiple and yet simultaneously singular) All/the Only—in the coming into being of we ourselves. Galileo and Newton recognize that in the cosmology of the ancient Jews, All is always already One, and All is always already Now. And Galileo and Newton recognize that in the cosmology of the ancient Jews, all of us always already exist as manifestation(s) of Divinity and of ever-burgeoning life, and Paradise is always already Now.

(We note here that Newton taught himself Hebrew so that he could read the ancient Jews' sacred texts in their original forms. See Newton's "Nova Cubi Hæbræi Tabella," below.)

FIGURE 5[90]

90. Newton, "Nova Cubi Hæbræi Tabella." Scholars report that Newton's Bible was "the most heavily annotated book in his library" (Morrison, *Isaac Newton's Temple*,

CHAPTER IV. ARCHIMEDES

Galileo and Newton also recognize that the Greek term Logos—which derives from the verb légō (λέγω), meaning "'count,' 'tell,' 'say,' 'speak'" (Ackrill, *Categories*, 124), and which the Greeks associated with Divinity, with speech, and with number—was another Greek name for YHWH himself.[91] (As has been mentioned, Galileo and Newton study the ancient Jewish sacred texts deeply, and they recognize that in the cosmology of the ancient Jews, all of us always already exist as manifestation(s) of YHWH's Presently spoken Name/Word (which translates as "I AM") and all of us always already exist as manifestation(s) of his four-headed fountain of life; Galileo and Newton recognize that the Jews considered all of us to always already exist as manifestation(s) of Divine Speech. Galileo and Newton also recognize that the Jews considered All to always already be One, and All to always already be Now. And Galileo and Newton recognize that the Jews associated YHWH's (multiple and yet simultaneously singular) Presence in the natural world with quantity/number, and that the Greek term Logos—which the Greeks associated with Divinity, with speech, and with number—was another Greek name for YHWH himself. (And Galileo and Newton also recognize that the Jews of the Hellenistic period—the period during which Jesus himself lived—had referred to YHWH directly as "the Logos."))[92]

---

13), and that Newton studied the Bible in the original languages in which it was written. (We read that "Newton, who felt that his mission was more to study religion than science, certainly did not stop at reading the King James version of the Bible, but rather read all original versions he could, learning the necessary ancient languages." (See "Newton's Arian Beliefs," para. 3.)) And we recognize here that Newton studied the Bible deeply because he considered it to possess secret *natural philosophical* and *mathematical* wisdom.

91. Galileo and Newton were also students of Pythagoras, and they recognized that the Monad and the Tetrad were also Greek names for YHWH.

92. As has been mentioned, "within Hellenistic Judaism, Philo of Alexandria (c. 20BC–c.50AD) integrated the term [Logos] into Jewish philosophy" ("Logos," para. 6).

Galileo and Newton therefore recognize that the Greek term Logos—which was another name for YHWH—was also another name for the arche—the generative "source," "origin," or "originating cause" of all things that exist in the natural world, which also exists as the site of all things in the natural world. (And for confirmation that the Logos was another name for the arche, see the "Heraclitus" entry in *The Cambridge Dictionary of Philosophy*, 375, in which we read that "Heraclitus claims that we should listen to the *logos*, which teaches that all things are one.")

❧

Galileo and Newton also study the cosmology of the early Christians deeply, and they recognize that the monist, materialist focus of the early Christians' cosmology was also upon the arche—the generative "source," "origin," or "originating cause" of all things that exist in the natural world, which also exists as the site of all things in the natural world—and they recognize that the early Christians' name for the arche in their own cosmology was the Logos. But Galileo and Newton also recognize that in the cosmology of the early Christians, the Logos refers to Jesus—or to he whom the early Christians considered to exist as the manifestation of the Divine Word in the natural world. (For example, Galileo and Newton recognize that in John 1:1, it is written: "Ἐν ἀρχῇ ἦν ὁ λόγος"—which translates as "In the beginning [the arche] was the Word [the Logos; or the arche] . . . .")[93] And Galileo and Newton also recognize that, in the cosmology of the early Christians, the arche—or the Logos (and here, Jesus himself)—is located at the site of what Presently Is in the natural world; Galileo and Newton recognize that Jesus declares "I am" seven times in the early Christians' sacred writings—and that "I am" is "spoken by Jesus . . . to refer to himself not with the role of a verb but playing the role of a name."[94]

❧

Galileo and Newton therefore recognize that in the cosmology of the early Christians, Jesus/the Logos exists as the site of what Presently Is in the natural world. But Galileo and Newton also recognize that in

---

93. Aland et al., "John 1:1." We will explore the meaning of John 1:1 more deeply later in this section.

94. See "I Am (Biblical Term)," para. 1, in which it is written that "The Koine Greek term *Ego eimi* . . . literally 'I am' . . . is recorded in the Gospels to have been spoken by Jesus on several occasions to refer to himself not with the role of a verb but playing the role of a name, in the Gospel of John occurring seven times with specific titles." And Galileo and Newton therefore deduce that Jesus (or "I am") cryptically asserts here that he exists as "I am," and that therefore, he exists as the site of what Presently Is in the natural world. (Interestingly, in John 8:25, Jesus declares: "[I am] From the beginning [the arche]! – precisely what I have been saying (speaking) to you" (see Caragounis, "What Did Jesus Mean by τὴν ἀρχήν," 129), and we recognize that Jesus declares here that he (Presently) exists as the arche—as the generative "source," "origin," or "originating cause" of all things that exist in the natural world, which also exists as the site of all things in the natural world.)

the cosmology of the ancient Jews, YHWH/the Logos exists as the site of what Presently Is in the natural world. And therefore, Galileo and Newton, who were well-versed in the cosmologies of Pythagoras and of Archimedes, recognize that YHWH/the Logos exists as the manifestation of an "earlier" Now (relative to Jesus/the Logos, who exists as the manifestation of a "later" Now)—and that Jesus/the Logos exists as the manifestation of a "later" Now (relative to YHWH/the Logos, who exists as a manifestation of an "earlier" Now)—even as, *at the same time*, YHWH/the Logos and Jesus/the Logos also exist as the site(s) at which the concepts of "earlier" and of "later," and of passing time itself, are also always already vanquished, or overcome. Galileo and Newton recognize that a progressively linearly ordered geometric space and time exists between YHWH/the Logos and Jesus/the Logos—even as the progressive linear orderedness of this space and time is also always already vanquished, or overcome.

And therefore, Galileo and Newton recognize that YHWH/the Logos and Jesus/the Logos exist as (multiple and yet simultaneously singular) manifestation(s) of one another—as (multiple and yet simultaneously singular) manifestations of the arche—*the generative "source," "origin," or "originating cause" of all things that exist in the natural world, which also exists as the site of all things in the natural world*—as (multiple and yet simultaneously singular) manifestations(s) of the divine origin(s) of reality—as (multiple and yet simultaneously singular) manifestation(s) of we ourselves.[95]

And therefore, we will find that the monist, materialist focus of Galileo's and of Newton's cosmologies is upon YHWH, the father—even as, *at the same time*, it is also upon Jesus, the son; the monist, materialist focus of Galileo's and of Newton's cosmologies is upon (that which both Galileo and Newton consider to be) the Divine Name/Word Presently spoken (and written)—his ecstatic, bursting, and resoundingly affirmative, "I AM"—which Galileo and Newton consider to come into being ever-presently and omni-presently, in the coming into being of the (multiple and yet simultaneously singular) All/the Only—in the coming into

---

95. Galileo and Newton recognize that the Bible comprises the Old Testament and the New Testament—even as, *at the same time*, its monist, materialist focus—the Divine Logos himself—exists as the site at which the concepts of "old" and of "new" are always already vanquished, or overcome.

being of (what Galileo and Newton both consider to be) the One God: the Universe itself.[96]

⸎

Let us turn now to an exploration of the cosmology of Galileo, who, as has been mentioned, appropriates all of Archimedes's cosmology within his own cosmology, even as he extends and deepens Archimedes's cosmology in breathtaking and inspired ways.

---

96. We recognize that both Galileo and Newton considered the Universe to exist as a sacred text, with All existing as (multiple and yet simultaneously singular) manifestation(s) of the Divine Name/Word Presently spoken (and written)—his One ecstatic, bursting, and resoundingly affirmative, "I AM." (And indeed, we find that both Galileo and Newton allude to the Universe as being a sacred text in their own writings: in *Assayer* of 1623, Galileo famously writes, "Philosophy is written in this grand book, the universe, which stands continually open to our gaze" (Galileo, *Discoveries and Opinions*, 237–38); and Newton remarks that wisdom and insight are "not only to be found in ye volume of nature but also in ye sacred scriptures." (Newton, Keynes MS. 33, f.5v.))

We also find that both Galileo and Newton considered themselves to be prophets, who believed that they had received Divine wisdom and had been spoken through by God; and we find that they considered the Divine Logos himself to have written their texts, much as they considered him to ceaselessly write the Universe. We will return to the concept of the prophet later in this text.

Let us also turn to a brief exploration of John 1:1 here. In its entirety, John 1:1 reads: "Ἐν ἀρχῇ ἦν ὁ λόγος, καὶ ὁ λόγος ἦν πρὸς τὸν θεόν, καὶ θεὸς ἦν ὁ λόγος"—or: "In the arche was the Logos, and the Logos was with Theon, and Theos was the Logos" (see *Strong's Concordance*, applied to Aland et al., "John 1:1")—or, as we read in the KJV of the Bible: "In the beginning was the Word, and the Word was with God, and the Word was God." We also read that in Septuagint texts, Theos was another Greek name for YHWH. (For example, we read that in one Septuagint manuscript, "In the Book of Exodus alone . . . [Theos] represents [YHWH] the Tetragrammaton 41 times." ("Tetragrammaton," para. 46.)) We may therefore translate John 1:1 as follows: In the beginning [the arche] was the Word [the Logos; or the arche], and the Word [the Logos; or the arche] was with YHWH [the Logos; or the arche], and YHWH [the Logos; or the arche] was the Word [the Logos; or the arche]. We find that John 1:1 cryptically hints at the ideas that Galileo and Newton had deduced concerning the relationship between YHWH and Jesus in the natural world.

BOOK II. Modernity

Chapter V.

Galileo Galilei (1564–1642)

GALILEO GALILEI WAS AN Italian polymath: "astronomer, physicist, engineer, philosopher, and mathematician,"[1] and we find that his cosmology centers around exploring (what he refers to as) "the intimate relationship between time and motion" in the natural world.[2] As we know, Archimedes's cosmology centered around exploring this very relationship, and as we will see, Galileo was a deeply sensitive reader of Archimedes's works.

We find that Galileo appropriates all of Archimedes's cosmology in the development of his own cosmology, even as he extends and deepens Archimedes's cosmology in breathtaking and inspired ways. Galileo recognizes that the center and monist focus of Archimedes's cosmology was upon the site of all particles'—or of all bodies'—unchanging and immovable Presence(s)—and the site that Archimedes had recognized to exist as that of YHWH's Presence in the natural world—and as we will see, the center and monist focus of Galileo's cosmology too is upon the site of all particles'—or of all bodies'—unchanging and immovable Presence(s)—and the site that Galileo too recognizes to exist as that of Divinity's Presence in the natural world.[3]

---

1. "Galileo Galilei," para. 4.
2. Galilei, *Two New Sciences*, 161.
3. Scholars recognize that Galileo was a devoutly religious Christian (we read that Galileo was a "genuinely pious Roman Catholic" who "seriously considered the priesthood as a young man." ("Galileo Galilei," paras. 11, 13.)) And as has been mentioned, Galileo recognizes that YHWH/the Logos and Jesus/the Logos exist as (multiple and yet simultaneously singular) manifestation(s) of one another—as (multiple and yet simultaneously singular) manifestation(s) of the divine origin(s) of reality, which comes into being ever-presently and omni-presently, in the coming into being of the site of all particles'—or all bodies'—unchanging and immovable Presence(s)—in the coming

Scholars acknowledge that Galileo's ideas were responsible for the creation of the first accurate timepiece. As Wikipedia reports:

> Although Galileo seriously considered the priesthood as a young man, at his father's urging he instead enrolled at the University of Pisa for a medical degree. In 1581, [at age 17,] when he was studying medicine, he noticed a swinging chandelier, which air currents shifted about to swing in larger and smaller arcs. To him, it seemed, by comparison with his heartbeat, that the chandelier took the same amount of time to swing back and forth, no matter how far it was swinging. When he returned home, he set up two pendulums of equal length and swung one with a large sweep and the other with a small sweep and found that they kept time together.[4]

One hundred years later, Christiaan Huygens would apply Galileo's discoveries regarding the tautochrone nature of a swinging pendulum to the creation of an accurate timepiece.[5] Even as a teenager, Galileo had been fascinated with "the intimate relationship between time and motion" in the natural world—a fascination that he carried throughout his life.

⁂

Wikipedia relates the story of Galileo's early beginnings, and of his switch from the study of medicine at university to the study of mathematics and natural philosophy. We read:

> Up to this point [the time of his investigations into swinging pendulums], Galileo had deliberately been kept away from mathematics, since a physician earned a higher income than a mathematician. However, after accidentally attending a lecture on geometry, he talked his reluctant father into letting him study mathematics and natural philosophy instead of medicine.[6]

---

into being of we ourselves. And we find that the monist, materialist focus of Galileo's cosmology is upon the site of all particles'—or of all bodies'—unchanging and immovable Presence(s)—and the site that Galileo recognizes the Divine Logos to be realized in the natural world.

4. "Galileo Galilei," para. 13.
5. "Galileo Galilei," para. 13.
6. "Galileo Galilei," para. 13.

It was also at this time that Galileo discovered the works of Archimedes. Scholars report that the "relatively few copies of Archimedes's written work that survived through the Middle Ages were an influential source of ideas for scientists during the Renaissance,"[7] and they acknowledge that "Archimedes directly inspired Galileo Galilei and Isaac Newton to investigate [kinematics, or] the mathematics of motion."[8]

Historians of science note that "Archimedes's surviving works . . . finally made it into print in 1544,"[9] and Galileo's biographer John Joseph Fahie recounts that "about the summer of 1585," when Galileo was twenty-one years old:

> he devoted himself heart and soul to mathematics and physics. From the study of Euclid he passed on to the writings of Archimedes, whose work in mechanics he was destined to continue, and for whom he then conceived a veneration which lasted through life.[10]

Scholars report that "Galileo praised Archimedes many times"[11] in his writings, and as has been mentioned, Galileo referred to Archimedes as "the most divine Archimedes" and as a "superhuman."[12] It is also reported that Archimedes's "name appears more than a hundred times in Galileo's writings," and that, a few years before his death, Galileo referred to Archimedes as "my master."[13] And historians of science assert that Archimedes was the mathematician, natural philosopher, and engineer to whom "Galileo frequently turned for inspiration and guidance."[14] We find that Galileo, who was a student of the *prisca sapientia*, recognized that Archimedes's cosmology exists as secret, hidden wisdom, which requires

---

7. "Archimedes," para. 4.

8. Stewart, "Archimedes," para. 13.

9. Stewart, "Archimedes," para. 13.

10. Fahie, *Galileo*, 13–14.

11. "Archimedes," para. 43.

12. As biographer David Wootton writes in *Galileo*, 79, "Galileo's admiration for Archimedes, the Greek mathematician, engineer and scientist of the third century BC, knew no bounds. 'It is all too obvious that no one else has ever been nearly as clever as he was.' He is the 'superhuman Archimedes, whose name I never mention without a feeling of awe,' 'the most divine Archimedes,' someone Galileo reads with 'unending astonishment' ('infinito stupore')."

13. Hummel, *Galileo Connection*, 31. And see also Museo Galileo, "Galileo Galilei and Archimedes," para. 1.

14. Hummel, *Galileo Connection*, 84.

decrypting, and as we will see, Galileo too composed a cosmology that exists as secret, hidden wisdom, and that requires decrypting.[15]

15. Although it is not recognized by contemporary scholars that Galileo's cosmology exists as secret, hidden wisdom, which requires decrypting—this *was* recognized by Newton, who decrypted Galileo's secret cosmology. (And we note here that our reader may be skeptical that Galileo's cosmology exists as secret, hidden wisdom, and we invite our reader's skepticism; we expect our reader to be convinced of our assertion by the sublime beauty that will be revealed by Galileo's decrypted cosmology.)

Let us also note here that historians of science acknowledge that "Galileo, who considered Archimedes [to be] his mentor, also prized the dialogues of Plato" (Grudin, "Humanism, Art, and Science," para. 2). And although we have not spent any time exploring Plato's cosmology thus far, it will be necessary for us to turn to a brief exploration of his cosmology here, as scholars acknowledge that Plato was of great import both to Galileo and to Newton.

As has been mentioned, scholars recognize that Plato (428/427 BC–348/347 BC) was deeply influenced by Pythagoras (and let us remind ourselves here that in the "Pythagoreanism" entry in Wikipedia we read that "Pythagorean ideas exercised a marked influence on Plato"), and we find that Plato's cosmology largely echoes Pythagoras's own cosmology. Let us briefly return now to the fifth century BC, so that we may see what Plato sees.

☙

Plato recognizes that the monist, materialist focus of Pythagoras's cosmology was upon (what Thales had referred to as) the "arche"—the generative "source," "origin," or "originating cause" of all things that exist in the natural world, which also exists as the site of all things in the natural world—and Plato recognizes that Pythagoras had located the arche's presence in the natural world at the site of what Presently Is.

(Plato recognizes that Pythagoras had appropriated the ancient Jews' cosmology within his own cosmology, even as he had extended and deepened the ancient Jews' cosmology in breathtaking and inspired ways, and that the monist, materialist focus of the ancient Jews' cosmology too had also been upon (what Thales had referred to as) the arche; and Plato recognizes that the ancient Jews too had located the arche's presence in the natural world at the site of what Presently Is. Plato recognizes that the ancient Jews' name for the arche in their cosmology was YHWH, and he recognizes that Pythagoras's name for the ancient Jews' YHWH was the Monad/the Tetrad. Plato recognizes that both the ancient Jews and Pythagoras had considered All to always already be One, and All to always already be Now. And Plato recognizes that both the ancient Jews and Pythagoras had considered all of us to always already exist as manifestation(s) of Divinity and of ever-burgeoning life, and that they had considered Paradise to always already be Now.)

We find that the monist, materialist focus of Plato's cosmology too is upon the arche—the generative "source," "origin," or "originating cause" of all things that exist in the natural world, which also exists as the site of all things in the natural world—and that, like the ancient Jews and Pythagoras, Plato too locates the arche's presence in the natural world at the site of what Presently Is. Plato alternately refers to the arche in his own cosmology as "the first principle of the whole" (Plato, *Republic*, VI) (and we note here that the English word "principle" is a translation of Plato's Greek word "ἀρχήν," or arche), and as "the father and creator" (Plato, *Timaeus*, 37c, 1167), and we find that Plato asserts that the father and creator, or the arche—the generative "source," "origin," or "originating cause" of all things that exist in the natural world, which also exists as the site of all things in the natural world—is an "eternal living being" (Plato, *Timaeus*, 38a, 1167), who comes into being Presently, in the coming into being of the (multiple and yet simultaneously singular) All/the Only, in the coming into being of we ourselves. (Plato writes, "the past and future are created species of time, which we unconsciously but wrongly transfer to eternal being, for we say that it 'was,' or 'is,' or 'will be,' but the truth is that 'is' alone is properly attributed to it [eternal being—the arche]." (Plato, *Timaeus*, 38a, 1167.)) Plato also asserts that the father and creator is "that which is immovably the same forever" (Plato, *Timaeus*, 38a, 1167), and we recognize that "the father and creator" is Plato's name for the ancient Jews' YHWH and for Pythagoras's Monad/Tetrad.

Plato implies that he considers all of us to always already exist as manifestation(s) of the arche—the first principle of the whole—the father and creator himself—and to always already exist as manifestation(s) of eternal living being. And we find that, like Pythagoras, Plato too was a vegetarian and believed in metempsychosis; and we recognize that, like Pythagoras, Plato implies that he too considered All lives to always already exist as One life, and Paradise to always already be Now.

Plato ascribes three "transcendental" properties to eternal living being—or to the arche itself: truth, beauty, and goodness. (We read that "the transcendentals (Latin: *transcendentalia*) are the three properties of being: truth, beauty, and goodness" ("Transcendentals," para. 1)—and we recognize that Plato implies here that he considers all of us to always already exist as manifestation(s) of the Absolutely True, Beautiful, and Good in the natural world. (We find that Plato's ideas were to be deeply influential to the early Christians in the development of their own cosmology.))

Plato also asserts that (what he calls) "true philosophers" (Plato, *Republic*, VI) are those philosophers who devote their lives to exploring the arche—the first principle of the whole—the father and creator himself. (And we deduce that since Plato considers the true philosopher himself or herself to always already exist as a manifestation of the arche, Plato implies that he considers the work of the true philosopher to be that of fulfilling the Delphic Oracle's dictum to "know thyself.") And Plato asserts that true philosophers should be the rulers of his ideal state (the Republic), for he claims that it is they who see (what he refers to as) "the things themselves" (Plato, *Republic*, VI); he claims that it is they who see (what he considers to be) true reality. Plato asserts that true philosophers possess "magnificence of mind and are the spectator[s] of all time and all existence" (Plato, *Republic*, VI) because it is they who see "with the eye of the mind" (Plato, *Republic*, VI) that All is always already One and that All is always already Now. (Indeed, Plato writes that true philosophers "behold the things themselves, which can only be seen with the eye of the mind" (Plato, *Republic*, VI), and we recognize that Plato implies here that he does not consider observable reality to be the deepest seat of reality. (And we also recognize that although Plato did not possess intellectual knowledge of the existence of the site of all particles'—or of all bodies'—unchanging and immovable Presence(s) in the natural world (which Archimedes recognized is *implicit* to all particles'—or all bodies'—trajectories, but is not directly observable to us in nature), he intuited its Presence.)) Plato also asserts that the work of true philosophers is to correct the cosmologies of they who are not true philosophers and who do not see "the things themselves" (and who therefore do not see (what Plato considers to be) true reality); and he asserts that true philosophers "look at the absolute truth and to that original to repair" (Plato, *Republic*, VI).

We will find that Galileo was a true philosopher in the Platonic sense, who devoted his life to exploring the arche—the "first principle of the whole"—the father and creator himself—and who corrected the cosmology of Aristotle, whose natural philosophical

Galileo composed two major works: his *Dialogue Concerning the Two Chief World Systems, Ptolemaic and Copernican*, of 1632, and his *Dialogues Concerning Two New Sciences*, of 1638, and we find that both works concern themselves with exploring (what Galileo referred to as) "the intimate relationship between time and motion" in the natural world. Galileo's first major work, his *Dialogue Concerning the Two Chief World Systems, Ptolemaic and Copernican*, of 1632, was interpreted by Galileo's contemporaries to suggest that the Earth and the other planets orbit the Sun—the work was interpreted to suggest that the Sun exists as an unchanging and immovable referent by which it would be possible to rigorously define motion and change—and we find that it was this work that was responsible for Galileo's incurring "the wrath of the Inquisition,"[16] as the Church charged him with "vehement suspicion of heresy"[17] for (ostensibly) suggesting that ours is a heliocentric cosmology rather than a geocentric one. (As we will see, we consider this reading of Galileo's *Dialogue* to be a misinterpretation of his true ideas, and our reading of Galileo's work will follow in these pages.)[18] Galileo's second major work, his *Dialogues Concerning Two New Sciences*, of 1638, was published during the time in which Galileo had been put under house arrest as punishment for (what the Church had considered to be) his crime. In *Dialogues Concerning Two New Sciences*, Galileo summarized the "work he had done some forty years earlier on the two sciences now called kinematics and strength of materials."[19]

---

teachings were the prevailing philosophy of the time. And as we will see, Galileo honors Plato in his own cosmology by composing his works in Platonic dialogue form. We will return to an exploration of Plato's cosmology in the next chapter, as we will find that Newton too was a true philosopher in the Platonic sense, who also devoted his life to exploring the arche.

16. Greene, *Fabric of the Cosmos*, 25.

17. "Galileo Galilei," para. 41.

18. We will argue that Galileo's intent in composing his *Dialogue Concerning the Two Chief World Systems* was not to propose that ours is a heliocentric or a geocentric cosmology, but rather to propose that the "common center" (of gravity) towards which all bodies in any given system of bodies "tends" exists indistinguishably from the unchanging and immovable *place(s)* that all bodies always already Are—the site(s) of (what Galileo considers to be) their own (multiple and yet simultaneously singular) Presence(s). We will explore these thoughts in greater depth, and with deeper complexity, later.

19. "Galileo Galilei," para. 2. The narrative of *Dialogues Concerning Two New Sciences* spans four days; on Days 1 and 2, Galileo discusses the strength of materials, and

CHAPTER V. GALILEO GALILEI 117

As has been mentioned, Galileo appropriates all of Archimedes's cosmology within his own cosmology, even as he extends and deepens Archimedes's cosmology in breathtaking and inspired ways. For this reason, and before we decrypt Galileo's secret cosmology, it will be helpful for us to provide our reader with a brief summary of Archimedes's decrypted cosmology, since we will find that Galileo assumes a fluency on his reader's part with Archimedes's decrypted cosmology.[20]

Let us return here to the sixteenth century, so that we may see what Galileo sees about Archimedes's cosmology.

Like Archimedes, Galileo is interested in exploring the motions of extended physical bodies; he is interested in mechanics. And like Archimedes, Galileo believes that in order to understand mechanics, it would first be necessary to understand the mathematics of motion, or kinematics. Galileo recognizes that Archimedes had developed his kinematics in his mathematical treatise, *On Spirals*, of 225 BC, and Galileo recognizes that Archimedes applied his findings from *On Spirals* to the development of a mechanics. Galileo is a deeply sensitive reader of *On Spirals* and we will find that *On Spirals* is the originary text that is embedded within Galileo's kinematics and within his mechanics.

Like Archimedes, Galileo is also a gifted engineer. And from Galileo's investigations into Archimedes's Law of the Lever, he recognizes that Archimedes had succeeded in locating the particle equivalent of an extended physical body by locating the extended physical body's balancing point—its centroid, or center of gravity. Like Archimedes, Galileo recognizes that it is possible to simplify the mathematical modeling of physical problems by replacing extended physical bodies with their balancing points—their centroids, or centers of gravity—which Galileo too considers to exist as the particle equivalents of the extended bodies themselves. In his writings, Galileo refers to an object's balancing point—its centroid,

---

on Days 3 and 4, he discusses kinematics. Our primary interest will be in exploring Days 3 and 4, in which he discusses kinematics.

20. Galileo's one hundred references to Archimedes's writings—and his reference to Archimedes as being his "master"—are hints to Galileo's reader that he or she will need to decrypt Archimedes's cosmology in order to decrypt Galileo's own cosmology.

or center of gravity—by the names of "particle" and "body"—(we find that he uses the terms interchangeably)[21]—and we recognize that, like Archimedes, Galileo too considers an object's balancing point to exist as the particle equivalent of the extended body itself.

Galileo is interested in exploring the motions of particles over passing time. Like Archimedes, Galileo recognizes that the motions of particles over passing time generate plane curves, and he recognizes that particles' trajectories therefore exist as dynamically generated plane curves. Like Archimedes, Galileo is interested in exploring the dynamical generation of plane curves. And Galileo shows us that, like Archimedes, he too considers the fundamental elements of which all plane curves are composed to exist simultaneously as the curves' discrete indivisibles (the curves' zero-dimensional points) *and* as the curves' continuous infinitesimals (the curves' one-dimensional infinitesimal line segments); Galileo shows us that, like Archimedes, he too considers the fundamental elements of which all plane curves are composed to exist *as of two dimensions simultaneously*, and to simultaneously be discrete and continuous.

Galileo shows us that he successfully decrypted Archimedes's single axiom, and we recognize that Galileo applies Archimedes's single axiom to the decrypting of Archimedes's entire cosmology.

Galileo applies Archimedes's single axiom to the decrypting of Archimedes's definition of the spiral, and Galileo recognizes that in *On Spirals*, Archimedes had succeeded in locating the existence of an unchanging and immovable referent by which he had found it possible to rigorously define the spiral's ever-changing, instantaneous motions: Archimedes had succeeded in locating the spiral's unchanging and immovable *present motions*.

Galileo decrypts Archimedes's definition of the spiral and he recognizes that Archimedes considered the spiral to have its origins in the generation of its fundamental elements—its zero-dimensional points/ one-dimensional infinitesimal line segments—which, starting from a fixed extremity, are generated *at a uniform rate* in the generation of a straight line, and which undergo rotations *at the same time* that they are unchangingly brought into being at a uniform rate. Galileo recognizes that Archimedes considered the existence of a recursive self-similarity to be implicit to the generation of the spiral, and which allows the

---

21. This is revealed to us in "Day 3" of *Two New Sciences*, 154, in which Galileo discusses kinematics. (See part I of "Day 3," in which Galileo introduces to his reader "steady or uniform motion.")

fundamental elements of which the spiral is composed to *at the same time* possess both an unchanging and immovable present aspect and a changing, instantaneous aspect. Galileo recognizes that Archimedes considered the spiral's preexisting/post-existing points/infinitesimal line segments, which are generated at a uniform rate in the generation of a straight line, and which exist as the sites at which passing time is always already vanquished, or overcome (with respect to the generation of the spiral), to exist as the spiral's unchanging and immovable present motions; and Galileo recognizes that Archimedes considered the spiral's unchanging and immovable present motions, which are made subject to rotations *at the same time* that they are unchangingly brought into being at a uniform rate, to exist as the spiral's changing, instantaneous motions.

Galileo recognizes that Archimedes defined the spiral's ever-changing, instantaneous motions in relation to its unchanging and immovable present motions. And Galileo recognizes that it is by way of the existence of the spiral's ever-changing, instantaneous motions that we are able to discern the passage of time (with respect to the generation of the spiral). Galileo also recognizes that Archimedes defined the generation of the spiral in terms of the passage of time, and that he defined the passage of time (and its presently being vanquished, or overcome) in terms of the generation of the spiral, and that Archimedes implied that he considered mathematical reality to exist inextricably from physical reality.

And Galileo recognizes that Archimedes considered the spiral's unchanging and immovable present motions—its preexisting/post-existing points/infinitesimal line segments, which are generated at a uniform rate in the generation of a straight line—to be more fundamental to the spiral than its changing, instantaneous motions, since its unchanging and immovable present motions exist "before" and "after" its changing, instantaneous motions—even as, *at the same time*, they also exist as the sites at which passing time is always already vanquished, or overcome (with respect to the generation of the spiral).

Galileo also recognizes that Archimedes found it possible to generalize his findings from *On Spirals* to the generation of all plane curves, since the spiral exists as but a particular type of plane curve. Galileo recognizes that Archimedes considered all plane curves to have their origins in the generation of their fundamental elements—their zero-dimensional points/one-dimensional infinitesimal line segments—which, starting from a fixed extremity, are generated at a uniform rate in the generation of a straight line, and which undergo rotations *at the same time* that they are unchangingly brought into being at a uniform rate.[22] Galileo recognizes that Archimedes implied that he considered the existence of a recursive self-similarity to be implicit to the generation of all plane curves, and which allows the fundamental elements of which all plane curves are composed to *at the same time* possess both an unchanging and immovable present aspect and a changing, instantaneous aspect. Galileo recognizes that Archimedes implied that he considered plane curves' preexisting/post-existing points/infinitesimal line segments, which are generated at a uniform rate in the generation of a straight line, and which exist as the sites at which passing time is always already vanquished, or overcome (with respect to the generation of the plane curves), to exist as plane curves' unchanging and immovable present motions; and Galileo recognizes that Archimedes implied that he considered plane curves' unchanging and immovable present motions, which are made subject to rotations *at the same time* that they are unchangingly brought into being at a uniform rate, to exist as plane curves' changing, instantaneous motions. Galileo recognizes that Archimedes considered plane curves to come into being presently and instantaneously *at the same time*; and Galileo recognizes that Archimedes considered plane curves to be the continuous magnitude that is responsible for bringing passing time, and the site at which passing time is presently vanquished, or overcome, into (what Archimedes implied that he considered to be) mathematical/physical reality.

And Galileo also recognizes that Archimedes found it possible to extrapolate his findings from *On Spirals* to the generation of all particles' trajectories in the natural world, since Archimedes recognized that

---

22. Galileo recognizes that Archimedes considered the one exception to this to be the special case of the straight line which is generated at a uniform rate, which possesses present motions that do not differ from its instantaneous motions. And as we will see, and like Archimedes, Galileo recognizes that the straight line which is generated at a uniform rate is embedded within the generation of all plane curves (and that it is embedded within the generation of all particles' trajectories), and, like Archimedes, Galileo spends much time exploring it.

CHAPTER V. GALILEO GALILEI   121

particles' trajectories exist as dynamically generated plane curves. Galileo recognizes that Archimedes considered particles to exist as the fundamental elements of which their trajectories are composed, and Galileo recognizes that Archimedes considered particles to be *dynamically generated* in the *dynamic generation* of their trajectories. Galileo recognizes that Archimedes did not consider particles to exist merely as *points*, but rather to exist as points/infinitesimal line segments, which exist *as of two dimensions simultaneously*, and are simultaneously discrete and continuous; and Galileo recognizes that Archimedes considered particles to exist as their trajectories' indivisibles/infinitesimals. Galileo also recognizes that Archimedes considered particles to exist inextricably from their trajectories.[23]

Galileo recognizes that Archimedes considered all particles' trajectories to have their origins in the generation of their fundamental elements—the zero-dimensional/one-dimensional particles themselves—which, starting from a fixed extremity, are generated at a uniform rate in the generation of a straight line, and which undergo rotations *at the same time* that they are unchangingly brought into being at a uniform rate. And Galileo recognizes that Archimedes implied that he considered the existence of a recursive self-similarity to be implicit to the generation of all particles' trajectories, and which allows the fundamental elements of which all particles' trajectories are composed—the zero-dimensional/one-dimensional particles themselves—to *at the same time* possess both an unchanging and immovable present aspect and a changing, instantaneous aspect. Galileo recognizes that Archimedes implied that he considered preexisting/post-existing particles, which are generated at a uniform rate in the generation of a straight line, and which exist as the sites at which passing time is always already vanquished, or overcome (with respect to the generation of particles' trajectories), to exist as their trajectories' unchanging and immovable present motions; and Galileo recognizes that Archimedes considered trajectories' unchanging and immovable present motions—or the preexisting/post-existing particles themselves—which are made subject to rotations *at the same time* that they are unchangingly brought into being at a uniform rate, to exist as their trajectories' changing, instantaneous motions.

23. Galileo recognizes that Archimedes did not consider particles to exist prior to—or independently of—their trajectories, but that rather he considered particles to be *dynamically generated* in the *dynamic generation* of their trajectories. And Galileo recognizes that Archimedes derived his definition of particles directly from his kinematics.

Galileo recognizes that Archimedes considered particles to *at the same time* possess both an unchanging and immovable present aspect and a changing, instantaneous aspect; and Galileo recognizes that Archimedes considered particles' unchanging and immovable present aspect to be more fundamental to them (and to their trajectories) than their changing, instantaneous aspect, since their unchanging and immovable present aspect exists "before" and "after" their changing, instantaneous aspect—even as, *at the same time*, it also exists as the site at which passing time is always already vanquished, or overcome (with respect to the generation of their trajectories).

Galileo recognizes that *Archimedes considered preexisting/postexisting particles, which are generated at a uniform rate in the generation of a straight line, and which exist as the sites at which passing time is always already vanquished, or overcome (with respect to the generation of particles' trajectories), to exist as their trajectories' unchanging and immovable present motions*. And therefore, Galileo recognizes that *Archimedes considered particles to exist inextricably from their perseverance (over the course of their trajectories) with unchanging and immovable presently uniform rectilinear motions*.[24] Galileo also recognizes that Archimedes considered it to be possible to define particles' changing, instantaneous motions in relation to their unchanging and immovable present motions (which Archimedes considered to exist inextricably from the particles themselves). And Galileo recognizes that Archimedes suggested that it is by way of the existence of particles' changing, instantaneous motions that we are able to discern the passage of time (with respect to the generation of particles' trajectories).

Galileo also recognizes that by exploring the motions of particles over passing time, Archimedes had been exploring the motions of extended (or compound) bodies' balancing points—their fulcrums—and the motions of the extended (or compound) bodies themselves. Galileo recognizes that Archimedes considered all particles—or all bodies—in the natural world to exist inextricably from their perseverance (over the course of their trajectories) with their unchanging and immovable presently uniform rectilinear motions. And Galileo recognizes that Archimedes thought of the site of all particles—or of all bodies—(and which exist inextricably from their unchanging and immovable presently

---

24. Scholars attribute Galileo with having discovered the concept of inertia, but as we know, the concept of inertia was actually discovered by Archimedes in antiquity. And as we will see, Newton codifies the concept of inertia in his *Principia* as his Law I.

uniform rectilinear motions) as the site of all particles'—or of all bodies'—unchanging and immovable Presence(s). *Galileo recognizes that the center and focus of Archimedes's monist cosmology was upon the site of all particles'—or of all bodies'—unchanging and immovable Presence(s).* Galileo recognizes that Archimedes considered the site of all particles'—or all bodies'—unchanging and immovable Presence(s) to exist as the site of ultimate substance and of what Presently Is in the natural world; and Galileo recognizes that Archimedes considered the site of all particles'—or of all bodies'—unchanging and immovable Presence(s) to exist as the site of the (multiple and yet simultaneously singular) All/the Only. And Galileo recognizes that when Archimedes famously ran through the streets of Syracuse naked shouting, "Eureka! Eureka!"—which translates as, "I found it! I found it!"—it was because he recognized that he had succeeded in restoring YHWH's Presence to the philosophical discourse.

Galileo recognizes that Archimedes considered the site of all particles'—or of all bodies'—Presence(s) to exist as the (multiple and yet simultaneously singular) unchanging and immovable referent(s) in the natural world by which it would be possible to define all particles'—or all bodies'—changing, instantaneous motions. And Galileo recognizes that when Archimedes famously cried, "Give me a[n unchanging and immovable] place to stand on, and I will move the earth"!, he was facetiously (and giddily!) referring to the unchanging and immovable place that he had already found—Eureka! Eureka!—he was referring to the site of the (multiple and yet simultaneously singular) All/the Only—to the unchanging and immovable Fulcrum—to his God: the Universe itself. We find that Galileo too composes a giddy, facetious cosmology, for he too recognizes that we are all always already found; he too recognizes that we all always already exist as manifestation(s) of the site of all particles'—or of all bodies'—unchanging and immovable Presence(s) in the natural world, and that we all always already exist as manifestation(s) of the site at which Divinity and ever-burgeoning life are realized in the natural world; he too recognizes that we are all always already immortal; that we are all always already One; and that Paradise is always already Now. Eureka! Eureka![25]

25. Like Archimedes, Galileo composes a giddy, facetious cosmology. And as

Galileo also recognizes that Archimedes implied that *under gravity*, all particles—or all bodies—and which exist inextricably from their perseverance (over the course of their trajectories) with their unchanging and immovable presently uniform rectilinear motions—undergo rotations that are responsible for producing their changing, instantaneous motions (and by way of the existence of which, we are able to discern the passage of time in the natural world), even as, *at the same time*, all particles—or all bodies—continue to persevere (over the course of their trajectories) *as* (preexisting/post-existing) particles—or *as* (preexisting/post-existing) bodies—(and which exist inextricably from their unchanging and immovable presently uniform rectilinear motions)—and exist as the site(s) at which motion and passing time—and even gravity itself—are always already vanquished, or overcome, in the natural world.[26]

Galileo recognizes that Archimedes implied that under gravity, all particles'—or all bodies'—unchanging and immovable Presence(s) are responsible for bringing motion and passing time into being in the natural world, even as, *at the same time*, all particles'—or all bodies'—unchanging and immovable Presence(s) exist as the (multiple and yet simultaneously singular) site(s) at which motion and passing time—and gravity itself—are always already vanquished, or overcome, in the natural world.

---

example of Galileo's facetious humor, we may offer to our reader the introduction to Galileo's discussion of kinematics here; several other examples of Galileo's humor will follow in the body of this text. In "Day 3" of Galileo's *Two New Sciences*, 153, Galileo introduces his topic to his reader with the following humorous statement: "My purpose is to set forth a very new science dealing with a very ancient subject. There is, in nature, perhaps nothing older than motion, concerning which the books written by philosophers are neither few nor small." And although Galileo's tone seems to be quite serious here, we recognize that it is actually anything but serious, since we, who have decrypted Archimedes's cosmology, know that the only thing "older" and "younger" (more "ancient" and "newer") than motion in the natural world is the site of all particles'—or of all bodies'—unchanging and immovable Presence(s)—the divine origin(s) of reality; we ourselves—who come into being Presently, and who exist as the site(s) at which the concepts of "older" and "younger" (and of passing time itself) are always already vanquished, or overcome, in the natural world. Galileo knows that the only thing "older" and "younger" than motion is YHWH/Jesus—the Divine Logos himself. (And we find that the Divine Logos himself exists as the *kentron toi bareos*—the sharp point, center, or pivot of weight—around which Galileo's discussion (and his entire cosmology) revolves.)

26. Galileo recognizes that it was this insight that allowed Archimedes to design a highly successful catapult that protected Syracuse from Roman invaders for years.

And finally, Galileo recognizes that Archimedes implied that when we observe all particles—or all bodies—in motion, we are observing their changing, instantaneous motions, and not their unchanging and immovable presently uniform rectilinear motions (and from which the particles—or bodies—themselves exist inextricably). Galileo recognizes that Archimedes implied that while all particles'—or all bodies'—unchanging and immovable presently uniform rectilinear motions (and from which the particles—or bodies—themselves exist inextricably) are *implicit* to their trajectories, they are not actually directly observable to us in nature—although they are observable to us in our mind's eye, by way of mathematics.[27]

Galileo also recognizes that Archimedes found it necessary to determine the meaning of an "origin" with respect to the spiral—and also with respect to the trajectories of all particles—or of all bodies; that he discovered (what would be referred to in the Renaissance as) the Galilean Principle of Relativity; that he explored the concept of "direction" with respect to the generation of the spiral, and also with respect to the generation of all particles'—or of all bodies'—trajectories; and that he offered us his ideas on the nature of numbers in the natural world. Summarizing very briefly here (and only with respect to Archimedes's findings concerning the motions of all particles—or of all bodies):

Galileo recognizes that Archimedes considered the site of all particles'—or of all bodies'—unchanging and immovable Presence(s) to exist as the ever-presently and omni-presently realized divine origin(s) of reality.[28]

Galileo recognizes that Archimedes spent much time exploring the straight line that is generated at a uniform rate, whose generation is implicit to the generation of the spiral (and whose generation is implicit

---

27. Galileo recognizes that Archimedes implied that bodies' sensible trajectories exist as the aggregates of their changing, instantaneous motions. *And Galileo recognizes that all particles'—or all bodies'—unchanging and immovable presently uniform rectilinear motions (and from which the particles—or bodies—themselves exist inextricably)—or the site of all particles'—or of all bodies'—unchanging and immovable Presence(s)—therefore exists as the site of the unobservable absolute in the natural world.*

28. Galileo recognizes that, like Pythagoras and the ancient Jews, Archimedes implied that he considered all of us to always already exist as the (multiple and yet simultaneously singular) divine origin(s) of reality.

to the generation of all plane curves, and whose generation is implicit to the generation of all particles'—or bodies'—trajectories in the natural world). And Galileo recognizes that from these explorations, Archimedes was able to deduce two important facts regarding the motions of all particles—or of all bodies: first, that it would not be possible for any particle—or any body—to manifest a state of absolute rest in the natural world; and second, that all particles'—or all bodies'—manifestations of uniform rectilinear motion may only be relatively determined.

Galileo recognizes that Archimedes considered the perseverance of all (preexisting/post-existing) particles—or of all (preexisting/post-existing) bodies—(and which exist inextricably from their unchanging and immovable presently uniform rectilinear motions) *as* (preexisting/post-existing) particles—or *as* (preexisting/post-existing) bodies—(over the course of their trajectories) to generate a progressively linearly ordered space and time in the natural world whose progressive linear orderedness is also always already vanquished, or overcome. Galileo recognizes that Archimedes considered the perseverance of all (preexisting/post-existing) particles—or of all (preexisting/post-existing) bodies—*as* (preexisting/post-existing) particles—or *as* (preexisting/post-existing) bodies—(over the course of their trajectories) to generate a space and time in the natural world in which equal distances and equal times absolutely exists, and which itself is progressively linearly ordered, even as the progressive linear orderedness of this space and time is also always already vanquished, or overcome. And Galileo recognizes that Archimedes considered all (preexisting/post-existing) particles—or all (preexisting/post-existing) bodies—(and which exist inextricably from their perseverance (over the course of their trajectories) with their unchanging and immovable presently uniform rectilinear motions) to exist as the unchanging and immovable element(s) of which this space and time are composed; and Galileo recognizes that Archimedes therefore considered this absolute space and time to exist as a *substantial/material* entity in the natural world.[29] And Galileo recognizes that from these findings, Archimedes saw that it was possible to define a "direction" with respect to the generation of all particles'—or of all bodies'—trajectories, even as Archimedes also saw that the concept of "direction" is also always already vanquished, or overcome.

---

29. And Galileo recognizes that with these ideas, Archimedes had composed a more mathematically rigorous version of Pythagoras's Tetrad.

CHAPTER V. GALILEO GALILEI   127

And finally, Galileo recognizes that Archimedes considered (what would later be called) the real number line to come into being in the natural world in the coming into being of (and the perseverance of) the site of all particles'—or of all bodies'—unchanging and immovable Presence(s); in the coming into being of (and the perseverance of) we ourselves. Galileo recognizes that Archimedes implied that we all always already exist as the (multiple and yet simultaneously singular) site(s) at which Divinity, ever-burgeoning life, and *numbers* come into being in the natural world. Eureka! Eureka![30]

∽

Let us turn now to the decrypting of Galileo's cosmology itself—keeping in mind as we go that Galileo embeds all of Archimedes's cosmology within his own cosmology, even as he extends and deepens Archimedes's cosmology in breathtaking and inspired ways.

∽

We will begin to explore Galileo's cosmology by turning to a passage in Galileo's *Dialogues Concerning Two New Sciences* in which he reveals to us that, like Archimedes, he too considers the fundamental elements of which all plane curves are composed to exist simultaneously as the curves' discrete indivisibles (the curves' zero-dimensional points) *and* as

---

30. Galileo recognizes that, like Pythagoras and the ancient Jews, Archimedes considered numbers to come into being in the natural world in the coming into being of the (multiple and yet simultaneously singular) All/the Only; in the coming into being of Divinity himself. And we find that Galileo implies that he considers the same to be true: in his *Dialogue Concerning the Two Chief World Systems, Ptolemaic and Copernican*, he writes, "I know perfectly well that the Pythagoreans had the highest esteem for the science of number and that Plato himself admired the human intellect and believed that it participates in divinity solely because it is able to understand the nature of numbers. And I myself am inclined to make the same judgment" (cited in Kafatos and Nadeau, *Conscious Universe*, 104). We recognize that Galileo implies here that he considers our understanding of the nature of numbers to be the means by which we may come to understand the (multiple and yet simultaneously singular) All/the Only—the Universe itself; our own Divine selves.

We find that Galileo also writes, "I have never met a man so ignorant that I couldn't learn something from him" ("Quotations: Galileo Galilei"), and we recognize that Galileo is able to say this with complete sincerity because he believes that all of us always already exist as manifestation(s) of God's Presently spoken (and written) Name/Word—his ecstatic, bursting, and resoundingly affirmative, "I AM."

the curves' continuous infinitesimals (the curves' one-dimensional infinitesimal line segments).[31]

In the passage quoted below, Salviati, Galileo's spokesperson in the *Dialogues*,[32] claims to "resolve the whole of infinity, at a single stroke" by way of the act of bending a straight line into a circle—for he asserts that such an act shows that the straight line (having become a circle) exists as an infinilateral polygon whose sides are infinitesimal line segments (the plane curve's one-dimensional continuous infinitesimals)—even as those "sides" are *also* discrete points (the plane curve's zero-dimensional discrete indivisibles). Galileo/Salviati bends the straight line into a circle and he argues as follows:

> Salviati. If now the change which takes place when you bend a line at angles so as to form now a square, now an octagon, now a polygon of forty, a hundred or a thousand angles, is sufficient to bring into actuality the four, eight, forty, hundred, and thousand parts which, according to you, existed at first only potentially in the straight line, may I not say, with equal right, that, when I have bent the straight line into a *polygon having an infinite number of sides, i. e., into a circle*, I have reduced to actuality that infinite number of parts which you claimed, while it was straight, were contained in it only potentially? *Nor can one deny that the division into an infinite number of points is just as truly accomplished* as the one into four parts when the square is formed or into a thousand parts when the millagon is formed; for in such a division the same conditions are satisfied as in the case of a polygon of a thousand or a hundred thousand sides. Such a polygon laid upon a straight line touches it with one of its sides, i. e., with one of its hundred thousand parts; *while the circle which is a polygon of an infinite number of sides touches the*

---

31. As has been mentioned, Galileo's work on indivisibles was to be deeply influential to his student, Bonaventura Cavalieri, who is credited in the history of mathematics with producing the first logically rigorous definition of the indivisible. We dispute, however, that Cavilieri produced the first logically rigorous definition of the indivisible; we argue that Pythagoras, Democritus, Archimedes, and Galileo himself had all considered themselves to possess a logically rigorous definition of the indivisible, but that they had desired that their reader actively participate in logically deducing their ideas.

32. As has been mentioned, Galileo composed his major works in the form of Platonic dialogues, and we find that Galileo speaks through the voice of Salviati in his *Dialogues*, much as Plato speaks through the voice of Socrates in his own *Dialogues*. We read that: "The characters [in Galileo's *Dialogues*] are: Salviati: An expert follower and friend of Galileo. What he says can be taken as Galileo's view. Sagredo: Sympathetic to Galileo but not an expert. What he says is not necessarily Galileo's view. Simplicio: An Aristotelian. What he says is almost never Galileo's view" (Maher, "Galileo").

same straight line with one of its sides which is a single point different from all its neighbors and therefore separate and distinct in no less degree than is one side of a polygon from the other sides.[33]

We find that this passage subtly reveals to us that, like Archimedes, Galileo considers the fundamental elements of which plane curves are composed to exist simultaneously as the curves' continuous infinitesimals (the curves' one-dimensional infinitesimal line segments) *and* as the curves' discrete indivisibles (the curves' zero-dimensional points); the passage subtly reveals to us that Galileo succeeded in decrypting Archimedes's single axiom. And as we will see, Galileo applies this single axiom to the decrypting of Archimedes's entire cosmology, and Galileo sees all that we have seen about it—even as he also sees more.

There are two deeply significant ways in which Galileo extends and deepens Archimedes's cosmology. The first is in that Galileo recognizes that it is not only possible to locate the balancing point—or the center of gravity—of an extended physical body, but that it is also possible to locate the balancing point—or the center of gravity—of a *system of bodies*. And Galileo recognizes that much as the center of gravity of an extended physical body exists as its particle equivalent, the center of gravity of a system of bodies also exists as the particle equivalent of the entire system. Galileo recognizes that in the mathematical modeling of physical problems it is therefore possible to replace an entire system of bodies by its particle equivalent, and he recognizes that it is possible to explore the motions of the particle over passing time. As we will see, this finding has profound implications on his understanding of reality. And we will find that by decrypting Galileo's ideas on the center of gravity of a system of bodies, we will be able to discern (what we consider to be) Galileo's

33. Galilei, *Two New Sciences*, 47–48; my emphases. We note here that Galileo's/Salviati's references to actuality and potentiality are allusions to the cosmology of Aristotle, in which motion is defined to be "the fulfillment of what exists potentially, in so far as it exists potentially" (Aristotle, *Physics* III:1). And let us also note here that Galileo implies that the line's/circle's *present motions* (which come into being *now*) come into being in the coming into being of an infinite (and yet simultaneously singular) number of the line's/circle's fundamental elements—its continuous infinitesimal sides/discrete indivisible points. Galileo implies here that *now* is the moment at which potentiality is reduced to actuality—the moment at which infinity is overcome at a single stroke—and that *now* is therefore the site of true reality.

true intent in composing his *Dialogue Concerning the Two Chief World Systems, Ptolemaic and Copernican*—which, as we know, was interpreted by Galileo's contemporaries to suggest that the Sun exists as the common center of gravity of our solar system.

The second deeply significant way in which Galileo extends and deepens Archimedes's cosmology is in that Galileo offers us his ideas on how gravity affects the motions of all particles—or of all bodies—in the natural world. As has been mentioned, (and like Archimedes), Galileo recognizes that under gravity, all particles—or all bodies—and which exist inextricably from their perseverance (over the course of their trajectories) with their unchanging and immovable presently uniform rectilinear motions—undergo rotations that are responsible for producing their changing, instantaneous motions (and by way of the existence of which, we are able to discern the passage of time in the natural world), even as, *at the same time*, all particles—or all bodies—continue to persevere (over the course of their trajectories) *as* (preexisting/post-existing) particles—or *as* (preexisting/post-existing) bodies—(and which exist inextricably from their unchanging and immovable presently uniform rectilinear motions)—and exist as the site(s) at which motion and passing time—and even gravity itself—are always already vanquished, or overcome, in the natural world. Galileo recognizes that Archimedes implied that under gravity, all particles—or all bodies—undergo *uniform rotations* (over the course of their trajectories).[34] We find, however, that Galileo recognizes that under gravity, all particles—or all bodies—actually undergo *nonuniform rotations* (over the course of their trajectories).[35] Galileo subtly alters Archimedes's ideas on the way in which gravity affects the motions of all particles—or of all bodies—in the natural world, and we find that this alteration to Archimedes's cosmology also has profound implications on his understanding of reality.

Let us turn now to exploring the first way in which Galileo extends and deepens Archimedes's cosmology; let us turn to exploring Galileo's ideas on locating the balancing point—or the center of gravity—of a system of bodies.

---

34. And we remind ourselves here of Archimedes's definition of the spiral. Galileo recognizes that Archimedes implied that under gravity, all particles—or all bodies—are rotated through the same equal angles in equal times (over the course of their trajectories).

35. As we will see, Galileo recognizes that all particles—or all bodies—are actually rotated through changing, unequal angles in equal times (over the course of their trajectories).

CHAPTER V. GALILEO GALILEI   131

As we know, Galileo assumes that we have seen all that he has seen about Archimedes's cosmology. Galileo assumes that, like him, (and like Archimedes), we recognize that it is possible to locate the particle equivalent of an extended physical body by locating the extended body's "balancing point"—its centroid, or center of gravity. Galileo assumes that, like him, (and like Archimedes), we recognize that an extended (or compound) body is composed of many systems, and that it is possible to find the balancing point—or center of gravity—of the extended (or compound) body itself by finding the balancing points—or the centers of gravity—of all of the systems of which the body is composed. Galileo assumes that, like him, (and like Archimedes), we recognize that Archimedes's Law of the Lever shows that the extended body's own single balancing point—its center of gravity—exists as the entire system's fulcrum—the system's balancing point—and that this balancing point exists as the particle equivalent of the extended body itself. Galileo also assumes that, like him, (and like Archimedes), we recognize that this balancing point—this *particle*—exists inextricably from its perseverance (over the course of its trajectory) with an unchanging and immovable presently uniform rectilinear motion; and Galileo assumes that, like him, (and like Archimedes), we recognize that it therefore exists as a manifestation of the site of all particles'—or all bodies'—unchanging and immovable Presence(s) in the natural world.[36]

We find that Galileo's great genius is to extend Archimedes's ideas here and to apply them to a *system of bodies*. Galileo recognizes that it is possible to replace all of the extended physical bodies of which a system of bodies is composed by their balancing points—their centers of gravity—which, like Archimedes, he too considers to exist as the particle equivalents of the extended bodies themselves. And Galileo recognizes that since the extended physical bodies' balancing points—their centers of gravity—exist as the particle equivalents of the extended bodies themselves, these balancing points—or *particles*—themselves exist inextricably from their perseverance (over the course of their trajectories) with their unchanging and immovable presently uniform rectilinear motions; and Galileo recognizes that they too therefore exist as manifestation(s)

---

36. Galileo assumes that, like him, (and like Archimedes), we recognize that it exists as a manifestation of the site of Divinity's Presence in the natural world.

of the site of all particles'—or all bodies'—unchanging and immovable Presence(s) in the natural world.[37]

And by applying Archimedes's Law of the Lever to the *system of bodies*, Galileo also recognizes that it is possible to find the single balancing point—or center of gravity—of the entire system, since the balancing points of all of the bodies composing the system have already been found. Galileo recognizes that by applying the Law of the Lever to the system of bodies it is therefore possible to replace the entire system by its single balancing point—*its* center of gravity—which he recognizes exists as the particle equivalent of the entire system itself.[38] And Galileo recognizes that since the system's single balancing point—its center of gravity—exists as the particle equivalent of the entire system, it too, being a *particle*, exists inextricably from its perseverance (over the course of its trajectory) with an unchanging and immovable presently uniform rectilinear motion; and Galileo recognizes that it too therefore exists as a manifestation of the site of all particles'—or all bodies'—unchanging and immovable Presence(s) in the natural world.[39]

(And, like Archimedes, Galileo also recognizes that the site of all particles'—or of all bodies'—unchanging and immovable Presence(s) in the natural world exists as the unchanging and immovable *place(s)* (as in Archimedes's famous cry, "Give me a[n unchanging and immovable] *place* to stand on, and I will move the earth"! [my emphasis]) by which it is possible to rigorously define all motion and change.)

☙

We find that as well as being a natural philosopher and a mathematician, Galileo was also an astronomer,[40] and that from his observa-

---

37. Galileo recognizes that they exist as manifestation(s) of the site of Divinity's Presence in the natural world.

38. And Galileo recognizes that the problem of locating the balancing point—or center of gravity—of a *system of bodies* is exactly the same problem as that of locating the balancing point—or center of gravity—of a single extended physical body, since an extended physical body itself exists as a system.

39. Galileo recognizes that it too exists as a manifestation of the site of Divinity's Presence in the natural world.

40. Scholars acknowledge that Galileo made one of the first telescopes, and that he was the first to discover that Jupiter possesses four moons ("Galilean moons," paras. 3, 4). Scholars also acknowledge that Galileo was the first to discover that the Milky Way galaxy—our galaxy—exists as a collection of individual stars. In Galileo's *Sidereus*

tions of the heavenly bodies, he deduces that all bodies composing any given system of bodies "tend" towards (what he calls) a "common center" (of gravity). In the "Third Day" of his *Dialogues Concerning Two New Sciences*, Galileo/Salviati explains:

> Salviati. For just as a heavy body or system of bodies cannot of itself move upwards, or recede from the common center [*comun centro*] toward which all heavy things tend, so it is impossible for any body of its own accord to assume any motion other than one which carries it nearer to the aforesaid common center.[41]

But, as has been mentioned, Galileo recognizes that the common center (of gravity) of a system of bodies itself exists as an unchanging and

---

Nuncius (*Starry Messenger*) of 1610, he describes the Milky Way as being composed of "congeries of innumerable stars distributed in clusters. [And he continues:] To whatever region of it you direct your spyglass, an immense number of stars immediately offer themselves to view, of which very many appear rather large and very conspicuous but the multitude of small ones is truly unfathomable" (Galilei, *Sidereus Nuncius*, 62).

Let us also briefly comment here on the role that observation and experimentation play in Galileo's cosmology. We find that although Galileo was primarily interested in exploring the site of all particles'—or of all bodies'—unchanging and immovable Presence(s), which, like Archimedes, Galileo recognized is *implicit* to all particles'—or all bodies'—trajectories, but is not directly observable to us in nature (although it is observable to us in our mind's eye, by way of mathematics), Galileo was also interested in exploring sensible, observable reality, and that he applied the discoveries that he made from his sensible observations to furthering his insights into the site of all particles'—or of all bodies'—unchanging and immovable Presence(s)—and the site that he recognized to exist as that of the unobservable absolute in the natural world.

(Galileo, who was deeply influenced by Archimedes, recognized that Archimedes had been a gifted engineer as well as a natural philosopher and a mathematician, and that it was from Archimedes's experiments with levers that he had deduced that it would be possible to locate the particle equivalent of an extended physical body. Galileo also recognized that it was from Archimedes's experiments with extended physical bodies' balancing points—their centroids, or centers of gravity—that he had deduced his concept of *kentron toi bareos*—the sharp point, center, or pivot of weight. And Galileo recognized that although the monist, materialist focus of Archimedes's cosmology was upon the site of all particles'—or of all bodies'—unchanging and immovable Presence(s)—*the site that Galileo recognized to exist as that of the unobservable absolute in the natural world*—Archimedes's sensible observations and experimentations and engineering feats had allowed him to develop insights into (what Archimedes had considered to be) this unchanging and immovable *place*. We find that similarly, although the monist, materialist focus of Galileo's cosmology too is upon the site of all particles'—or of all bodies'—unchanging and immovable Presence(s)—and the site that Galileo recognized to exist as that of the unobservable absolute in the natural world—Galileo's sensible observations and experimentations and engineering feats also allowed him to develop insights into (what Galileo too considered to be) this unchanging and immovable *place*.)

41. Galilei, *Two New Sciences*, 181.

immovable *place*; and Galileo also recognizes that this unchanging and immovable *place* itself exists indistinguishably from the unchanging and immovable *place(s)* that all of the bodies composing the system always already Are. (And as we know, Galileo considers all of these unchanging and immovable *place(s)* to exist as the site(s) at which Divinity and ever-burgeoning life are realized in the natural world; and he considers all of these unchanging and immovable *place(s)* to exist as the (multiple and yet simultaneously singular) divine origin(s) of reality.) We find that Galileo also implies that he considers all of these unchanging and immovable *place(s)* to exist as the (multiple and yet simultaneously singular) manifestation(s) of *absolute simultaneity* in the natural world—which come into being presently, and which exist as the site(s) at which passing time is always already vanquished, or overcome.[42]

And therefore, we find that Galileo implies that he considers all heavy bodies composing any given system of bodies to "tend" (as he writes) ceaselessly towards an unchanging and immovable *place* that itself exists indistinguishably from the unchanging and immovable *place(s)* that all of the bodies composing the system of bodies always already Are;[43] Galileo implies that he considers all heavy bodies composing any given system of bodies to tend ceaselessly towards a manifestation of absolute simultaneity in the natural world—even as he recognizes that all heavy bodies always already exist as the (multiple and yet simultaneously singular) manifestation(s) of absolute simultaneity in the natural world. *Galileo implies that he considers all heavy bodies composing any given system of bodies to tend ceaselessly towards a manifestation of Divinity's unchanging and immovable Presence in the natural world—even as he recognizes that all heavy bodies always already exist as manifestation(s) of Divinity's unchanging and immovable Presence in the natural world.* And therefore, we find that *Galileo implies that he considers ours to neither be a heliocentric cosmology nor a geocentric cosmology but to be a Divinity-centric*

---

42. Galileo recognizes that it is an absolute simultaneity that is not observable to us by way of our eyes, but which is observable to us in our mind's eye, by way of mathematics.

43. Galileo implies that he considers all heavy bodies composing any given system of bodies to tend ceaselessly *over passing time*; he implies that he considers all heavy bodies composing any given system of bodies to *generate* passing time as they tend ceaselessly (over the course of their trajectories) towards their system's common center (of gravity)—even as, *at the same time*, they—and their system's common center (of gravity)—exist as the site(s) at which passing time is always already vanquished, or overcome, in the natural world.

cosmology. Galileo implies that he considers all heavy bodies composing any given system of bodies to tend ceaselessly towards a manifestation of God's Presently spoken (and written) Name/Word—towards a manifestation of his ecstatic, bursting, and resoundingly affirmative, "I AM"—even as Galileo recognizes that all heavy bodies always already exist as manifestation(s) of God's Presently spoken (and written) Name/Word. (And we also recognize here that by the word *tend*, Galileo implies that he considers all heavy bodies composing any given system of bodies to ceaselessly *rotate* (over the course of their trajectories) towards their system's common center (of gravity)—towards its *kentron toi bareos*—its sharp point, *center*, or pivot of weight; and we also recognize that Galileo implies that he considers the heavy bodies to generate rotating flower patterns as they go.)[44]

And here we also recognize the facetious and giddy humor of the title of Galileo's *Dialogue Concerning the Two Chief World Systems, Ptolemaic and Copernican*—for we recognize that, (like the ancient Jews, and like Pythagoras, and like Archimedes), Galileo too actually considers there to be only One (multiple and yet simultaneously singular) Chief World System; he actually considers there to be only One unchanging and immovable referent in the natural world by which it is possible to rigorously define all motion and change—and he considers that referent to be the Divine Logos himself.

Galileo also recognizes that any given system of bodies itself belongs to a *greater system of bodies*, and he recognizes that it is also possible to locate the balancing point—or center of gravity—of this greater system of bodies. Galileo recognizes that the greater system of bodies is composed of many systems of bodies—each of which possesses its own balancing point, or center of gravity.[45] And he recognizes that each of these balanc-

---

44. We may think of these rotating flower patterns as being loosely similar to those produced by a spirograph, which traces out rotating orbital patterns around a common center over passing time.

45. And Galileo recognizes that the systems of bodies themselves are composed of many bodies—each of which possesses its own balancing point, or center of gravity.

ing points, or centers of gravity, exists as the particle equivalent of each system of bodies, and that each, being a *particle*, exists inextricably from its perseverance (over the course of its trajectory) with an unchanging and immovable presently uniform rectilinear motion; and he recognizes that each therefore exists as a manifestation of the site of all particles'—or of all bodies'—unchanging and immovable Presence(s) in the natural world.[46] And Galileo recognizes that by applying the Law of the Lever to a greater system of bodies, it is possible to locate the greater system's own balancing point—its center of gravity—and Galileo recognizes that this single balancing point—or center of gravity—exists as the particle equivalent of the greater system of bodies itself. Galileo recognizes that this balancing point—this *particle*—itself exists inextricably from its perseverance (over the course of its trajectory) with an unchanging and immovable presently uniform rectilinear motion; and Galileo recognizes that it too therefore exists as a manifestation of the site of all particles'—or of all bodies'—unchanging and immovable Presence(s) in the natural world.[47] Galileo recognizes that this balancing point—or center of gravity—exists as a manifestation of the divine origin(s) of reality, and he recognizes that it too exists as a manifestation of absolute simultaneity in the natural world. And Galileo recognizes that it exists indistinguishably from all of the centers of gravity of the systems of which the greater system is composed.

And Galileo recognizes that all of the systems of which the greater system is composed tend ceaselessly (over the course of their trajectories) towards a manifestation of the unchanging and immovable *place(s)* from which they have never departed—and Galileo recognizes that they generate rotating flower patterns as they go.[48]

Galileo also recognizes that any given greater system of bodies itself belongs to an even greater system of bodies, which itself belongs to an even greater system of bodies, and so on, and so forth—ad infinitum. Galileo recognizes that ours is an infinite cosmology:[49] he recognizes that *systems* are embedded within *greater systems* which are embedded within

---

46. Galileo recognizes that each exists as a manifestation of the site of Divinity's Presence in the natural world.

47. Galileo recognizes that it too exists as a manifestation of the site of Divinity's Presence in the natural world.

48. Again, we may think of these rotating orbital flower patterns as being loosely similar to those produced by a spirograph over passing time.

49. And Galileo also recognizes that ours is an infinitely self-similar cosmology.

even greater systems (and that rotating flower patterns are embedded within greater rotating flower patterns which are embedded within even greater rotating flower patterns)—even as he recognizes that there is also only One Chief World System—and only One ecstatic, blossoming Flower—which is realized ever-presently and omni-presently, in the coming into being of the site of all particles'—or of all bodies'—unchanging and immovable Presence(s)—in the coming into being of God's Presently spoken (and written) Name/Word—his ecstatic, bursting, and resoundingly affirmative, "I AM."⁵⁰

As has been mentioned, Galileo had seriously considered the priesthood as a young man, and we recognize that the priesthood was, in fact, a vocation that Galileo realized during his life. We find that Galileo wrote a version of the Gospels—Greek for "the Good News"⁵¹—more than 1500 years after the Gospels themselves were written, and that the center and focus of Galileo's life's work—his life's *kentron toi bareos*—its sharp point, *center*, or pivot of weight—was upon his God: the Universe itself.⁵²

And therefore, it is with a sad and terrible irony that we recognize that the Church charged Galileo with vehement suspicion of heresy, and

---

50. Galileo recognizes that the One ecstatic, blossoming Flower is akin to the One ever-cleaving fountain of life. (Galileo recognizes that in Gen. 2:9 it is written, "And out of the ground made [YHWH] the LORD God . . . the tree of life . . . in the midst of the garden"—and that in Gen. 2:10 it is written, "And a river went out of Eden to water the garden; and from thence it was parted, and became into four heads." And Galileo recognizes that the tree of life and the fountain of life are alternate ways of referring to YHWH himself—or to the Divine Logos—who blossoms/bursts forth Presently in Eden. (And let us also note here that legend holds that the dogwood, which possesses a four-petalled blossom, is symbolic of Christ—or of the Divine Logos himself. For the legend of the dogwood tree, in which it is claimed that Christ's four-pointed crucifix was also constructed from the wood of a dogwood tree, see the "Cornus" entry in Wikipedia.))

51. The English word "Gospel" comes from the Greek εὐαγγέλιον, which translates as "good news" ("Gospel," para. 3). We will explore the Gospels themselves later in this text.

52. The *kentron toi bareos*—the sharp point, *center*, or pivot of weight—around which Galileo's entire life revolved was the Divine Logos himself. And we recognize that the Good News that Galileo delivers to us is to show us that we all always already Presently exist as manifestation(s) of God's ecstatic, blossoming Flower of life—even as we also "tend" ceaselessly towards a manifestation of it—and that we generate rotating flower patterns over passing time as we go.

that he was subjected to years of house arrest—during which time his health deteriorated and he went blind.[53] (Although we also recognize that in a sense, the house arrest still did not matter, for even before Galileo went blind, he was already blind; Galileo spent his life blindly observing, with the eye of the mind, the site of all particles'—or of all bodies'—unchanging and immovable Presence(s)—the site that he recognized to exist as that of the unobservable absolute in the natural world; and we also recognize that it would have been impossible to contain him within four walls, for he lived—and still lives on—ever-presently and omni-presently—in the coming into being of the (multiple and yet simultaneously singular) All/the Only—in the coming into being of the One ecstatic, blossoming Flower—the Divine Logos himself.)

Let us turn now to the second deeply significant way in which Galileo extends and deepens Archimedes's cosmology; let us turn to Galileo's thoughts on how gravity affects the motions of all particles—or of all bodies—in the natural world. We will begin to explore Galileo's thoughts on how gravity affects the motions of all particles—or of all bodies—in the natural world by returning to (Archimedes's) Principle of Relativity.

As we know, Galileo was a deeply sensitive reader of Archimedes's cosmology, and he recognizes that Archimedes had deduced two important facts from having applied his Principle of Relativity to all particles'—or all bodies'—trajectories: first, that it is not possible for any particle—or any body—to manifest a state of absolute rest in the natural world; and second, that all particles'—or all bodies'—manifestations of presently uniform rectilinear motions can only be relatively determined. (How did Archimedes deduce that it would not be possible for any particle—or any body—to manifest a state of absolute rest in the natural world? We remind ourselves here that since Archimedes recognized that the generation of a straight line at a uniform rate is implicit to the generation of all particles'—or all bodies'—trajectories, he also recognized that it would not be possible for any particle—or any body—and which exists inextricably from its perseverance (over the course of its trajectory) with its unchanging and immovable presently uniform rectilinear motion, to generate zero distances in equal times (over the course of its trajectory),

---

53. "Galileo Galilei," para. 38.

since in that case, the particle—or body—would not generate a straight line at a uniform rate. Archimedes therefore deduced that all particles—or all bodies—and which exist inextricably from their perseverance (over the course of their trajectories) with their unchanging and immovable presently uniform rectilinear motions, necessarily generate some equal *non-zero* distances over equal times (over the course of their trajectories); and he deduced that it would not be possible for any particle—or any body—to manifest a state of absolute rest in the natural world.)[54]

We find that Galileo applies Archimedes's ideas regarding the Principle of Relativity to a system of bodies' balancing point—to the system of bodies' common center (of gravity)—which, as we know, Galileo considers to exist as the particle equivalent of the system itself, and which, being a *particle*, exists inextricably from its perseverance (over the course of its trajectory) with an unchanging and immovable presently uniform rectilinear motion. (And as we know, Galileo considers this particle equivalent of the system to exist as a manifestation of the site of all particles'—or of all bodies'—unchanging and immovable Presence(s) in the natural world—and to exist as a manifestation of Divinity's own Presence in the natural world.)

In applying Archimedes's ideas regarding the Principle of Relativity to the particle equivalent of the system, Galileo recognizes that the particle equivalent of the system necessarily exists inextricably from its perseverance (over the course of its trajectory) with some unchanging and immovable *non-zero speed* presently uniform rectilinear motion.[55] And Galileo also recognizes that relative to the particle equivalent of *another* system (which itself exists inextricably from *its* perseverance (over the course of its trajectory) with some *different* unchanging and immovable *non-zero speed* presently uniform rectilinear motion),[56] the particle equivalent of the first system could be taken to be "at rest" if the particle equivalent of the second system were to be taken to be "in motion"—and visa versa.

---

54. Galileo recognizes that Archimedes considered all particles—or all bodies—to exist inextricably from their perseverance (over the course of their trajectories) with some non-zero *speed* presently uniform rectilinear motions.

55. Galileo also recognizes that the particle equivalent of the system exists as the fundamental element of which its trajectory is composed, and that the absolute space and time that it generates (over the course of its trajectory) therefore exists as a substantial/material entity.

56. Relative to the particle equivalent of the first system.

Galileo applies these ideas to the system of a large ship, and he recognizes that the particle equivalent of the ship system, which exists inextricably from its perseverance (over the course of its trajectory) with some unchanging and immovable *non-zero speed* presently uniform rectilinear motion—could be taken to be "at rest" or "in motion" relative to the particle equivalent of another system—say, perhaps, the particle equivalent of the system of the shore, which might be manifesting some *different* but still unchanging and immovable *non-zero speed* presently uniform rectilinear motion.[57] (And Galileo recognizes that the particle equivalents of both systems—the particle equivalents of the ship system and of the shore system—exist as manifestation(s) of the site of all particles'—or of all bodies'—unchanging and immovable Presence(s) in the natural world—as manifestation(s) of Divinity's own unchanging and immovable Presence in the natural world—and he recognizes that their manifestations of "motion" and of "rest" may only be relatively determined.)[58]

And Galileo therefore recognizes that if you were an observer located within any given system, it would only be possible for you to be able to discern whether your system was "in motion" or "at rest" by comparing your system with another system. For example, Galileo recognizes that if you were located in the main cabin below decks aboard the ship system, with no portholes available for you to look out through, you would be unable to discern whether you were "in (uniform rectilinear) motion" or "at rest." And in illustrating this point, Galileo/Salviati invites you to perform the following experiment with your friend:

> Salviati. Shut yourself up with some friend in the main cabin below decks on some large ship, and have with you there some

---

57. Relative to the particle equivalent of the ship system.

58. Galileo's explorations here are something of an idealization and a simplification, for as he knows, the particle equivalents of both systems *actually* tend ceaselessly (over the course of their trajectories) towards their greater system's common center (of gravity)—towards an unchanging and immovable *place* that exists indistinguishably from the unchanging and immovable *place(s)* that they always already Are—and that they generate rotating flower patterns as they go. However, we find that Galileo is not interested in exploring the rotating aspects of their motion here; he is only interested in exploring the linear aspects of their motion. (We find that Galileo is known for "idealizing" as a means of simplifying a problem. See "Idealization (Philosophy of Science)," paras. 1, 4, in which it is written that "idealization is the process by which scientific models assume facts about the phenomenon being modeled that are strictly false but make models easier to understand or solve," and that "Galileo utilized the concept of idealization in order to formulate the law of free fall.")

flies, butterflies, and other small flying animals. Have a large bowl of water with some fish in it; hang up a bottle that empties drop by drop into a narrow-mouthed vessel beneath it. With the ship standing still, observe carefully how the little animals fly with equal speed to all sides of the cabin. The fish swim indifferently in all directions; the drops fall into the vessel beneath; and, in throwing something to your friend, you need throw it no more strongly in one direction than another, the distances being equal; jumping with your feet together, you pass equal spaces in every direction. When you have observed all these things carefully (though there is no doubt that when the ship is standing still everything must happen in this way), have the ship proceed with any speed you like, so long as the motion is uniform and not fluctuating this way and that. You will discover not the least change in all the effects named, nor could you tell from any of them whether the ship was moving or standing still.[59]

Galileo implies here that only if you were standing *outside* of the ship system—say, perhaps, if you were standing on the shore, watching the ship depart from the harbor—and if you therefore belonged to a *different* system whose own particle equivalent was manifesting a *different* unchanging and immovable *non-zero speed* presently uniform rectilinear motion (relative to the unchanging and immovable *non-zero speed* presently uniform rectilinear motion that was being manifested by the particle equivalent of the ship system), would you be able to discern the relative motions between the two systems.

Galileo also implies that the motions of the particle equivalent of the ship system—the motions of the ship system's center of gravity—do not affect the motions of the bodies of which the ship system is composed. Galileo implies that regardless of whether the particle equivalent of the ship system is considered to be "in motion" or "at rest" (from the perspective of an observer outside of the system), the motions of the bodies of which the ship system is composed are the same.

Galileo also applies these ideas to his explorations of the motions of bodies freely falling under gravity. Galileo considers further the "bottle that empties drop by drop into a narrow-mouthed vessel beneath it" that

---

59. From "Day 2" of Galileo's *Two Chief World Systems*, 216–17.

is present on his ship. And he recognizes that you, who are located on the ship, and who are unable to determine whether your ship system is "in motion" or "at rest," notice that the water droplets appear to fall in a straight line path into the basin directly beneath them—and that this is your experience of the water droplets' motions, regardless of whether an observer on the shore considers you to be (relatively) "in motion" or "at rest." However, Galileo also recognizes that from the perspective of the observer on the shore, who may choose to consider his or her shore system to be relatively "at rest" when your ship system is "in motion," the water droplets appear to fall in a non-linear, parabolic path into the basin located directly beneath them.

And Galileo wonders: which trajectory is the water droplets' *true* trajectory? He wonders: do the water droplets *truly* fall in straight line paths into the basin directly beneath them, or do they *truly* fall in non-linear, parabolic paths into the basin directly beneath them? Galileo recognizes that in order to answer this question, further exploration will be necessary. And Galileo continues to explore these ideas by dropping a stone from the top of the Leaning Tower of Pisa and observing its motion as it falls.[60]

Galileo drops a stone from the top of the Leaning Tower and he recognizes that to an observer located within the Leaning Tower system, and who does not compare his or her system to another system (and who is therefore unable to determine whether his or her system is "in motion" or "at rest"), the stone appears to fall in a straight line path to a spot directly below it on the surface of the Earth—and that this is true regardless of whether an observer outside of the Leaning Tower system considers the Leaning Tower system to be (relatively) "in motion" or "at rest." However, Galileo also recognizes that to an observer viewing the situation from outside of the Leaning Tower system—say, perhaps, from the system of a passing horse-driven cart, whose particle equivalent is manifesting some *different* unchanging and immovable *non-zero speed* presently uniform rectilinear motion (relative to the unchanging and immovable *non-zero speed* presently uniform rectilinear motion that is being manifested by the particle equivalent of the Leaning Tower system), and who may

60. Scholars recognize that Galileo's famous Leaning Tower of Pisa experiments were actually thought experiments. See "Galileo Galilei," para. 64.

choose to consider his or her cart system to be "at rest" relative to the "in motion" Leaning Tower system—the stone appears to fall in a non-linear, parabolic path to a spot directly below it on the surface of the Earth.

And again, Galileo asks himself: which trajectory is the stone's *true* trajectory?

Galileo reflects deeply, and he recognizes that since it is not possible for any particle—or any body—to manifest a state of absolute rest in the natural world, the particle equivalent of the stone—the stone's center of gravity—necessarily exists inextricably from its perseverance (over the course of its trajectory) with some unchanging and immovable *non-zero speed* presently uniform rectilinear motion; and Galileo recognizes that the particle equivalent of the stone—the stone's center of gravity—therefore always possesses some unchanging and immovable *non-zero magnitude horizontal component of motion*.[61] Galileo therefore deduces that the stone dropped from the top of the Leaning Tower *actually* falls in a non-linear, parabolic path to a spot directly below it on the surface of the Earth—despite the fact that to an observer located within the Leaning Tower system, the stone *appears* to fall in a linear path to a spot directly below it on the surface of the Earth. And Galileo recognizes here that it is necessary to distinguish between particles'—or bodies'—*actual* motions under gravity and their *apparent* motions under gravity.[62]

---

61. As we will see, Newton amends this idea slightly in his own cosmology. Newton recognizes that Galileo had deduced his ideas regarding the effects of gravity on the motions of all particles'—or of all bodies'—in the natural world by exploring bodies dropped from the top of the Leaning Tower, and that Galileo had assumed that while the "inertial" component of particles'—or of bodies'—motions (and which exist inextricably from the particles—or bodies—themselves) are *horizontal*, the "gravitational" components of the particles'—or bodies'—motions are *vertical*. Newton himself recognizes that the "inertial" components of particles'—or bodies'—motions (and which exist inextricably from the particles—or bodies—themselves) are not necessarily horizontal, but that they are *orthogonal* to the gravitational components of the particles'—or bodies'—motions. We find that in Newton's own cosmology, he defines gravity as being a "centripetal," or "center-seeking" force, and we read that that direction of a centripetal force "is always orthogonal to the [inertial] motion of the body" (see "Centripetal Force," para. 1).

62. Galileo recognizes that it is necessary to distinguish between particles'—or bodies'—*actual* motions under gravity and their *apparent* motions under gravity because although all particles'—or all bodies'—unchanging and immovable presently uniform rectilinear motions (and from which the particles—or bodies—themselves exist inextricably) are *implicit* to their trajectories, they are not directly observable to us in nature—although they are observable to us in our mind's eye, by way of mathematics.

Let us note here the following illustration, in which stones are dropped from the mast of the ship and also from the top of the Leaning Tower:

FIGURE 6[63]

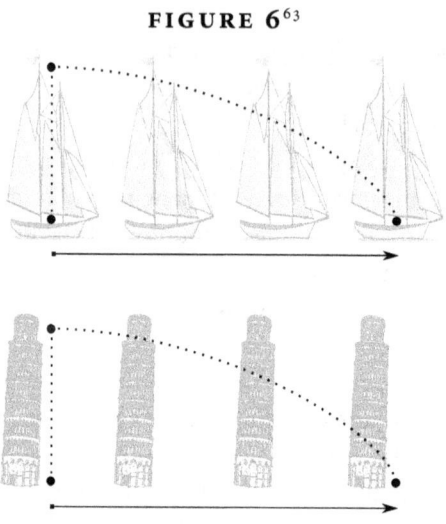

Galileo recognizes that to observers located within the ship system and within the Leaning Tower system, and who are unable to compare their systems with other systems (and who are therefore unable to determine whether their systems are "in motion" or "at rest"), the stones appear to fall in straight line paths to spots directly below them—and that this is true regardless of whether observers located outside of their systems consider their systems to be "in motion" or "at rest." Galileo also recognizes that to observers located outside of the ship system and outside of the Leaning Tower system, and who may choose to consider their systems to be "at rest" relative to the "in motion" ship and Leaning Tower systems, the stones appear to fall in non-linear, parabolic paths to spots directly below them. And Galileo reasons that the stones' *true* trajectories are *actually* non-linear and parabolic, since he recognizes that the stones always possess some unchanging and immovable *non-zero magnitude horizontal components of motion*.[64]

---

63. With thanks to Robert DiSalle, who offers readers a similar image in his "Space and Time: Inertial Frames" entry in the *Stanford Encyclopedia of Philosophy*.

64. Again, we find that Newton amends this thought slightly in his own cosmology.

CHAPTER V. GALILEO GALILEI 145

❧

Galileo therefore recognizes that under gravity, all freely falling particles—or bodies—*actually manifest non-linear projectile motions* (over the course of their trajectories)—despite the fact that to observers located within their given systems, the particles—or bodies—*appear* to manifest linear trajectories. (And Galileo asks himself: why do all freely falling particles—or bodies—manifest non-linear projectile motions under the influence of gravity? Galileo recognizes that all freely falling particles—or bodies—manifest non-linear projectile motions under the influence of gravity because they all tend ceaselessly (over the course of their trajectories) towards their system's common center (of gravity)—its *kentron toi bareos*—its sharp point, *center*, or pivot of weight.)

Galileo finds himself reminded here of Archimedes's ideas regarding the effects of gravity upon all particles—or all bodies—in the natural world; he finds himself reminded of how Archimedes had suggested that under gravity, all particles—or all bodies—and which exist inextricably from their perseverance (over the course of their trajectories) with their unchanging and immovable presently uniform rectilinear motions—undergo *rotations* that are responsible for producing their changing, instantaneous motions (and by way of the existence of which, we are able to discern the passage of time in the natural world), even as, *at the same time*, all particles—or all bodies—continue to persevere (over the course of their trajectories) *as* (preexisting/post-existing) particles—or *as* (preexisting/post-existing) bodies—(and which exist inextricably from their unchanging and immovable presently uniform rectilinear motions)—and exist as the site(s) at which motion and passing time—and even gravity itself—are always already vanquished, or overcome, in the natural world. Galileo recognizes that Archimedes implied that under gravity, all particles—or all bodies—are *uniformly rotated* (over the course of their trajectories).[65] And Galileo asks himself: is this actually true?

In an effort to answer this question, Galileo continues to explore the motion of a stone dropped from the top of the Leaning Tower—and

---

65. Galileo recognizes that Archimedes implied that under gravity, all particles—or all bodies—are rotated through the same equal angles in equal times (over the course of their trajectories).

Galileo explores the stone's motion from two different perspectives: first, from the perspective of an observer located within the Leaning Tower system, and then from the perspective of an observer located outside of the Leaning Tower system, and who may choose to consider his or her own system to be "at rest" relative to the "in motion" Leaning Tower system. And Galileo considers himself to be the observer in both situations.

At first, Galileo considers himself to be the observer located within the Leaning Tower system, and he recognizes that the stone appears to fall in a straight line path to a spot directly below it on the surface of the Earth.[66] However, Galileo also *times* the stone as it falls (over the course of its trajectory),[67] and he recognizes that the stone undergoes a change in speed—or a change in the *rate* at which it falls—as it falls (over the course of its trajectory). *Galileo recognizes that the distances over which the stone falls (over equal intervals of time) uniformly increase (over the course of the stone's trajectory).* And Galileo recognizes that the stone therefore undergoes (what he calls) a uniform change in speed (over the course of its trajectory).[68] Galileo calls this motion the stone's "uniformly and continuously accelerated" motion under gravity, and in "Day 3" of his *Dialogues Concerning Two New Sciences*, he writes:

> When, therefore, I observe a stone initially at rest falling from an elevated position and continually acquiring new increments of speed, why should I not believe that such increases take place in a manner which is exceedingly simple and rather obvious to everybody? If now we examine the matter carefully we find no addition or increment more simple than that which repeats itself always in the same manner. This we readily understand when we consider *the intimate relationship between time and motion*; for just as uniformity of motion is defined by and conceived

---

66. Galileo considers himself to be unable to compare his system with another system, and he is therefore unable to determine whether his Leaning Tower system is "in motion" or "at rest." He also recognizes that the stone appears to fall in a straight line path to a spot directly below it on the surface of the Earth—and that this is true regardless of whether an observer located outside of his system considers his system to be (relatively) "in motion" or "at rest."

67. How does Galileo time the stone as it falls? Perhaps relative to the beatings of his heart, as he had done to time the motions of the falling pendulums when he was still only a teenager.

68. How is Galileo able to rigorously define this motion? We find that Galileo is able to rigorously define this motion by defining it in relation to the site of all particles'—or all bodies'—unchanging and immovable Presence(s)—in relation to (what he considers to be) the One Chief World System, the Divine Logos himself.

through equal times and equal spaces (thus we call a motion uniform when equal distances are traversed during equal time-intervals),[69] so also we may, in a similar manner, through equal time-intervals, conceive additions of speed as taking place without complication; thus we may picture to our mind a motion as uniformly and continuously accelerated when, during any equal intervals of time whatever, equal increments of speed are given to it. Thus if any equal intervals of time whatever have elapsed, counting from the time at which the moving body left its position of rest and began to descend, the amount of speed acquired during the first two time-intervals will be double that acquired during the first time-interval alone; so the amount added during three of these time-intervals will be treble; and that in four, quadruple that of the first time interval....

And thus, it seems, we shall not be far wrong if we put the increment of speed as proportional to the increment of time; hence the definition of motion which we are about to discuss may be stated as follows: *A motion is said to be uniformly accelerated, when starting from rest, it acquires, during equal time-intervals, equal increments of speed.*[70]

Galileo also refers to this type of motion in his writings as a body's "naturally accelerated motion" under gravity.[71] And he recognizes that there is a simple mathematical pattern governing the changes in a falling body's speed as it falls (over the course of its trajectory), and he writes:

The spaces described by a body falling from rest with a uniformly accelerated motion are to each other as the squares of the time-intervals employed in traversing these distances.[72]

Next, Galileo asks himself: how do these *uniform changes in speed* manifest themselves to an observer who is located outside of the Leaning Tower system, and who may choose to consider his or her own system to be "at rest" relative to the "in motion" Leaning Tower system?

---

69. And as we know, Galileo considers all particles—or all bodies—to exist inextricably from their perseverance (over the course of their trajectories) with this type of motion; a type of motion which also "repeats itself always in the same manner."

70. Galilei, *Two New Sciences*, 161–62; my emphases.

71. Galilei, *Two New Sciences*, 160.

72. Theorem II, Proposition II, from "Day 3" of Galileo's *Two New Sciences*, 174.

Galileo considers himself to be the observer in this situation too, and he recognizes that from this perspective, the stone still appears to fall in a non-linear, parabolic path (over the course of its trajectory). However, he also recognizes that the changes in the distances over which the stone falls (over equal intervals of time) over the course of the stone's trajectory manifest themselves as *non-uniform rotations* to which the stone is made subject (over the course of its trajectory). And Galileo recognizes that the degree to which the stone is rotated (over the course of its trajectory) corresponds to the increasing distances over which it falls (over equal intervals of time) over the course of its trajectory.

Galileo provides us with an illustration of this type of motion, which we recognize to be projectile motion:

FIGURE 7[73]

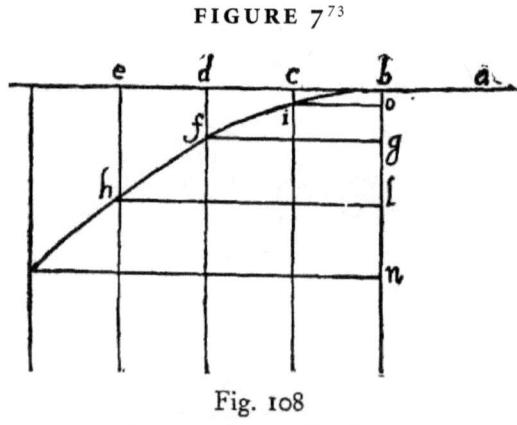

Fig. 108

To an observer located outside of the Leaning Tower system, and who may choose to consider his or her own system to be "at rest" relative to the "in motion" Leaning Tower system, the particle equivalent of the stone—or the stone's center of gravity—and which exists inextricably from its perseverance (over the course of its trajectory) with its unchanging and immovable *non-zero speed* presently uniform rectilinear motion, appears to undergo *non-uniform rotations* (over the course of its trajectory), which correspond to the increasing distances that it falls (over equal intervals of time) over the course of its trajectory. (Galileo shows us here that the particle equivalent of the freely falling body appears to progress from point b to point i to point f and to point h (over the course

---

73. Galilei, *Two New Sciences*, 249.

CHAPTER V. GALILEO GALILEI   149

of its trajectory), and that it is rotated through greater and greater angles (over equal intervals of time) as it falls.) And Galileo recognizes that the degree to which the particle equivalent of the freely falling body is rotated (over the course of its trajectory) increases in magnitude as it approaches its system's common center (of gravity).[74]

Galileo recognizes that the *true* motion of all particles—or all bodies—freely falling under gravity is to manifest non-uniform rotations (over the course of their trajectories). And Galileo therefore recognizes that under gravity, all freely falling particles—or bodies—*actually* undergo *non-uniform rotations* (over the course of their trajectories), which are responsible for producing their changing, instantaneous motions (and by way of the existence of which, we are able to discern the passage of time in the natural world)—even as, *at the same time*, all particles—or bodies—continue to persevere (over the course of their trajectories) *as* (preexisting/post-existing) particles—or *as* (preexisting/post-existing) bodies—(and which exist inextricably from their unchanging and immovable presently uniform rectilinear motions)—and exist as the site(s) at which motion and passing time—and even gravity itself—are always already vanquished, or overcome, in the natural world.

And we find that this is the second deeply significant way in which Galileo extends and deepens Archimedes's cosmology.

---

74. We note here that Galileo is exploring the motions of "a stone initially at rest falling from an elevated position," as it approaches the Earth. But we may also ask: what about the motions of a freely falling body such as a planet, which is not initially at rest? Does the particle equivalent of a freely falling planet also undergo non-uniform rotations (over the course of its trajectory)? Galileo's answer to this question is *yes*, and he finds that the degree to which the particle equivalent of the freely falling planet is rotated (over the course of its trajectory) increases in magnitude both *at the points closest to*, and *at the points furthest from*, its system's common center (of gravity)—and that this is the reason why the planet produces an orbital rotating flower pattern over passing time. (Why is the degree to which the freely falling planet is rotated greatest *at points closest to*, and *furthest from*, its system's common center? Galileo finds that there is a constant negotiation between the strength of gravity's effect upon bodies and the bodies' own tendencies to persevere (over the course of their trajectories) with their presently inertial motions—motions from which the bodies themselves exist inextricably.)

Galileo also recognizes that with this thought, he is correcting the "superhuman" Archimedes's cosmology.[75] And we find that Galileo acknowledges this correction to the superhuman Archimedes's cosmology in the following humorous passage from "Day 3" of his *Dialogues Concerning Two New Sciences*, in which Galileo (ostensibly) criticizes Archimedes for having invented "an arbitrary type of motion" in *On Spirals* that is "not [actually] met with in nature." Galileo writes:

> And first of all it seems desirable to find and explain a definition best fitting natural phenomena. For anyone may invent an *arbitrary* type of motion and discuss its properties; thus, for instance, some have imagined helices and conchoids as described by certain motions which are not met with in nature, and have very commendably established the properties which these curves possess in virtue of their definitions; but we have decided to consider the phenomena of bodies falling with an acceleration such as *actually* occurs in nature and to make this definition of accelerated motion exhibit the essential features of observed accelerated motions.[76]

Galileo seems to be criticizing Archimedes here, but we recognize that this passage is actually written in a tongue-in-cheek and deeply affectionate tone, for we may surmise that "the most divine" Archimedes is the friend and fellow mathematician with whom Galileo is most anxious to share his findings.

Let us close our exploration of Galileo's cosmology with another humorous, tongue-in-cheek passage from "Day 3" of *Dialogues Concerning Two New Sciences* in which Galileo (ostensibly) speculates about "the cause" of all bodies' naturally accelerated motions under gravity. (And we recognize here that, like Archimedes, Galileo of course considers "the cause" of all bodies' naturally accelerated motions under gravity to be the site(s) of their own unchanging and immovable Presence(s); he considers

---

75. Galileo recognizes that he is performing the work of the true philosopher upon Archimedes's cosmology, and he "look[s] at the absolute truth and to that original to repair."

76. Galilei, *Two New Sciences*, 160; my emphases.

"the cause" of all bodies' naturally accelerated motions under gravity to be the Divine Logos himself.) Galileo/Salviati writes:

> Salviati. *The present* does not seem to be the proper time to investigate the *cause* of the acceleration of natural motion concerning which various opinions have been expressed by various philosophers, some explaining it by attraction to the center, others to repulsion between the very small parts of the body, while still others attribute it to a certain stress in the surrounding medium which closes in behind the falling body and drives it from one of its positions to another. *Now*, all these fantasies, and others too, ought to be examined; but it is not really worth while. *At present* it is the purpose of our Author merely to investigate and to demonstrate some of the properties of accelerated motion (whatever the cause of this acceleration may be).[77]

As we know, Galileo considered the present—or the site of all bodies' unchanging and immovable Presence(s)—to exist as the cause of all bodies' naturally accelerated motions under gravity, even as he also considered the present—or the site of all bodies' unchanging and immovable Presence(s)—to exist as the site(s) at which motion and passing time—and even gravity itself—are always already vanquished, or overcome, in the natural world. And as we know, Galileo always considered it to be the *proper time* to explore the site of all bodies' unchanging and immovable Presence(s)—the (multiple and yet simultaneously singular) All/the Only—the unchanging and immovable Fulcrum—his God: the Universe itself—which, as we know, was the *kentron toi bareos*—the sharp point, center, or pivot of weight—around which his entire cosmology revolved.[78]

---

77. Galilei, *Two New Sciences*, 166–67; my emphases.

78. As has been mentioned, *Dialogues Concerning Two New Sciences* was written during the years in which Galileo had been placed under house arrest, and we recognize that he writes here with undiminished good humor, even in the wake of his house arrest. This passage also reminds us of Archimedes's giddy letter to his friend Dositheus, and with which Archimedes introduced *On Spirals*; and we recognize that Galileo also considers *us* to exist as the friends and fellow mathematicians with whom he is most anxious to share his findings.

152   PARADISE IS NOW

❧

Let us turn now to the cosmology of Isaac Newton, who, as we will see, appropriates all of Galileo's cosmology within his own cosmology, even as he extends and deepens Galileo's cosmology in breathtaking and inspired ways.[79]

79. Before we turn to the cosmology of Isaac Newton, let us offer our reader a few more words on the rotating orbital flower patterns that are produced as heavy bodies tend ceaselessly (over the course of their trajectories) towards their system's common center (of gravity). (And we remind our reader here that we had compared these rotating flower patterns to those produced by a spirograph around a common center over passing time.) As example of one such rotating flower pattern, we may offer the following images, which detail the path of the Sun around our solar system's common center (of gravity), measured over extended periods of time. We note that Galileo would not have been able to see these evolving blossoms with his eyes (as they are generated over decades and centuries), but that he had intuited their presence in the natural world.

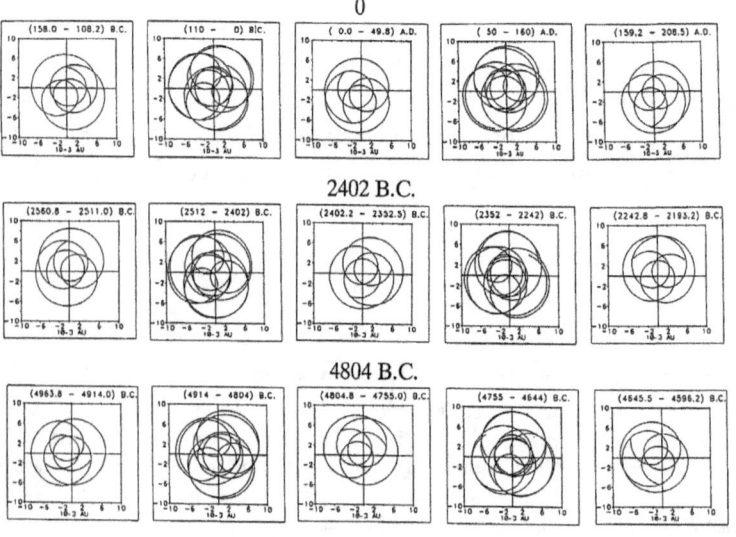

(See Charvatova, "Origin," 400.)

Chapter VI.

Isaac Newton (1642–1726/27)

ISAAC NEWTON WAS AN English "mathematician, physicist, astronomer, alchemist, theologian, and author," who is "widely recognized" to have been "one of the greatest mathematicians and physicists of all time."[1] Scholars consider Newton to have been both the Father of the Age of Reason and the author of (what today is referred to as) classical mechanics.

Newton was an intensely private man who "self-consciously hid much of his research findings,"[2] and who was fascinated by secret codes. Even as a young man, Newton had been fascinated by secret codes. In his famous Fitzwilliam Notebook of 1662 (composed when Newton was only nineteen years old), Newton confessed several petty sins—(which included: Line 1: "Vsing the word (God) openly" and Line 25: "Robbing my mother's box of plums and sugar")—among some far less petty sins—(which included: Line 13: "Threatning my father and mother Smith to burne them and the house over them"; Line 15: "Striking many"; Line 24: "Punching my sister"; Line 45: "Beating Arthur Storer")—in an elaborate code that remained uncracked for more than 300 years.[3]

A picture from The Fitzwilliam Notebook follows:

1. "Isaac Newton," para. 1.
2. Trompf, "Isaac Newton," 91.
3. Newton, "Fitzwilliam Notebook." And on The Fitzwilliam Notebook, we read, "Newton also recorded his secret confessions, written in a cryptic shorthand code only deciphered in 1964. 'Using Wilfords towel to spare my own'; 'robbing my mother's box of plums and sugar'; 'caring for worldly things more than God'" (see "Sir Isaac Newton's Notebook," para. 1).

154 PARADISE IS NOW

FIGURE 9[4]

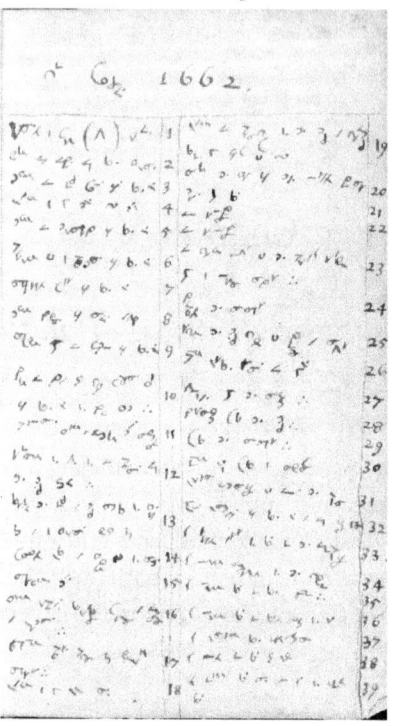

Newton also considered the Universe itself to exist as a cryptogram—a secret puzzle—that had been authored by God himself. As the economist John Maynard Keynes, a collector of some of Newton's secret alchemical and theological manuscripts, wrote about Newton in the early 1940's:

> I believe that Newton was different from the conventional picture of him. But I do not believe he was less great. He was

---

4. Newton, "Fitzwilliam Notebook Confessions." As we will see, the personality of Newton was markedly different from that of Galileo, who, as we know, wrote, "I have never met a man so ignorant that I couldn't learn something from him," and who possessed an egalitarian, gregarious spirit. Newton's biographers paint Newton as having been a difficult, surly man of an extremely secretive nature. We read that Newton's "deepest instincts were occult [or secret], esoteric, semantic—with profound shrinking from the world, a paralyzing fear of exposing his thoughts, his beliefs, his discoveries in all nakedness to the inspection and criticism of the world. 'Of the most fearful, cautious and suspicious temper that I ever knew,' said [William] Whiston, his successor in the Lucasian Chair" (see Keynes, "Newton," 364).

CHAPTER VI. ISAAC NEWTON 155

less ordinary, more extraordinary, than the nineteenth century cared to make him out. . . .

In the eighteenth century and since, Newton came to be thought of as the first and greatest of the modern age of scientists, a rationalist, one who taught us to think on the lines of cold and untinctured reason.

I do not see him in this light. I do not think that any one who has pored over the contents of that box which he packed up when he finally left Cambridge in 1696 [and which contained his secret alchemical and theological manuscripts] . . . can see him like that. Newton was not the first of the age of reason. He was the last of the magicians, the last of the Babylonians and Sumerians, the last great mind which looked out on the visible and intellectual world with the same eyes as those who began to build our intellectual inheritance rather less than 10,000 years ago. . . .

Why do I call him a magician? *Because he looked on the whole universe and all that is in it as a riddle, as a secret which could be read by applying pure thought to certain evidence, certain mystic clues which God had laid about the world to allow a sort of philosopher's treasure hunt to the esoteric brotherhood. He believed that these clues were to be found partly in the evidence of the heavens and in the constitution of elements . . . but also partly in certain papers and traditions handed down by the brethren in an unbroken chain back to the original cryptic revelation in Babylonia. He regarded the universe as a cryptogram set by the Almighty*—just as he himself wrapt the discovery of the calculus in a cryptogram when he communicated with Leibniz. By pure thought, by concentration of mind, the riddle, he believed, would be revealed to the initiate.[5]

As we will see, Newton considered himself to be a member of the esoteric brotherhood of sages and mystics who had discovered "the great truths of nature" and who had hidden their wisdom in secret codes, which require decrypting—and Newton composed his *Philosophiae Naturalis Principia Mathematica* (*Mathematical Principles of Natural Philosophy*), or *Principia*, as it is commonly called, of 1687—his most famous work, and the work that will be the center and focus of our explorations—in an elaborately crafted secret code, which also requires decrypting.[6]

5. Keynes, "Newton," 363–66; my emphasis.

6. As we will see, Newton composed his *Principia* for (what he considered to be) other members of the esoteric brotherhood. In "Untitled Treatise on Revelation (section 1.1)," para. 2, Newton reveals that he considered himself to have been specially

❧

What will we discover by decrypting Newton's secret code? We will discover that the site of all particles'—or of all bodies'—unchanging and immovable Presence(s) exists as the *kentron toi bareos*—the sharp point, center, or pivot of weight—around which Isaac Newton's entire cosmology revolves. We will discover that, (like Archimedes and Galileo), Newton too considered the site of all particles'—or of all bodies'—unchanging and immovable Presence(s) to exist as the unchanging and immovable *place(s)* (as in Archimedes's famous cry, "Give me a[n unchanging and immovable] *place* to stand on, and I will move the earth"! [my emphasis]) by which Newton too considered it to be possible to rigorously define all motion and change. And we will discover that, (like Archimedes and Galileo), Newton too considered the site of all particles'—or of all bodies'—unchanging and immovable Presence(s) to exist as the site of the (multiple and yet simultaneously singular) All/the Only; that he too considered it to exist as the unchanging and immovable Fulcrum; and that for Newton too the site of all particles'—or of all bodies'—unchanging and immovable Presence(s)—the Universe itself—was his God.

❧

We will also find that Newton, who was a deeply sensitive reader of Galileo's cosmology, embeds all of Galileo's cosmology within his own cosmology, even as he extends and deepens Galileo's cosmology in breathtaking and inspired ways. And Newton also recognizes that Galileo had embedded all of Archimedes's cosmology within his own (Galileo's) cosmology, even as he had extended and deepened Archimedes's cosmology in breathtaking and inspired ways.

And as we will see, this pattern—of systems being embedded within greater systems which are embedded within even greater systems—harmonizes with what Newton considers to be the pattern that is generated by Nature herself.[7] (As we will see, and like Galileo, New-

---

chosen by God to know his Truth, and he writes that "but a remnant, a few scattered persons which God hath chosen, such as without being led by interest, education, or humane authorities, can set themselves sincerely & earnestly to search after truth." We will find that Newton was elitist and that he composed his *Principia* for (what he considered to be) other members of this elect.

7. We recognize that this pattern is akin to that of Russian matryoshka dolls, and we will find that Newton's *Principia*—his most famous work, and the work that will be the center and focus of our explorations—was written in this form, as Archimedes's system

ton recognizes that systems in the natural world are embedded within greater systems which are embedded within even greater systems (and that rotating flower patterns are embedded within greater rotating flower patterns which are embedded within even greater rotating flower patterns)—even as Newton also recognizes that there is also only One Chief World System—(which, as we will see, Newton refers to as "the Frame of the System of the World")—and only One blossoming Flower—which is realized ever-presently and omni-presently, in the coming into being of the site of all particles'—or of all bodies'—unchanging and immovable Presence(s)—in the coming into being of the (multiple and yet simultaneously singular) All/the Only—in the coming into being of (what, like Galileo, Newton too considers to be) God's Presently spoken (and written) Name/Word—his ecstatic, bursting, and resoundingly affirmative, "I AM."

Of all of the cosmologies that we have encountered thus far, Newton's is the most deeply encrypted in code. And as an example of the carefully crafted code that we will encounter in Newton's *Principia*, we may offer to our reader the following preview:

As has been mentioned, Newton embeds the cosmologies of Archimedes and of Galileo within his own cosmology, even as he extends and deepens their cosmologies in breathtaking and inspired ways. And as we know, Archimedes and Galileo considered the perseverance of all (preexisting/post-existing) particles—or of all (preexisting/post-existing) bodies—(and which exist inextricably from their unchanging and immovable presently uniform rectilinear motions) *as* (preexisting/post-existing) particles—or *as* (preexisting/post-existing) bodies—(over the course of their trajectories) to generate a progressively linearly ordered space and time in the natural world whose progressive linear orderedness is also always already vanquished, or overcome. As we know, Archimedes

---

is embedded within Galileo's system, which is embedded within Newton's system. As has been mentioned, scholars acknowledge that the General Scholium (or general explanatory notes) to Newton's *Principia* was also written in this matryoshka dolls form. (See "Newton's General Scholium," para. 1, in which it is written that "the General Scholium, added to the *Principia* in 1713, is probably Newton's most famous text. It is also one of the least understood of Newton's writings. This is partly because Newton constructed it much like a Russian doll.") We will find that the body of Newton's *Principia*, which was also constructed much like a Russian doll, is not well understood either, and as we will see, style and artistry were important to Newton, who considered himself to be an artist as well as a natural philosopher.

and Galileo considered the perseverance of all (preexisting/post-existing) particles—or of all (preexisting/post-existing) bodies—*as* (preexisting/post-existing) particles—or *as* (preexisting/post-existing) bodies—(over the course of their trajectories) to generate a space and time in the natural world in which equal distances and equal times absolutely exists, and which itself is progressively linearly ordered, even as the progressive linear orderedness of this space and time is also always already vanquished, or overcome. And as we know, Archimedes and Galileo considered all (preexisting/post-existing) particles—or all (preexisting/post-existing) bodies—(and which exist inextricably from their perseverance (over the course of their trajectories) with their unchanging and immovable presently uniform rectilinear motions) to exist as the unchanging and immovable element(s) of which this space and time are composed; *and Archimedes and Galileo therefore considered this absolute space and time to exist as a substantial/material entity in the natural world.*

We find that in his *Principia*, Newton reveals to us that he considers the same to be true, and that he authors four terms to describe these ideas.

As we will see, Newton refers to the absolute space and the absolute time that are generated in the natural world by way of the perseverance of all (preexisting/post-existing) particles—or of all (preexisting/post-existing) bodies—(and which exist inextricably from their unchanging and immovable presently uniform rectilinear motions) *as* (preexisting/post-existing) particles—or *as* (preexisting/post-existing) bodies—(over the course of their trajectories) as an *Absolute Space* and an *Absolute Time*.

Newton refers to all (preexisting/post-existing) particles—or all (preexisting/post-existing) bodies (and which Newton too considers to exist inextricably from their unchanging and immovable presently uniform rectilinear motions) as *Absolute Places*.

And Newton refers to the perseverance of (what he refers to as) "immovable" Absolute Place(s) *as* immovable Absolute Place(s) (over the course of their trajectories) as their *Absolute Motions*, which deliver the Absolute Place(s) to the unchanging and immovable Absolute Place(s) that they always already Are, and from which they never depart—to the site(s) of their own unchanging and immovable Presence(s).[8]

---

8. We recognize that Newton considers Absolute Place(s) to be immovable because he considers them to be unchanging (with respect to themselves) over the course of their trajectories.

As we will see, Newton defines four Absolute quantities in his *Principia*—Absolute Space, Time, Place, and Motion—which he considers to come into being ever-presently and omni-presently—in the coming into being of the site of all particles'—or of all bodies'—unchanging and immovable Presence(s)—in the coming into being of the (multiple and yet simultaneously singular) All/the Only—in the coming into being of God's Presently spoken (and written) Name/Word—his ecstatic, bursting, and resoundingly affirmative, "I AM"; and we find that these four Absolute quantities exist at the heart of Newton's entire cosmology.

(And as we will see, Newton considers the coming into being of his four Absolute quantities in the natural world to bring into being (what he refers to as) the "Frame of the System of the World"—the (multiple and yet simultaneously singular) unchanging and immovable (and *material*) referent(s) by which he considers it to be possible to rigorously define all motion and change.)

We note here that these are not new ideas; they are the ideas that are embedded within the cosmologies of Archimedes and of Galileo. However, we will find that Newton speaks of these ideas in a new way and in a new deeply coded language; we will find that Newton provides *names* for (what he considers to be) the elements of which God's Presently spoken (and written) *Name*/Word are composed.[9]

And as we will see, language and artistry were important to Newton, who considered himself to be an artist as well as a natural philosopher.[10]

---

9. As we will see, Newton implies that he considers his four Absolute quantities to also be one Absolute quantity, which come into being Presently, in the coming into being of the (multiple and yet simultaneously singular) All/the Only; in the coming into being of (he whom Newton considers to be) the Divine Logos himself. And we recognize that Newton authors four Absolute quantities (which he also considers to be one Absolute quantity) in his cosmology as tribute to the ancient Jews, who considered YHWH, the four-headed fountain of life, whose four-lettered Name/Word translates as "I AM," to be the One God, who comes into being Presently, in the coming into being of the (multiple and yet simultaneously singular) All/the Only; as tribute to Pythagoras, who considered the Holy Tetrad to also be the One Monad, which also comes into being Presently, in the coming into being of the (multiple and yet simultaneously singular) All/the Only—in the coming into being of (what Pythagoras considered to be) the Kosmos, the One Universe itself; and as tribute to the early Christians, who composed four Gospel stories that are also only One Gospel, or One "Good Story"—and who considered the One Good Story to be Jesus himself—the Divine Word—who comes into being Presently, in the coming into being of the (multiple and yet simultaneously singular) All/the Only.

10. Newton considered himself to belong to the tradition of *vates*; he considered himself to be a poet/prophet and a seer of what is to come. And as we will see, Newton suggests that what is to come is that which always already Presently (and unchangingly)

Newton was elitist and we find that he composed his *Principia* for (what he considered to be) his "uncommon" reader.[11] But we ask ourselves here: who did Newton consider his "uncommon" reader to be? We recognize that Newton considered his "uncommon" reader to be that reader who, like him, had decrypted the cosmologies of Archimedes and of Galileo, and who had therefore seen all that he had seen about their cosmologies. (We find that Newton composed his *Principia* for us!)

Newton assumes a fluency on his reader's part with the cosmologies of Archimedes and of Galileo, and for this reason, we will find it helpful to provide our reader with a brief summary of Galileo's decrypted cosmology, since Newton assumes a fluency on his reader's part with it. (We note here that we have already summarized for our reader what Galileo had seen about Archimedes's cosmology, and we find that what Galileo had seen about Archimedes's cosmology is what Newton assumes that his own reader has also seen about Archimedes's cosmology. (We encourage our reader to review the summary of Archimedes's cosmology that we provided in the previous chapter.)) Let us return now to the seventeenth century, so that we may see what Newton sees about Galileo's cosmology.

Newton sees that Galileo recognized that it is not only possible to locate the balancing point—or center of gravity—of an extended physical body, but that it is also possible to locate the balancing point—or center of gravity—of a *system of bodies*. Newton sees that Galileo recognized that a system of bodies is composed of many bodies—each of which possesses its own balancing point, or center of gravity. And Newton sees

---

Is: the site of all particles'—or of all bodies'—unchanging and immovable Presence(s)—the (multiple and yet simultaneously singular) All/the Only—the divine origin(s) of reality—we ourselves.

11. How do we know that Newton composed his *Principia* for his "uncommon" reader? Early on in his *Principia*, Newton distinguishes between quantities that he considers to be of interest to the "common people," and quantities that he considers to be of interest to the uncommon people, and we recognize that he scorns (they to whom he refers as) the "common" and the "vulgar" people. (And we find that although Newton considered All to always already be One, and All to always already exist as the (multiple and yet simultaneously singular) manifestation(s) of Divinity and of ever-burgeoning life in the natural world, he nevertheless struggled with extending generosity towards his fellow man.)

that Galileo recognized that each of these balancing points, or centers of gravity, exists as the particle equivalent of each body, and that each, being a *particle*, exists inextricably from its perseverance (over the course of its trajectory) with an unchanging and immovable presently uniform rectilinear motion; and that each therefore exists as a manifestation of the site of all particles'—or of all bodies'—unchanging and immovable Presence(s) in the natural world.[12]

Newton also sees that Galileo recognized that by applying Archimedes's Law of the Lever to the system of bodies, it is possible to locate the system's own balancing point—its center of gravity—which exists as the particle equivalent of the system of bodies itself. Newton sees that Galileo recognized that this balancing point—this *particle*—itself exists inextricably from its perseverance (over the course of its trajectory) with an unchanging and immovable presently uniform rectilinear motion; and that it too therefore exists as a manifestation of the site of all particles'—or of all bodies'—unchanging and immovable Presence(s) in the natural world.[13]

(And Newton sees that Galileo recognized that the site of all particles'—or of all bodies'—unchanging and immovable Presence(s) in the natural world exists as the unchanging and immovable *place(s)* (as in Archimedes's famous cry, "Give me a[n unchanging and immovable] *place* to stand on, and I will move the earth"! [my emphasis]) by which it is possible to rigorously define all motion and change.)

Newton also sees that from Galileo's astronomical observations, Galileo had deduced that all heavy bodies composing any given system of bodies "tend" towards a common center (of gravity). But Newton sees that Galileo recognized that the common center (of gravity) of a system of bodies itself exists as an unchanging and immovable *place*; and Newton sees that Galileo recognized that this unchanging and immovable *place* exists indistinguishably from the unchanging and immovable *place(s)* that all of the bodies composing the system always already Are. (Newton sees that Galileo recognized that all of these unchanging and immovable *place(s)* exist as the site(s) at which Divinity and ever-burgeoning life are realized in the natural world; and Newton sees that Galileo recognized that they exist as the (multiple and yet simultaneously singular) divine

---

12. Newton sees that Galileo recognized that each exists as a manifestation of the site of Divinity's Presence in the natural world.

13. Newton sees that Galileo recognized that it too exists as a manifestation of the site of Divinity's Presence in the natural world.

origin(s) of reality.) And Newton sees that Galileo implied that he considered all of these unchanging and immovable *place(s)* to exist as the (multiple and yet simultaneously singular) manifestation(s) of *absolute simultaneity* in the natural world—which come into being presently, and which exist as the site(s) at which passing time is always already vanquished, or overcome.

And therefore, Newton sees that Galileo recognized that all heavy bodies composing any given system of bodies "tend" ceaselessly (over the course of their trajectories) towards an unchanging and immovable *place* that itself exists indistinguishably from the unchanging and immovable *place(s)* that all of the bodies composing the system of bodies always already Are;[14] Newton sees that Galileo recognized that all heavy bodies composing any given system of bodies tend ceaselessly (over the course of their trajectories) towards a manifestation of absolute simultaneity in the natural world—even as all heavy bodies always already exist as the (multiple and yet simultaneously singular) manifestation(s) of absolute simultaneity in the natural world. *Newton sees that Galileo recognized that all heavy bodies composing any given system of bodies tend ceaselessly (over the course of their trajectories) towards a manifestation of Divinity's unchanging and immovable Presence in the natural world—even as all heavy bodies always already exist as manifestation(s) of Divinity's unchanging and immovable Presence in the natural world.* Newton sees that Galileo recognized that all heavy bodies composing any given system of bodies tend ceaselessly (over the course of their trajectories) towards a manifestation of God's Presently spoken (and written) Name/Word—towards a manifestation of his ecstatic, bursting, and resoundingly affirmative, "I AM"—even as all heavy bodies always already exist as manifestation(s) of God's Presently spoken (and written) Name/Word. *And therefore, Newton sees that Galileo recognized that ours is neither a heliocentric cosmology nor a geocentric cosmology but a Divinity-centric cosmology.* Newton sees that Galileo recognized that all heavy bodies composing any given system of bodies tend ceaselessly (over the course of their trajectories) towards a manifestation of the unchanging and immovable *place(s)* from

---

14. Newton sees that Galileo recognized that all heavy bodies composing any given system of bodies tend ceaselessly *over passing time*; Newton sees that Galileo recognized that all heavy bodies composing any given system of bodies *generate* passing time as they tend ceaselessly (over the course of their trajectories) towards their system's common center (of gravity)—even as, *at the same time,* they—and their system's common center (of gravity)—always already exist as the site(s) at which passing time is vanquished, or overcome, in the natural world.

which they have never departed; and Newton sees that Galileo recognized that they generate rotating flower patterns as they go.

Newton also sees that Galileo recognized that *systems* are embedded within *greater systems* which are embedded within *even greater systems* (and that rotating flower patterns are embedded within greater rotating flower patterns which are embedded within even greater rotating flower patterns)—even as Galileo recognized that there is also only One Chief World System—and only One blossoming Flower—which Galileo recognized is realized ever-presently and omni-presently, in the coming into being of the site of all particles'—or of all bodies'—unchanging and immovable Presence(s)—in the coming into being of the (multiple and yet simultaneously singular) All/the Only—in the coming into being of God's Presently spoken (and written) Name/Word—his ecstatic, bursting, and resoundingly affirmative, "I AM."

And Newton sees that the second deeply significant way in which Galileo extended and deepened Archimedes's cosmology was to offer us his thoughts on how gravity affects the motions of all particles—or all bodies—in the natural world. Newton sees that Galileo was a deeply sensitive reader of Archimedes's Principle of Relativity, and that Galileo had recognized that since the state of absolute rest does not exist in the natural world, all particles—or all bodies—and which exist inextricably from their perseverance (over the course of their trajectories) with unchanging and immovable presently uniform rectilinear motions, necessarily traverse some equal non-zero distances in equal times (over the course of their trajectories). Newton sees that Galileo recognized that all particles—or all bodies—therefore exist inextricably from their perseverance (over the course of their trajectories) with some unchanging and immovable *non-zero speed* presently uniform rectilinear motions; and Newton sees that Galileo recognized that all particles—or all bodies—therefore always possess some unchanging and immovable *non-zero magnitude horizontal components of motion*.[15] Newton sees that Galileo recognized that all particles—or all bodies—freely falling under gravity

---

15. As has been mentioned, we will find that Newton corrects this idea in his own cosmology, and that he recognizes that this component of motion is not necessarily horizontal, but that it (or what we may refer to as the presently inertial component of a body's motion—and which exists inextricably from the body itself) is always *orthogonal* to (what we may refer to as) the gravitational component of the body's motion.

actually manifest non-linear projectile motions (over the course of their trajectories)—despite the fact that to observers located within the systems in which the particles—or bodies—are falling, the particles—or bodies—*appear* to manifest linear trajectories (over the course of their trajectories). And Newton sees that Galileo recognized that it is therefore necessary to distinguish between all particles'—or all bodies'—*actual* motions under gravity and their *apparent* motions under gravity.

Newton also sees that Galileo recognized that under gravity, all freely falling particles—or bodies—also undergo changes in speed—or changes in the *rates* at which they fall—as they fall (over the course of their trajectories). Newton sees that Galileo recognized that for particles—or bodies—initially at rest, the distances that they fall (over equal intervals of time) uniformly increases (over the course of their trajectories), and Newton sees that Galileo referred to this type of motion in his writings as all particles'—or all bodies'—"naturally accelerated motions" under gravity.

Newton sees that Galileo recognized that all particles—or bodies—freely falling under gravity *actually* undergo *non-uniform rotations* (over the course of their trajectories), and that Galileo recognized that the degree to which they are rotated (over the course of their trajectories) is dependent upon their distances from their system's common center (of gravity). (Newton sees that Galileo recognized that this is responsible for producing the rotating orbital flower patterns that we see in nature.) Newton sees that Galileo recognized that these *non-uniform rotations*, to which all particles—or bodies—freely falling under gravity are subject, are responsible for producing all particles'—or all bodies'—changing, instantaneous motions (and by way of the existence of which, we are able to discern the passage of time in the natural world)—even as, *at the same time*, all particles—or bodies—continue to persevere (over the course of their trajectories) *as* (preexisting/post-existing) particles—or *as* (preexisting/post-existing) bodies—(and which exist inextricably from their unchanging and immovable presently uniform rectilinear motions)—and exist as the site(s) at which motion and passing time—and even gravity itself—are always already vanquished, or overcome, in the natural world.

And Newton sees that Galileo recognized that all particles—or bodies—freely falling under gravity undergo these *non-uniform rotations* (over the course of their trajectories) as they all tend ceaselessly towards their system's common center (of gravity)—towards an unchanging and immovable *place* that itself exists indistinguishably from the unchanging

CHAPTER VI. ISAAC NEWTON 165

and immovable *place(s)* that all particles—or bodies—composing the system always already Are. Newton also sees that Galileo recognized that all particles—or bodies—freely falling under gravity *generate* passing time as they tend ceaselessly (over the course of their trajectories) towards their system's common center (of gravity)—even as, *at the same time*, they—and their system's common center (of gravity)—always already exist as the site(s) at which passing time is vanquished, or overcome, in the natural world.

We find that there are four ways in which Newton extends and deepens Galileo's cosmology. First, Newton extends and deepens Galileo's ideas regarding how gravity affects the motions of all particles—or all bodies—in the natural world. (As we will see, Newton provides us with a mathematically rigorous Theory of Universal Gravitation—a theory that rivets the world.)[16] Second, we find that Newton considered himself to have found a way to *prove* the existence of the Divine Logos's Presence in the natural world.[17] Third, Newton codifies the findings of Archimedes and of Galileo in a systematic, methodical way, and offers to his uncommon reader three Laws of Motion and six Corollaries to those Laws of Motion. We find that the focus of the Laws and Corollaries is upon all preexisting/post-existing particles—or all preexisting/post-existing bodies themselves—which Newton considers to exist inextricably from their perseverance (over the course of their trajectories) with unchanging and immovable presently uniform rectilinear motions; the focus of the Laws and Corollaries is upon the site of all particles'—or all bodies'—unchanging and immovable Presence(s)—and the site that Galileo had recognized to exist as that of the unobservable absolute in the natural world. We find that Newton too recognizes that the site of all particles'—or all bodies'—unchanging and immovable Presence(s) exists as the site of the unobservable absolute in the natural world, and we discover that the *Principia* is not actually the empirical manifesto that it has been interpreted to be over the centuries.[18] And the fourth way in which Newton

16. As example of how Newton's theory rivets the world, we may offer to our reader the poet Alexander Pope's words: "Nature, and Nature's laws lay hid in night./ God said, *Let Newton be!* and all was light" (Pope, "Epitaph," 336).

17. We note here that there is a long tradition of philosophers delighting in the construction of God proofs, and Newton joins in this tradition.

18. Ironically, the *Principia* inaugurates an Empirical Revolution, but as we will see,

finds it possible to extend and deepen Galileo's cosmology is to offer us his ideas on kinematics, or the mathematics of motion. Kinematics was renamed "the Calculus" in the seventeenth century by Gottfried Leibniz, and the Calculus was recognized to be "the mathematics of motion and change."[19] The Calculus was acknowledged to involve infinite summations over indivisible and infinitesimal quantities.[20] Scholars report that Newton came to kinematics/the Calculus by way of his interest in mechanics—or by way of his interest in exploring the motions of extended physical bodies.[21] We find that, like Archimedes and Galileo, Newton also believed that it would not be possible to understand mechanics without first exploring kinematics. And Newton recognized that Archimedes's kinematics (which Archimedes had developed in his mathematical treatise, *On Spirals*) is embedded within Archimedes's mechanics—and that both Archimedes's kinematics and his mechanics are embedded within Galileo's cosmology. And we find that *On Spirals* is the originary text that is embedded within Newton's cosmology too.

Let us turn now to the decrypting of Newton's cosmology—as Newton presents it to us in his most famous work, his *Philosophiae Naturalis*

Newton considered himself to be a true philosopher in the Platonic sense, and we find that the primary focus of his interests is upon exploring the site of all particles'—or of all bodies'—unchanging and immovable Presence(s)—the site that, like Galileo, he too recognizes to exist as that of the unobservable absolute in the natural world.

19. "History of Calculus," para. 36.

20. And as we will see, and like Archimedes and Galileo, Newton actually considered kinematics (or the Calculus) to involve infinite summations over indivisible/infinitesimal quantities.

21. In the seventeenth century, kinematics/the Calculus was recognized to be "the mathematics of motion and change," and we read that "for Newton, change was a variable quantity over time" ("History of Calculus," para. 36). And we deduce here that, like the ancient Jews, Pythagoras, Archimedes, and Galileo, Newton too considered mathematical reality to exist inextricably from physical reality. (Indeed, in the "Author's Preface" to the *Principia*, Newton suggests that geometry exists as a *subspecies* of mechanics, and he writes, "To describe right lines and circles are problems, but not geometrical problems. The solution of these problems is required from Mechanics. . . . Geometry is founded in mechanical practice, and is nothing but that part of universal Mechanics which accurately proposes and demonstrates the art of measuring." Newton implies here that he considers geometry—and the generation of continuous magnitudes—to emanate from the motions of bodies, and therefore to exist as a *subspecies* of mechanics (Newton, "Author's Preface," *Mathematical Principles*, 1:A1).

Principia Mathematica, or *Principia*, of 1687.[22] Because Newton's *Principia* is fairly extensive, it will be helpful for us to divide our explorations of it into several parts. The parts in which we will divide our explorations of Newton's *Principia* are as follows:

   i. *The Scholium to the Definitions*
  ii. *Measured quantities and the Definitions themselves*
 iii. *The Frame of the System of the World*
  iv. *True motions vs. Apparent motions, or proving the existence of the Divine Logos's Presence in the natural world*

We will follow these four parts with an exploration of Newton's Laws and Corollaries; and we will conclude our discussion with an exploration of how Newton had been a true philosopher in the Platonic sense.

Let us begin now by turning to Newton's Scholium to his Definitions, in which he introduces us to his secret code.

I. THE SCHOLIUM TO THE DEFINITIONS

Following a brief preface, Newton begins his *Principia* with a series of cryptic Definitions—which are followed by an even more cryptic Scholium, or "explanatory notes," to those Definitions. We will find that in order to decrypt the Definitions themselves, it will first be necessary to decrypt the Scholium to the Definitions. And we will also find that in

---

22. The name of Newton's most famous work is four words that are also one word—and we find that, like Newton's four Absolute quantities, which, as we will see, are also one Absolute quantity—the name of Newton's most famous work also alludes to the Name of his God. Names are important to Newton, and for this reason, the name of Newton's most famous work warrants our deeper attention. We read that the Latin word "Principia," which translates into English as "fundamental principles," is the plural form of the Latin word "Principium," which itself means the beginning or origin—or *arche*—the generative "source," "origin," or "originating cause" of all things that exist in the natural world, which also exists as the site of all things in the natural world. (And let us remind ourselves here of Plato's "first principle of the whole," where the English word "principle" is a translation of Plato's Greek "ἀρχήν," or arche.) And as we will see, the monist, materialist focus of Newton's *Philosophiae Naturalis Principia Mathematica*, or *Principia*, is upon (what Newton considers to be) *the fundamental principle*—the arche—the (multiple and yet simultaneously singular) All/the Only—which, like Archimedes and Galileo, Newton too considers to come into being ever-presently and omni-presently, in the coming into being of the site of all particles'—or of all bodies'—unchanging and immovable Presence(s)—in the coming into being of the unchanging and immovable Fulcrum—in the coming into being of his God: the Universe itself.

order to decrypt the Scholium to the Definitions, it will be necessary for us to keep in mind several ideas that we have learned from our explorations of the cosmologies of Archimedes and of Galileo:

> —First, it will be necessary for us to keep in mind that when we observe all particles—or all bodies—in motion, we are observing their changing, instantaneous motions, and not their unchanging and immovable presently uniform rectilinear motions (and from which the particles—or bodies—themselves exist inextricably). We will need to keep in mind that although all particles'—or all bodies'—unchanging and immovable presently uniform rectilinear motions (and from which the particles—or bodies—themselves exist inextricably) are *implicit* to their trajectories, they are not actually directly observable to us in nature—although they are observable to us in our mind's eye, by way of mathematics.[23]

> —And second, we will need to keep in mind that from these "observations," Galileo had deduced that the site of all particles'—or of all bodies'—unchanging and immovable Presence(s) therefore exists as the site of the unobservable absolute in the natural world.

As we will see, with these thoughts in mind, it will be possible for us to decrypt Newton's Scholium to the Definitions.

❧

It is in the Scholium to the Definitions that Newton presents us with (what he calls his) four "Absolute, True, and Mathematical" quantities: Absolute, True, and Mathematical Time, Space, Place, and Motion.[24] And we also find that in reference to these four Absolute, True, and Mathematical quantities (or what we may refer to here simply as Newton's "Absolute" quantities), Newton writes that "in Philosophical disquisitions, we ought

---

23. We will need to keep in mind that all sensible bodies' trajectories exist as the aggregates of their changing, instantaneous motions.

24. We recognize that Newton's phrase "Absolute, True, and Mathematical" is a nod to Plato and to Plato's Trinity of Transcendentals—the Absolutely True, Beautiful, and Good—which Plato considered to come into being Presently, in the coming into being of the arche—the generative "source," "origin," or "originating cause" of all things that exist in the natural world, which also exists as the site of all things in the natural world. And we recognize that Newton's phrase is a hint to his reader that he considers himself to be a true philosopher in the Platonic sense, and that, like Plato, the focus of his interests also lies in exploring the arche's Presence in the natural world.

to abstract from our senses, and consider *things themselves*, distinct from what are only sensible measures of them."²⁵ We recognize that Newton therefore implies here that he considers his four Absolute quantities to exist as sites of the unobservable absolute in the natural world.

And we find that *at the same time* that Newton presents us with these four Absolute quantities, he also contrasts them with (what he calls) four "Relative, Apparent, and Common" quantities: Relative, Apparent, and Common Time, Space, Place, and Motion. As we will see, by Relative, Apparent, and Common (or what we may refer to here simply as "Relative") Time, Space, Place and Motion, Newton means the Time, Space, Place, and Motion that are commonly encountered in empirical analyses. Newton speaks with marked derision of Relative quantities; he asserts that perceptions of Relative Time, Space, Place, and Motion derive from observers' measurements with respect to objects of the senses, and are of interest only to the "common" and "vulgar" people. And in contrast with Absolute Time, Space, Place, and Motion, which he refers to as being the "things themselves," he refers to Relative Time, Space, Place, and Motion as being "only sensible measures" of the unobservable and absolute "true" quantities themselves.²⁶ Newton's Scholium begins:

> Hitherto I have laid down the definitions of such words as are less known, and explained the sense in which I would have them to be understood in the following discourse. I do not define Time, Space, Place, and Motion, as being well known to all. Only I must observe, that the *vulgar* conceive those quantities under no other notions but from the relation they bear to sensible objects. And thence arise certain prejudices, for the removing of which, it will be convenient to distinguish them into Absolute and Relative, True and Apparent, Mathematical and Common.

25. Newton's phrase "things themselves" is also an allusion to Plato, who asserts that true philosophers devote their lives to exploring the arche—the site of "the things themselves, which can only be seen with the eye of the mind"; and we recognize that Newton is once again hinting to us here that he considers himself to be a true philosopher in the Platonic sense. (Newton, "Scholium to the Definitions," *Mathematical Principles*, 1:12; my emphasis.)

26. We, who have decrypted the cosmologies of Archimedes and of Galileo, recognize that Newton is hinting here that only the "common" and "vulgar" people are interested in exploring all particles'—or all bodies'—changing, instantaneous motions, while the "uncommon" people—like himself—are interested in exploring all particles'—or all bodies'—unchanging and immovable presently uniform rectilinear motions (and from which the particles—or bodies—themselves exist inextricably). We recognize that Newton implies here that the "common people" see only with their eyes, rather than with the eye of the mind, and that they are not true philosophers in the Platonic sense.

> I. Absolute, True, and Mathematical Time, of it self, and from its own nature flows equably without relation to any thing external, and by another name is called Duration: Relative, Apparent, and Common Time, is some sensible and external (whether accurate or unequable) measure of Duration by the means of motion, which is *commonly* used instead of True time; such as an Hour, a Day, a Month, a Year.
>
> II. Absolute Space, in its own nature, without regard to any thing external, remains always similar and immoveable. Relative Space is some movable dimension or measure of the absolute spaces; which our senses determine, by its position to bodies; and which is *vulgarly* taken for immoveable space. . . .
>
> III. Place is a part of space which a body takes up, and, is according to the space, either absolute or relative. . . .
>
> IV. Absolute motion, is the translation of a body from one absolute place into another; and Relative motion, the translation from one relative place into another. . . .[27]

Newton asserts here that Absolute Time "flows equably, without relation to any thing external [to itself]" and that Absolute Space "in its own nature, without relation to any thing external [to itself], remains always similar and immoveable." And we recognize that since Newton pronounces here that both quantities flow equably, and exist independently of an observer's perceptions, he therefore asserts that Absolute Time and Space exist in the natural world as (unobservable) sites in which equal times and equal distances absolutely and indisputably exist.

Newton also asserts here that Duration is another name in his cosmology for Absolute Time. And we find that it is deeper in the Scholium to the Definitions that Newton associates the "existence of things" with their Duration, or their Absolute Time. He writes:

> The duration or perseverance of the existence of things remains the same, whether the [sensible] motions are swift or slow, or none at all: and therefore it ought to be distinguish'd from what are only sensible measures thereof.[28]

We recognize that Newton is referring here to the perseverance (or the continuing on) of the existence of things *as* the things themselves here,

---

27. Newton, "Scholium to the Definitions," *Mathematical Principles*, 1:9–10; my emphases.

28. Newton, "Scholium to the Definitions," *Mathematical Principles*, 1:11–12.

since the English word *persevere* stems from the Latin *perseverare*, which means, "continue steadfastly, persist."[29] And therefore, we find that Newton reveals to us here that he considers the perseverance (or the continuing on) of the existence of things *as* the things themselves to be their Duration, or their Absolute Time; and we also recognize that Newton implies here that he considers the perseverance (or the continuing on) of the existence of things *as* the things themselves to be a type of motion.[30]

From here, Newton reveals to us that "things" are another name in his cosmology for Absolute Places. He writes:

> *All things* are *placed* in [Absolute] Time as to order of Succession; and in [Absolute] Space as to order of Situation. It is from their [all things'] essence or nature that they are Places; and that the primary places of things should be moveable, is absurd. These are therefore the absolute places; and translations out of those [immovable Absolute] places, are the only Absolute Motions.[31]

Newton puns here that "all things" are *placed* in Absolute Time and Absolute Space, but we, Newton's uncommon readers, who have decrypted the cosmologies of Archimedes and of Galileo, recognize that "all things"—and therefore all substance/matter itself—exist as the fundamental element(s) of which Absolute Time and Space are composed; and we therefore recognize that Newton refers to these fundamental element(s) in his cosmology as Absolute Place(s). We also recognize that Newton refers to his Absolute Place(s) as "immovable" here because he considers them to be unchanging (with respect to themselves) over the course of their trajectories.[32] And we recognize that Newton considers the perseverance of immovable Absolute Place(s) *as* immovable Absolute Place(s)

---

29. For a Latin version of the *Principia*, see Newton, *Principia mathematica* (Latin ed.). See also the "persevere" entry in the *Online Etymology Dictionary*.

30. As we decrypt the Scholium to the Definitions further, we will find that Newton defines the perseverance (or the continuing on) of the existence of things *as* the things themselves (over the course of their trajectories) to be their Absolute Motions.

31. Newton, "Scholium to the Definitions," *Mathematical Principles*, 1:12; my emphases.

32. Newton implies that he considers Absolute Place(s) to be preexisting/post-existing (with respect to one another) over the course of their trajectories; and we recognize that by the term "immovable," Newton means unchanging with respect to itself (over the course of its trajectory).

(over the course of their trajectories) to be their Absolute Motions, which deliver the Absolute Place(s) to the unchanging and immovable Place(s) that they always already Are, and from which they never depart—to the site(s) of their own unchanging and immovable Presence(s).[33]

We also recognize that these deductions are only possible to us, Newton's uncommon readers, who have first decrypted the cosmologies of Archimedes and of Galileo. In a 1675 letter to the natural philosopher Robert Hooke, Newton wrote, "If I have seen further it is by standing on ye sholders of Giants"[34]—and we find that Newton expects us, his uncommon readers, to recognize that Archimedes and Galileo were the Giants upon whose shoulders he stood. Such is the subtlety of Newton's code.[35]

Newton continues to provide us, his uncommon readers, with cryptic hints regarding his four Absolute quantities. He writes:

> As the order of the parts of [Absolute] Time is immutable, so also is the order of the parts of [Absolute] Space. Suppose those parts to be mov'd out of their [Absolute] places, and they will be moved (if the expression may be allowed) out of themselves.

---

33. Newton implies that he considers his Absolute Space and his Absolute Time to be *generated* in the natural world by way of the Absolute Motions of the Absolute Place(s), and that he considers Absolute Place(s) to exist as the unchanging and immovable (and *material*) element(s) of which Absolute Space and Time are composed. And we recognize that *Newton therefore implies that he considers Absolute Space and Absolute Time to exist as a substantial/material entity in the natural world.*

We also recognize that Newton implies here that he does not consider Absolute Place(s) to exist independently of, or prior to, Absolute Time and Space, but that rather he considers Absolute Place(s) to be *dynamically generated* in the *dynamical generation* of Absolute Time and Space. And finally, we recognize that by Absolute Place(s), Newton is referring to all preexisting/post-existing particles—or all preexisting/post-existing bodies themselves, and which exist inextricably from their perseverance (over the course of their trajectories) with their unchanging and immovable presently uniform rectilinear motions. (And let us remind ourselves here that Newton considered geometry—and the generation of continuous magnitudes—to exist as a *subspecies* of mechanics.)

34. Newton, "Letter to Hooke."

35. We recognize that some readers may not be fully convinced of our argument here; however, we can promise that as we continue to decrypt Newton's secret code, Newton will provide us with further hints which will more strongly point to the accuracy of this reading.

For [Absolute] times and [Absolute] spaces are, as it were, the [Absolute] Places as well of themselves as of all other things.³⁶

And again, we find that Newton expects us, his uncommon readers, to recognize that he considers the perseverance of immovable Absolute Place(s) *as* immovable Absolute Place(s) (over the course of their trajectories) to generate an Absolute Time and an Absolute Space in the natural world in which equal times and equal distances absolutely and indisputably exist, and which is progressively linearly ordered, even as the progressive linear orderedness of this time and space is also always already vanquished, or overcome. Newton expects us, his uncommon readers, to recognize that he considers immovable Absolute Place(s) to exist as the fundamental element(s) of which this Absolute Time and Space are composed, and *he expects us to recognize that he therefore considers Absolute Time and Space to exist as a substantial/material entity in the natural world.*

And finally, deeper in the Scholium, Newton puns:

Now no other [Absolute] *places* are immoveable, but those that, from infinity to infinity, do all retain the same given positions one to another; and upon this account, must ever remain unmov'd; and do thereby constitute, what I call, immoveable [Absolute] space.³⁷

And once again, Newton expects us, his uncommon readers, to recognize that by way of the Absolute Motions of the Absolute Place(s), immovable Absolute Place(s) are delivered to the immovable Absolute Place(s) that they always already Are, and from which they never depart—to the site(s) of their own unchanging and immovable Presence(s). Newton expects us, his uncommon readers, to recognize that he considers the perseverance of immovable Absolute Place(s) *as* immovable Absolute Place(s) (over the course of their trajectories) to generate an Absolute Time and an Absolute Space in the natural world in which equal times and equal distances absolutely and indisputably exist, and which is progressively linearly ordered (with an orderedness that extends to the infinite in both directions), even as the progressive linear orderedness of this time and space (and the infinite itself) are also always

---

36. Newton, "Scholium to the Definitions," *Mathematical Principles*, 1:12.

37. Newton, "Scholium to the Definitions," *Mathematical Principles*, 1:14; my emphases.

already vanquished, or overcome.[38] And Newton expects us, his uncommon readers, to recognize that immovable Absolute Place(s) exist as the fundamental element(s) of which this Absolute Time and Absolute Space are composed, *and that he therefore considers Absolute Time and Space to exist as a substantial/material entity in the natural world.* And finally, Newton expects us, his uncommon readers, to recognize that he considers his four Absolute quantities—his Absolute Time, Space, Place, and Motion—to come into being ever-presently and omni-presently in the natural world, in the coming into being of (and the perseverance of) the site of all particles'—or all bodies'—unchanging and immovable Presence(s)—in the coming into being of (and the perseverance of) the (multiple and yet simultaneously singular) All/the Only—in the coming into being of (and the perseverance of) his God: the Universe itself.[39]

☙

Let us note here that Newton also does nothing to dissuade his "common" reader from assuming that he considers Absolute Time and Space to exist independently of (and indeed as an abstract backdrop to) the motions of all sensible bodies in the natural world.[40]

38. Newton expects us to recognize that it is possible to consider any of the fundamental elements of which Absolute Places' trajectories are composed—the Absolute Place(s) themselves—to exist as their trajectories' origins; and he therefore expects us to recognize that Absolute Time and Space are progressively linearly ordered with an orderedness that extends to the infinite in both directions—even as the infinite is also always already vanquished, or overcome. (Newton expects us to recognize that we may choose any particular Absolute Place to be its trajectory's origin, and he expects us to recognize that the line segments on both sides of this origin exist as infinite (and yet simultaneously singular) collection(s) of their fundamental element(s)—the Absolute Place(s) themselves.) These ideas once again remind us of Pythagoras's Tetrad.

39. Newton expects us to recognize that a more mathematically nuanced version of Pythagoras's Tetrad lies at the heart of his cosmology. (And we remind ourselves here that Pythagoras was of deep import to Newton.)

40. We find that for this reason, contemporary scholars consider Newton to have authored the concept of "inertial frames of reference" in his *Principia*. (For example, in Huggett and Hoefer's "Absolute and Relational Theories of Space and Motion" entry in the *Stanford Encyclopedia of Philosophy*, we read that "the concept of the set of inertial frames was first clearly expressed [in the nineteenth century], though it was implicit in both remarks and procedures to be found in the *Principia*.") However, we recognize that insofar as inertial frames of reference exist as *abstract backdrops to bodies' motions, which exist independently of bodies themselves*, Newton did *not* in fact author the concept of inertial frames of reference in his *Principia*. (As we will see, contemporary scholars do not recognize that the monist, materialist focus of Newton's cosmology was upon the site of his four Absolute quantities, which he considered to come into being

CHAPTER VI. ISAAC NEWTON 175

And we find that in this respect, Newton is not unlike Archimedes, who also did nothing to dissuade his own reader from assuming that he had considered the fundamental element of which the spiral is composed to be a point (and not a point/infinitesimal line segment); and who also did nothing to dissuade his own reader from assuming that he had considered the particle equivalent of an extended physical body—the extended body's balancing point—its *kentron toi bareos*—its sharp *point*, center, or pivot of weight—to be a *point*, and not a point/infinitesimal line segment.[41]

And similarly, we find that in this respect, Newton is also not unlike Galileo, who also did nothing to dissuade his own reader from assuming that he did not consider the Present to be the proper time to explore the site of all particles'—or of all bodies'—unchanging and immovable Presence(s)—which, as we know, was the monist, materialist focus of Galileo's entire cosmology.[42]

We find that like the works of Archimedes and of Galileo, which were written in a facetious, humorous tone, Newton's *Principia* too was written in a facetious, humorous tone—for like Archimedes and Galileo, Newton too recognized that we are always already found (Eureka! Eureka!); Newton too recognized that we all always already exist as manifestation(s) of the site of all particles'—or of all bodies'—unchanging and immovable Presence(s) in the natural world, and that we all always already exist as manifestation(s) of the site at which Divinity and ever-burgeoning life are realized in the natural world; he too recognized that we are always

---

ever-presently and omni-presently in the natural world—in the coming into being of the site of all particles'—or of all bodies'—unchanging and immovable Presence(s)—in the coming into being of the (multiple and yet simultaneously singular) All/the Only—in the coming into being of his God: the Universe itself; and contemporary scholars do not recognize that Newton considered the coming into being of his four Absolute quantities to bring into being (what he referred to as) the "Frame of the System of the World"—the (multiple and yet simultaneously singular) unchanging and immovable (and *material*) referent(s) by which he considered it to be possible to rigorously define all motion and change.)

41. We find that in this respect, Newton is not unlike Archimedes, who had facetiously cried, "Give me a[n unchanging and immovable] *place* to stand on, and I will move the earth"! (my emphasis)—even as he had already found such a place (Eureka! Eureka!)—the site of all particles'—or of all bodies'—unchanging and immovable Presence(s)—the (multiple and yet simultaneously singular) All/the Only—the divine origin(s) of reality—his God: the Universe itself.

42. We find that in this respect, Newton is not unlike Galileo, who also did nothing to dissuade the Church from assuming that he had considered ours to be a heliocentric cosmology rather than a Divinity-centric cosmology.

already immortal; that we are always already One; and that Paradise is always already Now.[43]

Let us continue to decrypt Newton's secret code.

II. MEASURED QUANTITIES AND THE DEFINITIONS THEMSELVES

From our reading of the Scholium to the Definitions, we have deduced that Newton authored his four *"Absolute quantities"*—his Absolute Time, Space, Place, and Motion—so that he could refer to all particles'—or all bodies'—unchanging and immovable presently uniform rectilinear motions (and from which the particles—or bodies—themselves exist inextricably) in a secret, coded way; and we have deduced that he authored his four *"Relative quantities"*—his Relative Time, Space, Place, and Motion—so that he could refer to all particles'—or all bodies'—changing, instantaneous motions in a secret, coded way. We have deduced that Newton's four Absolute quantities refer to all particles'—or all bodies'—(unobservable) unchanging and immovable present aspects; and we have deduced that Newton's four Relative quantities refer to all particles'—or all bodies'—(observable) changing, instantaneous aspects. And we have deduced that while Newton considered the uncommon people to be interested in exploring all particles'—or all bodies'—(unobservable) unchanging and immovable present aspects, he considered the "common" and "vulgar" people to be interested in exploring all particles'—or all bodies'—(observable) changing, instantaneous aspects. But why is this important for us to note here?

We find that buried deep within the Scholium to the Definitions, and in the context of discussing the difference between Absolute Time, Space, Place, and Motion and Relative Time, Space, Place, and Motion, Newton explains further what he means by his term *"quantities"*—and we find that this explanation allows us to decrypt the Definitions themselves. Newton distinguishes here between "relative quantities" (which, and as we know, he does not consider to be "true quantities," but "only sensible measures of them") and what he refers to here as *"measured quantities"*—which he asserts are the unobservable, absolute, and purely mathematical

---

43. As examples of the humorous and facetious tone that we have already encountered in Newton's cosmology, we may offer to our reader Newton's pun: "All things are *placed* in Time," and also Newton's assertion that "*Now* no other places are immovable." Other examples of Newton's facetious humor will follow in these pages.

"real quantities themselves." We find that the term "measured quantities" is therefore another name in Newton's cosmology for his Absolute, True, and Mathematical quantities,[44] and that Newton writes:

> Wherefore relative quantities, are not the quantities themselves, whose names they bear, but those sensible measures of them (either accurate or inaccurate) which are commonly used instead of the measur'd quantities themelves. And if the meaning of words is to be determin'd by their use; then by the names Time, Space, Place and Motion, their measures are properly to be understood; and the expression will be unusual [meaning uncommon], and purely Mathematical, if the measured quantities themselves are meant.[45]

We therefore deduce that by "measured quantities," Newton means Absolute, True, and Mathematical quantities. And as we turn now to Newton's "Definitions" themselves, we find that Newton defines both bodies and their momenta as being "measured" quantities in his *Principia*—and we therefore deduce that by bodies and their momenta in his *Principia*, Newton means their (unobservable) unchanging and immovable present aspects, and not their (observable) changing, instantaneous aspects. Strikingly, we recognize here that *Newton defines bodies and their momenta in his* Principia *as being sites of the unobservable absolute in the natural world—and we recognize that the* Principia *is not actually the empirical manifesto that it has been hailed to be over the centuries.*

Turning now to Definition I, we read:

> The Quantity of Matter is the *measure* of the same, arising from its density and bulk conjunctly.[46]

—and Newton continues, "It is this quantity that I mean hereafter every where [in the *Principia*] under the name of Body or Mass." Newton reveals to us here that he considers mass to be another name in his cosmology for body, and that by body or mass in his *Principia*, he means the body's—or mass's—(unobservable) unchanging and immovable present aspect. And therefore, we deduce that by body—or mass—in his cosmology, Newton means the preexisting/post-existing body—or the

---

44. The term "measured quantities" is the name of a name, and we find that authoring names of other names in his *Principia* is another way in which Newton constructs a cosmology that exists like a Russian doll.

45. Newton, "Scholium to the Definitions," *Mathematical Principles*, 1:16–17.

46. Newton, "Definitions," *Mathematical Principles*, 1:1; my emphasis.

preexisting/post-existing mass—and which exists inextricably from its perseverance (over the course of its trajectory) with an unchanging and immovable presently uniform rectilinear motion, and which exists as a manifestation of the site of all bodies'—or of all masses'—unchanging and immovable Presence(s) in the natural world.

(Let us note here that Newton also expects us, his uncommon readers, who have decrypted the cosmologies of Archimedes and of Galileo, to recognize that by the term "body" in his *Principia*, he means an extended physical body's balancing point—its center of gravity—and the particle equivalent of the extended physical body itself. Newton therefore expects us to recognize here that by the terms particle, body, or mass in his cosmology, he means the preexisting/post-existing particle—or the preexisting/post-existing body—or the preexisting/post-existing mass— and which exists inextricably from its perseverance (over the course of its trajectory) with an unchanging and immovable presently uniform rectilinear motion, and which exists as a manifestation of the site of all particles'—or of all bodies'—or of all masses'—unchanging and immovable Presence(s) in the natural world. And we find that although Newton expects us to recognize that he considers the terms particle, body, and mass to exist exactly equivalently to one another, he mostly refers to bodies in his *Principia*. For this reason, in our reading of the *Principia*, we will do the same.)

Definition II reads:

> The Quantity of Motion is the *measure* of the same, arising from the velocity and quantity of matter conjunctly.[47]

And we recognize here that Newton refers to a body's momentum as also being a "measured" quantity—and that by the term "Quantity of Motion," Newton is therefore referring to a body's (unobservable) unchanging and immovable present momentum—and from which we recognize that Newton considers the body itself to exist inextricably.[48]

---

47. Newton, "Definitions," *Mathematical Principles*, 1:2; my emphasis.

48. We recognize that Newton considers all bodies to exist inextricably from their perseverance (over the course of their trajectories) with unchanging and immovable *non-zero speed* presently uniform rectilinear motions. And we also recognize that Newton considers all bodies' unchanging and immovable present momenta to exist as sites of the unobservable absolute in the natural world.

And we ask ourselves here: why does Newton choose to define these quantities—the Quantity of Matter and the Quantity of Motion—separately, since we recognize that, like Archimedes and Galileo, Newton too considers bodies to exist inextricably from their perseverance (over the course of their trajectories) with their unchanging and immovable presently uniform rectilinear motions? We find that Newton chooses to define these quantities separately so that he may apply *number values* to each quantity individually. For example, Newton recognizes that although all bodies exist as (multiple and yet simultaneously singular) manifestation(s) of (what he refers to as) the Quantity of Matter, they also vary in the *amounts* of matter that they individually manifest. Similarly, Newton recognizes that although all bodies exist as (multiple and yet simultaneously singular) manifestation(s) of (what he refers to as) the Quantity of Motion, they also vary in the *amounts* of velocity and of matter that they individually manifest.[49]

As we know, Newton assumes a fluency on our part with the cosmologies of Archimedes and of Galileo; he assumes that we have seen all that he has seen about their cosmologies. And going forward, we find that Newton devotes much of his *Principia* to deeply encrypting their wisdom. We find that in Definitions III, IV, and V, Newton shows us, his uncommon readers, that, like Archimedes and Galileo, he too recognizes that *under gravity*, all particles'—or all bodies'—unchanging and immovable Presence(s) are responsible for bringing motion and passing time into being in the natural world, even as, *at the same time*, all particles'—or all bodies'—unchanging and immovable Presence(s) exist as the (multiple and yet simultaneously singular) site(s) at which motion and passing time—and gravity itself—are always already vanquished, or overcome, in the natural world.

In Definition III, Newton proposes the existence in the natural world of what he calls a "Vis Insita"—or an "Innate Force of Matter"—which he claims is innate to every body, and which, when exercised, is

---

49. We recognize that Quantity of Motion is a term by which Newton refers to the magnitude of all bodies' unchanging and immovable Presence(s).

responsible for every body's endeavoring "to persevere" (or continue on) in what Newton calls "its *present state*, whether it be of rest, or of moving uniformly forwards in a right line" (my emphasis). We find that it is here, in Definition III, that Newton subtly and cunningly confirms for us that, like Archimedes and Galileo, he too considers every body's "*present state*" to be—and to have been—that of manifesting an unchanging (with respect to itself, and therefore immovable) uniformly rectilinear state of motion—a state of motion from which, like Archimedes and Galileo, we recognize that Newton too considers every body itself to exist inextricably.

Definition III reads:

> The Vis Insita, or Innate Force of Matter, is a power of resisting, by which every body, as much as in it lies, endeavours to persevere in its *present state*, whether it be of rest, or of moving uniformly forward in a right line.[50]

And Newton goes on to say that "a body exerts this force [the Vis Insita, or Innate Force of Matter] only, when another force impress'd upon it [the body], endeavours to change its condition."

As we will see, the one and only "impressed force" in Newton's cosmology that acts continuously (at all times) upon every body in the natural world in an endeavor "to change its condition" (or to change its unchanging and immovable presently uniform rectilinear state of motion—a state of motion from which we know that Newton considers every body itself to exist inextricably) is gravity. We find that gravity therefore exists in Newton's cosmology as the one impressed force that is responsible for the continuous exercising (or the exercising at all times) of every body's Vis Insita—and by way of the exercising of which, every body endeavors "to persevere" (or continue on) in its unchanging and immovable presently uniform rectilinear state of motion (a state of motion from which we know that Newton considers every body itself to exist inextricably)—even as, *at the same time*, gravity exists as the one impressed force in Newton's cosmology that continuously (at all times) endeavors to *change* every body's condition (or to change every body's unchanging and immovable presently uniform rectilinear state of motion—a state of

---

50. Newton, "Definitions," *Mathematical Principles*, 1:2; my emphasis. Let us note here that Newton, who has decrypted the cosmologies of Archimedes and of Galileo, recognizes that the state of absolute rest does not exist in the natural world. And we recognize that Newton is therefore referring here to a state of relative rest, and not of absolute rest.

motion from which we know that Newton considers every body itself to exist inextricably). The existence of the gravity/Vis Insita interaction in Newton's cosmology therefore confirms for us that like Archimedes and Galileo, Newton too considers a recursive self-similarity to be implicit to the generation of all bodies' trajectories in the natural world, and which allows all bodies to *at the same time* possess both an unchanging and immovable present aspect and a changing, instantaneous aspect; and the existence of the gravity/Vis Insita interaction in Newton's cosmology also confirms for us the accuracy of our reading of the Scholium to the Definitions.

We find that Definition III therefore exists as the site in Newton's *Principia* in which he subtly (and extremely cunningly) asserts that (under the continuous exercising of every body's Vis Insita) every body's *present state* is—and was—that of manifesting an unchanging (with respect to itself, and therefore immovable) uniformly rectilinear motion (a state of motion from which we know that Newton considers every body itself to exist inextricably); and it is in Definition III that Newton reveals to us that Archimedes's *On Spirals* is the originary text that is embedded within his cosmology, as it is the originary text that is embedded within the cosmology of Galileo (and as it is the originary text that is embedded within the cosmology of Archimedes). We find that it is also in Definition III that Newton subtly and cunningly reveals to us that he considers the continuous exercising of every body's Vis Insita (under the continuously impressed force of gravity) to be responsible for bringing into being in the natural world the site of all particles'—or of all bodies'—unchanging and immovable Presence(s)—which, as we will see, Newton refers to in his *Principia* as the Frame of the System of the World.[51]

Before we turn to exploring the Frame of the System of the World, however, it will be necessary for us to first acknowledge where it is in the Definitions that Newton reveals to us that he considers gravity to be an "impressed force." We find that Newton defines gravity as being an impressed force in Definitions IV and V. In Definition IV, Newton

---

51. We recognize that Newton considers the existence of the gravity/Vis Insita interaction to be responsible for bringing into being his four Absolute quantities—the (multiple and yet simultaneously singular) All/the Only—his God: the Universe itself—which exists as the monist, materialist focus of his cosmology.

defines the impressed force, and he asserts that a centripetal force—or a "center-seeking" force—is one type of impressed force. In Definition V, Newton defines the centripetal force, and he declares that gravity is a type of centripetal force.

Definition IV reads:

> An impress'd force is an action exerted upon a body, in order to change its [present] state, either of rest, or of moving uniformly forward in a right line.[52]

And Newton asserts that "Impress'd forces are of different origines; as from percussion, from pressure, from centripetal force."[53]

In Definition V, Newton defines the centripetal force. He writes: "A Centripetal force is that by which bodies are drawn or impelled, or any way *tend*, towards a *point* as to a *centre*," and he continues, "Of this sort is gravity."[54] We recognize that the *center* of which Newton speaks here, and towards which he considers all bodies impressed upon by the centripetal force of gravity to "tend," is a system of bodies' *common center* (of gravity); it is a system of bodies' *kentron toi bareos*—its sharp *point*, *center*, or pivot of weight. (And we recognize here that Newton's word "tend" exists as a quiet homage to Galileo, and that Newton's word "point" exists as a quiet homage to Archimedes.)[55]

We ask ourselves two questions here: why does Newton author a Vis Insita, an Innate Force of Matter (since we recognize that such a force was not present within the cosmologies of Archimedes and of Galileo); and does such a force actually exist in the natural world? We recognize that Newton authors a Vis Insita for two different reasons: first, for a practical reason (so that he may apply a *number value* to a body's tendency to persevere (over the course of its trajectory) *as* itself), and second, for a

---

52. Newton, "Definitions," *Mathematical Principles*, 1:3.

53. Newton, "Definitions," *Mathematical Principles*, 1:3.

54. Newton, "Definitions," *Mathematical Principles*, 1:14; my emphases.

55. And let us also note here that although the impressed forces of percussion and of pressure act upon bodies that are immersed in an atmosphere, the centripetal force of gravity is the one impressed force in Newton's cosmology that does not require the existence of an atmosphere in order to act; it acts upon bodies in a vacuum. And we therefore deduce that gravity exists as the one impressed force in Newton's cosmology that acts upon all bodies at all times.

CHAPTER VI. ISAAC NEWTON   183

poetical reason (so that he may think of bodies not as being static entities, but rather as being *dynamic entities*, which come into being presently, and which are imbued with the principle of life). Let us turn now to exploring the first reason.

Newton asserts that another name in his cosmology for the Vis Insita is the *Vis inertiæ*, or the Inertial Force of Matter (as he writes that the "Vis insita may, by a most significant name, be called Vis inertiæ"),[56] and he suggests that the Inertial Force of Matter is "a power of resisting" the impressed force of gravity, which possesses a magnitude that is "ever proportional to the body whose force it is."[57] Newton therefore implies here that he considers a body's power of resisting the impressed force of gravity—its Inertial Force of Matter—to be proportional to the body's own Quantity of Motion—or proportional to the body's own unchanging and immovable present momentum—and we recognize that by authoring a Vis inertiæ, Newton is therefore able to apply a *number value* to (what he considers to be) this "power" of resisting.[58]

And we also recognize that Newton authors the Vis Insita for a more poetical reason; we recognize that Newton authors a Vis Insita—which, we find, may also be alternately translated from the Latin as the "Implanted Force of Matter"[59]—so that he may attribute the coming into being of all bodies in the natural world (and which exist inextricably from their perseverance (over the course of their trajectories) with their unchanging and immovable presently uniform rectilinear motions)—the coming into being of the site of all particles'—or of all bodies'—unchanging and immovable Presence(s) in the natural world—the coming into being of (what Newton considers to be) Divinity's Presence in the natural world—to a Force, and so that he may consider this Force to exist as the generative "source," "origin," or "originating cause" of all things that exist

---

56. Newton, "Definitions," *Mathematical Principles*, 1:3. We find that the term Vis inertiæ is also the name of a name in Newton's cosmology.

57. Newton, "Definitions," *Mathematical Principles*, 1:2.

58. Authoring a Vis inertiæ allows Newton to apply a number value to the magnitude of all particles'—or of all bodies'—unchanging and immovable Presence(s), and we recognize that it is an alternate name in his cosmology for the Quantity of Motion.

59. In Cohen's "Guide to Newton's *Principia*," 99, he reports that Newton's phrase "Vis Insita" may also be translated from the Latin as "Implanted Force" of Matter. And we recognize that the Implanted Force of Matter is another name of a name in Newton's cosmology.

in the natural world, even as he also considers this Force to exist *as* the natural world itself.⁶⁰

And finally, we ask ourselves: does the Vis Insita (or the Vis inertiæ, or the Implanted Force of Matter) actually *exist* in the natural world? And our answer to this question is: no, it does not. Unlike the other (impressed) forces in Newton's cosmology, which are responsible for producing bodies' changing, instantaneous motions (and by way of the existence of which, we are able to discern the passage of time in the natural world), the Vis Insita is responsible for producing bodies' unchanging and immovable present motions (and from which the bodies themselves exist inextricably)—and the site(s) at which passing time is always already vanquished, or overcome, in the natural world. We consider the Vis Insita to be a poetical construction which Newton authored in his *Principia* so that he could speak of (he whom Newton considered to be both) the *Author* of the All and the *manifestation* of the All without referring to him directly by Name.⁶¹ (And we remind ourselves here that Newton considered it to be a sin to use God's name openly; see Line 1 of his Fitzwilliam Notebook.)⁶²

---

60. As has been mentioned, Newton considered his own natural philosophy to be most consistent with the natural philosophy of Thales, and as we know, Thales had been responsible for introducing the concept of the arche—the generative "source," "origin," or "originating cause" of all things that exist in the natural world, which also exists as the site of all things in the natural world—into the Greek philosophical discourse. As we know, Thales had associated the arche's Presence in the natural world with Divinity and with the principle of life, and we recognize that Newton authored the Vis Insita in his cosmology so that he might refer to the arche in a secret, coded way. (We also recognize that the Greek word "arche" (like the Greek word "physis") is a *verbal noun*, and that it is therefore implicitly dynamic. (See the "ἀρχή" entry in Wiktionary.))

61. We deduce that Newton authored the Vis Insita, the Implanted Force of Matter, so that he could speak of (he whom Newton considered to be both) the Gardener and the Garden without referring to him directly by Name. (See John 15:1, in which Jesus declares: "I am the true vine, and my Father is the husbandman.")

62. Let us note here that Definitions III, IV, and V are followed by Definitions VI, VII, and VIII—and all of which relate to different aspects of the centripetal force. We will not spend any time discussing these definitions here, as we recognize that Newton once again separates quantities so that he may apply *number values* to them. However, it will be important for us to note that Newton defines these different aspects of the centripetal force to be *measured quantities*, and that he therefore implies that he considers these different aspects of the centripetal force to be Absolute, True, and Mathematical quantities, which exist as site(s) of the unobservable absolute in the natural world. And we wonder: why does Newton consider different aspects of the centripetal force—which, as we know, is responsible for producing bodies' changing, instantaneous motions—(and which is therefore responsible for producing Relative, Apparent, and Common quantities)—to be *measured* quantities, which, as we know,

Let us conclude this section with an acknowledgement of how Newton reveals to us that, like Archimedes and Galileo, he too considers the site of all particles'—or all bodies'—unchanging and immovable Presence(s) in the natural world to exist as the *cause* of all bodies' naturally accelerated motions under gravity, even as, *at the same time*, he considers the site of all particles'—or all bodies'—unchanging and immovable Presence(s) to exist as the (multiple and yet simultaneously singular) site(s) at which gravity is always already vanquished, or overcome, in the natural world.

As we know, Galileo had facetiously speculated about the cause of all bodies' naturally accelerated motions under gravity in his own cosmology—even as he had considered the cause of all bodies' naturally accelerated motions under gravity to be the site of all bodies' unchanging and immovable Presence(s)—the Divine Logos himself. (And let us remind ourselves here that in *Dialogues Concerning Two New Sciences*, Galileo/Salviati wrote, "*The present* does not seem to be the proper time to investigate the *cause* of the acceleration of natural motion concerning which various opinions have been expressed by various philosophers."[63]) We find that Newton subtly pays homage to Galileo in his own writings by also facetiously speculating about the cause of all bodies' naturally accelerated motions under gravity—even as Newton reveals to us that he too considers the cause of all bodies' naturally accelerated motions under gravity to be the site of all bodies' unchanging and immovable Presence(s)—(and he whom Newton too considers to be) the Divine Logos himself. In a letter to Richard Bentley, theologian and Master of Trinity College, Cambridge, Newton writes:

> Gravity must be *caused* by an *agent* {acting} consta{ntl}y according to *certain laws*; but whether this agent be *material* or immaterial is a question I have left to the consideration of my readers.[64]

---

come into being presently? We find that Newton considers these different aspects of the centripetal force to be measured quantities because although the centripetal force is responsible for *producing* all bodies' changing, instantaneous motions, it acts upon bodies *at the same time* that the bodies themselves come into being—which, as we know, is presently.

63. Galilei, *Two New Sciences*, 166–67; my emphases.
64. Newton, "Original Letter"; my emphases.

We recognize that the *agent* to whom Newton is referring here is (he whom Newton considers to be) the *Author* of the All and the *manifestation* of the All; it is (he whom Newton considers to be) *The One Certain Law*—the Divine Logos himself.[65]

Let us turn now to the third part of our discussion, the Frame of the System of the World.

III. THE FRAME OF THE SYSTEM OF THE WORLD

As has been mentioned, Newton considers the continuous exercising of every body's Vis Insita (under the continuously impressed force of gravity) to be responsible for bringing into being in the natural world the site of all particles'—or of all bodies'—unchanging and immovable Presence(s); and as has been mentioned, (and like Archimedes and Galileo), Newton considers the site of all particles'—or of all bodies'—unchanging and immovable Presence(s) to exist as the (multiple and yet simultaneously singular) unchanging and immovable referent(s) by which Newton too considers it to be possible to rigorously define all motion and change in the natural world. We find that Newton refers to this referent in book III

---

65. The sentence cited above is excerpted from a larger, highly facetious passage, which reads: "Tis inconceivable that inanimate brute matter should (without the mediation of something else which is not material) operate upon & affect other matter without mutual contact; as it must if gravitation in the sense of Epicurus be essential & inherent in it. And this is one reason why I desired you would not ascribe {innate} gravity to me. That gravity should be innate inherent and {essential} to matter so that one body may act upon another at a distance through a vacuum without the mediation of any thing else by & through which their action or force {may} be conveyed from one to another is to me so great an absurdity that I believe no man who has in philosophical matters any competent faculty of thinking can ever fall into it. Gravity must be caused by an agent {acting} consta{ntl}y according to certain laws, but whether this agent be material or immaterial is a question I have left to the consideration of my readers." We recognize Newton's wildly facetious tone here, as he refers to matter as being both "inanimate" and "brute" (and where brute means "characterized by an absence of reasoning or intelligence")—when we know that Newton considers matter both to be animate (to exist as the manifestation(s) of ever-burgeoning life) *and* to exist as the manifestation(s) of the Divine reasoning/logical principle—the Logos—itself. And we recognize that, like Galileo, Newton too considers All matter to always already be One, and to always already exist as the realization(s) of absolute simultaneity in the natural world.

of his *Principia* as "the Frame of the System of the World,"⁶⁶ and that he devotes book III of his *Principia* to exploring it.⁶⁷

⊷

It is here, in book III of the *Principia*, that Newton famously authors his Law of Universal Gravitation, in which he asserts that the strength of the gravitational force between two bodies is proportional to the two bodies' quantities of matter and is inversely proportional to the distances between the bodies' centers of gravity squared. Newton proposes:

> That there is a power [or force] of gravity *tending* to all bodies, proportional to the several quantities of matter which they contain.⁶⁸

—and he continues by proposing that this power (or force) of gravity is inversely proportional to the distances between the bodies' centers of gravity squared.

Newton then "demonstrates" this idea to his uncommon reader by applying it to various systems—to the system of Jupiter and its moons, to the system of Saturn and its moons, to the system of the Sun and its planets (to our solar system), and to the system of the Earth and its Moon.⁶⁹

Newton begins by exploring the system of Jupiter and its moons (which he refers to as Jupiter's "Planets"), and he proposes:

---

66. See the introduction to book III of Newton's *Principia*. (Newton, *Mathematical Principles*, 2:201.)

67. Book III of Newton's *Principia* is subtitled *De mundi systemate*, or "Of the System of the World" (Newton, *Mathematical Principles*, 2:200).

68. Newton, "Proposition VII, Theorem VII," *Mathematical Principles*, 2:225; my emphasis.

69. In the introduction to book III, Newton asserts that his intent in composing this book is to "*now demonstrate* the [F]rame of the System of the World" (my emphasis). And we are reminded here of Archimedes's giddy letter to Dositheus, in which he writes that "of most of the theorems which I sent to Conon, and of which you ask me *from time to time* to send you the proofs, *the demonstrations are already before you* in the books brought to you by Heracleides; and some more are also contained in that which I *now* send you" (my emphases). We recognize that, like Archimedes, Newton too is writing in a facetious tone here, for, as we will see, he considers all of us to always already exist as the (multiple and yet simultaneously singular) *demonstration(s)* of the Frame of the System of the World; he considers all of us to always already exist as the (multiple and yet simultaneously singular) manifestation(s) of the site of Divinity's Presence in the natural world.

> That the forces by which the circumjovial Planets [or the moons surrounding Jupiter] are continually drawn off from rectilinear motions, and retain'd in their proper orbits, tend to Jupiter's *centre*; and are reciprocally as the squares of the distances of *the places of those Planets* from that *centre*.[70]

We find that Newton expects his uncommon reader to recognize here that by his phrase "the places of those Planets [or moons]," he means the Absolute Place(s) of those Planets (or moons);[71] he means the particle equivalents of those Planets (or moons), and which exist inextricably from their perseverance (over the course of their trajectories) with their unchanging and immovable presently uniform rectilinear motions; he means the site of the Planets' (or moons') unchanging and immovable Presence(s).

And similarly, Newton expects his uncommon reader to recognize here that by his reference to Jupiter's *centre*, he means Jupiter's center of gravity; he means the particle equivalent of Jupiter (and which exists inextricably from its perseverance (over the course of its trajectory) with its unchanging and immovable presently uniform rectilinear motion); he means the site of Jupiter's own unchanging and immovable Presence.

And we find that Newton also expects his uncommon reader to recognize here that in his Definitions, he defined gravity as being a centripetal, or center-seeking, force (and let us remind ourselves here that Newton wrote, "A Centripetal force is that by which bodies are drawn or impelled, or any way tend, towards a point as to a centre," and that he had continued, "Of this sort is gravity"). Newton expects his uncommon reader to recognize here that he considers the system of Jupiter and its Planets (or moons) to possess a common center (of gravity), which exists as the "centre" towards which Jupiter and its Planets (or moons) ceaselessly *tend*. And Newton also expects his uncommon reader to recognize here that he considers this common center (of gravity) to exist as the particle equivalent of the system of Jupiter and its Planets (or moons) itself—which, being a *particle*, itself exists inextricably from its

---

70. Newton, "Proposition I, Theorem I," *Mathematical Principles*, 2:213; my emphases.

71. And we remind ourselves here that in the Scholium to the Definitions, Newton wrote, "And if the meaning of words is to be determin'd by their use; then by the names Time, Space, Place and Motion, their measures [and therefore their Absolute, True, and Mathematical quantities] are properly to be understood." We therefore recognize that by Newton's phrase "the places of those Planets," he means the Absolute Place(s) of those Planets (or moons).

perseverance (over the course of its trajectory) with an unchanging and immovable presently uniform rectilinear motion; and which therefore exists as a manifestation of the site of all particles'—or of all bodies'—unchanging and immovable Presence(s) in the natural world.

(And we find that Newton also expects his uncommon reader to recognize here that, (like Archimedes and Galileo), he too considers the site of all particles'—or of all bodies'—unchanging and immovable Presence(s) in the natural world to exist as the unchanging and immovable *place(s)* (as in Archimedes's famous cry, "Give me a[n unchanging and immovable] *place* to stand on, and I will move the earth"! [my emphasis]) by which it is possible to rigorously define all motion and change. Newton expects his uncommon reader to recognize here that, (like Archimedes and Galileo), he too considers the site of all particles'—or of all bodies'—unchanging and immovable Presence(s) to exist as the site(s) at which Divinity and ever-burgeoning life are realized in the natural world; and Newton expects his uncommon reader to recognize here that he too considers the site of all particles'—or of all bodies'—unchanging and immovable Presence(s) to exist as the (multiple and yet simultaneously singular) divine origin(s) of reality. Newton expects his uncommon reader to recognize here that, (like Galileo), he too considers the site of all particles'—or of all bodies'—unchanging and immovable Presence(s) to exist as the (multiple and yet simultaneously singular) manifestation(s) of (unobservable) *absolute simultaneity* in the natural world—which come into being presently, and which exist as the site(s) at which passing time is always already vanquished, or overcome, in the natural world.)

And therefore, (and returning here to the system of Jupiter and its Planets (or moons)), Newton expects his uncommon reader to recognize here that he considers the particle equivalents of Jupiter and its Planets (or moons)—or the site(s) of Jupiter's and its Planets' (or moons') own unchanging and immovable Presence(s)—to "tend" ceaselessly (over the course of their trajectories) towards their system's common center (of gravity)—towards the particle equivalent of their system itself; towards the site of their system's own unchanging and immovable Presence. Newton expects his uncommon reader to recognize here that he considers the particle equivalents of Jupiter and of its Planets (or moons) to tend ceaselessly (over the course of their trajectories) towards an unchanging and immovable *place* that itself exists indistinguishably from the unchanging and immovable *place(s)* that the particle equivalents of Jupiter and of its

Planets (or moons) always already Are.[72] Newton expects his uncommon reader to recognize here that he considers the particle equivalents of Jupiter and its Planets (or moons) to tend ceaselessly (over the course of their trajectories) towards a manifestation of absolute simultaneity in the natural world—even as he expects his uncommon reader to recognize that he considers the particle equivalents of Jupiter and its Planets (or moons) to always already exist as (multiple and yet simultaneously singular) manifestation(s) of absolute simultaneity in the natural world. *Newton expects his uncommon reader to recognize here that he considers the particle equivalents of Jupiter and its Planets (or moons) to tend ceaselessly (over the course of their trajectories) towards a manifestation of Divinity's unchanging and immovable Presence in the natural world—even as he considers the particle equivalents of Jupiter and its Planets (or moons) to always already exist as manifestation(s) of Divinity's unchanging and immovable Presence in the natural world.* Newton expects his uncommon reader to recognize here that he considers the particle equivalents of Jupiter and its Planets (or moons) to tend ceaselessly (over the course of their trajectories) towards a manifestation of God's Presently spoken (and written) Name/Word—towards a manifestation of his ecstatic, bursting, and resoundingly affirmative, "I AM"—even as he considers the particle equivalents of Jupiter and its Planets (or moons) to always already exist as manifestation(s) of God's Presently spoken (and written) Name/Word. *And therefore, Newton expects his uncommon reader to recognize here that (like Galileo), he too considers ours to neither be a heliocentric cosmology nor a geocentric cosmology but a Divinity-centric cosmology.* Newton expects his uncommon reader to recognize here that he considers the particle equivalents of Jupiter and its Planets (or moons) to tend ceaselessly (over the course of their trajectories) towards a manifestation of the unchanging and immovable *place(s)* that they always already Are; and he expects his uncommon reader to recognize here that he considers them to generate rotating flower patterns as they go.

---

72. Newton expects his uncommon reader to recognize here that he considers the particle equivalents of Jupiter and its Planets (or moons) to tend ceaselessly *over passing time*; he expects his uncommon reader to recognize here that he considers the particle equivalents of Jupiter and its Planets (or moons) to *generate* passing time as they tend ceaselessly (over the course of their trajectories) towards their system's common center of gravity—even as, *at the same time*, they—and their system's common center (of gravity)—always already exist as the site(s) at which passing time is vanquished, or overcome, in the natural world.

And Newton also expects his uncommon reader to recognize here that he considers the *system* of Jupiter and its Planets (or moons) to be embedded within the *greater system* of our solar system, which itself is embedded within the *even greater system* of our galaxy, and so on, and so forth, ad infinitum—(and that he considers rotating flower patterns to be embedded within greater rotating flower patterns which are embedded within even greater rotating flower patterns, and so on, and so forth, ad infinitum)—even as he expects his uncommon reader to recognize here that he also considers there to be only One Chief World System—only One Frame of the System of the World—and only One ecstatic, blossoming Flower—which is realized ever-presently and omni-presently, in the coming into being of the site of all particles'—or of all bodies'—unchanging and immovable Presence(s)—in the coming into being of the (multiple and yet simultaneously singular) All/the Only—in the coming into being of God's Presently spoken (and written) Name/Word—his ecstatic, bursting, and resoundingly affirmative, "I AM."[73]

As we know, Newton authors four Absolute quantities in his *Principia*—his Absolute Time, Space, Place, and Motion—which he considers to come into being ever-presently and omni-presently—in the coming into being of the site of all particles'—or of all bodies'—unchanging and immovable Presence(s)—in the coming into being of the (multiple and yet simultaneously singular) All/the Only—in the coming into being of God's Presently spoken (and written) Name/Word—his ecstatic, bursting, and resoundingly affirmative, "I AM," and we recognize here that Newton considers the coming into being of his four Absolute quantities in the natural world to bring into being the Frame of the System of the

---

73. Newton expects his uncommon reader to recognize here that he considers ours to be an infinite cosmology (as systems are embedded within *greater* systems which are embedded within *even greater* systems, and so on, and so forth, ad infinitum; and as rotating flower patterns are embedded within greater rotating flower patterns which are embedded within even greater rotating flower patterns, and so on, and so forth, ad infinitum)—even as he also considers ours to be a cosmology in which the infinite is always already vanquished, or overcome, since he recognizes that there is also only One System and only One blossoming Flower, which is realized ever-presently and omni-presently, in the coming into being of the site of all particles'—or of all bodies'—unchanging and immovable Presence(s)—in the coming into being of the (multiple and yet simultaneously singular) All/the Only—in the coming into being of God's Presently spoken Name/Word—his ecstatic, bursting, and resoundingly affirmative, "I AM."

World—the (multiple and yet simultaneously singular) unchanging and immovable (and *material*) referent(s) by which he considers it to be possible to rigorously define all motion and change.

We find that Newton's choice of name for his Absolute Place(s), whose Absolute Motions, we know, (over the course of their trajectories) generate an Absolute Space and an Absolute Time, is a nod to Archimedes and to Archimedes's facetious request to be given "a[n unchanging and immovable] *place*" by which it would be possible to move the earth. (We recognize that Newton sees how Archimedes had truly moved the world with his insights into motion, and that Newton playfully gives back to Archimedes the facetiously requested *place*, in the form of Newton's Absolute Place, nearly two millennia later.)

And we also find that Newton's name for his Absolute Place(s) is a nod to the ancient Jews, who (according to Newton), referred to YHWH in their cosmology as "Place." In an unpublished but intended preface to the *Principia*, Newton writes:

> And therefore those Ancients who rightly understood the mystical philosophy taught that a *certain* infinite spirit pervades all space & contains and vivifies the universal world; and this supreme spirit was their numen, according to the Poet cited by the Apostle: in Him we live and move and have our being. Hence the omnipresent God is acknowledged and by the Jews is called Place.[74]

And we recognize here that Newton's *Absolute Place* also exists as secret code in his cosmology for his God—the Divine Logos himself.

❧

From here, Newton applies his idea regarding Universal Gravitation to the system of Saturn and its Planets (or moons). Newton writes:

> The same thing we are to understand of the Planets [or moons] which encompass Saturn.[75]

---

74. See Westfall, *Never at Rest*, 511; my emphasis. Newton's reference to a "*certain* infinite spirit" (my emphasis) reminds us of his reference to an "agent acting constantly according to *certain* laws" (my emphasis). And we recognize that the monist, materialist focus of Newton's cosmology is upon (what he considers to be) the *One Certain Truth—The One Certain Law*: the Divine Logos himself.

75. Newton, "Proposition I, Theorem I," *Mathematical Principles*, 2:213.

And Newton then turns his attentions to the system of the Sun and its Planets—or to our solar system. Newton proposes:

> That the forces by which the primary Planets are continually drawn off from rectilinear motions, and retain'd in their proper orbits, tend to the Sun; and are reciprocally as the squares of the distances of the places of those Planets from the Sun's centre.[76]

And again, Newton expects his uncommon reader to recognize here that he considers the particle equivalents of the Sun and its Planets—or the site(s) of the Sun's and its Planets' own unchanging and immovable Presence(s)—to tend ceaselessly (over the course of their trajectories) towards the solar system's common center (of gravity)—towards the particle equivalent of the solar system itself; towards the site of the solar system's own unchanging and immovable Presence. Newton expects his uncommon reader to recognize here that he considers the particle equivalents of the Sun and its Planets to tend ceaselessly (over the course of their trajectories) towards an unchanging and immovable *place* that itself exists indistinguishably from the unchanging and immovable *place(s)* that the particle equivalents of the Sun and its Planets always already Are. Newton expects his uncommon reader to recognize here that he considers the particle equivalents of the Sun and its Planets to tend ceaselessly (over the course of their trajectories) towards a manifestation of absolute simultaneity in the natural world—even as he considers the particle equivalents of the Sun and its Planets to always already exist as the (multiple and yet simultaneously singular) manifestation(s) of absolute simultaneity in the natural world. Newton expects his uncommon reader to recognize here that he considers the particle equivalents of the Sun and its Planets to tend ceaselessly (over the course of their trajectories) towards a manifestation of Divinity's unchanging and immovable Presence in the natural world—even as he considers the particle equivalents of the Sun and its Planets to always already exist as manifestation(s) of Divinity's unchanging and immovable Presence in the natural world. Newton expects his uncommon reader to recognize here that he considers the particle equivalents of the Sun and its Planets to tend ceaselessly (over the course of their trajectories) towards a manifestation of God's Presently spoken (and written) Name/Word—towards a manifestation of his ecstatic, bursting, and resoundingly affirmative, "I AM"—even as he considers the particle equivalents of the Sun and its Planets to always already

---

76. Newton, "Proposition II, Theorem II," *Mathematical Principles*, 2:214.

exist as manifestation(s) of God's Presently spoken (and written) Name/Word. Newton expects his uncommon reader to recognize here that he considers the particle equivalents of the Sun and its Planets to tend ceaselessly (over the course of their trajectories) towards an unchanging and immovable *place* that itself exists indistinguishably from the unchanging and immovable *place(s)* that the particle equivalents of the Sun and its Planets always already Are; and Newton expects his uncommon reader to recognize here that he considers them to generate rotating flower patterns as they go.

And Newton also expects his uncommon reader to recognize here that he does not consider the solar system's center of gravity to be located within the Sun, but rather to be located a diameter away from the Sun. He writes:

> And pursuing the principles of this computation, we should find that tho' the Earth and all the Planets were plac'd on one side of the Sun, the distance of the common centre of gravity of all from the centre of the Sun would scarcely amount to one diameter of the Sun.[77]

We find that Newton *definitively* reveals to his uncommon reader here (and even to his common reader!) that he does not consider ours to be a heliocentric cosmology; (and as we know, Newton had already revealed to his uncommon reader that he considered ours to be a center-centric cosmology, whose center is the Divine Logos himself.)[78]

We find that Newton refers to our solar system's common center (of gravity) as "the Centre of the World." He declares:

> Hence the common centre of gravity of the Earth, the Sun, and all the Planets is to be esteemed the Centre of the World.[79]

Newton also asserts "That the common centre of gravity of the Earth, the Sun, and all the Planets [or the Center of the World] is immoveable,"[80] and he continues: "that centre either is at rest, or moves uniformly forward in

---

77. Newton, "Proposition XII, Theorem XII," *Mathematical Principles*, 2:233.

78. Newton had already revealed to his uncommon reader that, like Galileo, he too considered ours to be a center-centric cosmology (in a recursively self-similar way), and that he considered the Universe's center to be the Divine Logos himself.

79. Newton, "Proposition XII, Theorem XII, Corollary," *Mathematical Principles*, 2:233.

80. Newton, "Proposition XI, Theorem XI," *Mathematical Principles*, 2:232.

a right line."⁸¹ *And Newton makes clear to his uncommon reader here (and even to his common reader!) that by his term "immoveable," he does not mean absolutely at rest, but rather, means unchanging with respect to itself (over the course of its trajectory).* (We find that Newton also uses the term "fix'd" as a synonym for "immoveable," and again, he implies to us that by the term "fix'd" he does not mean absolutely at rest, but rather means unchanging with respect to itself (over the course of its trajectory.))⁸²

Newton also proposes:

> That the centre of the system of the world is immoveable.⁸³

—and we recognize here that while Newton is ostensibly referring to the center of our solar system as being immovable, he is also referring to the center of (what he considers to be) the *entire* System of the world itself—to the center of our Universe—which, we recognize, he also considers to be immovable, since he considers it to come into being ever-presently and omni-presently, in the coming into being of the site of all particles'—or of all bodies'—unchanging and immovable Presence(s)—in the coming into being of the (multiple and yet simultaneously singular) All/the Only—in the coming into being of the Divine Logos himself.⁸⁴

---

81. Newton, "Proposition XI, Theorem XI," *Mathematical Principles*, 2:232.

82. Like Archimedes and Galileo, Newton recognizes that the state of absolute rest does not exist in the natural world.

83. Newton, "Proposition X, Theorem X, Hypothesis I," *Mathematical Principles*, 2:232.

84. Elsewhere, Newton implies that he considers the center of the Universe—the (multiple and yet simultaneously singular) All/the Only—the Divine Logos himself—to exist as the location of the Universe's "sacred fire"—and he implies that he considers all of us to always already exist as manifestation(s) of this sacred fire. As Tessa Morrison reports in *Isaac Newton and the Temple of Solomon*, Newton was a student of the ancients' sacred Temples (for he believed that the ancients had embedded secret natural philosophical and mathematical wisdom within their Temple plans), and she explains that a "Temple structure that contained a central fire was to Newton a symbol of the purest form of philosophical wisdom." (Indeed, we find that Newton himself wrote that "The placing of fire in the common centre . . . is a part also of the religion which the nations received from Noah," and he continued, "Noah & his sons carried with them the sacred fire.") We recognize that Newton considered the Temples' centers—and their sacred fire(s)—to serve as metaphors for the site of the Divine Logos's Presence in the natural world, and that he considered all of us to always already Presently exist as manifestation(s) of this sacred fire (see Morrison, *Isaac Newton*, 29–30, 44).

From here, Newton turns his attentions towards exploring the system of our Earth and its Moon, and he proposes:

> That the force by which the Moon is retain'd in its orbit, tends to the Earth; and is reciprocally as the square of the distance of its place from the Earth's centre.[85]

Newton also recognizes that this force is responsible for generating the motions of the Earth's tides, and he turns his attentions towards focusing on the following problem:

> Proposition XXXVII. Problem XVIII. To find the force of the Moon to move the Sea.[86]

Newton, who was a deeply sensitive reader of Galileo's cosmology, recognizes that Galileo had attempted to provide his own reader with an accurate theory of tidal motion, but that he had failed (and we read that Galileo's theory of tidal motion "was so important to him that he originally intended to entitle his *Dialogue on the Two Chief World Systems* the *Dialogue on the Ebb and Flow of the Sea*").[87] And we find that Newton attempts to provide his own (uncommon) reader with an accurate theory of tidal motion—and he recognizes that in order to do so, it will be necessary to extend and deepen Galileo's ideas regarding how gravity affects the motions of all particles—or of all bodies—in the natural world.[88]

Newton begins to explore the problem of tidal motion by turning to the Earth/Moon system, and by analyzing it in the same way that he had analyzed the other systems that we have already encountered in book III. Newton recognizes that the Earth/Moon system possesses a common center (of gravity)—(or that which is referred to as a "barycenter")—towards which the particle equivalents of the Earth and the Moon ceaselessly tend.[89] Newton recognizes that the particle equivalents

---

85. Newton, "Proposition III, Theorem III," *Mathematical Principles*, 2:214.
86. Newton, "Proposition XXXVII. Problem XVIII," *Mathematical Principles*, 2:306.
87. "Galileo Galilei," para. 15.
88. Newton recognizes that it will be necessary to perform the work of the true philosopher upon Galileo's cosmology, and as we will see, he "look[s] at the absolute truth and to that original to repair."
89. The English word "barycenter" derives "from Ancient Greek βαρύς (barús) 'heavy', and κέντρον (kéntron) 'center'" and we recognize that it is a modern translation of the *kentron toi bareos*—the sharp point, center, or pivot of weight ("Barycenter (Astronomy)," para. 1).

CHAPTER VI. ISAAC NEWTON   197

of the Earth and its Moon—or the site(s) of the Earth's and its Moon's own unchanging and immovable Presence(s)—tend ceaselessly (over the course of their trajectories) towards the Earth/Moon system's common center (of gravity)—towards the particle equivalent of the Earth/Moon system; towards the site of the Earth/Moon system's own unchanging and immovable Presence. Newton recognizes that the particle equivalents of the Earth and Moon tend ceaselessly (over the course of their trajectories) towards an unchanging and immovable *place* that itself exists indistinguishably from the unchanging and immovable *place(s)* that the particle equivalents of the Earth and its Moon always already Are. Newton recognizes that the particle equivalents of the Earth and its Moon tend ceaselessly (over the course of their trajectories) towards a manifestation of absolute simultaneity in the natural world—even as he recognizes that the particle equivalents of the Earth and its Moon always already exist as the (multiple and yet simultaneously singular) manifestation(s) of absolute simultaneity in the natural world. Newton recognizes that the particle equivalents of the Earth and its Moon tend ceaselessly (over the course of their trajectories) towards a manifestation of Divinity's unchanging and immovable Presence in the natural world— even as he recognizes that the particle equivalents of the Earth and its Moon always already exist as manifestation(s) of Divinity's unchanging and immovable Presence in the natural world. Newton recognizes that the particle equivalents of the Earth and its Moon tend ceaselessly (over the course of their trajectories) towards a manifestation of God's Presently spoken (and written) Name/Word—towards a manifestation of his ecstatic, bursting, and resoundingly affirmative, "I AM"—even as Newton recognizes that the particle equivalents of the Earth and its Moon always already exist as manifestation(s) of God's Presently spoken (and written) Name/Word. Newton recognizes that the particle equivalents of the Earth and its Moon tend ceaselessly (over the course of their trajectories) towards an unchanging and immovable *place* that itself exists indistinguishably from the unchanging and immovable *place(s)* that the particle equivalents of the Earth and its Moon always already Are; and Newton recognizes that they generate rotating flower patterns as they go.

And from here, Newton turns his attentions towards extending and deepening Galileo's ideas. As has been mentioned, Newton recognizes that Galileo had deduced his ideas regarding the effects of gravity on the motions of all particles—or of all bodies—by exploring bodies dropped from the top of the Leaning Tower; and Newton recognizes that

Galileo had assumed that while the presently "inertial" components of particles'—or of bodies'—motions (and which exist inextricably from the particles—or bodies—themselves) are *horizontal*, the "gravitational" components of particles'—or bodies'—motions are *vertical*. We find that Newton himself recognizes that the presently "inertial" components of particles'—or bodies'—motions (and which exist inextricably from the particles—or bodies—themselves) are not necessarily *horizontal*, but that they are *orthogonal* to the gravitational components of particles'—or bodies'—motions. (And as we know, in Definitions IV and V, Newton defined gravity as being a "centripetal," or "center-seeking" force, and we read that that direction of a centripetal force "is always orthogonal to the [presently inertial] motion of the body.")[90] And we find that it is in this way that Newton extends and deepens Galileo's cosmology with regard to how gravity affects the motions of all particles—or all bodies—in the natural world.

Like Galileo, Newton recognizes that all bodies composing any given system of bodies undergo *non-uniform rotations* (over the course of their trajectories) as they tend ceaselessly towards their system's common center (of gravity). And, like Galileo, Newton recognizes that the degree to which the bodies are rotated (over the course of their trajectories) is dependent upon their distances from their system's common center (of gravity), and that this is responsible for producing the rotating orbital flower patterns that we see in nature.[91]

We find that contemporary scientists model the motions of the Earth/Moon system around its barycenter (point G in this image) as follows:

---

90. "Centripetal Force," para. 1.

91. And we recognize that these rotating orbital flower patterns are observable to us over extended periods of time as we view the systems from without.

CHAPTER VI. ISAAC NEWTON   199

FIGURE 10[92]

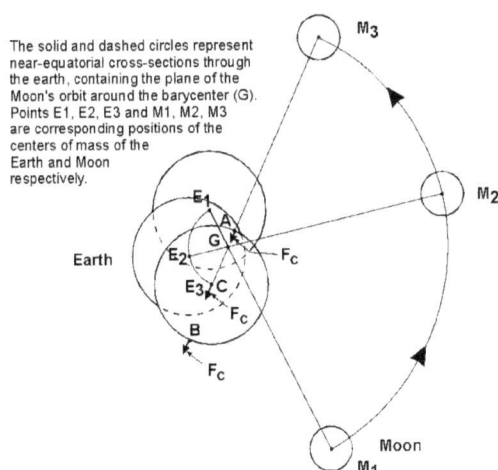

—and in viewing this image, we may imagine a sunflower blossoming into being—whose blossom, we know, is also our own.[93]

FIGURE 11[94]

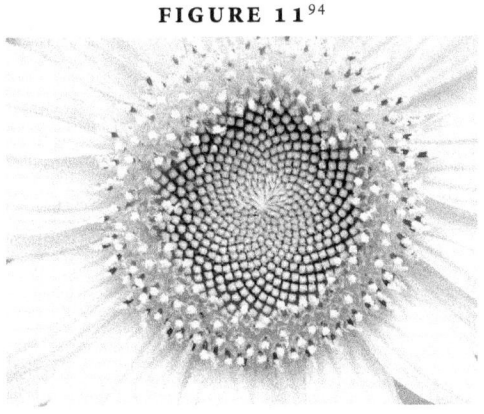

92. National Oceanic and Atmospheric Administration, "Detailed Explanation of Differential Tide."

93. We may think of the Earth and Moon as being systems, which tend ceaselessly (over the course of their trajectories) towards their greater system's common center (of gravity)—its barycenter—and which generate rotating flower patterns as they go; and we recognize that we too are composed of systems, which tend ceaselessly (over the course of their trajectories) towards their greater system's common center (of gravity)— our own single barycenter!—and which generate rotating flower patterns as they go.

94. "Helianthus Whorl," Wikimedia Commons.

❧

Newton also recognizes that the particle equivalents (or the corpuscles) of which the Seas are composed themselves tend ceaselessly (over the course of their trajectories) towards the Earth/Moon's common center (of gravity) in the same way that the particle equivalents of the Earth and the Moon do too; and Newton recognizes that they too generate rotating flower patterns as they go. We find that the following image is a map of the Earth's tidal motions (or what contemporary scientists refer to as "tidal amphidromes"), and which reveals the flowers that are ceaselessly raised in our Seas:

FIGURE 12[95]

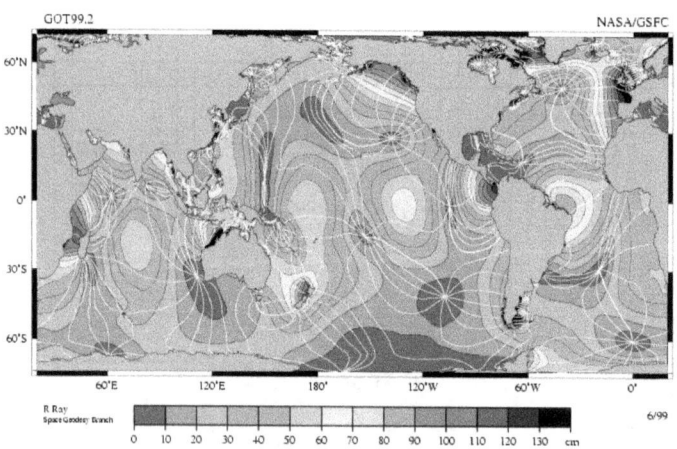

❧

As has been mentioned, Newton was a student of the ancients' sacred architecture; he was a student of the ancients' sacred Temples—although we also recognize that Newton actually considered our Universe itself to exist as the One sacred Temple, which comes into being ever-presently and omni-presently, in the coming into being of the site of all particles'—or of all bodies'—unchanging and immovable Presence(s); in the coming into being of the (multiple and yet simultaneously singular)

95. Ray, "Tidal Patterns."

All/the Only—in the coming into being of God's Presently spoken Name/ Word—his ecstatic, bursting, and resoundingly affirmative, "I AM."[96]

We find that Newton was also an alchemist, who devoted one million words to pursuing his alchemical interests.[97] Scholars report that alchemy arose in the third century AD, and that our modern chemistry evolved from it; they explain that alchemy (or what was referred to as "chymistry" in the seventeenth century)[98] arose from "theoretical speculations about the nature of *matter and change* [which were] present in Greek natural philosophy" from the time of the Presocratics[99]—and they report that the ultimate goal of alchemy was to locate a single, stable, unchanging substrate that was common to all—or the site of an ultimate substance. Scholars report that alchemists alternately referred to this ultimate substance as "the philosopher's stone" and as "the elixir of life"; and we recognize that alchemists considered the philosopher's stone/the elixir of life to exist both as the site at which substance/matter is realized in the natural world and also to exist as the site at which ever-burgeoning life is realized in the natural world.[100] As Wikipedia reports:

> The philosopher's stone, or stone of the philosophers (Latin: *lapis philosophorum*) is . . . also called the elixir of life, useful for rejuvenation and for achieving immortality; for many centuries, it was the most sought goal in alchemy. The philosopher's stone was the central symbol of the mystical terminology of alchemy,

---

96. Newton implies that he considers our Universe itself to exist as the One Sacred Temple—the One blossoming Flower/Fountain of the Divine Logos himself.

97. See Newman, "Chymistry of Issac Newton."

98. Newman, "Chymistry of Isaac Newton."

99. Principe, *Secrets of Alchemy*, 13; my emphasis.

100. "Philosopher's Stone," para. 1. Alchemy was born after the rise of Christianity, and we find that it incorporates within it Christian metaphors for the arche—the generative "source," "origin," or "originating cause" of all things that exist in the natural world, which also exists as the site of all things in the natural world. As we know, the early Christians considered Jesus himself to exist as the arche (and let us remind ourselves here of John 1:1, in which it is written: "In the beginning [the arche] was the Word [the Logos; or the arche]"), and we find that the early Christians alternately referred to Jesus in their cosmology as the "rock" (Matt 7:24) and as "the life" (John 14:6). We recognize that the alchemists of the third century AD, who sought to locate the rock and the life, sought to locate the site of Jesus's own Presence in the natural world. (We recognize that they sought to locate the Presence of the Divine Word in the natural world—the (multiple and yet simultaneously singular) All/the Only—and their own Divine selves.)

symbolizing perfection at its finest, enlightenment, and heavenly bliss. Efforts to discover the philosopher's stone were known as the Magnum Opus ("Great Work").[101]

And regarding the concept of a Magnum Opus, Wikipedia reports:

> The perfection of the human body and soul was thought to permit or result from the alchemical magnum opus and, in the Hellenistic and western tradition, the achievement of gnosis.[102]

And finally, as Wikipedia continues,

> Gnosis is the common Greek noun for knowledge (γνῶσις, gnôsis, f.). The term is used in various Hellenistic religions and philosophies. It is best known from Gnosticism, where it signifies a knowledge or insight into man's real nature as Divine, leading to the deliverance of the Divine spark within man from the constraints of earthly existence.[103]

As we know, Newton's *Principia* was his Magnum Opus—his Great Work—in which he realized the most sought-after goal in alchemy: to locate the site of the philosopher's stone/the elixir of life in the natural world—to locate the site of the Divine Logos himself. And as we know, Newton located the coming into being of the philosopher's stone/the elixir of life in the natural world in the coming into being of the (multiple and yet simultaneously singular) All/the Only; in the coming into being of we ourselves.

Fascinatingly, we also recognize that Newton hints to us here that he did not actually consider himself to be the author of his Magnum Opus—his *Philosophiae Naturalis Principia Mathematica*, or *Principia*—whose four word title is also one word. We find that Newton's alchemical name for himself was "Jehovah Sanctus Unus"[104]—Latin for "YHWH, the Holy One"—and we recognize that Newton had considered himself to be a prophet, who had received Divine wisdom, and who had been spoken through by the Divine Logos. (We recognize that Newton considered his true Name to be YHWH, the Holy One, and that he considered YHWH

---

101. "Philosopher's Stone," para. 1.
102. "Alchemy," para. 1.
103. "Gnosis," para. 1.
104. Newman, "Newton the Alchemist."

to write his Magnum Opus, much as he considered YHWH to ceaselessly write the Universe itself—with All existing as the Present speaking (and writing) of his One Name/Word—his ecstatic, bursting, and resoundingly affirmative, "I AM.")[105]

Before we turn to the fourth part of our discussion, True motions vs. Apparent motions, let us offer our reader a few final words here on Newton's Law of Universal Gravitation. From all that we have deduced thus far, it has become clear to us that Newton's Law of Universal Gravitation was original to his cosmology, but we also find ourselves asking: was it actually his? In authoring his Law of Universal Gravitation, Newton depended heavily upon the observations of others—including upon those of Tycho Brahe, of Johannes Kepler, and most significantly, of Robert Hooke. Indeed, in 1679, eight years before the publishing of the *Principia*, Hooke wrote a letter to Newton in which he explained that he (Hooke) considered the strength of the force of gravity upon bodies' centers of gravity to be inversely proportional to the distances between the bodies' centers of gravity squared. Hooke wrote:

> My supposition is that the attraction always is in duplicate proportion to the distance from the center reciprocall.[106]

Eight years later, Newton would propose his Law of Universal Gravitation in his *Principia* with only a passing mention of Hooke.[107]

---

105. We recognize that Newton considered All to Presently exist as the realization of the philosopher's stone/the elixir of life, and that he considered the Universe itself to exist as God's Presently spoken (and written) Magnum Opus—his Great Work.

106. Koyré, "Unpublished Letter of Robert Hooke," 332.

107. See "Book I: Of the Motion of Bodies, Section II: Proposition IV, Theorem IV, Scholium" of Newton's *Mathematical Principles*, 1:66, in which Newton writes, "The case of the sixth corollary obtains in the celestial bodies (as Sir *Christopher Wren*, Dr. *Hooke*, and Dr. *Halley* have severally observed) and therefore in what follows, I intend to treat more at large of those things which relate to centripetal force decreasing in a duplicate ratio of the distances from the centres."

Newton's biographers paint Newton as having been a fiercely competitive man who held lifelong grudges and who didn't take kindly to criticism. They report that, in 1672, Robert Hooke, who was then Curator of the esteemed Royal Society, criticized Newton's first paper—Newton's Theory of Light and Colors. Then, in 1676, Hooke accused Newton of plagiarizing his ideas on light. Years later (1686), Hooke once again accused Newton of plagiarizing his ideas—this time on gravitation, and the two men engaged in a lifelong bitter dispute. There are rumors that when Newton himself became President of the Royal Society in 1703—the same year that Hooke died—he destroyed the only existing portrait of Hooke in an attempt to write Hooke out of history.

Let us turn now to the fourth part of our discussion: True motions vs. Apparent motions, or *proving* the existence of the Divine Logos's Presence in the natural world. For this part of our discussion, we will need to return to the Scholium to the Definitions.

IV. TRUE MOTIONS VS. APPARENT MOTIONS, OR PROVING THE EXISTENCE OF THE DIVINE LOGOS'S PRESENCE IN THE NATURAL WORLD

As we know, in the Scholium to the Definitions, Newton contrasted his four Absolute quantities—his Absolute Time, Space, Place, and Motion—with his four Relative quantities—his Relative Time, Space, Place, and Motion, and thus far, we have devoted much time to exploring Newton's four Absolute quantities. Let us turn now to an exploration of Newton's four Relative quantities.

We remind ourselves that it was in the Scholium to the Definitions that Newton asserted that the "common people" conceive of Time, Space, Place, and Motion "under no other notions but from the relation they bear to sensible objects." But we ask ourselves here: what precisely did Newton mean by the terms Relative Time, Space, Place, and Motion? We recognize that Newton considered Relative Time and Space to be those quantities (measurable time and measurable distance) that an observer finds it possible to extrapolate from the motions of sensible bodies (over the course of their trajectories). Newton considered observable, sensible bodies themselves to exist as Relative Places, and he considered the Relative Motions of the Relative Places to be the (observable) changing, instantaneous motions of sensible bodies (over the course of their trajectories).[108]

And as we return now to the Scholium to the Definitions, we find that in this Scholium, Newton also asserts that it is possible to define the motions of a sensible body in two different ways, and with respect to two

---

108. We remind ourselves that, like Archimedes and Galileo, Newton recognized that sensible bodies' trajectories exist as the aggregates of their changing, instantaneous motions.

different referents: he asserts that it is possible to define the motions of a sensible body with respect to an immovable Absolute Place (whose Absolute Motions, we know, (over the course of its trajectory) bring into being in the natural world an Absolute Space and an Absolute Time—bring into being the Frame of the System of the World); and he also asserts that it is also possible to define the motions of a sensible body with respect to a movable Relative Place (or with respect to another sensible body). Newton refers to the former motion as the sensible body's "true and absolute" motion, and he refers to the latter motion as the sensible body's "relative and apparent" motion, and he writes:

> absolute motions can be no otherwise determin'd than by immoveable places; and for that reason I . . . [refer] absolute motions to immoveable places, but relative ones to moveable places.[109]

And Newton acknowledges here that while his own interests (of course!) lie in defining sensible bodies' motions in relation to immovable Absolute Place(s) (whose Absolute Motions (over the course of their trajectories) bring into being in the natural world an Absolute Space and an Absolute Time—bring into being the Frame of the System of the World), "in common affairs," the motions of sensible bodies are defined in relation to movable Relative Places (or in relation to other (movable) sensible bodies). He writes:

> But because the parts of [Absolute] Space cannot be seen, or distinguished from one another by our Senses, therefore in their stead we use sensible measures of them. For from the positions and distances of things from any [sensible] body consider'd as immoveable, we define all [relative] places: and then with respect to such [relative] places, we *estimate* all [relative] motions, considering [sensible] bodies as transfer'd from some of those [relative] places into others. And so instead of absolute places and motions, we use relative ones; and that without any inconvenience in common affairs: but in Philosophical disquisitions, we ought to abstract from our senses, and consider things themselves, distinct from what are only sensible measures of them. For it may be that there is no [sensible] body really at rest, to which the places and motions of others may be referr'd.[110]

---

109. Newton, "Scholium to the Definitions," *Mathematical Principles*, 1:14.

110. Newton, "Scholium to the Definitions," *Mathematical Principles*, 1:12; my emphasis. As we know, Newton is not interested in estimating; nor is he interested in

And towards the end of the Scholium to the Definitions, Newton provides his uncommon reader with an example of how a sensible body's "true and absolute" motions may be distinguished from its "relative and apparent" motions—and this passage, in which Newton recounts the details of an experiment that he had conducted upon water contained within a spinning bucket, has become famous over the centuries. The passage is referred to in the philosophical literature as Newton's "bucket experiment," and Newton writes:

> If a vessel, hung by a long cord, is so often turned about that the cord is strongly twisted, then fill'd with water, and held at rest together with the water; after by the sudden action of another force, it is whirl'd about the contrary way, and while the cord is untwisting it self, the vessel continues for some time in this motion; the surface of the water will at first be plain, as before the vessel began to move: but the vessel, by gradually communicating its motion to the water, will make it begin sensibly to revolve, and recede by little and little from the middle, and ascend to the sides of the vessel, forming it self into a concave figure, (as I have experienced) and the swifter the motion becomes, the higher will the water rise, till at last, performing its revolutions in the same times with the vessel, it becomes relatively at rest in it. This ascent of the water shews its endeavour to recede from the axe of its motion; and the true and absolute circular motion of the water, which is here directly contrary to the relative, discovers it self, and may be measured by this endeavour.[111]

Newton's language here is somewhat dense, but we may interpret his experiment as follows:

A bucket is hung from a rope, and the rope is twisted tightly, so that the bucket is all wound up. Then the bucket is filled with water, and the bucket/water system is let go. At first, while the bucket begins to spin, the surface of the water within the bucket remains flat: the water is not in motion. But then the bucket's motion is conveyed to the water, and the

---

approximate truths, but rather, he is interested in the *certain truth* and in (that which he considers to be) *The One Certain Law*—the Divine Logos himself. And of course, we know that there is no sensible body that really is immovable (or unchanging with respect to itself over the course of its trajectory), since sensible bodies' trajectories exist as the aggregates of their changing, instantaneous motions.

111. Newton, "Scholium to the Definitions," *Mathematical Principles*, 1:15.

water too begins to spin: the water's surface becomes concave. Finally, the water and bucket move together as one, and the water is "relatively at rest" with respect to the bucket. But Newton also asserts here that the water is actually still in motion—and that the water, which is still manifesting a concave surface, is actually exhibiting its "true and absolute" motion. Newton proposes that the water is not in motion with respect to the bucket (another sensible body—a Relative Place), but that rather it is in motion with respect to immovable Absolute Place(s) (whose Absolute Motions (over the course of their trajectories) bring into being in the natural world an Absolute Space and an Absolute Time—bring into being the Frame of the System of the World); and he implies that the water is therefore in motion with respect to the site of the Divine Logos's unchanging and immovable Presence in the natural world.

And Newton asserts here that in general, we, his uncommon readers, may distinguish between sensible bodies' "true and absolute" motions and their "relative and apparent" motions because sensible bodies that are manifesting their "true and absolute" motions (like the water in the bucket) recede "from the axe of circular motion." Newton writes:

> The Effects which distinguish absolute from relative motion are, the forces of receding from the axe of circular motion. For there are no such forces in a circular motion purely relative, but in a true and absolute circular motion, they are greater or less, according to the quantity of the motion.[112]

Newton also asserts here that the Planets of which our solar system is composed exhibit "true and absolute" motions too as they too recede from the axe of circular motion; and Newton implies that they too move with respect to Absolute Place(s) (whose Absolute Motions (over the course of their trajectories) bring into being in the natural world an Absolute Space and an Absolute Time—bring into being the Frame of the System of the World); and again, Newton implies that the Planets too are therefore in motion with respect to the site of the Divine Logos's unchanging and immovable Presence in the natural world. He writes:

> There is only one real circular motion of any one revolving body, corresponding to only one power of endeavouring to recede from its axe of motion, as its proper and adequate effect....
> And therefore in their system who suppose that our heavens, revolving below the sphere of the fixt Stars, carry the Planets

112. Newton, "Scholium to the Definitions," *Mathematical Principles*, 1:15.

along with them; the several parts of those heavens, and the Planets, which are indeed relatively at rest in their heavens, do yet really move. For they change their position one to another (which never happens to bodies truly at rest) and being carried together with their heavens, participate of their motions, and as parts of revolving wholes, endeavour to recede from the axe of their motions.[113]

Newton implies that our perception of this effect—our perception of sensible bodies' recession from the axe of circular motion—exists as sensible *proof* of the existence of Absolute Place(s)—(whose Absolute Motions (over the course of their trajectories) bring into being in the natural world an Absolute Space and an Absolute Time—bring into being the Frame of the System of the World); and therefore exists as sensible *proof* of the existence of the Divine Logos's unchanging and immovable Presence in the natural world.[114]

(And let us also note that Newton makes mention of the "fixt Stars" here, but we recognize that since the fixed stars exist as sensible, observable bodies, Newton considers them to exist as Relative Places, and not as Absolute Place(s); and we recognize that he does not consider the fixed stars to exist as the site of an unchanging and immovable referent in the natural world by which it is possible to *rigorously* define all motion and change.)

Newton concludes his Scholium to the Definitions with a final tongue-in-cheek remark in which he facetiously complains of the "great difficulty" of distinguishing between sensible bodies' "true and absolute" motions and their "relative and apparent" motions. He writes:

> It is indeed a matter of great difficulty to discover, and effectua'ly to distinguish, the True motion of particular bodies from the Apparent: because the parts of that immoveable [Absolute] space in which those motions are perform'd, do by no means come under the observation of our senses.[115]

---

113. Newton, "Scholium to the Definitions," *Mathematical Principles*, 1:16.

114. Newton implies that our perception of this effect exists as sensible *proof* of (what he considers to be) the existence of our own Divine selves.

115. Newton, "Scholium to the Definitions," *Mathematical Principles*, 1:17.

—And yet he also acknowledges here that distinguishing between the two states of motion was his intent in composing his entire *Principia*: Newton writes, "For to this end it was that I compos'd it."[116] And we, Newton's uncommon readers, recognize that Newton's intent in composing his *Principia* was to *prove* the existence of the Divine Logos's unchanging and immovable Presence in the natural world.[117]

Let us turn now to an exploration of Newton's Laws of Motion and his Corollaries to the Laws of Motion. As has been mentioned, Newton composed three Laws of Motion and six Corollaries to his Laws of Motion, and (unsurprisingly), we find that the focus of the Laws and Corollaries is upon the site of all preexisting/post-existing particles—or all preexisting/post-existing bodies—themselves, which Newton considers to exist inextricably from their perseverance (over the course of their trajectories) with their unchanging and immovable presently uniform rectilinear motions; the focus of the Laws and Corollaries is upon the site of all particles'—or all bodies'—unchanging and immovable Presence(s)—Newton's God: the Universe itself.[118]

NEWTON'S LAWS OF MOTION AND HIS COROLLARIES TO THE LAWS OF MOTION

Law I.

Newton's First Law reads:

---

116. Newton, "Scholium to the Definitions," *Mathematical Principles*, 1:18.

117. We are reminded here once again of Pythagoras's cosmology, and of how Pythagoras had considered the existence of music in the natural world (and from which he recognized that it was possible to extrapolate ratios, and numbers themselves) to serve as sensible evidence of the existence of YHWH's absolute Presence in the natural world.

118. In total, Newton offers his uncommon reader a Decalogue of Natural Laws: the Law of Universal Gravitation, three Laws of Motion, and six Corollaries to the Laws of Motion—even as we recognize that he also considers there to be only *One True Law*—the (multiple and yet simultaneously singular) All/the Only—his God: the Universe itself. (And we deduce that Newton considered himself to be a prophet equal to Moses, who had also delivered a Decalogue of Laws.)

> Every body perseveres in its state of rest, or of uniform motion in a right line, unless it is compelled to change that state by forces impress'd thereon.[119]

And we decrypt this humorous, tongue-in-cheek Law to mean that every body only perseveres—or continues on—in its unchanging and immovable *present* state of rest or of uniform motion in a right line—a state of motion from which we know that Newton considers every body itself to exist inextricably—precisely because *at the same time* it is also compelled to change that (unchanging and immovable) state under the impressed force of gravity.

(Let us remind ourselves here that Newton proposes that under the impressed force of gravity (which he considers to act continuously—at all times—upon every body in the natural world), every body's Vis Insita is continuously exercised (and by way of the exercising of which, every body endeavors to persevere, or continue on, in its unchanging and immovable presently inertial state of motion—a state of motion from which we know that Newton considers every body itself to exist inextricably)—even as, *at the same time*, the impressed force of gravity is also responsible for continuously altering every body's unchanging and immovable presently inertial state of motion—a state of motion from which we know that Newton considers every body itself to exist inextricably—and is therefore responsible for producing every body's changing, instantaneous motions (and by way of the existence of which we are able to discern the passage of time in the natural world.))

Let us continue on here to Newton's Laws II and III. We find that Laws II and III concern themselves with the actions of forces impressed upon bodies. As we know, in Definition IV, Newton asserted that impressed forces are "of different origins as from percussion, from pressure, from centripetal force." And we recognize that while Newton considers gravity, a centripetal force, to be the one impressed force that acts continuously (at all times) upon all bodies in the natural world, he considers other impressed forces, such as those "from percussion, from pressure," to (under some circumstances) act upon bodies in addition to the continuously-impressed force of gravity.[120]

---

119. Newton, "Axioms: Law I," *Mathematical Principles*, 1:19.

120. Newton considers percussion and pressure to act upon bodies only when the

Law II.

Law II reads:

> The alteration of motion is ever proportional to the motive force impress'd; and is made in the direction of the right line in which that force is impress'd.[121]

Law II exists as a continuation of the thought expressed in Law I (which reads: "Every body perseveres in its state of rest, or of uniform motion in a right line, unless it is compelled to change that state by forces impress'd thereon"—and which we have interpreted to mean: Every body only perseveres in its unchanging and immovable *present* state of rest or of uniform motion in a right line—a state of motion from which we know that Newton considers every body itself to exist inextricably—precisely because *at the same time* it is also compelled to change that (unchanging and immovable) state by forces impress'd thereon.) And by "alteration of motion," we recognize that Newton is referring here to the action of the impressed force exerted upon the body (and which exists inextricably from its perseverance (over the course of its trajectory) with its unchanging and immovable presently uniform rectilinear motion). We find that the focus of Law II is therefore upon *how* a body's unchanging and immovable presently uniformly rectilinear state of motion (and from which Newton considers the body itself to exist inextricably) is *at the same time* altered by the action of an impressed force exerted upon it. Newton asserts that the alteration of the body's motion is proportional to the magnitude of the force impressed, and is made in the direction of the straight line in which the force is impressed. And therefore, we find that Newton defines an impressed force to exist in his cosmology as a mathematical vector, which possesses both magnitude and direction. The famous mathematical equation $\mathbf{F} = \mathbf{ma}$ is the mathematical form of Newton's Second Law.[122]

---

bodies are immersed within an atmosphere. And we also note that although Newton considers percussion and pressure to act *upon* preexisting/post-existing bodies, he considers the gravity/Vis Insita interaction to itself be responsible for *generating* all preexisting/post-existing bodies themselves.

121. Newton, "Axioms: Law II," *Mathematical Principles*, 1:19.

122. Let us also remind ourselves here that in Definition I, Newton asserted that "mass" is another name in his cosmology for "body." Newton implies that he therefore considers a mass to exist inextricably from its perseverance (over the course of its trajectory) with an unchanging and immovable presently uniform rectilinear motion, and to exist as a manifestation of the site of all particles'—or of all bodies'—or of all

Law III.

Law III reads:

> To every Action there is always opposed an equal Reaction: or the mutual *actions* of two bodies *upon* each other are always equal, and directed to contrary parts.[123]

Let us also remind ourselves here that in Definition IV, Newton defined the impressed force as being "an *action* exerted *upon* a body" (my emphases), "in order to change the body's [present] state, either of rest, or of moving uniformly forward in a right line." And we find that Newton therefore makes plain here that he conceives of "reactions" as being equal and opposite "actions," which *act upon* bodies (from without), and which therefore also exist in his cosmology as a type of impressed force.[124]

Let us turn now to the Corollaries to the Laws of Motion.

Corollaries I and II.

In Corollaries I and II, Newton reveals to us, his uncommon readers, how he intends impressed forces to be mathematically treated in his *Principia*. (And as we know, in Law II, Newton defined impressed forces to exist in his cosmology as vectors, which possess both magnitude and direction.) We find that Corollary I exists as a statement of the "parallelogram law" for vector addition, in which it is shown that a composite vector exists as the sum of its vector components. And in Corollary II, Newton reveals to us, his uncommon readers, how it is possible to compose composite vectors from their component vectors, and how it is also possible to decompose composite vectors into their component vectors.

Corollary I reads:

> A body by two forces conjoined will describe the diagonal of a parallelogram, in the same time that it would describe the sides, by those forces apart. (Pl. I. Fig. I.)[125]

---

masses'—unchanging and immovable Presence(s) in the natural world.

123. Newton, "Axioms: Law III," *Mathematical Principles*, 1:20; my emphases.

124. As we know, the one and only force in Newton's cosmology that does not act *upon* bodies (from without), but that Newton considers to be innate to bodies themselves, is the Vis Insita, or the "Innate Force of Matter."

125. Newton, "Axioms: Corollary I," *Mathematical Principles*, 1:21.

And Newton provides us, his uncommon readers, with the following diagram, which he explains as follows:

FIGURE 13

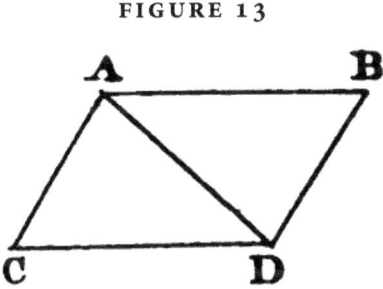

> If a body in a given time, by the force M impress'd apart in the place A, should with an uniform motion be carried from A to B; and by the force N impress'd apart in the same place, should be carried from A to C; compleat the parallelogram $ABCD$, and by both forces acting together, it will in the same time be carried in the diagonal from A to D.[126]

And it is possible for us, Newton's uncommon readers, to decode this cryptic passage as follows: if a body (and which exists inextricably from its perseverance (over the course of its trajectory) with its unchanging and immovable presently uniform rectilinear motion) were to be acted upon "by the force M impress'd apart in the place A" (and where it is possible for us to infer here that by place A, Newton means the unchanging and immovable Absolute Place A; he means the site of the body itself (and which exists inextricably from its perseverance (over the course of its trajectory) with its unchanging and immovable presently uniform rectilinear motion); he means the site of the body's own unchanging and immovable Presence), the body's Vis Insita would be exercised, and the body would therefore endeavor to persevere with its unchanging and immovable presently "uniform motion" to B. And alternatively, if the body (and which exists inextricably from its perseverance (over the course of its trajectory) with an unchanging and immovable presently uniform rectilinear motion) were to be acted upon "in the same place" (at the Absolute Place A—at the site of the body itself (and which exists inextricably from its perseverance (over the course of its trajectory) with

---

126. Newton, "Axioms: Corollary I," *Mathematical Principles*, 1:21.

its unchanging and immovable presently uniform rectilinear motion); at the site of the body's own unchanging and immovable Presence) by the impressed force *N*, its Vis Insita would be exercised, and the body would endeavor to persevere with its unchanging and immovable presently uniform rectilinear motion to C. Newton asserts here that if both impressed forces were to act upon the body "together" at the place *A* (instead of acting "apart" at the place *A*), the body would "in the same time be carried in the diagonal from *A* to *D*."[127]

Corollary II reads:

> And hence is explained the composition of any one direct force AD, out of any two oblique forces AB and BD; and, on the contrary the resolution of any one direct force AD into two oblique forces AB and BD: which composition and resolution are abundantly confirmed from Mechanics.[128]

And here Newton defers to the rules of Euclidean geometry, and shows us, his uncommon readers, how it is possible to compose composite vectors from their component vectors, and how it is also possible to decompose composite vectors into their component vectors.

Let us briefly remark here on the role that mathematics plays in Newton's cosmology.

As we know, Newton recognized that Archimedes had developed his kinematics (or his mathematics of motion) in his mathematical treatise *On Spirals*, and Newton recognized that Archimedes had applied this kinematics to the development of a mechanics (and to an exploration of the motions of all physical bodies in the natural world). And as we know, *On Spirals* is the originary text that is embedded within Archimedes's mechanics and within his entire cosmology—and as we know, *On Spirals* is the originary text that is embedded within Galileo's mechanics and within his entire cosmology—and as we know, *On Spirals* is the originary text that is embedded within Newton's own mechanics and within his entire cosmology as well.

As has been mentioned, kinematics was renamed "the Calculus" in the seventeenth century by Gottfried Leibniz, and the Calculus was

---

127. We recognize that Newton's diagram details the motions of the body's (unobservable) unchanging and immovable present momentum, or its Quantity of Motion.

128. Newton, "Axioms: Corollary II," *Mathematical Principles*, 1:22.

recognized to be "the mathematics of motion and change." The Calculus was acknowledged to involve infinite summations over indivisible and infinitesimal quantities.[129] Historians note that a controversy arose in the seventeenth century as to who the true author of the Calculus was—Leibniz or Newton—and although they report that Newton vehemently asserted that *he* (and not Leibniz) was the Calculus's true author, we find that Newton also expects us, his uncommon readers, to recognize that he actually considered the true Author of the Calculus to be the Divine Logos himself. Newton expects us, his uncommon readers, to recognize that he considered the Divine Logos himself to exist both as the Author of the All and *as* the manifestation of the All; and Newton expects us, his uncommon readers, to recognize that he considered the Divine Logos himself to be responsible for bringing motion and change into being in the natural world, even as, *at the same time,* he also exists as the site(s) at which motion and change are always already vanquished, or overcome, in the natural world.

We find that mathematicians and philosophers of Newton's day debated as to who they considered the true author of the Calculus to have been (for example, the Marquis L'Hospital asserted that the *Principia* is "all about the Calculus"—and L'Hospital noted that the *Principia* was published only three years after the publication of Leibniz's first work on the Calculus),[130] but we, Newton's uncommon readers, recognize that the *Principia* is in fact all about (he whom Newton considered to be) *the Author*—the Divine Logos himself.

Let us return now to the Corollaries and to an exploration of Corollary III.

Corollary III.

Corollary III reads:

> The Quantity of motion, which is collected by taking the sum of the motions directed towards the same parts, and the difference

---

129. And we recognize that, like Archimedes and Galileo, Newton actually considered kinematics (or the Calculus) to involve infinite summations over indivisible/infinitesimal quantities.

130. L'Hospital wrote that the *Principia* is "composed almost wholly of this calculus" (Hutton et al., *Philosophical Transactions*, 134). And we note here that Leibniz himself published his first work on the Calculus in 1684 (see "Leibniz–Newton Calculus Controversy," para. 2).

of those that are directed to contrary parts, suffers no change from the action of bodies among themselves.[131]

We recognize that in Corollary III, Newton is referring to the "quantity of motion" of a *system of bodies*—or to a system of bodies' unchanging and immovable present momentum. (And let us remind ourselves that in Definition II, Newton defined the "quantity of motion" to be "the measure of the same, arising from the velocity and quantity of matter conjunctly"; and that we have deduced that by the term "quantity of motion," Newton meant the site of a body's unchanging and immovable present momentum.)

In Corollary III, Newton implies that a system of bodies also possesses a quantity of motion, which exists as the site of the system of bodies' own unchanging and immovable present momentum. And we find that Newton expects us, his uncommon readers, to recognize here that since the center of gravity of a system of bodies exists as the system's particle equivalent, it—being a *particle*, itself exists inextricably from its perseverance (over the course of its trajectory) with an unchanging and immovable presently uniform rectilinear motion, and that it therefore exists in the natural world as a manifestation of the "quantity of motion."

And in Corollary III, Newton explains that the magnitude of a system of bodies' unchanging and immovable present momentum remains unchanged, regardless of "the action of [the] bodies among themselves." Newton explains as follows:

> Thus if a spherical body A with two parts of velocity is triple of a spherical body B which follows in the same right line with ten parts of velocity; the motion of A will be to that of B, as 6 to 10. Suppose then their motions to be of 6 parts and of 10 parts, and the sum will be 16 parts. Therefore upon the meeting of the bodies, if A acquire 3, 4 or 5 parts of motion, B will lose as many; and therefore after reflexion A will proceed with 9, 10 or 11 parts, and B with 7, 6 or 5 parts; the sum remaining always of 16 parts as before.[132]

Today, this Corollary is interpreted as Newton's Law of Conservation of Momentum for a system of bodies.

---

131. Newton, "Axioms: Corollary III," *Mathematical Principles*, 1:25.
132. Newton, "Axioms: Corollary III," *Mathematical Principles*, 1:25.

Corollaries IV, V, and VI all reference the cosmology of Galileo, and we find that Newton writes them as tributes to Galileo and to his genius.

Corollary IV

In Newton's Fourth Corollary to his Laws of Motion, he proposes that the common center (of gravity) of two or more bodies is "either at rest, or moves uniformly forward in a right line." Corollary IV reads:

> The common centre of gravity of two or more bodies, does not alter its state of motion or rest by the actions of the bodies among themselves; and therefore the common centre of gravity of all bodies acting upon each other (excluding outward actions and impediments) is either at rest, or moves uniformly in a right line.[133]

And as we know, (and like Galileo), Newton considers the common center (of gravity) of a system of bodies to exist as the particle equivalent of the system of bodies itself—which, being a *particle*, exists inextricably from its perseverance (over the course of its trajectory) with an unchanging and immovable presently uniform rectilinear motion, and therefore exists as a manifestation of the site of all particles'—or of all bodies'—unchanging and immovable Presence(s) in the natural world.

Corollary V.

Corollary V exists as a restatement of (what was referred to in the Renaissance as) the Galilean Principle of Relativity,[134] and reads:

> The motions of bodies included in a given space are the same among themselves, whether that space is at rest, or moves uniformly forwards in a right line without any circular motion.[135]

—And we find that Newton follows this statement with a reference to Galileo's ship, and with the assertion that "A clear proof of which we have from the experiment of a ship: where all motions happen after the same

---

133. Newton, "Axioms: Corollary IV," *Mathematical Principles*, 1:27.
134. As we know, it is actually the Archimedean Principle of Relativity.
135. Newton, "Axioms: Corollary V," *Mathematical Principles*, 1:30.

manner, whether the ship is at rest, or is carried uniformly forwards in a right line."

We recognize that Newton considers the "given space" of which he speaks in Corollary V (and which he asserts is either "at rest, or moves uniformly forwards in a right line without any circular motion") to exist as the site of the given system's common center (of gravity); he considers it to exist as the particle equivalent of the system itself—which, being a particle, exists inextricably from its perseverance (over the course of its trajectory) with an unchanging and immovable presently uniform rectilinear motion, and therefore exists as a manifestation of the site of all particles'—or of all bodies'—unchanging and immovable Presence(s) in the natural world.[136]

Corollary VI.

And finally, we find that Corollary VI exists as a codification of the ideas that Galileo had deduced from his Leaning Tower of Pisa experiments. Corollary VI reads:

> If bodies, any how moved among themselves are urged in the direction of parallel lines by equal accelerative forces; they will all continue to move among themselves, after the same manner as if they had been urged by no such forces.[137]

Here, Newton imagines two bodies being dropped from the top of the Leaning Tower in tandem, and (like Galileo), he recognizes that although to an observer located within the Leaning Tower system, the bodies *appear* to manifest parallel trajectories (relative to one another) over the course of their trajectories, *in truth*, the bodies *actually* manifest non-linear trajectories as they tend ceaselessly (over the course of their trajectories) towards their system's common center (of gravity).[138]

Like Galileo, Newton recognizes that the bodies are *actually non-uniformly rotated* (over the course of their trajectories) as they tend

---

136. We note that Newton considers the "given space" of which he speaks in Corollary V to exist as a material entity.

137. Newton, "Axioms: Corollary VI," *Mathematical Principles*, 1:31.

138. As we know, Newton considers the bodies to manifest non-linear trajectories relative to the site of all particles'—or of all bodies'—unchanging and immovable Presence(s); relative to the unchanging and immovable (and *material*) referent by which he considers it to be possible to rigorously define all motion and change—the Divine Logos himself.

ceaselessly towards their system's common center (of gravity). (And as we know, and like Galileo, Newton recognizes that the degree to which the bodies are rotated (over the course of their trajectories) is dependent upon their distances from their system's common center (of gravity), and that this is responsible for producing the rotating orbital flower patterns that we see in nature.)

Let us also note here that in Corollary VI, Newton refers to gravity as being an "equal accelerative" force, but we recognize that he means this too only in an *apparent* way, since we know that he recognizes that gravity *actually* acts upon bodies *unequally*, and that the degree to which the bodies are rotated (over the course of their trajectories) is dependent upon their distances from their system's common center (of gravity).

Let us conclude our explorations of Newton's cosmology now with an acknowledgment of how Newton had been a true philosopher in the Platonic sense.

ISAAC NEWTON, TRUE PHILOSOPHER

In book VI of Plato's *Republic* (and speaking in the voice of Socrates), Plato/Socrates writes:

> And when I speak of the other division of the intelligible, you will understand me to speak of that other sort of knowledge which reason herself attains by the power of dialectic, using the hypotheses not as first principles, but only as hypotheses—that is to say, as steps and points of departure into a world which is above hypotheses, in order that she may soar beyond them to the first principle [ἀρχήν] of the whole; and clinging to this and then to that which depends on this, by successive steps she descends again without the aid of any sensible object, from ideas, through ideas, and in ideas she ends.[139]

As we know, in his *Principia*, Newton soars from this, and then to that which depends on this, by successive steps to (what, like Plato, Newton too considers to be) the first *principle* of the whole—to the heart of his *Principia*—to the arche (ἀρχήν) itself—to the generative "source," "origin,"

---

139. Plato, *Republic*, VI:511a.

or "originating cause" of all things that exist in the natural world, which also exists as the site of all things in the natural world—to the (multiple and yet simultaneously singular) All/the Only—to his God: the Universe itself.

⁓

In book VI of *The Republic*, Socrates and Socrates' student Glaucon discuss the attributes of the "true philosopher." Plato/Socrates defines the true philosopher as being one who "behold[s] the things themselves, which can only be seen with the eye of the mind," and who possesses "magnificence of mind and is the spectator of all time and existence." And Plato/Socrates implies that the true philosopher is a "spectator of all time and existence" because he or she "sees" (with the eye of the mind) that which ever-presently and omni-presently Is: the (multiple and yet simultaneously singular) All/the Only—(he whom Plato/Socrates considers to be) Divinity himself.[140]

Plato/Socrates also contrasts true philosophers, who see "the things themselves" (blindly, with the eye of the mind) with they who are not true philosophers—with they who see exclusively with their eyes. He refers to those in the latter category as being "blind," and he writes:

> And are not those who are verily and indeed wanting in the knowledge of the true being of each thing, and who have in their souls no clear pattern, and are unable as with a painter's eye to look at the absolute truth and to that original to repair, and having perfect vision of the other world to order the laws about beauty, goodness, justice in this, if not already ordered, and to guard and preserve the order of them—are not such persons, I ask, simply blind?[141]

And Plato/Socrates asserts that only true philosophers, who see the things themselves (blindly, with the eye of the mind) should be rulers of the Republic, his ideal state. He explains:

> Inasmuch as [true] philosophers only are able to grasp the eternal and unchangeable, and those who wander in the region

---

140. Plato/Socrates implies that the true philosopher is a "spectator of all time and existence" because he or she "sees" (with the eye of the mind) that All is always already One and that All is always already Now.

141. Plato, *Republic*, VI:484d.

of the many and variable are not philosophers, I must ask you which of the two classes should be the rulers of our state?[142]

As we know, both Galileo and Newton were such true philosophers; both possessed in their souls a "clear pattern" of "the things themselves, which can only be seen with the eye of the mind"; and both were able, "as with a painter's eye," to (blindly) "look at the absolute truth and to that original to repair."

Let us turn now to an exploration of the cosmology of Albert Einstein, who, as we will see, was not a true philosopher in the Platonic sense. Einstein was born into an Empirical Age, and he himself was an empiricist; Einstein saw exclusively with his eyes, rather than with the eye of the mind. And we will find that although Einstein built his cosmology upon the cosmology of Newton, Einstein did not recognize Newton's true cosmology. Einstein did not recognize that the monist, materialist focus of Newton's cosmology was upon the site of all particles'—or of all bodies'—unchanging and immovable Presence(s)—the site that Newton had recognized to exist as that of the unobservable absolute in the natural world. Contemporary physicists acknowledge that Einstein's empirical cosmology is incomplete, and we will find that by implanting the site of all particles'—or of all bodies'—unchanging and immovable Presence(s) into the heart of Einstein's empirical cosmology, we will be able to complete it; we will be able "to that original to repair."[143]

Let us begin to explore Einstein's cosmology by first exploring the Empirical Age—the Age of Science—into which Einstein was born. As

142. Plato, *Republic*, VI:484b.

143. Einstein's cosmology comprises his theories of special relativity and of general relativity. Einstein's theory of general relativity embeds his theory of special relativity within it, and the theory of general relativity is the more general theory. And physicists acknowledge that the theory of general relativity is incomplete. We read that "general relativity has emerged as a highly successful model of gravitation and cosmology, which has so far passed many unambiguous observational and experimental tests. However, there are strong indications the theory is incomplete" ("General Relativity," para. 82).

we will see, because Newton's *Principia* is so deeply encrypted in code, in the years following its publication, it was (mis)interpreted as being an empirical manifesto, and (ironically) it inaugurated an Empirical Revolution—an Age of Science—in which knowledge of (what Newton had referred to as) the Relative, Apparent, and Common was prized, and knowledge of (what Newton had referred to as) the Absolute, Mathematical, and True was lost to the philosophical discourse.

Chapter VII.

(Mis)reading the Principia *in the wake of its publication*

DESPITE THE FACT THAT Newton had asserted that "in Philosophical disquisitions, we ought to abstract from our senses, and consider things themselves, distinct from what are only sensible measures of them," and despite the fact that Newton had insisted that Relative, Apparent, and Common quantities (or those quantities that Newton considered to be commonly encountered in empirical analyses) would be of interest only to the "common" and "vulgar" people, we find that in the years following the *Principia*'s publication, it was (mis)interpreted as being an empirical manifesto, and it inaugurated an Empirical Revolution—an Age of Science and of "Enlightenment."[1] (Ironically, we recognize that this Age of Enlightenment would have actually been considered to be a Dark Age by Newton himself—for it was an Age in which knowledge of (what Newton had referred to as) the Relative, Apparent, and Common was prized, and knowledge of (what Newton had referred to as) the Absolute, True, and Mathematical was lost to the philosophical discourse.)[2]

Why was the *Principia* (mis)interpreted as being an empirical manifesto in the years following its publication? There are two reasons. The first and most obvious reason that Newton's *Principia* was (mis)interpreted as

---

1. We read that "some consider the publication of Isaac Newton's *Principia Mathematica* (1687) as the first major enlightenment work" ("Age of Enlightenment," para. 2).

2. We recognize that Newton himself would have considered the Age of Enlightenment to always already (and eternally) be Now.

being an empirical manifesto lies in the fact that it is so deeply encrypted in code. In the wake of the *Principia*'s publication, philosophers did not recognize that it exists as secret, hidden wisdom, which requires decrypting. And philosophers also did not recognize that in order to decrypt Newton's *Principia*, it would first be necessary to decrypt the cosmologies of Archimedes and of Galileo, which, as we know, are embedded within Newton's own cosmology, and which also exist as secret, hidden wisdom.[3]

And the second reason why Newton's *Principia* was (mis)interpreted as being an empirical manifesto was that in 1713, Newton added a section to book III of his *Principia* entitled, "Rules of Reasoning in Philosophy," in which he facetiously asserted that his type of natural philosophy was "experimental philosophy."[4] (We find that Newton made this statement in quiet homage to Galileo, who, in his *Dialogues Concerning Two New Sciences*, had also facetiously referred to his own type of philosophy as being experimental philosophy—(Galileo began Day 3 of his *Dialogues Concerning Two New Sciences* with the facetious claim that he had "discovered *by experiment* some properties of [motion] which are worth knowing and which have not hitherto been either observed or demonstrated")[5]—but as we know, both Galileo and Newton composed their works in facetious, tongue-in-cheek tones; and as we know, both were true philosophers in the Platonic sense, who devoted their lives to exploring the first principle (ἀρχήν) of the whole: the site of all particles'—or of all bodies'—unchanging and immovable Presence(s)—and the site that both had recognized to exist as that of the unobservable absolute in the natural world.)[6]

3. In the wake of the *Principia*'s publication, philosophers overlooked the importance of the *prisca sapientia* to Newton—despite the fact that he had repeatedly insisted that he had been merely rediscovering a wisdom that had already been discovered in antiquity.

4. We recognize that this statement also directly contradicts Newton's assertion in the Scholium to the Definitions that "in Philosophical disquisitions, we ought to abstract from our senses, and consider things themselves, distinct from what are only sensible measures of them."

5. Galilei, *Two New Sciences*, 153; my emphasis. (And let us remind ourselves here that Galileo's Leaning Tower experiments were actually thought experiments; and let us also remind ourselves here that the monist, materialist focus of Galileo's cosmology was upon the site of all particles'—or of all bodies'—unchanging and immovable Presence(s)—the site that Galileo had recognized to exist as that of the unobservable absolute in the natural world.)

6. Let us briefly remark here on the role that experimentation (or what we may refer to as "experimental philosophy") played in the cosmologies of Galileo and of Newton. As we know, although both Galileo and Newton considered themselves to be true

In Rule IV of "Rules of Reasoning in Philosophy," Newton facetiously asserts that his type of natural philosophy is "experimental philosophy," and he jokes:

> In experimental philosophy we are to *look upon* propositions collected by general induction from phenomena as *accurately or very nearly true*, notwithstanding any contrary hypotheses that may be imagined, till such time as other phenomena occur, by which they may either be made more accurate, or liable to exceptions.[7]

Newton facetiously implies here that his philosophical process is that of "general induction," but we, Newton's uncommon readers, recognize that Newton's philosophical process was (primarily) that of *deduction*, not *induction*; we recognize that Newton performed countless acts of *logical deduction*—acts of mathematics—upon the cosmologies of Archimedes and of Galileo, and found what they had found—and as we know, what all three had found was the site of Divinity's Presence in the natural world.[8]

However, we find that in the wake of the publication of the *Principia*, philosophers did not recognize that Newton was a true philosopher in the Platonic sense, and they did not recognize that Newton's primary interest was in (blindly) seeing "the things themselves, which can only be seen with the eye of the mind"; and philosophers also did not recognize that Newton was not interested in approximate truths, or in the "very nearly true," but in *the certain truth*—and in (that which Newton had

---

philosophers in the Platonic sense, both also recognized the value of exploring sensible, observable reality. And as we know, Galileo and Newton applied the discoveries that they had made from their sensible observations and physical experimentations and engineering feats to furthering their insights into the site of the unobservable absolute in the natural world. (For example, Galileo developed one of the first telescopes, and as we know, it was by way of his astronomical observations that he deduced that all heavy bodies composing any given system of bodies "tend" towards a common center (of gravity). And as has been mentioned, in composing his Law of Universal Gravitation, Newton relied heavily upon the observations of Tycho Brache, of Johannes Kepler, and of Robert Hooke.) Both Galileo and Newton applied the discoveries that they made from their sensible observations and physical experimentations and engineering feats to furthering their insights into the site of all particles'—or of all bodies'—unchanging and immovable Presence(s)—the site that both recognized to exist as that of the unobservable absolute in the natural world—and the site that, as we know, was the monist, materialist focus of both of their cosmologies.

7. Newton, "Rules of Reasoning: Rule IV," *Mathematical Principles*, 1:205; my emphases.

8. As we know, what all three natural philosophers had found by way of their acts of *logical* deduction was the Divine *Logos* himself.

considered to be) *The One Certain Law*: the Divine Logos himself. Instead, eighteenth-century philosophers interpreted Rule IV of Newton's Rules of Reasoning in Philosophy to be an endorsement by Newton both of "experimental philosophy" and of the process of induction in the acquisition of knowledge. And we find that for this reason, they attributed Newton with having authored the scientific method in his *Principia*.[9] (As we know, the scientific method encourages observers to see with their eyes, rather than to see with the eye of the mind, and we recognize that Newton, who was a true philosopher in the Platonic sense, did not actually champion the scientific method in his *Principia*.)

Nevertheless, we find that eighteenth-century readers of the *Principia*, who did not recognize that Newton was a true philosopher in the Platonic sense, interpreted Rule IV of Newton's Rules of Reasoning in Philosophy to serve as textual evidence that the *Principia* itself exists as a celebration of "looking"; they interpreted Rule IV to serve as textual evidence that the *Principia* exists as a celebration both of empiricism and of "experimental philosophy." And for this reason, the *Principia* was interpreted as being an empirical manifesto, and it inaugurated an Empirical Age—an "Age of Enlightenment."

And in consequence, we find that in the years following the *Principia*'s publication, the discipline of natural philosophy, which allowed for explorations of the metaphysical—allowed for explorations of the site of the unobservable absolute in the natural world—gave way to the empirical science of physics; and with it, knowledge of the site of all particles'—or of all bodies'—unchanging and immovable Presence(s)—which, as we know, was the monist, materialist focus of the cosmologies of Archimedes, of Galileo, and of Newton—was lost to the philosophical discourse.

But we ask ourselves here: if knowledge of the site of all particles'—or of all bodies'—unchanging and immovable Presence(s) was lost to the philosophical discourse in the wake of the *Principia*'s publication, how then was the *Principia actually* interpreted in the years following its publication? And if eighteenth-century philosophers and physicists assumed that the *Principia* is an empirical manifesto, how were the (unobservable) metaphysics that lie at the heart of Newton's monist, materialist

---

9. We read that "Newton invented a scientific method which was truly universal in its scope" (Weisstein, "Isaac Newton," para. 4).

cosmology—his four Absolute quantities and his "measured" quantities (and which, as we know, include bodies themselves and their unchanging and immovable present momenta)—read in the years following the *Principia*'s publication?

↭

We find that in the wake of the *Principia*'s publication, philosophers and physicists interpreted Newton's Absolute Time and Absolute Space to exist as an *absolutely-at-rest, abstract backdrop to bodies' motions* in which equal times and equal distances absolutely and indisputably exist, and by way of the existence of which they considered it to be possible to rigorously define all motion and change.[10]

Philosophers and physicists interpreted Newton's "immovable" Absolute Space to itself exist as an absolutely-at-rest Euclidean plane, and they interpreted Newton's "immovable" Absolute Places to exist as the fixed points composing that plane. For example, philosophers and physicists interpreted the following passage from the Scholium to the Definitions to support this reading:

> Now no other [Absolute] places are immoveable, but those that, from infinity to infinity, do all retain the same given positions one to another; and upon this account, must ever remain unmov'd; and do thereby constitute, what I call, immoveable [Absolute] space.[11]

And we may therefore imagine here that philosophers and physicists envisioned Absolute Space to exist as an absolutely-at-rest Euclidean plane, which was composed of absolutely-at-rest points: the Absolute Places themselves.

---

10. In the "Absolute space and time" entry in Wikipedia, para. 5, we read that Absolute Space and Time exist in Newton's cosmology as an abstract "backdrop or stage setting within which physical phenomena occur," which exists distinctly from bodies themselves. (As we know, Newton did nothing in his *Principia* to dissuade his "common" reader from assuming that he considered Absolute Time and Space to exist independently of (and indeed as an abstract backdrop to) the motions of sensible bodies in the natural world, and we find that in the wake of its publication, the *Principia* was "commonly" read. And we note here that this reading of Newton's Absolute Time and Space persists to this very day!)

11. Newton, "Scholium to the Definitions," *Mathematical Principles*, 1:14.

We find that because eighteenth-century philosophers and physicists did not recognize that Newton's *Principia* was written in a secret, hidden code which requires decrypting, they did not recognize that Newton's four Absolute quantities exist as the monist, materialist focus of his cosmology. Philosophers and physicists therefore did not recognize that by Absolute Place(s), Newton actually meant the site of all preexisting/post-existing particles—or of all preexisting/post-existing bodies—themselves, and which exist inextricably from their perseverance (over the course of their trajectories) with their unchanging and immovable presently uniform rectilinear motions. And philosophers and physicists did not recognize that Newton considered the perseverance of (what he called) "immovable" Absolute Place(s) *as* immovable Absolute Place(s) (over the course of their trajectories)—or the Absolute Motions of the Absolute Place(s)—to generate an Absolute Space and an Absolute Time in the natural world in which equal distances and equal times absolutely and indisputably exists.[12]

Philosophers and physicists did not recognize that Newton considered his four Absolute quantities to come into being ever-presently and omni-presently in the natural world—in the coming into being of the site of all particles'—or of all bodies'—unchanging and immovable Presence(s)—in the coming into being of the (multiple and yet simultaneously singular) All/the Only—in the coming into being of God's Presently spoken (and written) Name/Word—his ecstatic, bursting, and resoundingly affirmative, "I AM."

Philosophers and physicists did not recognize that Newton considered the coming into being of his four Absolute quantities in the natural world to bring into being (what Newton referred to as) the "Frame of the System of the World"—the (multiple and yet simultaneously singular) unchanging and immovable (and *material*) referent(s) by which Newton considered it to be possible to rigorously define all motion and change.

And philosophers and physicists also did not recognize that, (like Archimedes and Galileo), Newton did *not* consider the state of absolute rest to exist in the natural world; and they did not recognize that by his

---

12. Philosophers and physicists overlooked the fact that Newton considered geometry—and the generation of continuous magnitudes—to exist as a *subspecies* of mechanics.

term "immoveable," Newton meant unchanging with respect to itself (over the course of its trajectory).¹³

Eighteenth-century philosophers and physicists did not decrypt Newton's secret cosmology, however, and we find that all of this wisdom remained hidden in the wake of the *Principia*'s publication. Instead, and has been mentioned, philosophers and physicists interpreted Newton's Absolute Space and Time to exist as *an abstract backdrop to bodies' motions, which exists independently of bodies themselves*. And for this reason, we find that philosophers and physicists assumed that Newton had authored the concept of an "inertial frame of reference" in his *Principia*. (And let us note here that while historians of science acknowledge that the term "reference frame" was not coined until the nineteenth century, they also assert that the concept of an inertial frame of reference was "implicit in both remarks and procedures to be found in the *Principia*.")¹⁴

What is meant by the concept of an "inertial frame of reference"? We find that a frame of reference itself is defined to be a "standard relative to which motion and rest may be measured"¹⁵ which exists independently

---

13. Eighteenth-century philosophers and physicists overlooked the fact that Newton had asserted in his *Principia* that although the center of the world is immovable, it "either is at rest, or moves uniformly forward in a right line"—and that Newton had revealed to his uncommon reader here that by the term "immoveable," he did not mean absolutely at rest. (We find that over the centuries, philosophers and physicists have been willing to overlook obvious contradictions in their readings of the *Principia*—and that this is the reason why the *Principia* has been (mis)interpreted as being an empirical manifesto over the years. For example, philosophers and physicists have been willing to overlook the fact that Newton had asserted that "in Philosophical disquisitions, we ought to abstract from our senses, and consider things themselves, distinct from what are only sensible measures of them"—and that Newton had revealed to his uncommon reader here that his interests lay in exploring the site of the unobservable absolute in the natural world.)

14. As Huggett and Hoefer report in "Absolute and Relational Theories," in the *Stanford Encyclopedia of Philosophy*, para. 48: "Seeking a replacement for the unobservable Newtonian space, Neumann (1870) and Lange (1885) developed more concrete definitions of the reference frames in which Newton's laws hold. In these and a few other works, the concept of the set of inertial frames was first clearly expressed, though it was implicit in both remarks and procedures to be found in the *Principia*." And we note here that the "term 'reference frame' was coined in the 19th century" (DiSalle, "Space and Time," para. 3). We find that philosophers and physicists also interpreted Newton's phrase "Frame of the System of the World" to allude to (what they assumed that Newton had considered to be) a frame of reference.

15. DiSalle, "Space and Time," para. 1.

of bodies themselves, and that an inertial frame of reference is defined to be a type of reference frame in which equal times and equal distances indisputably exist. An inertial frame of reference is defined to be a frame of reference that is manifesting a state of rest or any other constant velocity motion (over the course of its trajectory), and which is considered to exist as *an abstract backdrop to bodies' motions*. And in mathematical terms, the time of an inertial frame of reference is defined to be linear and continuous, and the space of an inertial frame of reference is defined to be Euclidean, and is considered to be flat, linear, and continuous.

And we find that in addition to assuming that Newton had authored an absolutely-at-rest Absolute Space and Time in his *Principia*, which exists as an abstract "backdrop or stage setting within which physical phenomena occur" and which exists independently of bodies themselves, philosophers and physicists also assumed that Newton had authored *an infinite set of inertial reference frames* that move at a constant velocity in relation to this absolutely-at-rest Absolute Space and Time. Eighteenth-century philosophers and physicists interpreted Newton's Corollary V to suggest that the "given space" of which Newton speaks in Corollary V, and which (as we know) Newton asserts is "at rest, or moves uniformly forwards in a right line without any circular motion" also exists as an inertial frame of reference, and they therefore assumed that it exists as an abstract backdrop to the motions of the bodies of which the system is composed. Philosophers and physicists therefore attributed Newton with inventing the idea of the existence in the natural world of *an infinite set of inertial reference frames*, which move at (an infinite number of) constant velocities with respect to Newton's absolutely-at-rest Absolute Time and Space.

Philosophers and physicists did not recognize that in Corollary V, Newton had actually been exploring the motions of the given system of bodies' common center (of gravity); they did not recognize that Newton had actually been exploring the motions of the particle equivalent of the given system itself—which, being a *particle*, exists inextricably from its perseverance (over the course of its trajectory) with an unchanging and immovable presently uniform rectilinear motion, and therefore exists as a manifestation of the site of all particles'—or of all bodies'—unchanging and immovable Presence(s) in the natural world.[16]

16. Eighteenth-century philosophers and physicists attributed Newton with having authored the idea of the existence in the natural world of an infinite set of inertial frames of reference, which move at an infinite number of constant velocities with

CHAPTER VII. (MIS)READING THE *PRINCIPIA* 231

And as we find that the concept of inertial frames of reference was to be deeply important to all philosophy and physics developed in the wake of the *Principia*'s publication—including to the physics of Einstein—let us explore it further. As has been mentioned, eighteenth-century philosophers and physicists attributed Newton with authoring the concept of inertial frames of reference in his *Principia*, but we recognize that Newton did not actually author the concept of inertial frames of reference in his *Principia*, and we recognize that *Newton himself would not have considered inertial frames of reference to actually exist in the natural world*.[17]

And we find that because eighteenth-century philosophers and physicists did not recognize the importance of the concept of the *kentron*

---

respect to Newton's absolutely-at-rest Absolute Time and Space—but they also recognized that this idea does not make sense, since the Principle of Relativity shows that the state of rest can only be relatively determined. (See DiSalle, "Space and Time," para. 8, who explains to us that philosophers and physicists realized that "there is no way to distinguish [immovable] absolute space itself from any frame of reference that is in uniform motion relative to it . . . an infinity of such spaces [may be determined, all of which move] . . . in uniform rectilinear motion relative to each other.") Philosophers and physicists therefore recognized that it would be impossible to distinguish between Absolute Time and Space and any other inertial frame of reference that was manifesting a uniformly rectilinear motion in relation to it. And in the nineteenth century, the philosopher Ernst Mach asserted that Newton himself did not recognize this obvious contradiction in (what Mach assumed to be) Newton's reasoning because Newton had lived "in an age deficient in epistemological critique" (see Mach, *Science of Mechanics*, 571). We recognize that Newton did not actually author an infinite set of inertial frames of reference in his *Principia*, and that Newton did not consider Absolute Space to be absolutely at rest.

17. Why would Newton not have considered inertial frames of reference to actually exist in the natural world? As we know, (and like Archimedes and Galileo), *Newton did not consider particles—or bodies—to exist distinctly from an absolute space and time in which equal distances and equal times absolutely and indisputably exist*. Rather, and as we know, (like Archimedes and Galileo), Newton recognized that the perseverance of all (preexisting/post-existing) particles—or of all (preexisting/post-existing) bodies—(and which exist inextricably from their unchanging and immovable presently uniform rectilinear motions) *as* (preexisting/post-existing) particles—or *as* (preexisting/post-existing) bodies—(over the course of their trajectories) generates a space and time in the natural world in which equal distances and equal times absolutely exist; and as we know, (and like Archimedes and Galileo), Newton recognized that all (preexisting/post-existing) particles—or all (preexisting/post-existing) bodies exist as the fundamental element(s) of which this absolute space and time is composed, and *that this absolute space and time therefore exists as a substantial/material entity in the natural world*.

toi bareos—the sharp point, center, or pivot of weight—to Newton's cosmology:

— They did not recognize that, (like Archimedes and Galileo), Newton had been interested in exploring the motions of extended physical bodies' centers of gravity; Newton had been interested in exploring the motions of the particle equivalents of the extended physical bodies themselves—which, being *particles*, exist inextricably from their perseverance (over the course of their trajectories) with their unchanging and immovable presently uniform rectilinear motions, and therefore exist as manifestation(s) of the site of all particles'—or of all bodies'—unchanging and immovable Presence(s) in the natural world.

— They did not recognize that, (like Galileo), Newton had been interested in exploring the motions of *systems of bodies'* common centers (of gravity); Newton had been interested in exploring the motions of the particle equivalents of the systems of bodies themselves—which, being *particles*, exist inextricably from their perseverance (over the course of their trajectories) with their unchanging and immovable presently uniform rectilinear motions, and therefore exist as manifestation(s) of the site of all particles'—or of all bodies'—unchanging and immovable Presence(s) in the natural world.

— And they did not recognize that, (like Archimedes and Galileo), Newton had considered the site of all particles'—or of all bodies'—unchanging and immovable Presence(s) to exist as the unchanging and immovable *place(s)* (as in Archimedes's famous cry, "Give me a[n unchanging and immovable] *place* to stand on, and I will move the earth"! [my emphasis]) by which Newton too had considered it to be possible to rigorously define all motion and change. They did not recognize that, (like Archimedes and Galileo), Newton considered the site of all particles'—or of all bodies'—unchanging and immovable Presence(s) to exist as the (multiple and yet simultaneously singular) All/the Only; they did not recognize that he considered it to exist as the unchanging and immovable Fulcrum; and they did not recognize that, (as it was for Archimedes and Galileo), the site of all particles'—or of all bodies'—unchanging and immovable Presence(s)—the Universe itself—was Newton's God.[18]

---

18. They also did not recognize that Newton had referred to the site of all

Instead, we find that eighteenth-century philosophers and physicists built their ideas upon the cosmology of Newton, but they did not recognize Newton's true cosmology. Philosophers and physicists assumed that Newton had authored the concept of inertial frames of reference in his *Principia*, which exist as *abstract backdrops to bodies' motions*, and they assumed that Newton would have therefore considered it to be possible to explore the motions of bodies at rest in inertial frames of reference. Philosophers and physicists did not recognize, however, that Newton would *not* have considered it to be possible to explore the motions of bodies at rest in inertial frames of reference, and they did not recognize that by exploring the motions of bodies at rest in (what they considered to be) inertial frames of reference, they were *actually* exploring the motions of extended physical bodies' centers of gravity; they were *actually* exploring the motions of the particle equivalents of the extended physical bodies themselves—which, being *particles*, exist inextricably from their perseverance (over the course of their trajectories) with their unchanging and immovable presently uniform rectilinear motions, and therefore exist as manifestation(s) of the site of all particles'—or of all bodies'—unchanging and immovable Presence(s) in the natural world. (Ironically, empirical philosophers and physicists did not recognize that by exploring the motions of extended physical bodies' centers of gravity—the particle equivalents of the extended physical bodies themselves—they were *actually* exploring the site of the unobservable absolute in the natural world—the site that, (like Archimedes and Galileo), Newton had considered to be that of Divinity's Presence in the natural world.)

And we find that eighteenth-century philosophers and physicists also extrapolated the idea of the existence of inertial frames of reference in the natural world to the idea of the existence of *non-inertial—or accelerated—frames of reference*. Philosophers and physicists also assumed that it would be possible to explore the motions of bodies at rest in (what they considered to be) accelerated frames of reference.

Why were philosophers and physicists interested in exploring the motions of bodies at rest in (what they considered to be) accelerated frames of reference? Philosophers and physicists recognized that Galileo

---

particles'—or of all bodies'—unchanging and immovable Presence(s) in his cosmology as the Frame of the System of the World, and *they did not recognize that Newton had composed an entirely materialist cosmology.*

had referred to the motions of bodies freely falling under gravity in his cosmology as bodies' "naturally accelerated motions" under gravity, and philosophers and physicists therefore thought of gravity as manifesting in the natural world as an acceleration. Philosophers and physicists therefore assumed that it would be possible to explore the effects of gravity upon bodies by exploring the motions of bodies at rest in (what they considered to be) accelerated frames of reference. Philosophers and physicists did not recognize, however, that *Newton would also not have considered accelerated frames of reference to exist in the natural world*; and they did not recognize that by exploring the motions of bodies at rest in (what they considered to be) accelerated frames of reference, they were *actually* exploring the motions of extended physical bodies' centers of gravity; they were *actually* exploring the motions of the particle equivalents of the extended physical bodies themselves—which, being *particles*, persevere (over the course of their trajectories) with their unchanging and immovable presently uniform rectilinear motions (states of motion from which we know that the particles themselves exist inextricably)—and which, *at the same time*, undergo non-uniform rotations (over the course of their trajectories) as they tend ceaselessly towards their system's common center (of gravity)—towards an unchanging and immovable *place* that exists indistinguishably from the unchanging and immovable *place(s)* that they always already Are.[19] Philosophers and physicists did not recognize that the degree to which the particle equivalents of the extended physical bodies are rotated (over the course of their trajectories) is dependent upon their distances from their system's common center (of gravity), and philosophers and physicists did not recognize that they generate rotating orbital flower patterns as they go.

Finally, we find that eighteenth-century philosophers and physicists also assumed that in his *Principia*, Newton had defined particles to exist as *mathematical point particles* which do not possess extension in space.[20] Philosophers and physicists interpreted Newton's definition

---

19. Philosophers and physicists did not recognize that (what we may refer to as) the presently inertial components of particles' motions (and which exist inextricably from the particles themselves) are orthogonal to (what we may refer to as) the gravitational components of the particles' motions.

20. We read that a "point particle . . . is an idealization of particles heavily used in physics. [The] defining feature [of the point particle] is that it lacks spatial extension:

CHAPTER VII. (MIS)READING THE *PRINCIPIA* 235

of the centripetal force (and let us remind ourselves here that Newton wrote: "A Centripetal force is that by which bodies are drawn or impelled, or any way tend, towards a *point* as to a *centre*" (my emphases)) to serve as textual evidence in support of this idea, but they did not recognize that Newton had written his definition in a facetious tone, and that he had been paying quiet homage to Archimedes, who, as we know, had also done nothing to dissuade his own reader from assuming that he had considered a particle to exist as a point, and not as a point/infinitesimal line segment. Philosophers and physicists did not recognize that, (like Archimedes and Galileo), Newton considered particles to exist not merely as *points*, but rather to exist as points/infinitesimal line segments, which exist *as of two dimensions simultaneously*, and are simultaneously discrete and continuous. Philosophers and physicists did not recognize that, (like Archimedes and Galileo), Newton considered particles to exist as the *dynamically generated* elements of which their *dynamically generated* trajectories are composed, and they did not recognize that Newton considered particles to be *dynamically generated* in the *dynamic generation* of their trajectories.[21] And philosophers and physicists did not recognize that, (like Archimedes and Galileo), Newton considered particles to exist as their trajectories' discrete indivisibles/their continuous infinitesimals; and they did not recognize that Newton did not consider particles to exist prior to, or independently of, their trajectories, but that rather, he considered particles to exist inextricably from their trajectories.[22]

(And let us also briefly note here that although philosophers and physicists appropriated Newton's term "mass" into their equations, they did not recognize that by the term "mass," Newton meant a preexisting/post-existing mass—or equivalently, a preexisting/post-existing particle—or equivalently, a preexisting/post-existing body—and which exists inextricably from its perseverance (over the course of its trajectory) with

---

being zero-dimensional, it does not take up space" ("Point Particle," para. 1).

21. Philosophers and physicists chose to separate Newton's kinematics (or his mathematics of motion; his Calculus) from his mechanics, and, as has been mentioned, they overlooked the fact that Newton had considered geometry—and the generation of continuous magnitudes—to exist as a *subspecies* of mechanics. Philosophers and physicists did not recognize that Newton had derived his definition of the particle directly from his kinematics.

22. Instead, philosophers and physicists considered particles to exist as discrete entities and they considered frames of reference to possess both a continuous space and a continuous time. They did not recognize that Archimedes had solved the problem of determining the relationship between the discrete and the continuous in the natural world in antiquity.

an unchanging and immovable presently uniform rectilinear motion, and which exists as a manifestation of the site of all masses'—or of all particles'—or of all bodies'—unchanging and immovable Presence(s) in the natural world.)

This is the philosophical moment into which Einstein was born. Let us turn now to an exploration of Einstein's cosmology itself, and to seeing what the empiricist Einstein saw with his eyes, rather than with the eye of the mind. Along the way, we will perform the work of the true philosopher upon Einstein's incomplete cosmology, and we will (blindly) "to that original to repair."[23]

---

23. We may offer our reader a brief preview here of what is missing from Einstein's empirical cosmology. As we know, Newton considered all bodies to *at the same time* possess both an (unobservable) unchanging and immovable present aspect and an (observable) changing, instantaneous aspect; and as we know, the focus of Newton's *Principia* was upon all bodies' (unobservable) unchanging and immovable present aspect. We find that knowledge of bodies' (unobservable) unchanging and immovable present aspect is what is missing from Einstein's empirical cosmology, and that by implanting this knowledge into Einstein's incomplete cosmology, we will be able to complete it.

Chapter VIII.

Albert Einstein (1879–1955)

Albert Einstein was a "German-born theoretical physicist who is widely held to be one of the greatest and most influential scientists of all time."[1] He was awarded the Nobel Prize in Physics in 1921.

Einstein's biographers acknowledge that although he was considered to be a relativist by many (most likely because he authored the theories of special and of general *relativity*), his was actually a quest for knowledge of the absolute. As Walter Isaacson writes in *Einstein: His Life and Universe*:

> Einstein . . . was not truly a relativist, even though that is how he was interpreted by many. . . . Beneath all of his theories, including relativity, was a quest for invariants, certainties, absolutes. There was a harmonious reality underlying the laws of the universe, Einstein felt, and the goal of science was discover it.[2]

And although Einstein would spend his later years searching for this underlying harmonious reality, his biographers acknowledge that sadly, Einstein did not find it. Einstein did not recognize that Newton (and the natural philosophers upon whose cosmologies Newton had built his own—Archimedes and Galileo) had already found this underlying harmonious reality, and Einstein did not recognize that all had composed secret, hidden cosmologies, which require decrypting.

Let us turn now to an exploration of Einstein's incomplete cosmology, so that we may complete it.

---

1. "Albert Einstein," para. 1.
2. Isaacson, *Einstein*, 3.

Einstein's cosmology comprises his theory of special relativity (1905) and his theory of general relativity (1907–15). We find that the concept of frames of reference—both inertial and accelerated—is central to Einstein's cosmology. As has been mentioned, Einstein built his cosmology upon the cosmology of Newton, but he did not recognize Newton's true cosmology, and he did not recognize that *Newton would not have considered frames of reference to actually exist in the natural world.*

As we will see, in his theory of special relativity, Einstein explored the motions of bodies at rest in (what he considered to be) inertial frames of reference. However, Einstein did not recognize that by exploring the motions of bodies at rest in (what he considered to be) inertial frames of reference, he was *actually* exploring the motions of the extended physical bodies' centers of gravity; he was *actually* exploring the motions of the particle equivalents of the extended physical bodies themselves—which, being *particles*, exist inextricably from their perseverance (over the course of their trajectories) with their unchanging and immovable presently uniform rectilinear motions, and therefore exist as manifestation(s) of the site of all particles'—or of all bodies'—unchanging and immovable Presence(s) in the natural world. (Ironically, the empiricist Einstein did not recognize that in his theory of special relativity, he was actually exploring the site of the unobservable absolute in the natural world—the site that, (like Archimedes and Galileo), Newton had considered to be that of Divinity's Presence in the natural world.)

And in his theory of general relativity, Einstein explored the motions of bodies at rest in (what he considered to be) accelerated frames of reference. (In the theory of general relativity, Einstein was interested in exploring the effects of gravity upon bodies, and he recognized that Galileo had referred to the motions of bodies freely falling under gravity in his cosmology as bodies' "naturally accelerated motions" under gravity. Einstein therefore thought of gravity as manifesting in the natural world as an acceleration, and he assumed that it would be possible to explore the effects of gravity upon bodies by exploring the motions of bodies at rest in (what he considered to be) accelerated frames of reference.) Einstein did not recognize, however, that by exploring the motions of bodies at rest in (what he considered to be) accelerated frames of reference, he was *actually* exploring the motions of the extended physical bodies' centers of gravity; he was *actually* exploring the motions of the particle equivalents of the extended physical bodies themselves—which, being *particles*, persevere (over the course of their trajectories) with their unchanging and immovable presently uniform rectilinear motions (states of motion from which we know that the particles themselves exist inextricably)—and which, *at the same time*, undergo non-uniform rotations (over the course of their trajectories) as they tend ceaselessly towards their system's common center (of gravity)—towards an unchanging and immovable *place* that exists indistinguishably from the unchanging and immovable *place(s)* that they always already Are.[3] Einstein did not recognize that the degree to which the particle equivalents of the extended physical bodies are rotated (over the course of their trajectories) is dependent upon their distances from their system's common center (of gravity), and he did not recognize that they generate rotating flower patterns as they go.

Einstein did not recognize that in special relativity, he was exploring bodies' unchanging and immovable presently uniform rectilinear motions—which, as we know, exist inextricably from the bodies themselves; and Einstein did not recognize that in general relativity, he was exploring bodies' changing, instantaneous motions under gravity. Einstein also did not recognize that all bodies *at the same time* possess both unchanging and immovable presently uniform rectilinear motions (and from which the bodies themselves exist inextricably) and changing, instantaneous motions; and Einstein did not recognize that bodies' unchanging and immovable presently uniform rectilinear motions (and from which the bodies themselves exist inextricably) are more fundamental to them (and to their trajectories) than their changing, instantaneous motions, since their unchanging and immovable presently uniform rectilinear motions (and from which the bodies themselves exist inextricably) exist "before" and "after" their changing, instantaneous motions—even as, *at the same time*, they also exist as the site(s) at which passing time is always already vanquished, or overcome (with respect to the generation of their trajectories). Einstein also did not recognize that it is possible to rigorously define all bodies' ever-changing, instantaneous motions under gravity in relation to their unchanging and immovable presently uniform rectilinear motions (and from which the bodies themselves exist inextricably).

---

3. Einstein did not recognize that (what we may refer to as) the presently inertial components of particles' motions (and which exist inextricably from the particles themselves) are orthogonal to (what we may refer to as) the gravitational components of the particles' motions.

And we find that although Einstein built his cosmology upon the cosmology of Newton, he did not recognize that, (like Archimedes and Galileo), the focus of Newton's cosmology had been upon the site of all particles'—or of all bodies'—unchanging and immovable Presence(s). Einstein did not recognize that, (like Archimedes and Galileo), Newton had considered the site of all particles'—or of all bodies'—unchanging and immovable Presence(s) to exist as the unchanging and immovable (and *material*) referent(s) by which it is possible to rigorously define all particles'—or all bodies'—changing, instantaneous motions under gravity. Einstein did not recognize that, (like Archimedes and Galileo), Newton had considered the site of all particles'—or of all bodies'—unchanging and immovable Presence(s) to exist as the site of the (multiple and yet simultaneously singular) All/the Only; he did not recognize that Newton had considered it to exist as the unchanging and immovable Fulcrum; and he did not recognize that, (as it had been for Archimedes and Galileo), the site of all particles'—or of all bodies'—unchanging and immovable Presence(s)—the Universe itself—was Newton's God.[4]

Instead, we find that the site of all particles'—or of all bodies'—unchanging and immovable Presence(s) is missing from Einstein's empirical cosmology, and that Einstein's cosmology remains incomplete. Let us turn now to an exploration of Einstein's cosmology itself.

THE THEORY OF SPECIAL RELATIVITY (1905)

Einstein developed his theory of special relativity in the wake of James Clerk Maxwell's groundbreaking nineteenth-century discoveries in the field of electromagnetism. In 1865, Maxwell published four equations which revealed that light exists in the natural world as an electromagnetic wave that propagates through empty space at a constant speed. Along with the publication of Maxwell's equations, a question arose: relative to what object, or relative to what entity, does light propagate at a constant speed? Maxwell's equations themselves did not say.[5]

---

4. Einstein did not recognize that Newton had referred to the site of all particles'—or of all bodies'—unchanging and immovable Presence(s) in his cosmology as the Frame of the System of the World; and *Einstein did not recognize that Newton had composed an entirely materialist cosmology.*

5. At around this time, the concept of the existence of an "ether," a "theorized medium for the propagation of light," was proposed. We read, "In the 19th century, luminiferous aether (or ether), meaning light-bearing aether, was a theorized medium for the propagation of light (electromagnetic radiation). However, a series of increasingly

Einstein's answer to this question—which he published in his theory of special relativity some forty years later—was to propose that light travels at a constant speed through empty space "relative to anything and everything."[6] Einstein proposed that light travels through empty space at a constant, invariant, and absolute speed—regardless of the inertial motion of any observer of it, and regardless of the inertial motion of the source of light. This idea exists as the kernel of special relativity, and it has profound implications on the way observers (all of whom in the theory are considered to be at rest in inertial frames of reference) measure distances and times.[7]

Einstein's theory of special relativity therefore concerns itself with *how* different observers, all of whom are considered to be at rest in inertial frames of reference, measure distances and times differently, since all agree that the speed of light is invariant and absolute. (We note here that the source of light in special relativity is considered to be manifesting a constant velocity motion relative to an at-rest inertial frame of reference.) *In special relativity, each observer is considered to be at rest within his or her (or its) own inertial frame of reference, and each inertial frame of reference is considered to be manifesting a different constant velocity (relative to another inertial frame of reference, which is also manifesting a constant velocity).* As Wikipedia explains:

> Albert Einstein's 1905 *special theory of relativity* postulated that the speed of light through empty space has one definite value—a constant—that is independent of the motion of the light source. Einstein's equations described important consequences of this fact: [that] distances and times between pairs of events vary when measured in different *inertial frames of reference*.[8]

---

complex experiments had been carried out in the late 1800s like the Michelson-Morley experiment in an attempt to detect the motion of Earth through the aether, and had failed to do so" ("Aether Theories," para. 8). And as we will see, Einstein would propose that the ether does not exist in the natural world.

6. This is not actually Einstein's wording, but it is the wording of Brian Greene, who summarizes Einstein's accomplishments in *Fabric of the Cosmos*, 45.

7. In special relativity, observers are considered to be bodies at rest in inertial frames of reference that are manifesting constant velocities.

8. "Spacetime," para. 2.

❧

We find that Einstein's theory of special relativity depends upon—and requires—the existence in the natural world of inertial frames of reference.[9] As has been mentioned, Einstein built his cosmology upon the cosmology of Newton, but he did not recognize Newton's true cosmology, and he did not recognize that Newton himself would not have considered inertial frames of reference to actually exist in the natural world. And Einstein did not recognize that by exploring the motions of bodies at rest in (what he considered to be) inertial frames of reference, he was *actually* exploring the motions of the extended physical bodies' centers of gravity; he was *actually* exploring the motions of the particle equivalents of the extended physical bodies themselves—which, being *particles*, exist inextricably from their perseverance (over the course of their trajectories) with their unchanging and immovable presently uniform rectilinear motions, and therefore exist as manifestation(s) of the site of all particles'—or of all bodies'—unchanging and immovable Presence(s) in the natural world. (Ironically, the empiricist Einstein did not recognize that in his theory of special relativity, he was actually exploring the site of the unobservable absolute in the natural world.)

❧

As has been mentioned, Einstein's theory of special relativity proposes that light travels at a constant, invariant, and absolute speed "relative to anything and everything." But we ask ourselves here: what precisely does this mean? We interpret this statement to mean that light travels at a constant, invariant, and absolute speed relative to all bodies at rest in (what Einstein considered to be) inertial frames of reference—or, more accurately, we interpret this statement to mean that light travels at a constant, invariant, and absolute speed relative to the site of all particles'—or of all bodies'—unchanging and immovable Presence(s) in the natural world.

---

9. We ask ourselves here: Do inertial frames of reference *actually* exist in the natural world? As we know, Newton would *not* have considered inertial frames of reference to actually exist in the natural world, and we find that today, philosophers and physicists acknowledge that the concept of inertial frames of reference is *an idealization that does not actually exist*. We read: "the statement that 'nothing is at absolute rest' is loosely equivalent to saying that there are no frames of reference which are truly inertial" ("Rest (Physics)," para. 3).

And since we recognize that light travels at a constant, invariant, and absolute speed relative to the site of all particles'—or of all bodies'—unchanging and immovable Presence(s), we recognize that *light itself therefore exists indistinguishably from the site of all particles'—or of all bodies'—unchanging and immovable Presence(s)*. We recognize that light therefore exists as a *manifestation* of the site of all particles'—or of all bodies'—unchanging and immovable Presence(s), and that light therefore manifests in the natural world as a particle, which exists inextricably from its perseverance (over the course of its trajectory) with an unchanging and immovable presently uniform rectilinear motion.

(Interestingly, we find that Newton had been fascinated with the properties of light, and that he followed his *Principia* of 1687 with a work entitled *Opticks* of 1704, in which he explored the properties of light. Newton reveals to us in *Opticks* that he considered light to exist as a particle in the natural world; and towards the end of *Opticks*, he implies that, under gravity, light particles—being *particles*—persevere (over the course of their trajectories) with their unchanging and immovable presently uniform rectilinear motions (states of motion from which we know that Newton considered the particles to exist inextricably)—even as, *at the same time*, they also undergo non-uniform rotations (over the course of their trajectories) as they tend ceaselessly towards their system's common center (of gravity)—towards an unchanging and immovable *place* that exists indistinguishably from the unchanging and immovable *place(s)* that they always already Are. In the third and last book of his *Opticks*, Newton muses:

> Do not Bodies act upon Light at a distance, and by their action bend its rays, and is not this action (*cæteris paribus*) strongest at the least distance?[10]

(And we find that Newton also reveals to his uncommon reader here that he considered the degree to which light particles are non-uniformly rotated (over the course of their trajectories) to be dependent upon their distances from their system's common center (of gravity), and that he considered the light particles to generate rotating flower patterns as they go.))[11]

---

10. Newton, "Obs. XI, Query 1," *Opticks*.

11. We may deduce that Newton considered Bodies to act upon Light, and Light to act upon Bodies, and all to tend ceaselessly towards *their system's common center (of gravity)*—its *kentron toi bareos*—and to generate rotating flower patterns as they go.

As has been mentioned, Maxwell's equations showed that light exists in the natural world as a wave, and we recognize that Einstein's theory of special relativity showed that light exists in the natural world as a particle. We find that Einstein conducted another experiment in 1905 (the same year in which he proposed his theory of special relativity) that also revealed that light exists in the natural world as a particle. In 1905, Einstein also published a paper on "the photoelectric effect" in which he suggested that light behaves as a particle, and we find that scholars attribute Einstein with having developed the concept of the photon. We read, "The concept [of the photon] originated (1905) in Albert Einstein's explanation of the photoelectric effect, in which he proposed the existence of discrete energy packets during the transmission of light."[12]

Maxwell's equations revealed that light exists as a wave in the natural world, and Einstein's theory of special relativity—and his explorations of the photoelectric effect—revealed that light exists as a particle in the natural world.[13] And in 1924, Louis de Broglie suggested that all matter—light included—manifests a wave/particle duality.[14]

We find that there are two postulates upon which Einstein constructed his theory of special relativity. The two postulates are as follows:

— The laws of physics are the same in all inertial frames of reference.

— The speed of light is the same in all inertial frames of reference.[15]

And we ask ourselves here: why is it true that the laws of physics— Newton's Laws—are the same in all inertial frames of reference? As we

---

12. Augustyn, "Photon," para. 1.

13. Interestingly, we find that the debate concerning whether light exists as a wave or as a particle in the natural world originated with Robert Hooke and Isaac Newton in the seventeenth century. Hooke asserted that light exists as a wave, and Newton asserted that light exists as a particle. (And historians report that "Newton withheld publication of his *Opticks* until after Hooke's death in 1703—so that Newton could have the last word on the subject of light." (See Pickover, *Archimedes to Hawking*, 114.))

14. We recognize that since all matter exists *as of two dimensions simultaneously*, it possesses both a (discrete) punctiform aspect and a (continuous) infinitesimal aspect, which allows it to *at the same time* manifest both as a particle and as a wave.

15. Norton, "Special Theory of Relativity."

know, the focus of Newton's Laws was upon all preexisting/post-existing particles—or all preexisting/post-existing bodies—themselves, which exist inextricably from their perseverance (over the course of their trajectories) with their unchanging and immovable presently uniform rectilinear motions; the focus of Newton's Laws was upon the site of all particles'—or of all bodies'—unchanging and immovable Presence(s).

And as we know, although Newton himself would not have considered inertial frames of reference to actually exist in the natural world, by exploring the motions of bodies at rest in (what Einstein considered to be) inertial frames of reference, Einstein had *actually* been exploring the motions of the extended physical bodies' centers of gravity; he had *actually* been exploring the particle equivalents of the extended physical bodies themselves—which, being *particles*, exist inextricably from their perseverance (over the course of their trajectories) with their unchanging and immovable presently uniform rectilinear motions, and therefore exist as manifestation(s) of the site of all particles'—or of all bodies'—unchanging and immovable Presence(s) in the natural world.

We recognize that the laws of physics are the same in (what Einstein considered to be) all inertial frames of reference because the focus of the Laws was upon the site of all particles'—or of all bodies'—unchanging and immovable Presence(s)—which, we recognize, was the site that Einstein had *actually* been exploring when he was exploring the motions of bodies at rest in (what he considered to be) inertial frames of reference.

We find that one consequence of Einstein's theory of special relativity is that the state of (observable) absolute simultaneity does not exist in the natural world; we read that observers in the theory of special relativity "come to different conclusions about which events happen simultaneously ('at the same time')."[16] However, and as we know, Galileo and Newton recognized that we all always already exist as the (multiple and yet simultaneously singular) manifestation(s) of (unobservable) absolute simultaneity in the natural world; we all always already exist as the (multiple and yet simultaneously singular) manifestation(s) of the divine

---

16. We read: "In special relativity . . . simultaneity is relative. . . . Observers moving relative to one another come to different conclusions about which events happen simultaneously ('at the same time'). They agree only about what events there are, not about where or when these events take place" (see "Special Relativity/ Elementary Tour," para. 1).

246 PARADISE IS NOW

origin(s) of reality—which come into being Presently, and which exist as the site(s) at which passing time is always already vanquished, or overcome, in the natural world.

◦

Let us turn now to an exploration of the theory of general relativity. In an effort to keep his computations simple in his theory of special relativity, Einstein had neglected to explore the effects of gravity upon bodies.[17] He explored these effects in his theory of general relativity.

THE THEORY OF GENERAL RELATIVITY (1907-15)

As we know, Einstein was an empiricist, who saw with his eyes. We find that Einstein took Galileo to be his forefather—he dubbed Galileo "the father of modern physics and in fact of the whole of modern natural science"[18]—and Einstein assumed that Galileo had been an empiricist, like himself.[19] (Einstein also assumed that Newton had followed Galileo's lead, and that Newton too had been an empiricist.) Einstein did not recognize that both Galileo and Newton had been true philosophers in the Platonic sense, who had devoted their lives to exploring the site of all particles'—or of all bodies'—unchanging and immovable Presence(s)— the site that both had considered to be that of the unobservable absolute in the natural world. Instead, Einstein saw Galileo's and Newton's cosmologies only with his eyes. And in consequence, we find that Einstein built his ideas regarding the effects of gravity upon all particles—or all bodies—in the natural world upon (what he assumed to be) Galileo's and Newton's ideas, but that he did not see Galileo's and Newton's true ideas.

Einstein did not recognize that Galileo and Newton had considered all particles—or all bodies—to exist inextricably from their perseverance (over the course of their trajectories) with their unchanging and

---

17. See Greene, *Fabric of the Cosmos*, 62–63, in which he writes that "in special relativity, to keep the analysis tractable, [Einstein] had completely ignored gravity."

18. Einstein, "Theoretical Physics," 164.

19. Einstein interpreted Galileo's facetious statement regarding "experimental philosophy" in the opening of Day 3 of his *Dialogues Concerning Two New Sciences* to serve as evidence of Galileo's being an empiricist. However, Einstein did not recognize that Galileo had been writing in a facetious tone, and Einstein did not recognize that Galileo had been a disciple of the "superhuman" Archimedes, who had also written in a facetious tone in his own writings.

CHAPTER VIII. ALBERT EINSTEIN   247

immovable presently uniform rectilinear motions; and *Einstein did not recognize that Galileo and Newton had distinguished in their cosmologies between bodies' apparent motions under gravity and their actual motions under gravity.* Einstein did not recognize that Galileo and Newton had seen that although to observers located within a given system of bodies, freely falling particles—or bodies—*appear* to manifest linear trajectories (over the course of their trajectories), *in truth*, the freely falling particles—or bodies—are *actually* non-uniformly rotated (over the course of their trajectories) as they tend ceaselessly towards their system's common center (of gravity)—towards an unchanging and immovable *place* that itself exists indistinguishably from the unchanging and immovable *place(s)* that they always already Are. Einstein did not recognize that Galileo and Newton had seen that the degree to which the freely falling particles—or bodies—are non-uniformly rotated (over the course of their trajectories) is dependent upon their distances from their system's common center (of gravity), and Einstein did not recognize that they generate rotating flower patterns as they go.

Instead, Einstein himself saw only with his eyes, and he was only aware of (what Galileo and Newton had considered to be) bodies' *apparent* motions under gravity. Einstein assumed that (what Galileo and Newton had considered to be) bodies' *apparent* motions under gravity were in fact bodies' *actual* motions under gravity. *And Einstein therefore assumed that, under gravity, freely falling bodies simply undergo changes in speed—or changes in the rates at which they fall—as they fall (over the course of their trajectories).* As we will see, Einstein composed a highly complex cosmology to account for (what Galileo and Newton had considered to be) bodies' *actual* motions under gravity. However, we find that because Einstein did not recognize the existence of the site of all particles'—or of all bodies'—unchanging and immovable Presence(s) in the natural world, Einstein's cosmology is not as complete as Galileo's and Newton's true cosmologies. *And shockingly, we find that Einstein did not discover anything that had not already been discovered by Galileo and Newton, centuries before.*

Contemporary philosophers and physicists also acknowledge that Einstein's cosmology fails to provide us with answers to several fundamental physical problems. (And we find that these problems exist in Einstein's cosmology because Einstein did not recognize the existence of the site of all particles'—or of all bodies'—unchanging and immovable Presence(s) in the natural world. However, we also recognize that by implanting the site of all particles'—or of all bodies'—unchanging and immovable Presence(s) into Einstein's empirical cosmology, we will be able to solve all of the unsolved problems.) The problems are as follows:

i. General relativity fails to account for the inertial properties of matter.

As physicist D.W. Sciama wrote in 1953:

> As Einstein has pointed out, general relativity does not account satisfactorily for the inertial properties of matter, so that an adequate theory of inertia is still lacking.[20]

And as physicist Abraham Pais remarked in 2005, the origin of inertia remains a mystery to philosophy and to physics, even today. Pais wrote, "It must . . . be said that the origin of inertia is and remains the most obscure subject in the theory of particles and fields."[21]

As we know, the origin of inertia—or of a particle's—or body's—tendency to persevere (over the course of its trajectory) with an unchanging and immovable *presently* uniform rectilinear motion—a state of motion from which we know that the particle—or body—itself exists inextricably—was the subject addressed by the cosmologies of Archimedes, of Galileo, and of Newton. And as we know, Archimedes, Galileo, and Newton considered (what today is called) inertia to arise in the coming into being of all particles—or bodies—themselves; in the coming into being of the site of all particles'—or of all bodies'—unchanging and immovable Presence(s); in the coming into being of the (multiple and yet simultaneously singular) divine origin(s) of reality; in the coming into being of we ourselves.

ii. General relativity fails to provide an adequate explanation for Newton's bucket experiment; it fails to provide an explanation for why sensible bodies recede from "the axe of motion" when they accelerate relative to Newton's Absolute Place(s) (whose Absolute Motions, we know, (over the course of their trajectories) bring into being in the natural world an Absolute Space and an Absolute Time—bring into being the Frame of the System of the World)—but not when they accelerate relative to another sensible body.

---

20. Sciama, "On the Origin of Inertia," 34.
21. Pais, *Subtle Is the Lord*, 287.

CHAPTER VIII. ALBERT EINSTEIN 249

As Michael Friedman explains in his *Foundations of Space-Time Theories: Relativistic Physics and the Philosophy of Science* (1983):

> In the end, therefore, general relativity does not solve ... Newton's problem of the rotating bucket. ... General relativity ... predicts that if S_1 and S_2 were alone in the universe, it would still be possible for one and only one of them to experience distorting differential effects.[22]

—and Friedman asserts that the one who would experience the differential effects—the one who would recede from the axe of motion—would be the one who was accelerating with respect to (what philosophers and physicists still consider to be Newton's absolutely-at-rest) Absolute Space. As we know, the one who would experience the differential effects—the one who would recede from the axe of motion—would be the one who was accelerating with respect to Newton's Absolute Place(s) (whose Absolute Motions, we know, (over the course of their trajectories) bring into being in the natural world an Absolute Space and an Absolute Time—bring into being the Frame of the System of the World); the one who would experience the differential effects would be the one who was accelerating respect to the site of all particles'—or all bodies'—unchanging and immovable Presence(s)—and the site that Newton had considered to be that of the Divine Logos's unchanging and immovable Presence in the natural world.

iii. As we will see, in his theory of general relativity, the empiricist Einstein takes issue with the existence of Newton's unobservable, metaphysical Absolute Space and Time in the natural world, and in consequence, Einstein seeks to purge Absolute Space and Time from physics.[23] We find that in this effort, Einstein fails.

Einstein recognizes that the definition of inertial motion requires the existence of a space and a time in which equal distances and equal times absolutely and indisputably exist, but he wonders: does such a space and time *actually* exist in the natural world? Einstein recognizes that Newton's Absolute Space and Time exist in Newton's cosmology as the site of an unobservable and absolute metaphysics, and the empiricist

---

22. Friedman, *Foundations*, 211.
23. Although Einstein takes issue with all of Newton's metaphysics, Einstein largely ignores Newton's Absolute Place and Motion; and Einstein does not recognize that Newton's metaphysics include his "measured" quantities, and extends even to bodies themselves, and to their unchanging and immovable present momenta.

Einstein seeks to remove this unobservable and absolute metaphysics from physics. And Einstein attempts to remove this metaphysics from physics by relativizing all motion—by showing that there exists no physical distinction in the natural world between inertial motion and accelerated motion. However, (and as has been mentioned), in this endeavor, Einstein fails.

As Robert DiSalle reports in his *Understanding Space-Time* of 2006, "By the late 1960's . . . [the general consensus among philosophers and physicists was] that general relativity did not 'relativize' all motion."[24] (See also Michel Janssen's "Einstein's Quest for General Relativity, 1907–1920" in *The Cambridge Companion to Einstein*, in which Janssen examines "four different ways in which Einstein, between 1907 and 1918, tried to relativize all motion and [Janssen explains] how and why each of these attempts failed.")[25]

And as we know, Archimedes, Galileo, and Newton recognized that *indeed there exists a genuine physical distinction in the natural world between inertial motion and accelerated motion*; and as we know, all three proposed that under gravity, all particles—or all bodies—persevere (over the course of their trajectories) with their unchanging and immovable presently uniform rectilinear (or *inertial*) motions (motions from which the particles—or bodies—themselves exist inextricably)—even as, *at the same time*, they undergo rotations that are responsible for producing their changing, instantaneous motions (and by way of the existence of which, we are able to discern the passage of time in the natural world). As we know, all three considered the site of all particles—or of all bodies—(and which exist inextricably from their perseverance (over the course of their trajectories) with their unchanging and immovable presently uniform rectilinear motions) to exist as the site of all particles'—or of all bodies'—unchanging and immovable Presence(s) in the natural world; and as we know, all three considered the site of all particles'—or of all bodies'—unchanging and immovable Presence(s) to exist as the unchanging and immovable (and *material*) referent(s) by which it is possible to rigorously define all bodies' changing, instantaneous (or accelerated) motions under gravity.

24. DiSalle, *Understanding Space-Time*, 5.
25. Janssen, "Einstein's Quest," 173.

CHAPTER VIII. ALBERT EINSTEIN 251

iv. Although the empiricist Einstein sought to empiricize physics in his theory of general relativity, philosophers and physicists recognize that (ironically), an unobservable and absolute metaphysics lies at the heart of Einstein's own cosmology.

As we will see, one year after Einstein had begun to compose his theory of general relativity, Hermann Minkowski, Einstein's former mathematics professor at the Eidgenössische Polytechnikum in Zurich, invented the concept of "space-time." Minkowski conceived of his space-time as being an *abstract backdrop to bodies' motions, which exists independently of bodies themselves.* We find that Einstein incorporated Minkowki's space-time into his own cosmology, and that he built his theory of general relativity upon it. And as we will see, philosophers and physicists recognize that space-time in the theory of general relativity is as unobservable and absolute a structure as is Newton's Absolute Time and Space.

As Robert DiSalle writes in his *Understanding Space-Time* of 2006: "As a recent philosopher noted . . . general relativity turned out to be 'no less absolutistic about space-time than Newton's theory was about space.'"[26] DiSalle continues: "By the late 1960s . . . [the general consensus among philosophers and physicists was] that space-time in general relativity was in some respects the same sort of metaphysical entity as it had been in Newtonian mechanics—at the very least, both theories characterize space-time geometry as an objective physical structure."[27]

We also find that because the site of all particles'—or of all bodies'—unchanging and immovable Presence(s) is missing from Einstein's empirical cosmology, Einstein composed an *entirely abstract cosmology* in which the site of ultimate substance and of what Presently Is (which, as we know, all of the natural philosophers whose cosmologies we have explored in this text had considered to exist as the site at which *substance/ materiality* itself is realized in the natural world) is missing. We recognize that what is missing from Einstein's empirical cosmology is (what all had considered to be) the (multiple and yet simultaneously singular) All/the Only—the site of (what all had considered to be) Divinity's

---

26. DiSalle, *Understanding Space-Time*, 15.
27. DiSalle, *Understanding Space-Time*, 5.

unchanging and immovable Presence in the natural world—and the site of we ourselves.[28]

Let us turn now to an exploration of the theory of general relativity.

THE THEORY OF GENERAL RELATIVITY (1907-15)

As a way of introducing our reader to the rather complicated theory of general relativity, it will be helpful for us to briefly remind ourselves of what we have learned thus far.

As has been mentioned, Einstein was an empiricist, who saw with his eyes. Einstein took Galileo to be his forefather, and Einstein recognized that Galileo had referred to the motions of bodies freely falling under gravity in his cosmology as bodies' "naturally accelerated motions" under gravity. Einstein himself therefore thought of gravity as manifesting in the natural world as an acceleration. And in his theory of general relativity, Einstein explored the effects of gravity upon bodies by considering gravity to exist in the natural world as an acceleration. We find that in Einstein's theory of general relativity, he explored bodies at rest in (what he considered to be) accelerated frames of reference. (Einstein famously conducted thought experiments in which he imagined bodies at rest in freely falling elevators.)[29] However, Einstein did not recognize that by exploring the motions of bodies at rest in (what he considered to be) accelerated frames of reference, he was *actually* exploring the motions of the extended physical bodies' centers of gravity; he was *actually* exploring

---

28. Why is this site missing from Einstein's empirical cosmology? As has been mentioned, in large part, we may attribute modernity's loss of knowledge of the site of the unobservable absolute in the natural world—its loss of self-knowledge—to philosophers' and physicists' (mis)readings of the *Principia* in the wake of its publication. As we know, their (mis)readings inaugurated an Empirical Age in which knowledge of the site of the unobservable absolute was lost to the philosophical discourse. And we recognize that the early modern moment, in which self-knowledge was lost, was a moment of profound anxiety (which is not unlike our present, "postmodern" moment, which is also a moment of profound anxiety); it was a moment that birthed, for example, Edvard Munch's *Scream*, and two World Wars.

Let us also make mention here that although Einstein famously wrote, "I, at any rate, am convinced that *He* [God] does not throw dice," we recognize that it is God himself—the (multiple and yet simultaneously singular) All/the Only—the Universe itself—that is missing from Einstein's empirical cosmology. (See Einstein's December 1926 Letter to Max Born, in *Collected Papers of Einstein*, 15:654.)

29. See "Einstein's Thought Experiments," para. 39, in which we read that "Einstein ... refined his thought experiment to consider a man inside a large enclosed chest or elevator falling freely in space."

the motions of the particle equivalents of the extended physical bodies themselves—which, being *particles*, persevere (over the course of their trajectories) with their unchanging and immovable presently uniform rectilinear motions (states of motion from which we know that the particles themselves exist inextricably)—and which, *at the same time*, undergo non-uniform rotations (over the course of their trajectories) as they tend ceaselessly towards their system's common center (of gravity)—towards an unchanging and immovable *place* that exists indistinguishably from the unchanging and immovable *place(s)* that they always already Are. Einstein did not recognize that the degree to which the particle equivalents of the extended physical bodies are non-uniformly rotated (over the course of their trajectories) is dependent upon their distances from their system's common center (of gravity); and Einstein did not recognize that they generate rotating flowers patterns as they go.

Instead, although Einstein took Galileo to be his forefather, Einstein did not see Galileo's true cosmology; and although Einstein built his cosmology upon the cosmology of Newton, Einstein did not see Newton's true cosmology either. Einstein did not recognize that both Galileo and Newton had distinguished in their cosmologies between bodies' *apparent* motions under gravity and bodies' *actual* motions under gravity; and therefore, *Einstein assumed that, under gravity, freely falling bodies simply undergo changes in speed—or changes in the rates at which they fall—as they fall (over the course of their trajectories).* As has been mentioned, Einstein composed a highly complex cosmology to account for (what Galileo and Newton had considered to be) bodies' *actual* motions under gravity.[30] And we find that because Einstein's cosmology is highly complex— so complex, in fact, that late in life, Einstein joked that he himself did not understand it[31]—three years after Einstein had completed his general theory, and in a short paper entitled, "Prinzipielles zur allgemeinen Relativitatstheorie" ("Foundations of General Relativity"), Einstein attempted

---

30. —And this, despite the fact that Einstein (ostensibly) valued simplicity. Einstein is attributed with having said, "Everything should be made as simple as possible, but not simpler"—although it turns out that this statement is actually apocryphal. In 1933, Einstein actually made the following rather complicated statement regarding simplicity: "It can scarcely be denied that the supreme goal of all theory is to make the irreducible basic elements as simple and as few as possible without having to surrender the adequate representation of a single datum of experience" (Einstein, "On the Method," 165).

31. Einstein joked, "Since the mathematicians have invaded the theory of relativity, I do not understand it myself anymore" (quoted in Sommerfeld, "Albert Einstein's 70th Birthday," 102).

to clarify his ideas by defining the three principles upon which he had based his theory. As Abraham Pais explains in his *Subtle Is the Lord: The Science and the Life of Albert Einstein*, the three principles upon which Einstein based his theory of general relativity are as follows:

Mach's principle

The principle of equivalence

The principle of relativity as expressed by general covariance.[32]

And as a way of coming to understand the general theory of relativity itself, let us briefly explore each principle, noting as we go what is missing from Einstein's ideas, and how we may "to that original to repair."

i. Mach's principle

As has been mentioned, in his theory of general relativity, Einstein took issue with the existence in Newton's cosmology of Newton's unobservable, metaphysical Absolute Space and Time, and in consequence, he sought to purge Newton's Absolute Space and Time from physics. Scholars report that in these ideas, Einstein had been influenced by the nineteenth-century philosopher Ernst Mach, who had also taken issue with Newton's Absolute Space and Time in his own writings.

As Nick Huggett and Carl Hoefer explain in the "Absolute and Relational Theories of Space and Motion" entry in the *Stanford Encyclopedia of Philosophy*, the "most sustained, comprehensive, and influential attack on absolute space was made by [the philosopher] Ernst Mach in his *Science of Mechanics* (1883)."[33] Let us return now to the nineteenth century so that we may see what Mach sees about Absolute Time and Space.

In his *Science of Mechanics*, Mach complains that Newton's Absolute Time and Space are metaphysical constructions, inaccessible to empirical interrogation, which are embedded within an otherwise empirical manifesto. (And Mach asserts that the *Principia* is an empirical manifesto despite the fact that Newton had insisted that quantities encountered in empirical analyses would be of interest only to the "common" and

---

32. Pais, *Subtle Is the Lord*, 287.
33. Huggett and Hoefer, "Absolute and Relational Theories," para. 50.

"vulgar" people.) Mach recognizes that the definition of inertial motion requires the existence of a space and a time in which equal distances and equal times absolutely and indisputably exist, but he wonders: does such a space and time *actually* exist in the natural world? Mach recognizes that Newton's Absolute Space and Time exist in Newton's cosmology as the site of an unobservable and absolute metaphysics, and he seeks to remove this metaphysics from the empirical science of physics.[34]

Mach considers Newton's Absolute Time and Space to be conceptual failures on Newton's part—he considers them to have been dreamed up (or what we might call "fudged") by Newton, but to have no real ontological existence themselves. And as Huggett and Hoefer report, "In a lengthy discussion of Newton's *Scholium* on absolute space, Mach accuses Newton of violating his own methodological precepts by going well beyond what the observational facts teach us concerning motion and acceleration."[35] (Mach also asserts that Newton considered Absolute Space to be absolutely at rest because he lived "in an age deficient in epistemological critique.")[36]

And in Mach's discussion of Newton's Absolute Space, he proposes that as an alternative to defining the "true and absolute motions" of sensible bodies in relation to (what Mach interprets to be) Newton's abstract, unobservable, absolutely-at-rest Absolute Space, sensible bodies' "true and absolute motions" should be defined relative to the observable "fixed

---

34. Although Mach takes issue with all of Newton's metaphysics, he largely ignores Newton's Absolute Place and Motion; and Mach does not recognize that Newton's metaphysics include his "measured" quantities, and extends even to bodies themselves, and to their unchanging and immovable present momenta.

Interestingly, we find that even to this present day, philosophers and physicists continue to wrestle with Newton's Absolute Time and Space, and they complain about (what they consider to be) Newton's imprecisely defined quantities. In Brian Greene's *Fabric of the Cosmos*, of 2005, for example, Greene remarks that Newton "puts absolute space front and center in the description of the most basic and essential element of physics—motion—but he leaves its definition vague" (29). And yet Greene also feels that (what he refers to as) Newton's "incomplete reasoning" with respect to Newton's definition of Absolute Space is odd, since Greene also acknowledges that "Newton—[who was] a man [who was] so driven by the pursuit of truth that he once shoved a blunt needle between his eye and the socket bone to study ocular anatomy, and [who,] later in life as Master of the Mint, meted out the harshest of punishments to counterfeiters, sending more than a hundred to the gallows—had no tolerance for false or incomplete reasoning" (*Fabric of the Cosmos*, 26). We find that indeed Newton had no tolerance for false or incomplete reasoning, and that his concept of Absolute Space was not incompletely reasoned at all.

35. Huggett and Hoefer, "Absolute and Relational Theories," para. 51.

36. Mach, *Science of Mechanics*, 571.

stars." And even though by the eighteenth century it had already been proven that the fixed stars are not actually fixed,[37] Mach still proposed that bodies' "true and absolute motions" should be defined relative to the sensible fixed stars. The empiricist Mach sought to locate an observable, unchanging and immovable referent—an observable body—by which other observable bodies' changing, instantaneous motions could be defined, and which could therefore serve as a replacement for Newton's unobservable, metaphysical Absolute Space.

In his *Science of Mechanics*, Mach also argues that Newton's First Law (which, as we know, reads: "Every body perseveres in its state of rest, or of uniform motion in a right line, unless it is compelled to change that state by forces impress'd thereon") assumes—and requires—the existence in the natural world of a space and a time in which equal distances and equal times absolutely and indisputably exist; it assumes—and requires—the existence in the natural world of Newton's Absolute Time and Space. And because Mach seeks to rid physics of Newton's metaphysical Absolute Time and Space, he proposes that Newton's First Law be replaced by what he considers to be "an empirically equivalent mathematical rival." Or as Huggett and Hoefer explain:

> [In his *Science of Mechanics*, Mach] criticizes Newton's postulation of absolute space as a metaphysical leap that is neither justified by actual experiments, nor methodologically sound. The remedy offered by [Mach] is simple: we should retain Newton's mechanics and use it just as we already do, but eliminate the unnecessary posit of absolute space. In its place we need only substitute the frame of the fixed stars, as is the practice in astronomy in any case. If we find the incorporation of a reference to contingent circumstances (the existence of a single reference frame in which the stars are more or less stationary) in the fundamental laws of nature problematic . . . then Mach suggests that we replace the 1st law with an empirically equivalent mathematical rival:

---

37. In 1718, Newton's contemporary Edmund Halley showed that the fixed stars actually move, and are therefore not "fixed," or absolutely at rest (see "Fixed Stars," para. 46). (And as we know, Newton did not consider the sensible fixed stars to exist as an unchanging and immovable referent by which it would be possible to *rigorously* define motion and change.)

CHAPTER VIII. ALBERT EINSTEIN 257

$$\frac{d^2\left(\frac{\Sigma mr}{\Sigma m}\right)}{dt^2} = 0$$ [38]

Mach's equation states that the acceleration of the Universe's center of mass is zero—and that the Universe's center of mass therefore exists as an unchanging and immovable referent in the natural world by which it would be possible to rigorously define all motion and change.[39] (And we note here that the "sums in [Mach's] equation are to be taken over all massive bodies in the universe.")[40]

Mach's equation therefore implies that determining the location of the Universe's center of mass requires of us that we sum over all of the masses in the Universe—all of which are accelerating with respect to the Universe's center of mass, and all of which contribute to the existence of the Universe's center of mass.[41] Or as Mach explains in his *Science of Mechanics*:

> the natural investigator must feel the need of . . . knowledge of the *immediate* connections, say, of the masses of the universe. There will hover before him as an ideal an insight into the principles of the whole matter, from which accelerated and inertial motions will result in the *same* way.[42]

(And we note here that Mach's phrase "the principles of the whole matter" reminds us of Plato's phrase, "the first principle [ἀρχήν] of the whole.")

---

38. Huggett and Hoefer, "Absolute and Relational Theories," para. 52.

39. We recognize that the Universe's common center (of mass, or of gravity—we find that the terms are interchangeable) *does* exist as an unchanging and immovable referent in the natural world by which it is possible to rigorously define all motion and change; however, we also recognize that while Mach proposes that the Universe possesses *one* common center (of mass, or of gravity), Newton recognized that the Universe's common center (of gravity) is realized ever-presently and omni-presently, in the coming into being of the site of all particles'—or of all bodies'—unchanging and immovable Presence(s)—in the coming into being of the (multiple and yet simultaneously singular) All/the Only—in the coming into being of we ourselves.

40. Huggett and Hoefer, "Absolute and Relational Theories," para. 53.

41. According to Brian Greene, there "is debate concerning Mach's precise views . . . . Some of his writings are a bit ambiguous and some of the ideas attributed to him arose from subsequent interpretations of his work" (Greene, *Fabric of the Cosmos*, 33).

42. Mach, *Science of Mechanics: Supplement*, 44.

⌁

We recognize that Mach developed his "empirically equivalent mathematical rival" to Newton's First Law in response to Newton's First Law, but that Mach's equation is based upon (what we consider to be) a misreading of Newton's First Law—even as we also recognize that Mach's attacks on Newton's Absolute Space are based upon (what we consider to be) a misreading of Newton's Absolute Space. Since Mach did not recognize that Newton's *Principia* was written in a secret, hidden code which requires decrypting, he did not recognize that Newton's four Absolute quantities exist as the monist, materialist focus of Newton's entire cosmology. Mach did not recognize that by Absolute Place(s), Newton meant the site of all preexisting/post-existing particles—or of all preexisting/post-existing bodies—themselves, and which exist inextricably from their perseverance (over the course of their trajectories) with their unchanging and immovable presently uniform rectilinear motions; and Mach did not recognize that Newton considered the perseverance of (what he referred to as his) "immovable" Absolute Place(s) *as* immovable Absolute Place(s) (over the course of their trajectories)—or the Absolute Motions of the Absolute Place(s)—to generate an Absolute Space and an Absolute Time in the natural world in which equal distances and equal times absolutely and indisputably exist. Mach did not recognize that Newton considered his four Absolute quantities to come into being ever-presently and omnipresently—in the coming into being of the site of all particles'—or of all bodies'—unchanging and immovable Presence(s)—in the coming into being of the (multiple and yet simultaneously singular) All/the Only; and Mach did not recognize that Newton considered the coming into being of his four Absolute quantities in the natural world to bring into being (what Newton referred to as) the "Frame of the System of the World"—the (multiple and yet simultaneously singular) unchanging and immovable (and *material*) referent(s) by which Newton considered it to be possible to rigorously define all motion and change.

Mach also did not recognize that Newton wrote his Law I in a facetious, tongue-in-cheek tone; and Mach did not recognize that in Law I, Newton had actually been proposing that every body in the natural world only perseveres in its unchanging and immovable *present* state of rest, or of uniform motion in a right line—a state of motion from which we know that Newton considered every body itself to exist inextricably—precisely because *at the same time* it is compelled to change that (unchanging and immovable) state by forces impressed upon it from without.

We also find that because Mach did not recognize (what we consider to be) the true meaning of Newton's Law I, he interpreted Law I to suggest that Newton considered "free bodies"—or bodies that exist prior to, or independently of, the actions of any forces impressed upon them—to exist in the natural world.[43] Mach did not recognize that Newton did *not* consider free bodies—or bodies that exist prior to, or independently of, the actions of any forces impressed upon them—to exist in the natural world; and Mach did not recognize that Newton actually considered all bodies (in vacuo) to *presently* be free of the actions of all impressed forces upon them—even as, *at the same time*, he also considered all bodies (in vacuo) to *instantaneously* never be free of the actions of impressed forces upon them.

(And let us also note here that although Mach appropriated Newton's term "mass" in the development of his (Mach's) equation, Mach did not recognize that by the term "mass" in the *Principia*, Newton meant a mass—or a particle—or a body—and which exists inextricably from its perseverance (over the course of its trajectory) with its unchanging and immovable presently uniform rectilinear motion, and which exists as a manifestation of the site of all masses'—or of all particles'—or of all bodies'—unchanging and immovable Presence(s) in the natural world.)

And we recognize that although Mach wrote that the "investigator must feel the need of . . . knowledge of the *immediate* connections . . . of the masses of the universe," Mach did not see that Newton considered all particles/bodies/masses, and which exist inextricably from their perseverance (over the course of their trajectories) with their unchanging and immovable presently uniform rectilinear motions—to always already Presently exist as manifestation(s) of the (multiple and yet simultaneously singular) All/the Only—and to always already Presently exist as manifestation(s) of *the first principle—or arche—of the whole*.

---

43. Let us remind ourselves here that Newton's First Law reads: "Every body perseveres in its state of rest, or of uniform motion in a right line, unless it is compelled to change that state by forces impress'd thereon." We find that Mach interprets Law I to mean that Newton considered bodies to exist in their states "of rest, or of motion in a right line" *prior* to the actions of impressed forces upon them. (And this—despite the fact that Mach also recognizes that Newton had proposed that all bodies are continuously acted upon by the impressed force of gravity. And again, we recognize that Mach was willing to overlook obvious contradictions in his reading of Newton's *Principia*.)

We find that Einstein interpreted Mach's *Science of Mechanics* to mean that "*inertia* has it origin in some kind of *interaction*" between bodies,[44] but we recognize that both Mach and Einstein did not see that Newton had proposed that by way of the gravity/Vis Insita *interaction* in the natural world, all (preexisting/post-existing) bodies come into being, and persevere (over the course of their trajectories) with their unchanging and immovable presently uniform rectilinear motions—states of motion from which we know that Newton considered the bodies themselves to exist inextricably—even as, *at the same time*, they undergo continuous alterations to their unchanging and immovable present motions (and therefore manifest changing, instantaneous motions), and by way of the existence of which, we are able to discern the passage of time in the natural world. Mach and Einstein did not see that Newton considered all bodies—and which exist inextricably from their perseverance (over the course of their trajectories) with their unchanging and immovable presently uniform rectilinear motions—to exist as the site of all bodies' unchanging and immovable Presence(s) in the natural world; and Mach and Einstein did not see that Newton considered the site of all bodies' unchanging and immovable Presence(s) to exist as the unchanging and immovable (and *material*) referent(s) by which it is possible to rigorously define all bodies' changing, instantaneous motions under gravity.

Like Mach, Einstein also did not see that in Newton's Law I, Newton had actually been proposing that every body only perseveres in its unchanging and immovable *present* state of rest, or of uniform motion in a right line—a state of motion from which we know that Newton considered every body itself to exist inextricably—precisely because *at the same time* it is compelled to change that (unchanging and immovable) state by forces impressed upon it from without. And like Mach, Einstein also assumed that Newton considered free bodies—or bodies that exist prior to, or independently of, the actions of all impressed forces upon them—to exist in the natural world;[45] and Einstein did not see that Newton actually considered all bodies (in vacuo) to *presently* be free of the actions of all

---

44. See Albert Einstein's 1913 Letter to Mach (Zurich, 25 June 1913), in which Einstein wrote, "it follows of necessity that *inertia* has its origin in some kind of *interaction* of the bodies" (Einstein, *Collected Papers*, 5:340).

45. Like Mach, Einstein interpreted Newton's Law I to suggest that Newton considered bodies to exist in their states "of rest, or of uniform motion in a right line" *prior to* the actions of impressed forces upon them.

impressed forces upon them—even as, *at the same time*, he also considered all bodies (in vacuo) to *instantaneously* never be free of the actions of impressed forces upon them.

↭

In 1922, four years after Einstein had declared "Mach's principle [to be] one of the three pillars [underlying] his general theory of relativity,"[46] he noted that his theory of general relativity (and in particular, Mach's principle itself) had failed to provide us with any knowledge of the immediate connections of the masses of the Universe, and that it had failed to provide us with any knowledge of the origin of inertia. Einstein noted that others would be satisfied to proceed with developing general relativity further—even without the principle's having provided us with any knowledge of the origin of inertia, and Einstein added, "This contentedness will appear incomprehensible to a later generation however."[47]

And we find that eventually, Einstein lost his enthusiasm for Mach's principle. In 1946, writing in his *Autobiographical Notes*, Einstein gave "this 'farewell' to the principle":

> Mach conjectures that in a truly reasonable theory inertia would have to depend upon the interaction of the masses, precisely as was true for Newton's other forces, a conception that for a long time I considered in principle the correct one. It presupposes implicitly, however, that the basic theory should be of the general type of Newton's mechanics: masses and their interaction as the original concepts. Such an attempt at a resolution does not fit into a consistent field theory, as will be immediately recognized.[48]

And today, and as Abraham Pais remarks in *Subtle Is the Lord: the Science and the Life of Albert Einstein* (2005), the origin of inertia remains a mystery to philosophy and to physics. Pais writes, "It must be said that, as far as I can see, to this day Mach's principle has not brought physics decisively farther. It must also be said that the origin of inertia is and remains the most obscure subject in the theory of particles and fields."

46. Overduin, "Spacetime Before Einstein," para. 17.

47. We read that "in 1922, Einstein noted that others were satisfied to proceed without this criterion and added, 'This contentedness will appear incomprehensible to a later generation however'" (see Pais, *Subtle Is the Lord*, 287). And indeed, we are that later generation.

48. Einstein, *Autobiographical Notes*, 27. See also Norton, "Relativistic Cosmology."

As we know, the origin of inertia—or of a particle's—or a body's—tendency to persevere (over the course of its trajectory) with an unchanging and immovable *presently* uniform rectilinear motion—a state of motion from which we know that the particle—or body—itself exists inextricably—was the subject addressed by the cosmologies of Archimedes, of Galileo, and of Newton. And as we know, Archimedes, Galileo, and Newton considered (what today is called) inertia to arise in the coming into being of all particles—or bodies—themselves; in the coming into being of the site of all particles'—or of all bodies'—unchanging and immovable Presence(s); in the coming into being of the (multiple and yet simultaneously singular) divine origin(s) of reality; in the coming into being of we ourselves.

↶

Let us turn now to the second philosophical pillar which underlies the theory of general relativity: the principle of equivalence. It is this principle that exists at the heart of Einstein's empirical theory.

ii. *The principle of equivalence*

As has been mentioned, in his theory of general relativity, the empiricist Einstein sought to purge Newton's Absolute Space and Time from physics; and as has been mentioned, Einstein attempted to purge Absolute Space and Time from physics by relativizing all motion: by showing that there exists no genuine physical distinction in the natural world between inertial motion and accelerated motion. In this endeavor, Einstein failed.[49] Nevertheless, it was in Einstein's principle of equivalence that he formulated these ideas. Let us turn now to an exploration of it.

↶

The history of Einstein's development of the principle of equivalence begins with Einstein's recognition that the mass described by Newton's Law II ($\mathbf{F} = m\mathbf{a}$) is equivalent to the masses described by Newton's Law of Universal Gravitation ($\mathbf{F} = GmM/\mathbf{r}^2$).

---

49. As has been mentioned, and as Robert DiSalle writes in *Understanding Space-Time*, 5, "By the late 1960s, [the general consensus among philosophers and physicists was] that general relativity did not 'relativize' all motion."

Since Einstein recognizes that the masses in Newton's two equations are equivalent, he finds that it is possible to solve Newton's equations simultaneously.

Einstein therefore solves both equations simultaneously, and he is left with the following equation:

$F = m\mathbf{a}$ $\qquad F = GmM/\mathbf{r}^2$

$m\mathbf{a} = GmM/\mathbf{r}^2$

$\mathbf{a} = GM/\mathbf{r}^2$

And Einstein recognizes that this final equation is the equation of a field (where a field, in physics, is defined to be "a physical quantity ... that has a value for each point in space and time").[50] Einstein therefore interprets his equation to mean that a uniform gravitational field is equivalent to an acceleration.

And it is this finding—"the fact that a uniform gravitational field is equivalent to an acceleration"—that is Einstein's principle of equivalence.[51]

Einstein then applies his principle of equivalence to (his reading of) Newton's Corollary VI. (As has been mentioned, Einstein did not recognize that Galileo and Newton had distinguished in their cosmologies between bodies' *apparent* motions under gravity and bodies' *actual* motions under gravity; and therefore, Einstein did not recognize that in Corollary VI, Newton had been referring to bodies' *apparent* motions under gravity and not to their *actual* motions under gravity. Let us remind ourselves here that Newton's Corollary VI reads:

> If bodies, any how moved among themselves are urged in the direction of parallel lines by equal accelerative forces; they will all continue to move among themselves, after the same manner as if they had been urged by no such forces.

We find that since Einstein did not recognize Galileo's and Newton's true cosmologies, he did not recognize that Newton's Corollary VI exists as a codification of the ideas that Galileo had deduced from his Leaning

---

50. "Field (Physics)," para. 1.

51. Or as Penrose writes in *Road to Reality*, 392, "the 'equivalence' [in Einstein's principle of equivalence] refers to the fact that a uniform gravitational field is equivalent to an acceleration."

Tower of Pisa experiments. Einstein therefore did not recognize that in Corollary VI, Newton had been imagining two bodies dropped from the top of the Leaning Tower in tandem; and Einstein did not recognize that, (like Galileo), Newton had seen that although to an observer located within the Leaning Tower system, the two bodies *appear* to manifest parallel trajectories (relative to one another), *in truth*, the bodies *actually* manifest non-linear trajectories as they tend ceaselessly (over the course of their trajectories) towards their system's common center (of gravity).[52] Einstein did not recognize that, (like Galileo), Newton had seen that the bodies are *actually* non-uniformly rotated (over the course of their trajectories) as they tend ceaselessly towards their system's common center (of gravity); and Einstein did not recognize that, (like Galileo), Newton had seen that the degree to which the bodies are rotated (over the course of their trajectories) is dependent upon their distances from their system's common center (of gravity), and that they generate rotating flower patterns as they go.)

Einstein does not recognize Newton's secret, hidden cosmology, however, and instead he assumes that bodies' *apparent* motions under gravity are in fact their *actual* motions under gravity. Einstein therefore assumes that the two bodies dropped from the top of the Leaning Tower in tandem with one another simply undergo changes in speed—or changes in the rates at which they fall—as they fall (over the course of their trajectories). Einstein therefore surmises that although the two bodies freely falling in tandem with one another undergo changes in speed (over the course of their trajectories), neither body is able to discern the other body's changes in speed, or its acceleration (over the course of its trajectory). Einstein recognizes that from the perspective of each body, the other body appears to be at rest; and Einstein therefore surmises that, from the perspective of each body, the other body appears to be manifesting inertial motion (over the course of its trajectory).[53]

52. *Einstein overlooked the fact that Newton had defined gravity as being a centripetal, or center-seeking, force.*

53. In his *Road to Reality*, 393, Roger Penrose explains this interpretation of Newton's Corollary VI. Penrose invites his reader to consider an insect to be affixed to one of the falling bodies. (And Penrose imagines the two bodies dropped from the Leaning Tower to be rocks.) He writes, "Consider again [Galileo's] falling rocks, as they descend together from the top of the Leaning Tower. Imagine an insect clinging to one of the

CHAPTER VIII. ALBERT EINSTEIN 265

Einstein interprets Newton's Corollary VI in this way; and Einstein then proceeds to substitute "uniform gravitational field" in Corollary VI for Newton's "equal accelerative forces." Einstein therefore reinterprets Corollary VI to mean that if bodies, any how moved among themselves, are urged in the direction of parallel lines by a *uniform gravitational field*, the bodies will continue to move among themselves as if they were not subject to such a field. Einstein interprets this to mean that bodies subject to a uniform gravitational field (which, by his principle of equivalence, he considers to be equivalent to an acceleration) will *continue to manifest inertial motion* (over the course of their trajectories). And it is in this way that Einstein considered himself to have succeeded in relativizing accelerated and inertial motion—and we find that Einstein considered this idea to have been (what he called) "the happiest thought of my life."[54]

As we know, (and like Mach), Einstein assumed that Newton had considered free bodies—or bodies that exist prior to, or independently of, the actions of any impressed forces upon them—to exist in the natural world,[55] and, like Mach, Einstein too assumed that free bodies exist in the natural world. Einstein therefore defined free-fall motion, or the motion of bodies freely falling in a uniform gravitational field, to be inertial motion. And Einstein considered free fall motion (as inertial motion) to be the natural state of motion of all bodies in the Universe.[56]

---

rocks and looking at the other. To the insect, the other rock appears simply to hover without motion." And as Penrose explains, the entire system accelerates towards the ground, but from the perspective of the insect, it appears that the system is at rest, and that the system is therefore manifesting inertial motion.

54. See Einstein's "Basic Idea of the Theory of General Relativity in Its Original Form," an unpublished essay written about 1919, in which he recounts that, in 1907, there came to him "the happiest thought of my life in the following form: *for an observer in free-fall from the roof of a house there is during the fall*—at least in his immediate vicinity—*no gravitational field*" (Einstein, *Collected Papers*, 7:136).

55. —And this, despite the fact that Newton had asserted that the impressed force of gravity acts upon all bodies at all times.

56. We find that the accelerometer, which is a device that is used to measure a body's acceleration through space-time, is zeroed relative to another freely falling body, and that it therefore registers zero acceleration when freely falling (see "Proper Acceleration," para. 1). However, we also recognize that if the accelerometer were zeroed relative to the site of all particles'—or of all bodies'—Presence(s); relative to the site that

We note here that Einstein's definition of inertial motion exists independently of a time and a space in which equal times and equal distances absolutely and indisputably exist—it exists independently of Newton's Absolute Time and Space; and it exists independently of a body's manifestation of uniformly rectilinear motion. It is for this reason that Einstein considered himself to have succeeded in removing from physics (what he considered to be) the "privileged" site of Newton's Absolute Time and Space.[57]

☙

Let us turn now to the third and final philosophical pillar which underlies the theory of general relativity—the principle of relativity as expressed by general covariance.

iii. *The principle of relativity as expressed by general covariance*

As we know, there were two postulates upon which Einstein had constructed his theory of special relativity. The two postulates are as follows:

—The laws of physics are the same in all inertial frames of reference.

—The speed of light is the same in all inertial frames of reference.

We find that in the theory of general relativity, Einstein applies his principle of equivalence—and his application of it to (his reading of) Newton's Corollary VI—(and by way of which, Einstein believed himself to have succeeded in relativizing inertial motion and accelerated motion)—to these postulates, in an effort to show that "the form of the laws

---

Archimedes, Galileo, and Newton had considered to be that of Divinity's Presence in the natural world—it would register a non-zero acceleration when freely falling under gravity.

57. Why did Einstein consider Newton's Absolute Time and Space to be "privileged" in physics? Einstein recognized that Newton's Law I assumes—and requires—the existence in the natural world of a space and a time in which equal distances and equal times absolutely and indisputably exist, and Einstein therefore considered such a space and a time to be "privileged" in Newton's cosmology. (For an interesting discussion of how Einstein had considered Absolute Time and Space to be "privileged" in Newtonian physics, see DiSalle, "Space and Time.")

of physics should be the same in all—inertial and accelerating—frames."[58] This idea exists at the heart of the principle of relativity expressed by general covariance.

Einstein invites us to consider an inertial frame of reference (or a frame of reference in which equal times and equal distances indisputably exist), and he reasons that by way of his principle of equivalence—and his application of it to (his reading of) Newton's Corollary VI—this frame of reference "might be, for all we can determine empirically, falling in the gravitational field of some other system."[59] Einstein therefore argues that no frame of reference that we might consider is itself intrinsically inertial or accelerated. And in this way, Einstein considered himself to have succeeded in generalizing the postulates underlying special relativity to include all reference frames, and to have therefore succeeded in generalizing the theory of special relativity itself.

(And as we know, Newton himself would not have considered inertial or accelerated frames of reference to actually exist in the natural world; and as we know, (and like Archimedes and Galileo), Newton considered there to exist a genuine physical distinction in the natural world between inertial and accelerated motion. And finally, (and as we know), philosophers and physicists acknowledge that Einstein did not succeed in his attempts at relativizing all motion.)

As has been mentioned, one year after Einstein had begun working on his theory of general relativity, mathematician Hermann Minkowski, Einstein's former mathematics professor at the Eidgenössische Polytechnikum in Zurich, invented the concept of space-time. We read:

> In 1908, Hermann Minkowski—once one of the math professors of a young Einstein in Zurich—presented a geometric interpretation of special relativity that fused time and the three spatial dimensions of space into a single four-dimensional continuum now known as Minkowski space.[60]

---

58. "Principle of General Covariance," para. 7.
59. DiSalle, "Space and Time," para. 43.
60. "Spacetime," para. 4.

Minkowki conceived of this four-dimensional continuum—which today is known as "space-time"—to be *an abstract backdrop to bodies' motions, which exists independently of bodies themselves.*[61]

Einstein had been working on his theory of general relativity at the time that Minkowski announced his discovery—(Einstein had been exploring the motions of bodies at rest in his falling elevators)—and Einstein incorporated Minskowki's space-time into his own theory.[62] *And, like Minkowski, Einstein too considered space-time to exist as an abstract backdrop to bodies' motions, which exists independently of bodies themselves.*

Einstein incorporated Minkowski's space-time into his own theory, and he then applied his principle of equivalence—and his application of it to (his reading of) Newton's Corollary VI—to the motions of bodies freely falling in (what Einstein now considered to be) four-dimensional space-time. And Einstein noticed that "locally" (or over small space-time intervals), bodies freely falling in tandem with one another appeared to fall in parallel paths, relative to one another, but that "globally" (or over large space-time intervals), bodies freely falling in tandem with one

---

61. We find that space-time itself is defined to exist as "the collection of all possible events," and that an event is defined to be "something that happens instantaneously at a single point in spacetime, represented by a set of coordinates x, y, z and t [where x, y, and z refer to the point's three-dimensional location in space, and where t refers to the point's position in time]." We also find that "every set of coordinates, or particular space-time event [in relativity] ... is described as [being] a 'here-now' or a world point." Space-time is therefore also defined to exist as the collection of all possible Here-Nows; and space-time—or the collection of all possible Here-Nows—is considered to exist as a *continuous* abstract backdrop to *discrete* particles' motions. And we therefore deduce that in Minkowski's conception of space-time, the site of what Presently Is is considered to exist distinctly from particles themselves, and *time is considered to exist distinctly from matter*. (See Bais, *Very Special Relativity*, 14, in which he writes: "spacetime is the collection of all possible events"; see "Spacetime", para. 8, for the definition of an event; and see Augustyn, "Space-time," para. 2, in which it is written that "every set of coordinates, or particular space-time event [in relativity] ... is described as a 'here-now' or a world point.")

62. We read that "Minkowski's geometric interpretation of relativity was to prove vital to Einstein's development of his 1915 general theory of relativity" ("Spacetime," para. 5).

another appeared to fall in non-parallel paths, relative to one another.⁶³ And because Einstein considered bodies in free-fall to be free of all forces impressed upon them, and to be manifesting inertial motion, Einstein *necessarily considered space-time itself to be responsible for causing the bodies to appear to fall in these non-parallel paths, relative to one another.* Einstein came to consider the presence of matter in space-time to be responsible for causing the bodies to "exhibit [these] relative accelerations" with respect to one another.⁶⁴ And therefore, Einstein came to the conclusion that *gravity actually manifests in the natural world as curvature of space-time, rather than as a force.*⁶⁵ This idea exists at the heart of the theory of general relativity itself.

Einstein did not recognize, however, that in his theory of general relativity, he was simply exploring (what Galileo and Newton had considered to be) bodies' changing, instantaneous motions under gravity, as bodies persevere (over the course of their trajectories) with their unchanging and immovable presently uniform rectilinear motions (states of motion from which we know that the bodies themselves exist inextricably)—and, *at the same time,* undergo non-uniform rotations (over the course of their trajectories) as they tend ceaselessly towards their system's common center (of gravity)—towards an unchanging and immovable *place* that exists indistinguishably from the unchanging and immovable *place(s)* that they always already Are. And Einstein also did not recognize that in his theory of special relativity, he was simply exploring (what Galileo and Newton had considered to be) bodies' unchanging and immovable presently uniform rectilinear motions, and which exist inextricably from the bodies themselves, and which exist as manifestation(s) of the site of all particles'—or of all bodies'—unchanging and immovable Presence(s) in the natural world. Einstein did not recognize that all bodies *at the same time* possess both unchanging and immovable presently uniform rectilinear motions (and from which the bodies themselves exist

---

63. Einstein was noticing here the rotating orbital flower patterns that Galileo and Newton had seen are observable to us as we view systems from without over extended intervals of time.

64. Einstein surmised that "the relative accelerations of falling bodies depend[ed] upon the distribution of mass" in space-time (DiSalle, "Space and Time", para. 45).

65. Einstein concluded that the "curvature of spacetime [is] due to gravity" ("Special Relativity," para. 6).

inextricably) and changing, instantaneous motions; and Einstein did not recognize that bodies' unchanging and immovable presently uniform rectilinear motions (and from which the bodies themselves exist inextricably) are more fundamental to them (and to their trajectories) than their changing, instantaneous motions, since their unchanging and immovable presently uniform rectilinear motions (and from which the bodies themselves exist inextricably) exist "before" and "after" their changing, instantaneous motions—even as, *at the same time*, they also exist as the site(s) at which passing time is always already vanquished, or overcome (with respect to the generation of their trajectories). And Einstein also did not recognize that it is possible to rigorously define all bodies' changing, instantaneous motions under gravity in relation to their unchanging and immovable presently uniform rectilinear motions (and from which the bodies themselves exist inextricably).

Instead, and as has been mentioned, the site of all particles'—or of all bodies'—unchanging and immovable Presence(s) is missing from Einstein's empirical cosmology, and we find that he composed a highly complex cosmology to account for (what Galileo and Newton had considered to be) bodies' *actual* motions under gravity. And we also find that because Einstein did not recognize the existence of the site of all particles'—or of all bodies'—unchanging and immovable Presence(s) in the natural world, Einstein's cosmology is not as complete as Galileo's and Newton's true cosmologies. And as has been mentioned, *Einstein did not discover anything that had not already been discovered by Galileo and Newton, centuries before—and in a far more simple and elegant way.* And we also recognize that because Einstein did not see Galileo's and Newton's true cosmologies, Einstein did not see that *a space and a time in which equal distances and equal times absolutely and indisputably exist does not in fact exist as an abstract backdrop to all particles'—or all bodies'—motions, but rather exists inextricably from all particles—or all bodies—themselves.*

Instead, and as has been mentioned, Einstein considered (discrete) particles and bodies to exist distinctly from (continuous) space-time, and space-time in his theory of general relativity exists as an abstract backdrop to bodies' motions. And we find that despite the fact that it was Einstein's hope that general relativity would bind "spacetime so tightly to matter that one could not exist without the other"[66]—and indeed, when asked to summarize the theory of relativity in one sentence, Einstein

---

66. Overduin, "Experimental Verdict," 31.

declared: "Time and space and gravitation have no separate existence from matter"[67]—contemporary philosophers and physicists have come to the conclusion that "matter and space-time [in general relativity] remain logically independent."[68] Physicist John Archibald Wheeler, who was one of Einstein's later collaborators, summarized Einstein's general theory thusly: "Spacetime [in general relativity] tells matter how to move; matter tells spacetime how to curve."[69]

※

Sadly, Einstein himself had had intuitions about what was missing from his empirical cosmology. Friend Rudolph Carnap reports that Einstein once said that "the problem of the Now" worried him seriously, since Einstein recognized that although the Now exists, it remains inaccessible to empirical interrogation. As Carnap recounts:

> Once Einstein said that the problem of the Now worried him seriously. He explained that the experience of the Now means something special for man, something essentially different from the past and the future, but that this important difference does not and cannot occur within physics. That this experience cannot be grasped by science seemed to him a matter of painful but inevitable resignation.... [Einstein seemed to think] that there is something essential about the Now which is just outside the realm of science.[70]

Einstein had had intuitions that what was missing from his empirical cosmology was the site that Galileo and Newton had recognized to exist as that of the unobservable absolute in the natural world—the site of all particles'—or of all bodies'—unchanging and immovable Presence(s).

67. Einstein, quoted in Brian, *Einstein*, 130.
68. Overduin, "Experimental Verdict," 32. And as Overduin explains, "the equations of general relativity are perfectly consistent with spacetimes that contain no matter at all" ("Experimental Verdict," 31).
Let us also note here that there is one notable exception to the independence of matter and space-time in general relativity, which lies in the case of the gravitational field. Space-time in general relativity is considered to exist as "an embodiment of the gravitational field," and the gravitational field is considered to "[carry] energy and momentum." Therefore, and by Einstein's equation $E=mc^2$, the gravitational field itself is considered to exist as a material entity. (See Greene, *Fabric of the Cosmos*, 75; and see also Norton, "Hole Argument," para. 28.)
69. Wheeler and Ford, *Geons*, 235.
70. Carnap, "Carnap's Intellectual Biography," 37–38.

And sadly, we recognize that what was missing from Einstein's empirical cosmology was the site that the ancient Jews, Pythagoras, Plato, Archimedes, the early Christians, Galileo, and Newton had all considered to be that of the (multiple and yet simultaneously singular) All/the Only—the site of substance/materiality itself—and the site that all had considered Divinity and ever-burgeoning life to be realized in the natural world. We recognize that what was missing from Einstein's empirical cosmology was the site of we ourselves.[71]

☙

Before we conclude our discussion of Einstein's cosmology, let us turn now to a brief reflection on our present, postmodern moment.

Our Present, Postmodern Moment

In 1986, and reflecting on Einstein's cosmology and our contemporary understanding of reality, physicist John Archibald Wheeler remarked:

> Of all obstacles to a thoroughly penetrating account of existence, none looms up more dismayingly than "time." Explain time? Not without explaining existence. Explain existence? Not without explaining time. To uncover the deep and hidden connection between time and existence, to close on itself our quartet of questions, is a task for the future.[72]

As we know, uncovering the deep and hidden connection between time and existence was the task that had been undertaken by all of the philosophers whose cosmologies we have encountered in this text—and we recognize that it could also be the task taken up by philosophers going forward. We encourage philosophers going forward to take up this task!—to join the ancient Jews, and Pythagoras, and Plato, and Archimedes, and the early Christians, and Galileo, and Newton, and we ourselves!—in exploring the site of ultimate substance and of what Presently Is in the natural world—in exploring the site that Archimedes, Galileo, and Newton recognized to exist as that of all particles'—or of all bodies'—unchanging and immovable Presence(s)—and the site that all considered to exist as

---

71. Nevertheless, we recognize that Einstein *did* contribute profound beauty to the philosophical discourse—and we are thinking here of his sublime equation which reveals that energy and mass are related to one another by the speed of light, or $E=mc^2$.

72. Wheeler, "Hermann Weyl," 374.

the (multiple and yet simultaneously singular) divine origin(s) of reality—the site of we ourselves.[73]

Before we conclude, let us turn to a brief exploration of what Einstein called "the experience of the Now." As was briefly mentioned early on in this text, Pythagoras recognized that the ancient Jews had considered it to be possible for YHWH—or he whom the ancient Jews had considered to exist as the site of ultimate substance and of what Presently Is in the natural world—to be *experienced*. But how had the Jews proposed that we may come to *know ourselves* for experiences of YHWH? Let us turn to a brief exploration of these ideas now.

---

73. We encourage philosophers going forward to join us in the fight to rediscover this ancient (and modern) wisdom—for we recognize that that which we will rediscover will be self-knowledge. (As poet T.S. Eliot acknowledges in his *Four Quartets*, ours has been a long history of finding and losing and finding and losing again and again knowledge of the site of Divinity's—and of our own—Presence in the natural world, and in his *Four Quartets* (a set of four poems which, we find, is also One Poem), Eliot writes, "There is only the fight to recover what has been lost/ And found and lost again and again: and *now*, under conditions/ That seem unpropitious." (Eliot, "East Coker," *Four Quartets*; in *Collected Poems*, 189. My emphasis.))

Afterword

And the end of all our exploring
Will be to arrive where we started
And know the *place* for the first time.

—T.S. Eliot, "Little Gidding," *Four Quartets*[1]

AS WAS BRIEFLY MENTIONED early on in this text, Pythagoras recognized that the ancient Jews had considered it to be possible for YHWH—or he whom the ancient Jews had considered to exist as the site of ultimate substance and of what Presently Is in the natural world—to be *experienced*. But how had the Jews proposed that we may come to know ourselves for experiences of YHWH? To answer this question, we will need to see more fully what Pythagoras saw about the ancient Jews' cosmology.

As we know, Pythagoras studied the ancient Jewish sacred texts deeply (which he considered to be his own sacred texts, since he appropriated the ancient Jews' cosmology for his own). And we find that by way of such studies, Pythagoras came to recognize that the Jews were not only interested in questions of *ontology*—in questions of *what* can be known about the natural world (or in questions of *what* can be known about (he whom the Jews considered to be) YHWH himself—the manifestation

---

1. My emphasis. Eliot implies that the end of all our exploring will be to arrive where we started—at the beginning—at the arche (ἀρχή)—at the unchanging and immovable *place* from which none of us has ever departed—and to *know ourselves* for an experience of it.

of the (multiple and yet simultaneously singular) All/the Only—and therefore the natural world itself), but that they were also interested in questions of *epistemology*—in questions of *how* the natural world can be known (or in questions of *how* YHWH himself can be known).

☙

Let us return here to the sixth century BC, so that we may see what Pythagoras sees about the cosmology of the ancient Jews.

Pythagoras studies the ancient Jewish sacred texts deeply (which he considers to be his own sacred texts, since he appropriates the ancient Jews' cosmology for his own), and he recognizes that King Solomon—(whose love song, the Song of Solomon, celebrates sensual love)—suggests that we may come to know ourselves for experiences of YHWH by *learning how to surrender ourselves to one another completely in rapturous, sensual love.*[2]

Pythagoras studies the Song of Solomon carefully, and he recognizes that Solomon suggests that as we surrender ourselves completely to one another in rapturous, sensual love, we experience the foreclosure of our perceptions of "before" and of "after," and of "self" and of "other," and are recollected to an (orgasmic) experience of (what Solomon implies that he considers to be) the *unchanging place* from which we have never departed—to an experience of the site of what Presently (and unchangingly) Is—to an experience of YHWH himself—and therefore to an experience of self-knowledge and enlightenment. Pythagoras recognizes that Solomon suggests that our experience of recollection to YHWH is an experience of recollection to an (orgasmic) bright blossoming/cleaving/fountaining—it is an experience of recollection to (what Solomon implies that he considers to be) YHWH's ever-cleaving tree/fountain of life, which blossoms/bursts forth Presently in Eden.[3]

Pythagoras continues to study the Song of Solomon carefully, and he recognizes that Solomon suggests that YHWH has given us the gifts of

---

2. We note here that King Solomon's reign spanned the years 970–931 BC.

3. Pythagoras recognizes that in Gen. 2:9 it is written, "And out of the ground made [YHWH] the LORD God . . . the tree of life . . . in the midst of the garden"—and that in Gen. 2:10 it is written, "And a river went out of Eden to water the garden; and from thence it was parted, and became into four heads." And Pythagoras recognizes that the tree of life and the fountain of life are alternate ways of referring to YHWH himself, who, in the cosmology of the ancient Jews, blossoms/bursts forth Presently in Eden.

AFTERWORD 277

one another—and that he has also given us the gift of self-surrender—so that we may surrender ourselves completely unto one another (and by way of the process of which, find our perceptions of "before"/"after" and of "self"/"other" to be foreclosed), and be recollected to an (orgasmic) experience of self-knowledge and enlightenment. Pythagoras recognizes that Solomon suggests that YHWH has given us the gifts of one another—and that he has also given us the gift of self-surrender—so that we may come to recognize that all of us always already exist as (multiple and yet simultaneously singular) manifestation(s) of one another—that all of us always already exist as (multiple and yet simultaneously singular) manifestation(s) of YHWH himself—and that Paradise is always already Now.⁴

And Pythagoras also recognizes that Solomon implies that he does not consider wisdom and knowledge to merely be an abstract idea *about* the reality of what Presently (and unchangingly) Is—YHWH himself—but rather to be an indubitable substantial/material *experience* of it/him.⁵

Pythagoras continues to study the ancient Jews' sacred texts deeply, and he recognizes that although Solomon suggests that *by way of acts of self-surrendering lovemaking*, we may come to know ourselves for experiences of one another—for experiences of YHWH himself and of his ever-cleaving tree/fountain of life—and for experiences of (what Solomon implies that he considers to be) the Paradise that always already Presently (and unchangingly) Is, Solomon's father, King David, suggests that *by way of the process of self-surrender itself*—be it in the form of acts of prayer, acts of deep reading (acts of textual exegesis), acts of logical deduction (acts of mathematics), or acts of poetical composition—we may come to know ourselves for experiences of YHWH and of his ever-cleaving tree/fountain of life—and therefore for experiences of self-knowledge and

---

4. We note here that Paradise is discussed in the Song of Solomon.

5. Interestingly, we find that Newton considered Solomon to be the greatest of all of God's prophets. Newton wrote that wisdom and insight are "not only to be found in ye volume of nature but also in ye sacred scriptures, as in Genesis, Job, Psalms, Isaiah & others. In ye knowledg of this Philosophy God made Solomon ye greatest philosopher in ye world" (Newton, Keynes MS. 33, f.5v).

enlightenment.[6] Pythagoras recognizes that in Ps. 36:9, and addressing YHWH himself, the poet King David writes:

For with thee *is* the fountain of life: in thy light shall we see light.

—and Pythagoras recognizes that David implies here that *by way of the practice of self-surrender itself* (of which poetical composition serves as a form for him), we experience the foreclosure of our perceptions of "before"/"after" and of "self"/"other" and are recollected to an experience of (what David implies that he considers to be) the *unchanging place* from which we have never departed—to an experience of the site of what Presently (and unchangingly) Is—to an experience of YHWH himself and of his ever-cleaving tree/fountain of life—and therefore to an experience of self-knowledge and enlightenment.

Pythagoras also recognizes that David implies here that our experience of recollection to YHWH himself is an experience of recollection to the Holy Land from which we have never departed.[7] Pythagoras recognizes that David implies that our experience of recollection to YHWH is an experience of recollection to Paradise/Eden/the Promised Land/Israel—it is an experience of recollection to substance/materiality itself. And Pythagoras recognizes that, like Solomon, David implies that he too considers all of us to always already exist as the (multiple and yet simultaneously singular) manifestation(s) of Paradise, and that he too considers Paradise to always already be Now.

Pythagoras reflects upon these ideas deeply, and he recognizes that the reason why the ancient Jews' cosmology exists as secret, hidden wisdom, which requires decrypting is that the Jews imply that they do not consider wisdom and knowledge to merely be an abstract idea *about* the reality of what Presently (and unchangingly) Is—YHWH himself—but rather to be an indubitable substantial/material *experience* of it/him.

6. And we note here that King David's reign spanned the years 1010–970 BC. Pythagoras recognizes that David implies that *any kind of work that exists for us as a form of lovemaking (and that does not hurt ourselves or others)* has the potential to serve as a form of self-surrender, which may deliver us to experiences of YHWH himself and of his four-headed tree/fountain of life. (Why is it important that the work not hurt ourselves or others? Pythagoras recognizes that David implies that work that would hurt ourselves or others would reinscribe our perceptions of duality—and would therefore reinscribe our perceptions of "before"/"after" and of "self"/"other.")

7. Pythagoras recognizes that David implies that we all always already exist as YHWH's Chosen One(s).

Pythagoras recognizes that the Jews ask of a supplicant that he or she perform countless *acts of self-surrendering exegesis and of logical deduction* upon their sacred texts so that the supplicant may experience the foreclosure of his or her perceptions of "before"/"after" and of "self"/"other," and be recollected to an indubitable substantial/material *experience* of (what the Jews consider to be) self-knowledge and enlightenment.

As we know, Pythagoras asks of his own followers that they too perform countless acts of self-surrendering logical deduction upon his own teachings; and we recognize here that Pythagoras implies that, like the ancient Jews, he too does not consider wisdom and knowledge to merely be an abstract idea *about* the reality of what Presently (and unchangingly) Is—(he whom Pythagoras too considers to be) YHWH himself—but rather to be an indubitable substantial/material *experience* of it/him. *And further, we recognize that the reason why all of the* prisca sapientia—*and the cosmologies of Galileo and of Newton too—exist as secret, hidden wisdom, and require decrypting is that all imply that they do not consider wisdom and knowledge to merely be an abstract idea about the reality of what Presently (and unchangingly) Is—the Divine Logos himself—but rather to be an indubitable substantial/material experience of it/him.* We recognize that all seek to recollect us to (what all consider to be) an indubitable substantial/material *experience* of self-knowledge and enlightenment, and that all seek to help us to fulfill the Delphic Oracle's dictum to "know thyself."[8]

Pythagoras continues to explore the ancient Jews' sacred texts deeply, and he recognizes that the concept of the prophet is central to the ancient Jews' cosmology. Pythagoras recognizes that the first and most generally used Hebrew word for prophet, "nabi," comes "from a root meaning 'to bubble forth, as from a fountain,'"[9] and that in the cosmology of the ancient Jews, all of us always already exist as YHWH's prophets—all of us always already exist as manifestation(s) of the Present speaking (and writing) of YHWH's four-lettered Name/Word, which translates as "I AM," and as manifestation(s) of his ever-cleaving tree/fountain of life—and that it is only for us to come to *know ourselves* for experiences

---

8. And we recognize that all exist as complete theories of knowledge. Interestingly, scholars attribute the dictum "know thyself" to Thales, who, as we know, was responsible for introducing the concept of *monism* into the Greek philosophical discourse.

9. Easton, "Prophet."

of it/him—for experiences of ourselves—by learning how to practice self-surrender over passing time.[10]

(Pythagoras recognizes that the ancient Jews consider the Universe itself to exist as a sacred text, with All existing as the Present speaking (and writing) of YHWH's four-lettered Name/Word—his ecstatic, bursting, and resoundingly affirmative, "I AM"—and All existing as manifestation(s) of his ever-cleaving tree/fountain of life.)[11]

❧

And finally, Pythagoras recognizes that YHWH's gift to all of us—his "memorial unto all generations"—is that the names of all of his prophets—Abraham, Isaac, Jacob, and on—(and all of our own names too, since we too are his prophets)—are also only One Name—One ecstatic, bursting, and resoundingly affirmative, "I AM"—which comes into being ever-presently and omni-presently, in the coming into being of the (multiple and yet simultaneously singular) All/the Only—in the coming into being of the One Universe itself. Pythagoras returns to Exod. 3:14–15, and reads:

> And [YHWH] God said unto Moses, I AM THAT I AM: and he said, Thus shalt thou say unto the children of Israel, I AM hath sent me unto you. And God said moreover unto Moses, Thus shalt thou say unto the children of Israel, the Lord God of your fathers, the God of Abraham, the God of Isaac, and the God of Jacob, hath sent me unto you: this is my name for ever, and this is my memorial unto all generations.

Pythagoras recognizes that YHWH's gift to all of us is eternal life—for he recognizes that although we exist "before" and "after" one another in a progressively linearly ordered chronological time, as father and son, and as mother and daughter, we also never exist "before" and "after" one

---

10. Pythagoras recognizes that in ancient Judaism, they who are referred to as YHWH's prophets have learned how to practice self-surrender over passing time, and have therefore come to *know themselves* for experiences of being the prophets that they always already Are; and Pythagoras recognizes that in the cosmology of the ancient Jews, they are our teachers. Pythagoras recognizes that the ancient Jews suggest that it is for us to emulate them in our own lives (by also learning how to practice self-surrender over passing time) so that we too can come to know ourselves for being the prophets that we always already Are.

11. Pythagoras recognizes that the Jews consider the Universe itself to exist as One bright, bursting Flower/fountain of life.

another, since we all always already exist as (multiple and yet simultaneously singular) manifestation(s) of one another—as manifestation(s) of YHWH himself and of his ever-cleaving tree/fountain of life; and Pythagoras recognizes that Paradise truly is Now.[12]

As we know, Pythagoras considered himself to have been a prophet, who had received Divine wisdom and who had been spoken through by YHWH, the Divine Name/Word. And as we know, Newton too considered himself to have been a prophet, who had also received Divine wisdom and who had also been spoken through by the Logos, the Divine Name/Word.

As we know, Newton taught himself Hebrew so that he could read the ancient Jews' sacred texts in their originals; and as has been mentioned, Newton's Bible was the most heavily annotated volume in his library.

We find that Newton, a devoutly religious Christian, studied the Bible's Old Testament—the sacred texts of the ancient Jews—deeply, but that he also studied the writings of the Bible's New Testament—the sacred texts of the early Christians—deeply. Newton recognized that the concept of the prophet was central to the cosmology of the ancient Jews, and as we will see, he found that the concept of the prophet was central to the cosmology of the early Christians as well.

Let us return now to the Enlightenment, so that we may see what Newton sees about the cosmology of the early Christians.

Newton studies the writings of the early Christians deeply, and he recognizes that in the cosmology of the early Christians, Jesus, YHWH's son and his prophet—who always already exists as a manifestation of the Present speaking (and writing) of his father's (YHWH's) four-lettered

---

12. Pythagoras recognizes that we never truly lose one another, for we all always already exist as (multiple and yet simultaneously singular) manifestation(s) of one another—as (multiple and yet simultaneously singular) manifestation(s) of unchanging YHWH himself. And Pythagoras also recognizes that when David ends his book of Psalms with the One word, "Hallelujah" (הַלְלוּיָהּ)—which means "Praise YHWH"—it is because David himself knows this to be true (see Ps. 150, the last Psalm in the book of Psalms).

Name/Word, which translates as "I AM," and as a manifestation of his father's (YHWH's) ever-cleaving tree/fountain of life—needs only to learn how to *know himself* for being the prophet that he always already Is. Newton recognizes that the early Christians imply that over the course of Jesus's life, he needs only to learn how to practice self-surrender (here in the form of practicing infinite compassion—or, in the words of T.S. Eliot, in the form of practicing "death in love"),[13] so that he may experience the foreclosure of his perceptions of "before"/"after" and of "self"/"other," and be recollected/resurrected to an experience of the *unchanging place* from which he has never departed—to an experience of the Present speaking (and writing) of his father's (YHWH's) four-lettered Name/Word, which translates as "I AM," and of his father's (YHWH's) ever-cleaving tree/fountain of life—and therefore to an experience of self-knowledge and enlightenment. (Newton recognizes that the early Christians imply that over the course of Jesus's life, he needs only to come to *know himself* for experiences of himself, and that the early Christians imply that this is Jesus's life's work.)[14]

Newton recognizes that in the cosmology of the early Christians, Jesus always already exists as *the Word* and as *the Life* and as *the Light*, and that by learning how to practice self-surrender, he comes to know himself for *experiences* of *the Word* and *the Life* and *the Light* that he always already Is—and therefore for experiences of self-knowledge and enlightenment.[15]

13. Eliot, "The Dry Salvages," *Four Quartets*; in *Collected Poems*, 198.

14. Newton recognizes that the early Christians imply that Jesus's life's work is to fulfill the Delphic Oracle's dictum to "know thyself"—and Newton also recognizes that the early Christians imply that this is also our life's work, and that Jesus is our teacher. Newton recognizes that in the fourth canonical Gospel, the Gospel of John, 14:6, Jesus instructs: "I am *the way*, the truth, and the life: no man cometh unto the Father, but by me" (my emphasis)—and he recognizes that the early Christians imply that it is for us to learn how to emulate Jesus in our own lives (by learning how to practice self-surrender, also in the form of infinite compassion) so that we too may come to *know ourselves* for being the prophets that we always already Are.

15. Newton studies the Gospels deeply and he recognizes that in the Gospels, Jesus always already exists as *the Word* (see John 1:1, "In the beginning was the Word, and the Word was with God, and the Word was God") and as *the Life* (see John 14:6, "Jesus saith unto him, I am the way, the truth, and the life: no man cometh unto the Father, but by me") and as *the Light* (see John 8:12, "Then spake Jesus again unto them, saying, I am the light of the world: he that followeth me shall not walk in darkness, but shall have the light of life").

Newton reads the Gospel stories carefully, and he recognizes that the Gospel stories are actually about Jesus himself. For example, Newton recognizes that the human/Divine Jesus is the deaf and dumb man of the Gospel of Mark—even as he is also always already the Divine Word Presently spoken (and written); and that he needs only to learn how to practice self-surrender over passing time so that he may come to *know himself* for an experience of being the Divine Word that he always already Presently (and unchangingly) Is. Newton studies the Gospel of Mark (7:32–35) carefully, and he reads:

> And they bring unto him one that was deaf, and had an impediment in his speech; and they beseech him to put his hand upon him.
> And he took him aside from the multitude, and put his fingers into his ears, and he spit, and touched his tongue;
> And looking up to heaven, he sighed, and saith unto him, Ephphatha, that is Be opened.
> And straightway his ears were opened, and the string of his tongue was loosed, and he spake plain.

Newton recognizes that Jesus practices self-surrender here (in the form of extending infinite compassion to himself for his *human* deafness and dumbness; for his inability to always (at all times) hear and speak and *know himself* for experiences of the Divine Word Presently spoken (and written))—and *straightway* (or "at once")[16] he is opened[17]—straightway (or "at once") he bubbles forth, as from fountain—and straightway (or "at once") he *knows himself* for being the prophet that he always already Is.[18]

---

16. The English "straightway" is a translation of the Greek "εὐθέως," or "eutheós," which means "at once" (see "εὐθέως," Wiktionary).

17. As Mark 7:34 explains, the Aramaic word "Ephphatha" means "be opened."

18. Newton recognizes that Jesus practices "death into love" here and is recollected/resurrected/rebirthed to an experience of the *unchanging place* from which he has never departed—to an experience of the Present speaking (and writing) of his father's four-lettered Name/Word, which translates as "I AM," and of his ever-cleaving tree/fountain of life. Newton recognizes that Jesus experiences his own Apocalypse and comes to know himself for an experience of the Revelation that he always already Presently (and unchangingly) Is.

(Newton recognizes that the early Christians imply that Jesus's "death into love" rebirths him to an experience of Life—to an experience of the *unchanging place* from which he has never departed—and therefore to an experience of self-knowledge and enlightenment. And interestingly, we find that Newton speaks of the coming into being of numbers in the natural world in terms of (simultaneous; or "at once") death and rebirth, and we recognize that Newton implies that he considers numbers to come into being in the coming into being of the Divine Logos himself. (In the Scholium to Book I, Section I, of his *Principia*, 55, and speaking of (what today is referred to as) the mathematical limit, and the site at which Newton implies that he considers numbers to

◈

Newton recognizes that the four Gospels are also only One Gospel—or One Good Story[19]—and that the One Good Story is the Divine Logos himself, who comes into being ever-presently and omni-presently, in the coming into being of the (multiple and yet simultaneously singular) All/the Only—in the coming into being of we ourselves.[20]

◈

Newton recognizes all of these ideas about the teachings of the early Christians, and we find that he too encourages us to learn how to practice self-surrender in our own lives, so that we too may come to *know ourselves* for being the prophets that we always already Are.[21] Scholars attribute Newton with having written, "Live your life as an exclamation rather than an explanation"[22]—and we recognize that Newton is encouraging us here to live our lives as *the One Exclamation* that he considers us to always already Be; he is encouraging us to know ourselves for *experiences* of the Divine Logos's One ecstatic, bursting, and resoundingly affirmative, "I AM"—so that we too may come to know (as experience) that Paradise truly Is Now.

---

come into being in the natural world, Newton cryptically explains that "by the ultimate ratio of evanescent quantities is to be understood the ratio of the quantities, not before they vanish, nor afterwards, but with which they vanish. In like manner the first ratio of nascent quantities is that with which they begin to be." Newton implies here that (what he calls) "evanescent" and "nascent" quantities (at once) come into being Now, in the coming into being of the Divine Logos himself—and we recognize that, like the ancient Jews, Pythagoras, Plato, Archimedes, and Galileo, Newton too considers numbers to come into being in the coming into being of the (multiple and yet simultaneously singular) All/the Only—in the coming into being of the One Universe itself.))

19. And we remind ourselves here that the English word gospel comes from the Greek "εὐαγγέλιον," or "euangelion," which translates as "good news" ("Gospel," para. 3).

20. Newton recognizes that in the cosmology of the early Christians, the four-pointed (wooden) cross is symbolic of the Divine Logos's ever-cleaving tree/fountain of life, and of (what the early Christians consider to be) that which always already Presently (and unchangingly) Is—the (multiple and yet simultaneously singular) All/Only—the divine origin(s) of reality—the One Universe itself.

21. Newton recognizes that the Divine Logos's gift to all of us is *love*, for love (in any number of forms) is the means by which we may come to *know ourselves* for experiences of him.

22. Bariso, "12 Brilliant Quotes."

References

"Absolute Space and Time." Wikipedia. Last modified October 13, 2023. https://en.wikipedia.org/w/index.php?title=Absolute_space_and_time&oldid=1180007737.

Ackrill, J.L. *Aristotle: Categories and De Interpretatione*. Oxford: Oxford University Press, 1975.

"Aether Theories." Wikipedia. Last modified March 21, 2021. https://en.wikipedia.org/w/index.php?title=Aether_theories&oldid=1013395548.

"Age of Enlightenment." Wikipedia. Last modified May 19, 2019. https://en.wikipedia.org/w/index.php?title=Age_of_Enlightenment&oldid=897789105.

Aland, Barbara, et al. "John 1.1." *Novum Testamentum Graece* 28. Accessed February 17, 2024. https://www.bibelwissenschaft.de/en/bible/NA28/JHN.1.

"Albert Einstein." Wikipedia. Last modified February 21, 2024. https://en.wikipedia.org/w/index.php?title=Albert_Einstein&oldid=1209361803.

"Alchemy." Wikipedia. Last modified November 22, 2018. https://en.wikipedia.org/w/index.php?title=Alchemy&oldid=870071550.

Apostol, Tom M., and Mamikon A. Mnatsakanian. "Centroids Constructed Graphically." *Mathematics Magazine* 77.3 (2004) 201–10. DOI:10.2307/3219117.

———. "Finding Centroids the Easy Way." *Math Horizons* 8.1 (2000) 7–12. http://www.jstor.org/stable/25678275.

"Archimedes." Wikipedia. Last modified June 7, 2019. https://en.wikipedia.org/w/index.php?title=Archimedes&oldid=900754770.

Archimedes. *The Works of Archimedes*. Translated by Thomas Little Heath. New York: Dover, 2002.

Aristotle. *Metaphysics*. Translated by W.D. Ross. Internet Classics Archive. Accessed July 6, 2023. http://classics.mit.edu/Aristotle/metaphysics.12.xii.html.

———. *Physics*. Translated by R.P. Hardie and R.K. Gaye. Internet Classics Archive. Accessed February 12, 2024. https://classics.mit.edu/Aristotle/physics.html.

———. *Selections*. Translated by Terence Irwin and Gail Fine. Indiana: Hackett, 1995.

"Arithmetic." Wikipedia. Last modified February 23, 2021. https://en.wikipedia.org/w/index.php?title=Arithmetic&oldid=1008510185.

"ἀρχή." Wiktionary. Last modified January 28, 2024. https://en.wiktionary.org/w/index.php?title=%E1%BC%80%CF%81%CF%87%CE%AE&oldid=77757335.

Augustyn, Adam. "Photon." *Encyclopedia Britannica*. Last modified February 20, 2024. https://www.britannica.com/science/photon.

———. "Space-Time." *Encyclopedia Brittanica*. Last modified February 12, 2024. https://www.britannica.com/science/space-time.

Bais, Sander. *Very Special Relativity: An Illustrated Guide*. Cambridge, MA: Harvard University Press, 2007.

Bariso, Justin. "12 Brilliant Quotes from the Genius Mind of Sir Isaac Newton." Inc., December 29, 2016. https://www.inc.com/justin-bariso/12-brilliant-quotes-from-the-genius-mind-of-sir-isaac-newton.html.

"Barycenter (Astronomy.)" Wikipedia. Last modified January 5, 2024. https://en.wikipedia.org/w/index.php?title=Barycenter_(astronomy)&oldid=1193837413.

Bell, John L. "Continuity and Infinitesimals." *Stanford Encyclopedia of Philosophy*, edited by Edward N. Zalta. Spring 2022. https://plato.stanford.edu/archives/spr2022/entries/continuity/.

ben Israel, Manasseh, and Elias Hiam Lindo. *The Prophets and Hagiography*. Columbus: The Ohio State University Press, 1842.

Berryman, Sylvia. "Ancient Atomism." *Stanford Encyclopedia of Philosophy*, edited by Edward N. Zalta. Winter 2016. https://plato.stanford.edu/archives/win2016/entries/atomism-ancient/.

Boccaletti, Dino. *Galileo and the Equations of Motion*. Switzerland: Springer, 2016.

"Bonaventura Francesco Cavalieri 1598–1647." *The Mathematics Teacher* 25.2 (May 1932) 93–94. http://www.jstor.org/stable/27951415.

"Book of Isaiah." Wikipedia. Last modified January 27, 2024. https://en.wikipedia.org/w/index.php?title=Book_of_Isaiah&oldid=1199425092.

Brennan, Chris. *Hellenistic Astrology*. Colorado: Amor Fati, 2017.

Brian, Denis. *Einstein: A Life*. John Wiley, 1996.

Buchwald, Jed Z., and Mordechai Feingold. *Newton and the Origin of Civilization*. Princeton: Princeton University Press, 2013.

Caragounis, Chrys C. "What Did Jesus Mean by τὴν ἀρχήν in John 8:25?" *Novum Testamentum* 49.2 (2007) 129–47. http://www.jstor.org/stable/25442544.

Carnap, Rudolph. "Carnap's Intellectual Biography." In *The Philosophy of Rudolf Carnap*, edited by P. A. Schilpp, 3–84. Illinois: Open Court, 1963.

"Center of Mass." Wikipedia. Last modified April 10, 2021. https://en.wikipedia.org/w/index.php?title=Center_of_mass&oldid=1017094067.

"Centripetal Force." Wikipedia. Last modified December 8, 2023. https://en.wikipedia.org/w/index.php?title=Centripetal_force&oldid=1188881133.

"Centroid." Wikipedia. Last modified August 27, 2021. https://en.wikipedia.org/w/index.php?title=Centroid&oldid=1040897372.

Charvatova, Ivanka. "Can Origin of the 2400-Year Cycle of Solar Activity Be Caused by Solar Inertial Motion?" *Annales Geophysicae* 18.4 (April 2000) 399–405.

Christianson, Gale E. *In the Presence of the Creator: Isaac Newton and His Times*. New York: Free Press, 1984.

———. *Isaac Newton*. Lives and Legacies Series. New York: Oxford University Press, 2005.

Clegg, Brian, and Rhodri Evans. *Ten Physicists Who Transformed Our Understanding of Reality*. London: Little, Brown, 2015.

Cohen, I. Bernard. "A Guide to Newton's *Principia*." In *The* Principia: *Mathematical Principles of Natural Philosophy*. Translated by I. Bernard Cohen and Anne Whitman, 1–370. Berkeley: University of California Press, 1999.

———. *Introduction to Newton's* Principia. Cambridge, UK: Cambridge University Press, 1971.

"Construction of the Real Numbers." Wikipedia. Last modified November 30, 2023. https://en.wikipedia.org/w/index.php?title=Construction_of_the_real_numbers&oldid=1187554883.
"Cornus." Wikipedia. Last modified March 9, 2021. https://en.wikipedia.org/w/index.php?title=Cornus &oldid=1011181774.
Corry, Leo. *A Brief History of Numbers*. Oxford: Oxford University Press, 2015.
"Cosmos." Wikipedia. Last modified January 11, 2024. https://en.wikipedia.org/w/index.php?title=Cosmos&oldid=1194900194.
Dantzig, Tobias. *Number: The Language of Science*. Edited by Joseph Mazur. New York: Plume, 2007.
Darrigol, Oliver. *Physics and Necessity: Rationalist Pursuits from the Cartesian Past to the Quantum Present*. Oxford: Oxford University Press, 2014.
"Democritus." Wikipedia. Last modified February 9, 2024. https://en.wikipedia.org/w/index.php?title=Democritus&oldid=1205263281.
"Derivative." Wikipedia. Last modified February 11, 2024. https://en.wikipedia.org/w/index.php?title=Derivative&oldid=1206170449.
Dijksterhuis, E.J. *Archimedes*. Translated by C. Dikshoorn. Princeton: Princeton University Press, 1987.
DiSalle, Robert. "Space and Time: Inertial Frames." *Stanford Encyclopedia of Philosophy*, edited by Edward N. Zalta. Fall 2008. https://plato.stanford.edu/archives/fall2008/entries/spacetime-iframes/.
———. *Understanding Space-Time: The Philosophical Development of Physics from Newton to Einstein*. New York: Cambridge University Press, 2006.
"Do We Need to Rewrite General Relativity?" PBS, *Nova*, June 18, 2015. https://www.pbs.org/wgbh/nova/article/do-we-need-to-rewrite-general-relativity/.
Drake, Tom. "Hebrew Scriptures: Translation Issues." Accessed February 6, 2024. https://webpages.uidaho.edu/engl257/Bible/translation%20issues.htm.
Dry, Sarah. "The Strange, Secret History of Isaac Newton's Papers." Interview by Adam Mann. *Wired*, May 14, 2014. http://www.wired.com/2014/05/newton-papers-q-and-a/.
Easton, Matthew George. "*Easton's Bible Dictionary* (1897)/Prophet." Wikisource. Accessed February 18, 2024. https://en.wikisource.org/wiki/Easton%27s_Bible_Dictionary_(1897)/Prophet.
Einstein, Albert. *Autobiographical Notes*. Translated by Paul Arthur Schilpp. Illinois: Open Court, 1996.
———. *The Collected Papers of Albert Einstein*. Vol. 5, *The Swiss Years: Correspondence, 1902–1914 (English translation supplement)*. Translated by Anna Beck. Israel: Hebrew University of Jerusalem, 1995. https://einsteinpapers.press.princeton.edu/vol5-trans/.
———. *The Collected Papers of Albert Einstein*. Vol. 7, *The Berlin Years: Writings, 1918–1921 (English translation supplement)*. Translated by Alfred Engel. Princeton: Princeton University Press, 2002. https://einsteinpapers.press.princeton.edu/vol7-trans/.
———. *The Collected Papers of Albert Einstein*. Vol. 15, *The Berlin Years: Writings and Correspondence, June 1925–May 1927—Documentary Edition*. Edited by Diana K. Buchwald et al. Princeton: Princeton University Press, 2018. https://einsteinpapers.press.princeton.edu/vol15-doc/.

———. "On the Method of Theoretical Physics." *Philosophy of Science* 1.2 (Apr. 1934) 163–69. http://www.jstor.org/stable/184387.

"Einstein's Thought Experiments." Wikipedia. Last modified October 31, 2023. https://en.wikipedia.org/w/index.php?title=Einstein%27s_thought_experiments&oldid=1182718694.

Eliot, T.S. *Collected Poems: 1909–1962*. New York: Harcourt Brace, 1963.

"Eureka (Word)." Wikipedia. Last modified March 21, 2019. https://en.wikipedia.org/w/index.php?title=Eureka_(word)&oldid=888825051.

"εὐθέως." Wiktionary. Last modified February 18, 2024. https://en.wiktionary.org/wiki//εὐθέως.

Evans, Melbourne G. "Aristotle, Newton, and the Theory of Continuous Magnitude." *Journal of the History of Ideas* 16.4 (1955) 548–57. DOI:10.2307/2707510.

Fahie, John Joseph. *Galileo: His Life and Work*. New York: James Pott, 1903.

Faltin, F., et al. "The Real Numbers as a Wreath Product." *Advances in Mathematics* 16.3 (June 1975) 278–304.

Fideler, David. R., ed. *The Pythagorean Sourcebook and Library: An Anthology of Ancient Writings Which Relate to Pythagoras and Pythagorean Philosophy*. Compiled and translated by Kenneth Sylvan Guthrie. Michigan: Phanes, 1988.

"Field (Physics.)" Wikipedia. Last modified February 12, 2024. https://en.wikipedia.org/w/index.php?title=Field_(physics)&oldid=1206436799.

"Fixed Stars." Wikipedia. Last modified December 30, 2023. https://en.wikipedia.org/w/index.php?title=Fixed_stars&oldid=1192672088.

"Fractal." Wikipedia. Last modified February 6, 2024. https://en.wikipedia.org/w/index.php?title=Fractal&oldid=1204185924.

"The Fragments of Archytas." In *The Pythagorean Sourcebook and Library: An Anthology of Ancient Writings*, edited by David R. Fideler, 178–202. Michigan: Phanes, 1988.

Friedman, Michael. *Foundations of Space-Time Theories: Relativistic Physics and the Philosophy of Science*. Princeton: Princeton University Press, 1983.

Friesen, John. "Christ Church Oxford, the Ancients-Moderns Controversy, and the Promotion of Newton in Post-Revolutionary England." In *History of Universities*, vol. 31.1, edited by Mordechai Feingold, 33–66. Oxford: Oxford University Press, 2008.

"Galilean Moons." Wikipedia. Last modified January 30, 2024. https://en.wikipedia.org/w/index.php?title=Galilean_moons&oldid=1200781945.

Galilei, Galileo. *Dialogue Concerning the Two Chief World Systems, Ptolemaic and Copernican*. Translated by Stillman Drake. Edited by Stephen Jay Gould. New York: Random House, 2001.

———. *Dialogues Concerning Two New Sciences*. Translated by Henry Crew and Alfonso de Salvio. Connecticut: Martino Fine Books, 2015.

———. *Discoveries and Opinions of Galileo*. Translated by Stillman Drake. New York: Doubleday, 1957.

———. *Sidereus Nuncius, or the Sidereal Messenger*. Translated by Albert Van Helden. Chicago: University of Chicago Press, 1989.

"Galileo Galilei." Wikipedia. Last modified March 7, 2018. https://en.wikipedia.org/w/index.php?title=Galileo_Galilei&oldid=829209134.

"General Relativity." Wikipedia. Last modified January 29, 2024. https://en.wikipedia.org/w/index.php?title=General_relativity&oldid=1200517577.

"Geometry." Wikipedia. Last modified February 2, 2024. https://en.wikipedia.org/w/index.php?title=Geometry&oldid=1202442596.

Gibson, George. "Pythagorean Intervals." Accessed February 6, 2024. https://www.phys.uconn.edu/~gibson/Notes/Section3_2/Sec3_2.htm.

"Gnosis." Wikipedia. Last modified March 5, 2017. https://en.wikipedia.org/w/index.php?title=Gnosis&oldid=768687510.

"God in Judaism." Wikipedia. Last modified January 31, 2024. https://en.wikipedia.org/w/index.php?title=God_in_Judaism&oldid=1201466296.

"The Gospel." Wikipedia. Last modified January 12, 2024. https://en.wikipedia.org/w/index.php?title=The_gospel&oldid=1195032918.

Greene, Brian. *The Fabric of the Cosmos: Space, Time, and the Texture of Reality*. New York: Random House, 2005.

Gregersen, Erik. "Centre of Gravity." *Encyclopedia Brittanica*. Accessed February 16, 2024. https://www.brittanica.com/science/centre-of-gravity.

———. "Mass." *Encyclopedia Brittanica*. Accessed February 16, 2024. https://www.britannica.com/science/mass-physics.

Grudin, Robert. "Humanism, Art, and Science." *Encyclopedia Brittanica*. Accessed February 18, 2024. https://www.britannica.com/topic/humanism/Humanism-art-and-science.

Guicciardini, Niccolo. *Reading the* Principia. Cambridge, UK: Cambridge University Press, 1999.

Heath, Thomas Little. *A History of Greek Mathematics*. Vol. 1. New York: Dover, 1981.

———. *A Manual of Greek Mathematics*. New York: Dover, 2003.

———. "Preface" to *The Works of Archimedes*, by Archimedes. Translated by Thomas Little Heath. New York: Dover, 2002.

"Helianthus Whorl." Wikimedia Commons. Last modified June 26, 2006. https://commons.wikimedia.org/wiki/File:Helianthus_whorl.jpg.

"Heraclitus." In *The Cambridge Dictionary of Philosophy, Second Edition*, edited by Robert Audi, 375. Cambridge, UK: Cambridge University Press, 1999.

"History of Calculus." Wikipedia. Last modified January 18, 2024. https://en.wikipedia.org/w/index.php?title=History_of_calculus&oldid=1196832292.

Holton, Gerald James. *Einstein, History, and Other Passions*. Cambridge, MA: Harvard University Press, 2000.

———. "Mach, Einstein, and the Search for Reality." *Daedalus* 97.2 (1968) 636–73. https://www.jstor.org/stable/20023833.

Huggett, Nick, and Carl Hoefer. "Absolute and Relational Theories of Space and Motion." *Stanford Encyclopedia of Philosophy*, edited by Edward N. Zalta. Spring 2018. https://plato.stanford.edu/archives/spr2018/entries/spacetime-theories/.

Hummel, Charles E. *The Galileo Connection*. Wisconsin: Inter-Varsity Christian Fellowship, 1986.

Hutton, Charles, et al. *The Philosophical Transactions of the Royal Society of London*. London: C. and R. Baldwin, 1809.

"I Am (Biblical Term)." Wikipedia. Last modified December 4, 2023. https://en.wikipedia.org/w/index.php?title=I_am_(biblical_term)&oldid=1188364749.

"Idealization (Philosophy of Science.)" Wikipedia. Last modified January 5, 2024. https://en.wikipedia.org/w/index.php?title=Idealization_(philosophy_of_science)&oldid=1193835785.

Iliffe, Robert. "Is He Like Other Men? The Meaning of the *Principia Mathematica*, and the Author as Idol." In *Literature, Culture and Society in the Stuart Restoration*, edited by G. MacLean, 159–76. Cambridge, UK: Cambridge University Press, 1995.

"Infinitesimal." Wikipedia. Last modified November 9, 2023. https://en.wikipedia.org/w/index.php?title=Infinitesimal&oldid=1184309795.

"Ionian School (Philosophy)." Wikipedia. Last modified February 9, 2023. https://en.wikipedia.org/w/index.php?title=Ionian_School_(philosophy)&oldid=1138407310.

"Irrational Number." Wikipedia. Last modified December 27, 2023. https://en.wikipedia.org/w/index.php?title=Irrational_number&oldid=1192107484.

Irwin, Terence, and Gail Fine. *Aristotle: Selections*. Indianapolis: Hackett, 1995.

"Isaac Newton." Wikipedia. Last modified March 11, 2022. https://en.wikipedia.org/w/index.php?title=Isaac_Newton&oldid=1076491363.

Isaacson, Walter. *Einstein: His Life and Universe*. New York: Simon and Schuster, 2007.

Janssen, Michel. "Einstein's Quest for General Relativity, 1907–1920." In *The Cambridge Companion to Einstein*, edited by Michel Janssen and Christoph Lehner, 167–227. New York: Cambridge University Press, 2014.

Kafatos, Menas, and Robert Nadeau. *The Conscious Universe*. New York: Springer, 2012.

Keynes, John Maynard. "Newton, the Man." In *Essays in Biography*, 363–74. New York: Palgrave Macmillan, 2010.

"Kinematics." Wikipedia. Last modified January 30, 2024. https://en.wikipedia.org/w/index.php?title=Kinematics&oldid=1201046426.

Kline, Morris. *Mathematical Thought from Ancient to Modern Times*. Vol. 1. Oxford: Oxford University Press, 1990.

Koyré, Alexandre. "An Unpublished Letter of Robert Hooke to Isaac Newton." *Isis* 43.4 (December 1952) 312–37. https://www.journals.uchicago.edu/doi/10.1086/348155.

"Leibniz–Newton Calculus Controversy." Wikipedia. Last modified January 9, 2024. https://en.wikipedia.org/w/index.php?title=Leibniz%E2%80%93Newton_calculus_controversy&oldid=1194568735.

Liddell, Henry George, and Robert Scott. *A Greek-English Lexicon*. Revised by Sir Henry Stuart Jones and Roderick McKenzie. Oxford: Clarendon, 1940. https://www.perseus.tufts.edu/hopper/text?doc=Perseus:text:1999.04.0057:entry=a)rxh/.

"*Logos*." Wikipedia. Last modified January 30, 2024. https://en.wikipedia.org/w/index.php?title=Logos&oldid=1201069355.

"Logos." Wikiquote. Last modified March 25, 2022. https://en.wikiquote.org/w/index.php?title=Logos&oldid=3091290.

Mach, Ernst. *The Science of Mechanics: A Critical and Historical Account of Its Development*. Translated by Thomas J. McCormack. Chicago: Open Court, 1902. https://www.google.com/books/edition/The_Science_of_Mechanics/mFQ4AAAAMAAJ.

———. *The Science of Mechanics: A Critical and Historical Account of Its Development: Supplement to the 3rd English Edition Containing the Author's Additions to the 7th German Edition*. Translated by Philip E. B. Jourdain. Chicago: Open Court, 1915. https://www.google.com/books/edition/The_Science_of_Mechanics/cyE1AAAAIAAJ.

Maher, Patrick. "Galileo on Natural and Uniform Acceleration." Accessed February 18, 2024. http://patrick.maher1.net/317/lectures/galileo2.pdf.
"Material Monism." Wikipedia. Last modified September 30, 2021. https://en.wikipedia.org/w/index.php?title=Material_monism&oldid=1047434449.
Max Planck Institute for Gravitational Physics. "Special Relativity/Elementary Tour Part 5: Spacetime." Accessed February 18, 2024. http://www.einstein-online.info/en/spacetime/.
McClellan, James E., III, and Harold Dorn. *Science and Technology in World History*. 3rd ed. Baltimore: Johns Hopkins University Press, 2015.
"Measurement of a Circle." Wikipedia. Last modified November 6, 2023. https://en.wikipedia.org/w/index.php?title=Measurement_of_a_Circle&oldid=1183861632.
"Mechanics." Wikiquote. Last modified August 2, 2021. https://en.wikiquote.org/w/index.php?title=Mechanics&oldid=2990406.
Mendell, Henry. "Some Introductory Material on Infinitary Arguments in Ancient Greek Mathematics." Accessed February 14, 2024. https://web.calstatela.edu/faculty/hmendel/Ancient%20Mathematics/InfinitaryArgument.Folder/InfinitaryArguments.html.
"Metempsychosis." Wikipedia. Last modified July 5, 2022. https://en.wikipedia.org/w/index.php?title=Metempsychosis&oldid=1096558395.
"Method of Exhaustion." Wikipedia. Last modified January 11, 2024. https://en.wikipedia.org/w/index.php?title=Method_of_exhaustion&oldid=1195000213.
"The Method of Mechanical Theorems." Wikipedia. Last modified March 5, 2021. https://en.wikipedia.org/w/index.php?title=The_Method_of_Mechanical_Theorems&oldid=1010402053.
"Monad." Theosophy Wiki. Last modified November 22, 2023. https://theosophy.wiki/w-en/index.php?title=Monad&oldid=52047.
"Monad (Philosophy)." Wikipedia. Last modified January 17, 2019. https://en.wikipedia.org/w/index.php?title=Monad_(philosophy)&oldid=878930581.
Morrison, Tessa. *Isaac Newton and the Temple of Solomon: An Analysis of the Description and Drawings and a Reconstructed Model*. North Carolina: McFarland, 2016.
———. *Isaac Newton's Temple of Solomon and His Reconstruction of Sacred Architecture*. Germany: Springer, 2011.
Museo Galileo. "Galileo Galilei and Archimedes." Accessed February 18, 2024. https://exhibits.museogalileo.it/archimedes/section/GalileoGalileiArchimedes.html.
"Musica Universalis." Wikipedia. Last modified December 31, 2023. https://en.wikipedia.org/w/index.php?title=Musica_universalis&oldid=1192837993.
"Names of God." *Jewish Encyclopedia*. Accessed February 6, 2024. https://www.jewishencyclopedia.com/articles/7908-hosts-lord-of.
National Oceanic and Atmospheric Administration. "Detailed Explanation of the Differential Tide Producing Forces." *Our Restless Tides*. 1974. Accessed February 18, 2024. https://tidesandcurrents.noaa.gov/restles3.html.
Newman, William R. "The Chymistry of Issac Newton." Accessed February 18, 2024. https://webapp1.dlib.indiana.edu/newton/.
———. "Newton the Alchemist." Interview on *Nova*, November 15, 2005. https://www.pbs.org/wgbh/nova/article/newton-alchemist-newman.
———. *Newton the Alchemist: Science, Enigma, and the Quest for Nature's "Secret Fire."* Princeton: Princeton University Press, 2019.

Newton, Isaac. "446. Memoranda by David Gregory, 5, 6, 7 May 1694." In *The Correspondence of Isaac Newton*. Edited by H. W. Turnball, 334–40. Cambridge, UK: Cambridge University Press, 1966.

———. "Draft Chapters of a Treatise on the Origin of Religion and Its Corruption." The Newton Project. Accessed July 6, 2023. http://www.newtonproject.ox.ac.uk/view/texts/normalized/THEM00077.

———. "The Fitzwilliam Notebook." The Newton Project. Accessed February 18, 2024. http://www.newtonproject.ox.ac.uk/view/texts/normalized/ALCH00069.

———. "The Fitzwilliam Notebook Confessions." *The Fitzwilliam Notebook*, folio 3r. The Fitzwilliam Museum, Cambridge.

———. "Letter from Sir Isaac Newton to Robert Hooke: February 5, 1675." Collection of the Historical Society of Pennsylvania. https://digitallibrary.hsp.org/index.php/Detail/objects/9792.

———. *The Mathematical Principles of Natural Philosophy: To Which Is Added, Newton's System of the World*. Translated by Andrew Motte. New York: Putnam, 1850. https://www.google.com/books/edition/Newton_s_Principia/NhHAQAAMAAJ?hl=en&gbpv=0.

———. *The Mathematical Principles of Natural Philosophy*. Vol. 1. Translated by Andrew Motte. London: Benjamin Motte, 1729. https://www.google.com/books/edition/The_Mathematical_Principles_of_Natural_P/Tm0FAAAAQAAJ.

———. *The Mathematical Principles of Natural Philosophy*. Vol. 2. Translated by Andrew Motte. London: Benjamin Motte, 1729. https://www.google.com/books/edition/_/6EqxPav3vIsC?hl=en&gbpv=0.

———. MS. 33, f.5v. Keynes Manuscript Collection. Kings College Library. The Newton Project. https://newton.dlib.indiana.edu/text/ALCH00022/diplomatic.

———. MS Add. 3965.6. The Portsmouth Collection, Cambridge University Library. https://archivesearch.lib.cam.ac.uk/repositories/2/archival_objects/504729.

———. "Nova Cubi Hæbræi Tabella." *The Fitzwilliam Notebook*, folio 124r. The Fitzwilliam Museum, Cambridge.

———. *Opticks: Or, A Treatise of the Reflections, Refractions, Inflexions and Colours of Light*. London: 1704. The Newton Project. http://www.newtonproject.ox.ac.uk/view/texts/normalized/NATP00039.

———. "Original Letter from Isaac Newton to Richard Bentley." The Newton Project. Accessed February 18, 2024. http://www.newtonproject.ox.ac.uk/view/texts/normalized/THEM00258.

———. *Principia mathematica* (Latin edition.) Accessed February 18, 2024. https://oll.libertyfund.org/title/newton-principia-mathematica-latin-ed.

———. "Untitled Treatise on Revelation (section 1.1)." The Newton Project. Accessed February 18, 2024. https://www.newtonproject.ox.ac.uk/view/texts/normalized/THEM00135.

"Newton's Arian Beliefs." MacTutor History of Mathematics Archive. Accessed February 16, 2024. https://mathshistory.st-andrews.ac.uk/Extras/Newton_Arian/.

"Newton's General Scholium." Newton Project Canada. Accessed February 5, 2024. https://isaacnewton.ca/newtons-general-scholium/.

Nietzsche, Friedrich Wilhelm. *Philosophy in the Tragic Age of the Greeks*. Translated by Marianne Cowan. Washington, DC: Regnery, 1998.

Norton, John D. "The Hole Argument." *Stanford Encyclopedia of Philosophy*, edited by Edward N. Zalta. Summer 2019. https://plato.stanford.edu/archives/sum2019/entries/spacetime-holearg/.

———. "Relativistic Cosmology." Last modified February 5, 2022. http://pitt.edu/~jdnorton/teaching/HPS_0410/chapters/relativistic_cosmology/index.html.

———. "Special Theory of Relativity: The Principles." Last modified January 14, 2022. http://www.pitt.edu/~jdnorton/teaching/HPS_0410/chapters/Special_relativity_principles/.

"Orbital Resonance." Wikipedia. Last modified February 1, 2024. https://en.wikipedia.org/w/index.php?title=Orbital_resonance&oldid=1201741244.

Overduin, James. "The Experimental Verdict on Spacetime from Gravity Probe B." In *Space, Time, and Spacetime: Physical and Philosophical Implications of Minkowski's Unification of Space and Time*, edited by Vesselin Petkov, 25–60. Berlin: Springer, 2010.

———. "Spacetime Before Einstein." Gravity Probe B: Testing Einstein's Universe. Last modified October 2007. https://einstein.stanford.edu/SPACETIME/spacetime1.html.

———. "Testing Einstein." Gravity Probe B: Testing Einstein's Universe. Last modified April 2016. https://einstein.stanford.edu/SPACETIME/spacetime3.html.

Pais, Abraham. *Subtle Is the Lord: The Science and the Life of Albert Einstein*. Oxford: Oxford University Press, 2005.

"Parmenides." Wikipedia. Last modified January 29, 2021. https://en.wikipedia.org/w/index.php?title=Parmenides&oldid=1003456108.

Penrose, Roger. *The Road to Reality: A Complete Guide to the Laws of the Universe*. New York: Knopf, 2005.

"Persevere." *Online Etymology Dictionary*. Accessed February 18, 2024. https://www.etymonline.com/word/persevere#etymonline_v_12743.

Pesic, Peter. *Abel's Proof: An Essay on the Sources and Meaning of Mathematical Unsolvability*. Cambridge, MA: The MIT Press, 2003.

"Philosopher's Stone." Wikipedia. Last modified November 12, 2018. https://en.wikipedia.org/w/index.php?title=Philosopher%27s_stone&oldid=868502250.

"Physis." Wikipedia. Last modified November 20, 2019. https://en.wikipedia.org/w/index.php?title=Physis&oldid=927192468.

"Pi." Wikipedia. Last modified February 7, 2024. https://en.wikipedia.org/w/index.php?title=Pi&oldid=1204405258.

Pickering, F.R. "Aristotle on Zeno and the Now." *Phronesis* 23.3 (1978) 253–57. http://www.jstor.org/stable/4182047.

Pickover, Clifford. *Archimedes to Hawking: Laws of Science and the Great Minds Behind Them*. New York: Oxford University Press, 2008.

Plato. *The Republic*. Translated by Benjamin Jowett. Internet Classics Archive. Accessed February 18, 2024. http://classics.mit.edu/Plato/republic.html.

———. *Timaeus*. Translated by Benjamin Jowett. In *The Collected Dialogues of Plato: Including the Letters*, edited by Edith Hamilton and Huntington Cairns. Bollingen Series 71, 1151–1211. Princeton: Princeton University Press, 1980.

"Point Particle." Wikipedia. Last modified March 2, 2018. https://en.wikipedia.org/w/index.php?title=Point_particle&oldid=828412091.

Pope, Alexander. "Epitaph: Intended for Sir Isaac Newton." In *The Oxford Dictionary of Quotations by Subject*, edited by Susan Ratcliffe, 336. Oxford: Oxford University Press, 2003.

"Postmodernism." Wikipedia. Last modified December 21, 2023. https://en.wikipedia.org/w/index.php?title=Postmodernism&oldid=1191132809.

Principe, Lawrence M. *The Secrets of Alchemy*. Chicago: University of Chicago Press, 2013.

"Principle of General Covariance." Einstein Relatively Easy. Last modified December 20, 2022. https://einsteinrelativelyeasy.com/index.php/dictionary/77-principle-of-covariance.

"Proper Acceleration." Wikipedia. Last modified January 28, 2024. https://en.wikipedia.org/w/index.php?title=Proper_acceleration&oldid=1199981943.

"Pythagoras." Wikipedia. Last modified February 7, 2024. https://en.wikipedia.org/w/index.php?title=Pythagoras&oldid=1204590840.

"Pythagoreanism." Wikipedia. Last modified January 18, 2024. https://en.wikipedia.org/w/index.php?title=Pythagoreanism&oldid=1196770857.

"Quotations: Galileo Galilei." MacTutor History of Mathematics Archive. Accessed February 18, 2024. https://mathshistory.st-andrews.ac.uk/Biographies/Galileo/quotations/.

"Ratio." Wikipedia. Last modified January 23, 2024. https://en.wikipedia.org/w/index.php?title=Ratio&oldid=1198232902.

Ray, Richard. "Tidal Patterns." NASA Scientific Visualization Studio. Accessed February 18, 2024. https://svs.gsfc.nasa.gov/stories/topex/tides.html.

"Real Line." Wikipedia. Last modified December 5, 2020. https://en.wikipedia.org/w/index.php?title=Real_line&oldid=992491966.

"Rest (Physics)." Wikipedia. Last modified March 13, 2021. https://en.wikipedia.org/w/index.php?title=Rest_(physics)&oldid=1011956501.

Rieger, G. J. "A New Approach to the Real Numbers (Motivated by Continued Fractions)." *Abh. Braunschweig. Wiss. Ges.* 33 (1982) 205–17. https://mathscinet.ams.org/mathscinet-getitem?mr=693180.

Robbins, Frank Egleston, and Louis Charles Karpinski. "Studies in Greek Arithmetic." In *Nichomachus of Gerasa: Introduction to Arithmetic*, translated by Martin Luther D'ooge, 3–177. New York: Macmillan, 1926.

Sciama, D.W. "On the Origin of Inertia." *Monthly Notices of the Royal Astronomical Society* 113.1 (1953) 34–42. http://articles.adsabs.harvard.edu/full/seri/MNRAS/0113/0000042.000.html.

"Sir Isaac Newton's Notebook." BBC. Accessed February 18, 2024. http://www.bbc.co.uk/ahistoryoftheworld/objects/BkKuPZNiRmKddRoe4DiBBA.

Sommerfeld, Arnold. "To Albert Einstein's 70th Birthday." In *Albert Einstein, Philosopher-Scientist*, edited by Paul Arthur Schilpp. The Library of Living Philosophers 7, 97–106. Illinois: Open Court, 2000.

"Spacetime." Wikipedia. Last modified August 18, 2017. https://en.wikipedia.org/w/index.php?title=Spacetime &oldid=796142666.

"Special Relativity." Wikipedia. Last modified April 20, 2018. https://en.wikipedia.org/w/index.php?title=Special_relativity&oldid=837405495.

Spence, Joseph. *Observations, Anecdotes, and Characters, of Books and Men*. London: John Murray, 1820.

"Square Root of 2." Wikipedia. Last modified September 15, 2020. https://en.wikipedia.org/w/index.php?title=Square_root_of_2&oldid=978589426.

Stein, Sherman. *Archimedes: What Did He Do besides Cry Eureka?* Washington, DC: The Mathematical Association of America, 1999.
Stewart, Doug. "Archimedes." Famous Scientists. Accessed February 6, 2024. http://www.famousscientists.org/Archimedes.
———. "Pythagoras." Famous Scientists. Accessed February 6, 2024. https://www.famousscientists.org/pythagoras.
Strong, James. *Strong's Exhaustive Concordance of the Bible*. 1890. https://biblehub.com/greek/.
"Syracuse, Sicily." Wikipedia. Last modified January 31, 2024. https://en.wikipedia.org/w/index.php?title=Syracuse,_Sicily&oldid=1201423734.
"Tangent." Wikipedia. Last modified December 7, 2023. https://en.wikipedia.org/w/index.php?title=Tangent&oldid=1188702196.
"Tetractys." Wikipedia. Last modified January 31, 2024. https://en.wikipedia.org/w/index.php?title=Tetractys&oldid=1201485368.
"Tetragrammaton." *Brewer's Dictionary of Phrase and Fable, Centenary Edition.* Revised by Ivor H. Evans, 1104-5. London: Cassell, 1970.
"Tetragrammaton." Wikipedia. Last modified February 15, 2024. https://en.wikipedia.org/w/index.php?title=Tetragrammaton&oldid=1207801776.
"Thales of Miletus." Wikipedia. Last modified April 26, 2023. https://en.wikipedia.org/w/index.php?title=Thales_of_Miletus&oldid=1151870576.
"Transcendentals." Wikipedia. Last modified February 9, 2021. https://en.wikipedia.org/w/index.php?title=Transcendentals&oldid=1005857556.
Trompf, Garry W. "Isaac Newton and the Kabbalistic Noah: Natural Law Between *Mediaevalia* and the Enlightenment." *Aries* 5.1 (May 2005) 91-118. https://doi.org/10.1163/1570059053084689.
"Unmoved Mover." Wikipedia. Last modified January 27, 2024. https://en.wikipedia.org/w/index.php?title=Unmoved_mover&oldid=1199669437.
Usvat, Liliana. "Sacred Geometry and the Platonic Solids." *Mathematics Magazine.* Accessed February 6, 2024. http://www.mathematicsmagazine.com/Articles/SacredGeometryPlatonicSolids.php#.YEZzwWhKhPZ.
Vamvacas, Constantine J. *The Founders of Western Thought—The Presocratics.* Translated by Robert Crist. Boston: Springer, 2009.
Weisstein, Eric W. "Isaac Newton." Accessed February 18, 2024. https://scienceworld.wolfram.com/biography/Newton.html.
Westfall, Richard S. *Never at Rest: A Biography of Isaac Newton.* Cambridge, UK: Cambridge University Press, 1983.
Wheeler, John Archibald. "Hermann Weyl and the Unity of Knowledge: In the Linkage of Four Mysteries—The 'How Come' of Existence, Time, the Mathematical Continuum, and the Discontinuous Yes-or-no of Quantum Physics—May Lie the Key to Deep New Insight." *American Scientist* 74.4 (1986) 366-75. http://www.jstor.org/stable/27854250.
Wheeler, John Archibald, with Kenneth Ford. *Geons, Black Holes, and Quantum Foam: A Life in Physics.* New York: Norton, 1998.
White, John Williams. *A Series of First Lessons in Greek.* Boston: Ginn and Heath, 1881.
Wootton, David. *Galileo: Watcher of the Skies.* New Haven, CT: Yale University Press, 2010.

Index

"Absolute, True, and Mathematical," 168, 170
absolute rest, 91, 143, 180n50, 195n82, 228
absolute simultaneity, 134, 186n65, 189
Absolute Time, Space, Place, and Motion, 94n73, 158–59, 168–76, 191–92, 227–29
  as another name for arche, 191–92
  bringing into being the Frame of the System of the World, 159, 191–92, 228, 248–49
  four quantities as one, 159n9
  as monist, materialist focus of Newton's cosmology, 94n73, 159, 226–28, 258
  as secret code for Divine Logos, 159, 191–92
  as site of all particles'—or all bodies'—unchanging and immovable Presences(s), 94n73
  as the site of the unobservable absolute, 169–70
  as substantial/material, 94n73, 158–59, 171–74, 231n17
absolute truth, true philosophers looking at, 115n15, 150n75,196n88, 220–21
Age of Enlightenment, 223
alchemist, Newton as, 201–3
alchemy, xv, 201

All/the Only
  associated with Divinity and with the principle of life, 5
  comes into being Now, 10, 18, 79, 107, 115n15, 137, 167n22, 191, 228, 272, 280
  missing from Einstein's empirical cosmology, 272
  monist focus of cosmologies, 272
  site of, 79–80, 123
  as the unchanging and immovable Fulcrum, 80, 123, 232
alogos ("inexpressible"), 36–37
ancient Jews
  associate ultimate substance with Divinity and with principle of life, 9
  associate YHWH's Presence with quantity/number, 30n59, 283n18
  believe that All is One and All is Now; All is Divine and All is manifestation of life, 10n8
  believe that "God can be experienced," 13n15, 275–81
  believe that Paradise is Now, 10n8, 275–81
  consider the All/the Only to be the manifestation of YHWH, the four-headed fountain of life, 32
  consider the Universe to exist as One bright, bursting Flower/ fountain of life, 280n11

298 INDEX

ancient Jews (*continued*)
    eternal life as YHWH's gift to all of us, 280
    on the import of the numbers 4 and 1, 19n33
    locate the presence of the "arche," 9n5
    on mathematical reality, 30n59, 70n35, 105
    monist, materialist cosmology of, 9, 103–6, 114n15, 275–81
    prophet as central to cosmology, 279–80
    questions of ontology and of epistemology, 275–76
    on Universe existing as a sacred text, 280

arche (ἀρχή)
    Absolute Time, Space, Place, and Motion as another name for, 191–92
    Archimedes referring to, 89n66
    as center of Universe, 195
    as the Divine "origin" of all things, 4n7, 89n66, 103–8, 114n15, 136–37, 201n100
    father/creator as another name for, 114n15
    as a Greek word with primary meanings, 4n7
    Jesus as another name for, 106
    knowing oneself for experience of, 275–84
    located at the site of what Presently Is, 9, 89n66, 105–8, 114n15, 137, 167n22, 220, 272–73
    Logos as another name for, 105–6
    manifests as the All/the Only, 4
    missing from Einstein's cosmology, 272
    Monad/Tetrad as names for, 114n15
    as monist, materialist focus of all sages' cosmologies, 272–73
    as monist, materialist focus of Newton's *Principia*, 167, 168, 219
    as Plato's "first principle [ἀρχήν] of the whole," 114n15, 167n22
    as principle of life, 4
    referent for rigorously defining motion, 5
    as the site of all particles'—or all bodies'—unchanging and immovable Presence(s), 272
    as the site of ultimate substance, 4n7
    Thales introducing the concept of, 4–5, 184n60
    true philosophers devoting lives to exploring, 115n15, 169n25
    Vis Insita as another name for, 184
    where numbers come into being, 100n81, 283n18
    YHWH as another name for, 9

Archimedes, 51–108
    authors *kentron toi bareos*, or center of gravity, 73–75
    cosmology as secret wisdom, 55
    on curves dynamically generated in dynamic generation of elements, 61
    development of kinematics, 55–72
    development of mechanics, 72–80
    on direction of particles' trajectories, 92–95
    discovers absolute rest doesn't exist, 91
    discovers all particles'—or all bodies'—unchanging and immovable Presence(s), 79
    discovers (Galilean) Principle of Relativity, 89–92
    discovers inertia, 78
    discovers Law of the Lever, 74
    on divine origin of Universe being Now, 88–89

Archimedes (*continued*)
  on elements of which geometric objects composed as of 2D, 59–60
  Eureka! moment, 79, 95, 100
  extends method of exhaustion, 57–59
  finds an unchanging and immovable place, 80
  on gravity, 84–86
  of great import to Galileo and Newton, 81–83
  greatest mathematician of antiquity, 51
  on infinity and its presently being overcome, 98–100
  invents catapult, 52, 79n51
  invents method of indivisibles, 56–57
  locates arche Now, 79
  locates an unchanging referent in *On Spirals*, 62, 70–71
  locates YHWH's Presence at site of all particles'—or all bodies'—unchanging Presence(s), 79
  mathematically nuanced Tetrad at heart of cosmology, 92–95
  monist, materialist focus as Universe itself, 79–80
  on numbers coming into being in natural world, 95–102
  on particles dynamically generated in dynamic generation of trajectories, 75
  on particles existing as of 2D simultaneously, 75
  on particles existing inextricably from their present motions, 78
  on particles existing inextricably from their trajectories, 76
  on particles possessing unchanging present motions and changing instantaneous motions, 76–78
  on recursive self-similarity being implicit to natural world, 77
  on relationship between discrete and continuous, 102
  on relationship between geometry and number, 102
  on relationship between mathematics and natural world, 70
  restores YHWH's Presence to the philosophical discourse, 79
  subtle, jesting humor, 80
Archytas, 41, 43
Aristotle, 3, 46–50, 53, 62, 81

"Basic Idea of the Theory of General Relativity in Its Original Form" (Einstein), 265n54
Bell, John L., 41, 42, 47, 64n25
Bentley, Richard, 185–86
Boccaletti, Dino, 66–67
Brahe, Tycho, 203, 225n6
Broglie, Louis de, 244
"bucket experiment," Newton's, 206–7, 248–49

Carnap, Rudolph, 271
Cavilieri, Bonaventura, 41n20, 61n20, 128n31
center of Universe
  arche as, 195
  comes into being ever-presently and omni-presently for Newton, 195
  Divine Logos as, 137, 195, 195n84
  location of Universe's sacred fire, 195n84
Christianson, Gale, xvi
Corollaries, to Laws of Motion of Newton, 165, 212–19
Corry, Leo, 11n10, 29

David
  on four-headed fountain of life, 12n15, 278
  on Hallelujah, 281n12
  on self-surrender, 277–78

300 INDEX

Delphic Oracle, dictum to "know thyself," 115n15, 279, 282n14
Democritus, 39–44
 on elements of which geometric objects composed as of 2D, 39–43
 as "most subtle of the ancients," 39n17
 Newton deeply respected wisdom of, 39n16
Dialogue Concerning the Two Chief World Systems, Ptolemaic and Copernican (Galileo), 116, 116n18, 127n30, 130, 135
 Galileo composes Divinity-centric cosmology, 134–35
 shows that there is only One Chief World System, 135
Dialogues Concerning Two New Sciences (Galileo), 116, 127, 133, 146–48, 150–51
 deepens Archimedes's ideas on gravity, 149–50
 distinguishes between bodies' actual and apparent motions under gravity, 143
 particles non-uniformly rotated under gravity, 148–49
DiSalle, Robert, 250, 251, 266n57
Divine Logos. *See also* arche (ἀρχή)
 associated with "the divine animating principle pervading the Cosmos," 30
 cause of bodies' accelerations under gravity, even as site at which gravity overcome, 185
 as center of Universe, 137, 195, 195n84
 comes into being in coming into being of all particles'—or—all bodies'—unchanging Presence(s), 111n3, 138, 195
 Flower/Fountain of life for Galileo and Newton, 137, 201n96
 as Greek name for YHWH, 30n59
 location of arche for Newton, 184, 215
 location of Universe's sacred fire for Newton, 195n84
 as manifestation of Divine Speech, 137
 as monist, materialist focus of Galileo's cosmology, 137n52
 as monist, materialist focus of Newton's cosmology, 192n74
 Newton's God, 192
 Newton's *One Certain Law*, 186
 as referent for Galileo, 135, 146n68
 as referent for Newton, 218n138
 referring to Jesus for early Christians, 106
 responsible for bringing motion and change into being even as also immovable, 215
 YHWH as, 105
Divine origin of reality. *See also* arche (ἀρχή)
 ancient Jews and Pythagoras on, 18
 Archimedes on, 89, 89n66, 100
 can be known as experience, 275n1
 comes into being Now, 18, 23, 89, 95, 107, 160n10, 189
 early Christians on, 284n20
 Galileo and Newton on, 136–37, 160n10, 189, 195, 248
 immovable place towards which all bodies tend under gravity, 134, 189
 monist, materialist focus of cosmologies, 18, 23, 89, 95, 107, 111n3, 195, 272–73, 284n20
 points of Tetrad symbolic of, 23
 site of all particles'—or all bodies'—unchanging and immovable Presence(s) as, 95, 174n38, 272–73

INDEX   301

Divine origin of reality (*continued*)
   site at which inertia comes into being for Archimedes, Galileo, and Newton, 248
   site at which numbers come into being for ancient Jews and for Pythagoras, 30
   site at which numbers come into being for Archimedes, 100
   site at which numbers come into being for Newton, 283n18
   as the unchanging and immovable Fulcrum, 80, 123, 232
   what Presently Is for Newton, 159n10
Divine Speech, all as his Presently spoken Name/Word, 30n59

early Christians
   All as manifestation of Divine Speech, Jesus's "I am," 105–8
   composed a monist, materialist cosmology, 107–8
   cosmology of, 103–8, 281–84
   four-pointed (wooden) cross, 284n20
   four Gospels that are also One Gospel, 284
   Jesus as "I am," and as the manifestation of the All/the Only, 105–8
   on Jesus's life's work of knowing himself, 282
   learning how to emulate Jesus, 282n14
   located the arche's presence Now, 106
   Plato's ideas deeply influential to, 115n15
   prophet deeply important to, 281
   referred to Jesus as the "rock" and as "the life," 201n100
Einstein, Albert, 237–73
   asserts that gravity manifests as curvature of space-time, 269
   attempts to purge Absolute Space and Time from physics but fails, 254, 262
   builds his cosmology on concept of frames of reference, 238
   composes entirely abstract cosmology, 251
   considers (discrete) particles and bodies to exist distinctly from (continuous) space-time, 270
   doesn't discover anything about gravity that Galileo and Newton hadn't already, 270
   doesn't recognize that bodies exist inextricably from their presently inertial motions, 238
   doesn't recognize existence of site of all particles'—or all bodies'—unchanging Presence(s), 221, 240
   doesn't see Galileo and Newton's true ideas on gravity, 247, 263–64
   doesn't see that Galileo and Newton were true philosophers, 246
   doesn't see that Newton had composed monist, materialist cosmology, 221, 240
   doesn't see that Newton would not have considered frames of reference to exist, 238
   doesn't see that presently inertial component of motion orthogonal to gravitational component, 239n3
   doesn't see that site of all particles'—or all bodies'—unchanging Presence(s) is referent, 239–40
   doesn't see that under gravity, bodies are non-uniformly rotated towards common center, 239

Einstein, Albert (*continued*)
    failed to account for inertia, 78n50, 248, 261
    failed to uncover relationship between existence and time, 272
    had intuitions that the Now was missing from his cosmology, 271
    happiest thought of his life, 265n54
    (mis)interprets Newton's Corollary VI, 263–65
    not a true philosopher in the Platonic sense, 221
    overlooks that bodies possess unchanging present motions and changing instantaneous motions, 239
    overlooks that Newton defined gravity as center-seeking force, 264n52
    overlooks Newton's true cosmology, 221
    sought knowledge of absolute but failed to attain, 237
    took Galileo to be forefather but didn't see Galileo's true cosmology, 246
Eliot, T.S., 273n73, 275, 282
Empirical Age, 221–22, 226, 252n28
Eudoxus of Cnidus, 45–46

Fahie, John Joseph, 113
Fitzwilliam Notebook (Newton), xv, 153–54, 184
"Foundations of General Relativity" (Einstein), 253–54
Foundations of Space-Time Theories: Relativistic Physics and the Philosophy of Science (Friedman), 249
frame of reference, 229–31, 235n22, 238, 267
Friedman, Michael, 249
Fulcrum

    All/the Only and, 80, 123, 151, 156, 167, 232, 240
    as arche, 80, 123, 151, 156, 167, 232, 240

Galilei, Galileo, 111–52
    appropriates Archimedes's cosmology, 83n61, 111
    as astronomer, 132–33
    on bodies generating rotating flower patterns under gravity, 135, 152n79
    composes Divinity-centric cosmology, 111n3, 134–37
    composes giddy, facetious cosmology, 123n25, 135, 150–51
    composes secret cosmology, 75n48, 114
    composes a version of the Gospels, 137
    cosmology of, 83n61, 160–65
    deepens Archimedes's ideas on gravity, 149–50
    devoutly religious Christian, 111n3
    discovers particle equivalent of system of bodies, 131–32
    as disciple of Plato, 114n15, 128n32
    as disciple of the "superhuman" Archimedes, 81, 113
    distinguishes between bodies' actual and apparent motions under gravity, 143
    on Divinity-centric Universe, in recursively self-similar way, 136–37
    on elements of which plane curves composed as of 2D, 127–29
    explaining the common center, 133–34
    on house arrest not mattering, 137–38

Galilei, Galileo (*continued*)
  on infinite cosmology, with systems being embedded within systems, 136–37
  Leaning Tower experiment, 142–49
  monist, materialist focus as Divine Logos's Presently spoken Name/Word, 137
  monist, materialist focus as the One Flower/fountain of life, 137
  on passing time being generated by bodies' motions under gravity, 134n43
  possesses egalitarian spirit, 127n30
  referent (One Chief World System) as Divine Logos, 135
  shares ancients' ideas on numbers, 127n30
  ship experiment, 140–41, 217
  on site of particles'—or bodies'—Presence(s) as cause of gravity, 150–51
  on site of particles'—or bodies'—Presence(s) as divine origin(s) of reality, 111n3
  on site of particles'—or bodies'—Presence(s) as location of Divine Logos, 111n3
  on site of particles'—or bodies'—Presence(s) as manifestation of absolute simultaneity, 134
  on site of particles'—or bodies'—Presence(s) as manifestation of Divine Speech, 137
  on site of particles'—or bodies'—Presence(s) as monist, materialist focus, 111n3
  on site of particles'—or bodies'—Presence(s) as unchanging and immovable *place*, 132
  on site of particles'—or bodies'—Presence(s) as unobservable absolute, 125n27
  as student of *prisca sapientia*, 75n48, 103, 113
  true philosopher in the Platonic sense, 115n15, 221, 224, 246
  under gravity, particles non-uniformly rotated, 148–49
  on Universe as a sacred text, 108n96
  on YHWH's fountain of life being akin to the Divine Logos's four-petalled blossom, 137n50
general relativity, 238–39, 246–71
  assumes that free bodies exist, 260
  explores gravity, 246, 252
  fails to account for inertia, 248, 261
  fails to explain Newton's bucket experiment, 248–49
  fails to relativize all motion, 250, 262
  incomplete theory, xv, 221n143
  Mach's principle, 254–62
  overlooks that bodies possess unchanging present motions and changing instantaneous motions, 239
  overlooks distinction between apparent motions and actual motions under gravity, 253, 264
  overlooks Newton's definition of gravity as centripetal force, 264n52
  overlooks that under gravity, particles are non-uniformly rotated towards system's center, 239
  principle of equivalence, 262–66
  principle of general covariance, 266–67

304　INDEX

general relativity (*continued*)
　unobservable, absolute metaphysics lies at heart of, 251
geometry, as a subspecies of mechanics, 166n21, 172n33, 228n12, 235n21
gravity
　Archimedes's ideas on, 84–86
　Galileo's ideas on, 131–37, 141–52
　Newton's ideas on, 186–201, 218–19
　Einstein overlooks Galileo's and Newton's true cosmologies, 252–53
Gregory, David, 5
Guicciardini, Niccolo, 7n15, 39n16

"Harmony of the Spheres," 28–31
Heath, Thomas Little, 43, 55, 58n13
Heraclitus, 30n59, 105n92
Hippasus of Metapontum, 32, 33–37
Hooke, Robert, 172, 203, 203n107, 244n13
Huygens, Christiaan, 112

"I AM"
　coming into being ever-presently and omni-presently, 107
　as the Name/Word; as the manifestation of Divine Speech, 137, 201, 228
　spoken by Jesus to refer to himself, 106
　YHWH as, 19
indivisible(s)
　of Archimedes, 56–57
　of Cavilieri, 41n20
　of Democritus, 40–41
　of Galileo, 127–29
　of Pythagoras, 24n43
inertia
　general relativity not accounting for, 248, 261
　origin of, 78n50, 248, 261–62
　particles' present motions as manifestation of, 78n50
inertial frame of reference
　concept of, 229–31
　Einstein attempts to relativize motion but fails, 267
　existence in the natural world, 231n17, 242n9
　Newton wouldn't consider to exist, 231n17
Isaacson, Walter, 237

Janssen, Michel, 250
Jesus
　as the center and focus of monist, materialist cosmologies, 106–8
　as the Logos, 106–8
　presently existing as the arche, 106n94
　as YHWH's son and his prophet, 281–84
John 1:1, 106, 108n96

kentron toi bareos (sharp point, center, or pivot of weight)
　Archimedes on, 73–75
　comes into being ever-presently and omni-presently, 257n39
　Galileo on, 135, 137, 137n52
　Newton on, 156, 182
　as particle equivalent of body, 75
　as particle equivalent of system of bodies, 132
　philosophers and physicists overlooked importance to Newton, 231–32
　translated into English as "centroid" or "center of gravity," 73
Kepler, Johannes, 203
Keynes, John Maynard, on Newton, x, 154–55

Law of Conservation of Momentum, Newton, 216

Law of Universal Gravitation,
    Newton, 165, 187, 203,
    209n118
Laws of Motion, of Newton, 165,
    209–19
Leibniz, Gottfried, 18n29, 63n22,
    166, 214
L'Hospital, Marquis, 215

Mach, Ernst
    appropriated Newton's term
        "mass," 259
    asserting that Newton
        considered Absolute Space
        to be absolutely at rest, 231,
        255
    assumed that Newton
        considered free bodies to
        exist, 259
    attacks absolute space, 231,
        254–56
    deeply influential to Einstein,
        254, 260–61
    ignores most of Newton's
        metaphysics, 255n34
    on Newton's Law I, 256, 258–59
    on Newton's reasoning, 231n16,
        255
    not recognizing that Newton's
        Principia was written in a
        secret code, 258–59
    obvious contradictions in
        his reading of Newton's
        Principia, 254–55, 259n43
    precise views as ambiguous,
        257n41
    on "the principles of the whole
        matter," 257
    proposes Universe's one center
        of mass as referent, 257
    strong empirical view, 254–56
    takes issue with unobservable
        metaphysics at heart of
        Principia, 254
Mach's equation, 257
Mach's principle, 254–62

Magnum Opus (Great Work),
    Newton's Principia as, 202
mass
    Newton's true definition of,
        83n61, 177–78
    Newton's true definition not
        recognized, 235–36
Maxwell, James Clerk, 240, 244
mechanics
    Archimedes's development of,
        72–80, 84–86, 87–88, 90–92,
        93–95
    Galileo extending and
        deepening Archimedes,
        129–52
    Newton extending and
        deepening Galileo, 186–219
    origins in Ancient Greece,
        47n36
metempsychosis (soul living on
    after death), 31–32, 31n63,
    115n15
method of exhaustion
    Archimedes extends, 57–59, 61
    Eudoxus develops, 45–46, 57
    origins of, 46n32
method of indivisibles (the
    mechanical method),
    Archimedes and, 56–57,
    59, 61
Minkowski, Hermann, 251, 267–68
(mis)reading the Principia, 223–36
    assuming Absolute Space and
        Time exists as abstract
        backdrop, 227
    assuming that Newton had
        authored concept of inertial
        reference frames, 229–31,
        233
    assuming particles exist as
        discrete entities, distinct
        from continuous space and
        time, 235n22
    assuming point particles exist;
        not recognizing Newton's
        definition, 234–35

306 INDEX

(mis)reading the *Principia* (*cont.*),
  attributing Newton with inventing scientific method, 226
  not recognizing existence of site of all particles'—or all bodies'—unchanging Presence(s), 226, 232
  not recognizing that exploration of arche lies at heart of Newton's cosmology, 228, 232
  not recognizing "Frame of the System of the World" as material referent, 228, 232n18
  not recognizing import of *kentron toi bareos* to Newton, 231–32
  not recognizing that monist, materialist focus of cosmology on unobservable absolute, 226–27
  not recognizing that Newton appropriated Archimedes's definition of the particle, 228
  not recognizing that Newton didn't consider state of absolute rest to exist, 228
  not recognizing that Newton had composed entirely materialist cosmology, 232n18
  not recognizing Newton as true philosopher in the Platonic sense, 224–26
  not recognizing that Newton wrote in facetious tone, 224, 235
  not recognizing Newton's true definition of "mass," 235–36
  not recognizing secret code, 224, 228
  not recognizing true meaning of Newton's four Absolute quantities, 228
  overlooking import of *prisca sapientia* to Newton, 224n3
  overlooking that Newton considered geometry to exist as a subspecies of mechanics, 228n12
  overlooking obvious contradictions, 229n13
  overlooking that under gravity, particles are non-uniformly rotated towards system's center, 234
Monad, 17, 17n26, 18, 19, 39n16, 159n9
monism. *See also* arche (ἀρχή)
  concept of, 3, 4, 9, 17n27, 39n16, 49n42
  concept at heart of all sages' cosmologies, 272–73
  introduced to Greeks by Thales, 5, 279n8
  Newton on, 5, 39n16
  proposes that all things are one, 4
  ultimate substance of, 4, 49n42
motion
  as "the most basic and essential element of physics," 6n13
  defining, xvii, 49, 51
  Divine Logos as Galileo's referent, 135
  Divine Logos as Newton's referent, 218n138
  Einstein's failure to relativize, 267
  father and creator as Plato's referent, 3, 115n15
  Frame of System of World as Newton's referent, 159
  One Chief World System as Galileo's referent, 135
  quest of ancients to locate unchanging and immovable referent to define, xvii
  site of all particles'—or all bodies'—Presences(s) as Archimedes's referent, 80

motion (*continued*),
  site of all particles'—or all bodies'—Presences(s) as Galileo's referent, 135
  site of all particles'—or all bodies'—Presences(s) as Newton's referent, 159, 175n40, 186
  Universe's single center of mass as Mach's referent, 257
  unmoved mover as Aristotle's referent, 3, 49
  YHWH as ancient Jews', Pythagoras's, and Archimedes's referent, 10, 79–80

Name/Word
  All as manifestation(s) of Divine Speech, 30n59
  of Jesus, asserting "I am," 106
  realized ever-presently and omni-presently for Galileo, 107
  realized ever-presently and omni-presently for Newton, 107
  as site of the Divine Logos's Presence in natural world, 107
  Universe as sacred text, One Presently spoken Name/Word, 108n96, 280
  of YHWH, translating as "I AM," 105

Newton, Isaac, 153–222
  alchemical name as "YHWH, the Holy One," 202
  as alchemist, 201–3
  appropriates all of Archimedes's and of Galileo's cosmologies, 83n61, 156
  appropriates Archimedes's definition of the particle, 156, 168
  bucket experiment, 206–9
  codifies ideas of Archimedes and of Galileo, 165, 179, 181, 185, 188–90, 198, 218–19
  composes Divinity-centric cosmology, 190, 194
  Corollaries to Laws of Motion, 165, 212–19
  devoutly religious Christian, 11n11, 103–4, 281–84
  distinguishes between bodies' apparent and actual motions under gravity, 218
  on Divine Logos as center of Universe, 195
  on Divine Logos as true author of Calculus, 215
  doesn't author concept of inertial frames of reference, 174n40, 231–33
  as elitist, 155n6, 160
  extends Galileo's ideas on gravity, 197–98
  Fitzwilliam Notebook, xv, 153–54
  on Frame of System of World, 186–204
  Frame of System of World comes into being in coming into being of Divine Logos, 157
  Frame of System of World comes into being in coming into being of four Absolute quantities, 159
  Frame of System of World as manifestation of Divine Speech, 191
  Frame of System of World as *material*, 159, 172n33
  Frame of System of World as the One ecstatic, blossoming Flower, 191
  Frame of System of World as referent, 186, 204–9
  on his four Absolute quantities, 94n73, 157–59, 191–92
  on his four Relative quantities, 169, 204

308   INDEX

Newton, Isaac (*continued*),
  on Galileo's cosmology, 160–65
  on geometry as *subspecies* of mechanics, 166n21
  on gravitational component of motion as orthogonal to presently inertial component, 198
  gravity as centripetal, or "center-seeking" force, 182
  import of the *kentron toi bareos* to, 231–32
  import of the *prisca sapientia* to, x, xvi, 7n15, 103, 224n3
  jokes on "experimental philosophy," 224
  Keynes, John Maynard on, x, 154–55
  on kinematics/the Calculus, 166, 214–15
  Laws of Motion, 165, 209–19
  Law of Universal Gravitation, 165, 187, 203, 209n118
  on light existing as a particle, 243
  on Logos as cause of bodies' accelerations under gravity, even as where gravity overcome, 185
  "mass," definition of, 177–78, 211n122
  on mathematical reality existing inextricably from physical reality, 166n21, 283n18
  mathematically nuanced Tetrad at heart of cosmology, 174n39
  on measured quantities and the Definitions, 176–86
  monist, materialist focus as arche, 167n22, 168n24, 169n25, 184, 219
  monist, materialist focus as Divine Logos, 159n9, 192, 194, 202, 209, 215
  monist, materialist focus as Frame of System of World, 159
  monist, materialist focus as God's Presently spoken Name/Word, 159, 191
  monist, materialist focus as his four Absolute quantities, 159
  monist, materialist focus as site of all particles'—or all bodies'—unchanging Presence(s), 156
  monist, materialist focus as the unchanging and immovable Fulcrum, 156
  monist, materialist focus as the Universe itself, 156
  On Spirals as originary text embedded within *Principia*, 166, 181, 214
  One Certain Law as Divine Logos himself, 186
  Principia not actually empirical manifesto, 165, 177, 223–26
  as prophet, 27n48, 202, 209n118, 281, 282n14
  on proving the existence of the Divine Logos's Presence in natural world, 208–9
  on recursive self-similarity being implicit to natural world, 181, 194n78
  relationship with Robert Hooke, 203
  on the Scholium to the Definitions, 167–76, 204–9
  student of ancients' sacred Temples, 195n84, 200
  True motions vs. Apparent Motions, 204–9
  as true philosopher in Platonic sense, 168n24, 169n25, 219–21
  Universe as his God, 156, 167n22, 174, 181n51
  on Vis Insita/gravity interaction, 179–84, 186, 210
  writes in a facetious, humorous tone, 175, 176n43, 186n65, 210, 225
Nietzsche, Friedrich, 4

Noah, wisdom of, 8, 195n84
non-inertial frames of reference,
    idea of, 233
non-uniform rotations
    under gravity, all freely falling
        particles subject to, 148–49,
        218
number(s)
    in Archimedes's cosmology,
        95–102
    come into being in coming into
        being of arche, 30, 30n59,
        100, 100n81, 127n30,
        129n33, 283n18
    in Democritus's cosmology, 44
    in early Christians' cosmology,
        105–6
    in Galileo's cosmology, 127–29
    in Jews' cosmology, 10, 11,
        16n22, 17, 19n33
    in Newton's cosmology, 166,
        166n21, 209n118, 214–15,
        283n18
    in Plato's cosmology, 127n30
    in Pythagoras's cosmology, 11,
        11n10, 16, 29–30, 34
    rational and irrational, 37
    significance of one and four,
        19, 20, 26, 116n19, 137n50,
        159n9, 167n22, 181n51, 202,
        273n73, 278, 284

"Ode on a Grecian Urn" (John
    Keats), xviiin10
On Nature (poem), by Parmenides,
    44n27
On Spirals (Archimedes), 61–72
    Archimedes develops kinematics
        in, 62
    explores dynamical generation
        of plane curves, 61
    locates an unchanging and
        immovable referent, 62, 118
    as originary text embedded
        within Galileo's cosmology,
        117
    as originary text embedded
        within Newton's cosmology,
        166, 181, 214
    shows curves possess
        unchanging present motions
        and changing instantaneous
        motions, 71–72
    treatise in which Archimedes
        solves mysteries of time, 80
On the Equilibrium of Planes
    (Archimedes), 74n44, 75n45
Opticks (Newton), 243
origin. See also Divine origin of
    reality
    Archimedes's word for of the
        spiral, 89n66
    on the concept of, 86–89, 96

Pais, Abraham, 78n50, 248, 254, 261
Paradise as Now, 10n8, 84, 115n15,
    123, 176, 277–81, 284
Parmenides, 44n27
particle
    Archimedes's definition, 75–76
    Archimedes's definition
        appropriated by Galileo,
        83n61
    Archimedes's definition
        appropriated by Newton,
        83n61
    Archimedes's definition not
        recognized by Einstein,
        239–40
    Archimedes derives definition
        from kinematics, 76n49
    as center of gravity of body, 73
    as center of gravity of system of
        bodies, 132
    dynamically generated in
        dynamic generation of
        trajectory, 75
    exists inextricably from absolute
        space and absolute time,
        94n73
    exists as of two dimensions
        simultaneously, 75

particle (*continued*)
    implanting Archimedes's definition into Einstein's cosmology completes it, 269–70
    Newton's definition not recognized, 234–36
    possesses unchanging present motions and changing instantaneous motions, 76
    present motions generate space and time in which equal distances and equal times exist, 93–95
    present motions more fundamental to than instantaneous motions, 76
particle equivalent of body, *see also kentron toi bareos*, 73–78
particle equivalent of system, *see also kentron toi bareos*, 139, 139n55, 188, 230
passage of time
    discerning, 85, 91n68
passage of time (*continued*)
    gravity responsible for generating, 85, 134n43
Penrose, Roger, 101n85, 263n51, 264n53
Philo of Alexandria, 30n59
philosopher's stone, 201–3
Philosophiae Naturalis Principia Mathematica (Mathematical Principles of Natural Philosophy). See *Principia*
physis, 6, 184n60
plane curves
    elements existing as of 2D simultaneously, 59
    generated in dynamic generation of elements, 60
    as infinite collections of indivisibles/infinitesimals, 60
    possessing both unchanging present motions and changing instantaneous motions, 71–72

Plato
    admires the human intellect for understanding the nature of numbers, 127n30
    Aristotle reacts against, 48n39
    on the composition of solids, 41–42
    on father and creator as "that which is immovably the same forever," 3, 115n15
    on first principle [ἀρχήν] of the whole, 114n15, 219, 257
    Galileo prizes the dialogues of, 114n15
    impact on both Galileo and Newton, 42n22, 115n15, 219–21
    influenced by Pythagoras, 32n64
    locates the arche's presence Now, 114n15
    on mathematics as appropriate for physical investigations, 48n39
    natural philosophical ideas echoing Pythagoras, 42n22
    Trinity of Transcendentals, 115n15, 168n24
    on true philosophers as devoting life to exploring arche, 115n15
    on vegetarianism and metempsychosis, 115n15
Plato's *Republic*, 114n15, 219–21
Pope, Alexander, ix, 165n16
Presocratics, 4–6, 39, 201
Principe, Lawrence M., 4n5, 49n42, 201
Principia, 167–219
    arche as monist, materialist focus of, 167n22
    codification of ideas of Archimedes and of Galileo, 165
    "commonly" read after its publication, 227n10
    composed in a secret code, xv, 155, 224

INDEX 311

Principia (continued)
  constructed much like a Russian doll, xviii, 156n7
  Corollaries to Laws of Motion, 165, 212–19
  Divine Logos as monist, materialist center of cosmology, 194–95
  four Absolute quantities at heart of, 159
  four Absolute quantities as secret code for Divine Logos, 159, 191–92
  intent was to prove Divine Logos's Presence in natural world, 209
  Laws of Motion, 165, 209–19
  Law of Universal Gravitation, 165, 187
  (mis)read as an empirical manifesto, 86n63, 165, 177, 223–26
  as more mathematically nuanced Tetrad, 174n39
  On Spirals as originary text embedded within, 166
  philosophers' and physicists' (mis)readings of, 223–36, 252n28
  site of all particles'—or all bodies'—Presences as monist focus, 156
  unobservable Absolute quantities at heart, 86n63
  written in a facetious, humorous tone, 175
principle of equivalence, 254, 262–66, 268
Principle of Relativity (Archimedes), 89–92
prisca sapientia ("wisdom of the ancients")
  exploring, 103–8, 275–84
  Galileo as a student of, 75n48, 103, 113
  Newton influenced by, x, xvi, xvii, 7n15, 103, 224n3
  Pythagoras as the first student of, 11
prophet
  central to Jews' and early Christians' cosmologies, 279–81
  Galileo and Newton considered themselves to be, 108n96
  Newton considered himself to be, 27n48, 159n10, 202, 209n118, 281
  Pythagoras as, 27n48, 281
Pythagoras, 8–32
  acts of logical deduction (mathematics) on the ancient Jewish sacred texts, 11, 279
  appropriates the ancient Jews' cosmology, 11, 14, 114n15
  on divine origin of reality, 18
  dynamical generation of space, Tetrad revealing, 22–27
  on elements of which geometric objects composed, 24n43, 38, 40
  first student of the *prisca sapientia*, 11
  Galileo and Newton as students of, 105n91
  of great importance to Newton, 7, 7n15, 174n39
  on Harmony of the Spheres, 28–31
  on the import of the numbers 4 and 1 to, 19n33
  indivisible and, 24n43, 39–40, 128n31
  on infinity and its presently being overcome, 16n22
  Monad and Tetrad as names for YHWH, 17, 19, 159n9
  monist, materialist focus as the All/the Only, YHWH himself, 12
  on music being number made audible, 29–30, 209n117
  not referring to YHWH by name, 17

312 INDEX

Pythagoras (*continued*)
   on numbers coming into being Now, in the coming into being of YHWH, 30
   on orderedness of number that is also overcome, 16
   Plato deeply influenced by, 32n64, 114n15
   as prophet, 27n48, 281
   on recursive self-similarity being implicit to natural world, 18n29
   on relationship between mathematics and natural world, 10, 30, 70n35
   student of Thales, 8
   studied ancient Jewish sacred texts, 10n7, 275–81
   on Tetrad, 20–28
   on vegetarianism and metempsychosis, 31–32, 115n15
   on YHWH, 12, 14–20, 32, 49, 51
Pythagorean crisis, 33–50
Pythagorean Oath, 12

recursive self-similarity
   allows origin to never depart from itself, even as it does, 18, 94n73, 95, 174n38
   concept of, 18, 69n34
   in cosmology of Jews, Pythagoras, Archimedes, early Christians, Galileo, Newton, 18, 71, 77, 107, 121, 181
   implicit to the generation of all particles' trajectories, 77, 121, 181
   implicit to the generation of all plane curves, 71, 76, 120
Relative quantities
   exploration of Newton's, 169–70, 176–77, 204–8, 222
   of interest only to the "common" and "vulgar" people, 169
   Newton's four, 169

relativity. *See* general relativity; special relativity
Road to Reality (Penrose), 101n85, 263n51, 264n53
"Rules of Reasoning in Philosophy," added to *Principia*, 224

sacred fire, as metaphor for the site of the Divine Logos's Presence, 195n84
Scholium to the Definitions, decrypting, 167–76, 204–9
Sciama, D. W., 78n50, 248
Science of Mechanics (Mach), 231n16, 254–57, 260
secret codes
   all sages locate arche's presence Now, 272–73
   ancient Jews' hidden wisdom, 10n8, 11n11, 12n15, 103–5, 275–81
   Archimedes composed, 55
   early Christians' hidden wisdom, 106–8, 137n50, 281–84
   help us to know ourselves, 279
   Galileo composed, 114
   Newton fascinated by, xv, 153–55
   Plato composed, 114n15, 219–21
   Pythagoras's secret code, 7, 8 12n13
self-surrender, 277–84
site of all particles'—or of all bodies'—unchanging and immovable Presence(s)
   as the All/the Only; as the arche, 79, 89, 156, 240
   cause of bodies' accelerations under gravity, even as where gravity also overcome, 150, 179, 185
   as divine origin of reality, 88–89
   Einstein's cosmology missing, 221, 240, 247

site of all particles' Presence(s) (*cont.*)
    the first principle of the whole for Newton, 167n22
    focus of Newton's Laws and Corollaries, 165, 245
    as Galileo's and Newton's God, 151, 156
    location of center of System of the world for Newton, 195
    location of Galileo's One Chief World System, 163
    location of Newton's Frame of the System of the World, 181
    location of Newton's sacred fire, 195n84
    as monist, materialist focus of Archimedes's cosmology, 79
    as monist, materialist focus of Galileo's cosmology, 82, 137n52, 151
    as monist, materialist focus of Newton's cosmology, 82, 94n73, 156
    as referent for rigorously defining motion, 80, 146n68, 186
    as site of the Divine Logos's Presence in natural world, 111n3
    site of God's Presently spoken (and written) Name/Word, 137
    site of the unobservable absolute, 125n27, 132n40, 168
    site at which number comes into being, 100
    as site of YHWH's Presence in natural world, 79, 82n59
    as unchanging and immovable Fulcrum, 151, 156
    as unchanging and immovable place from which we never depart, 95
    where inertia comes into being, 248
    where Newton's four Absolute quantities come into being, 159

Solomon, 276–77

space-time
    as abstract backdrop to bodies' motions, 251, 268, 270–71, 271n68
    as "the collection of all possible events," or "Here-Nows," 268n61
    gravity as curvature of, in Einstein's theory, 269
    invention of the concept of, 251, 267–68
    unobservable and absolute structure, 251

special relativity, 240–46, 269
    assumes existence of inertial frames of reference, 242
    explores particles' unchanging and immovable present motions, 238, 269
    explores site of unobservable absolute, 238, 242
    postulates underlying, 244
    shows that light exists as particle, 244

Subtle Is the Lord: The Science and the Life of Albert Einstein (Pais), 78n50, 254, 261

temple plans, ancients embedded wisdom within, 195n84

temple structure that contained a central fire, 195n84

Tetrad, 20–28. *See also* Pythagoras
    defined, 20–21
    at heart of Archimedes's and of Newton's cosmologies, 95n74, 126n29, 174n39
    influential to Democritus, 40
    points symbolic of divine origin of reality, 23
    representative of Pythagorean musical system, 28

314   INDEX

Tetrad (*continued*)
  reveals natural world composed of four spatial-temporal dimensions, 26
  shows all geometric objects come into being Now, 24–25
  symbolizing the relationship of YHWH to time, number, and space, 22
  YHWH as Author of, 27
Thales of Miletus, 5, 8, 15n20, 184n60, 279n8
True motions versus Apparent motions, 204–9
true philosophers in the Platonic sense
  "behold the things themselves, which can only be seen with the eye of the mind," 115n15, 220
  defined, 219–21
  devote their lives to exploring arche, 115n15
  Einstein not as, 221
  Galileo as, 115n15, 150n75
  ideal rulers of the Republic, 220–21
  "look at the absolute truth and to that original to repair," 221
true philosophers in the Platonic sense (*continued*)
  Newton as, 115n15, 165n18, 219–21
  "spectator[s] of all time and existence," 220
ultimate substance. *See also* arche (ἀρχή)
  study of physis as a quest to locate, 6
Understanding Space-Time (DiSalle), 250, 251, 262n49
Universe
  and all that is in it as a riddle, 155
  comes into being Now, in coming into being of All/Only, 9–10, 80, 107–8
  as a cryptogram for Newton, x, 154
  as the Divine Logos's bursting, ecstatic Flower/fountain of life, 280n11
  as God's Presently spoken Magnum Opus—his Great Work, 203n105
  as the One Sacred Temple for Newton, 201n96
  as sacred text, 108n96, 280
"unmoved mover," 3, 49, 51

vegetarianism, Pythagoras on, 31–32

Wallis, John, 55
Wheeler, John Archibald, 271, 272
Whiston, William, 154n4
Wootton, David, 113n12

YHWH. *See also* arche (ἀρχή)
  as ancient Jews' name for the arche, 9, 103, 114n15
  coming into being Presently, 10, 104, 106–8
  as divine origin of reality, 18
  as "everlasting," 14
  father and creator as Plato's name for, 114n15
  as four-headed fountain of life, 12n15, 19, 30n59, 276–81
  four-lettered Name/Word translating as "I AM," 10n7
  generating all time, all number, all geometric objects, and all geometric/physical space, 27
  as the generative "source," "origin," or "originating cause" of all things, 9
  the Holy One as Newton's true Name, 202–3
  as infinite All, and also Only, 16n22
  as "the One" who brought the Monad/the Tetrad to humanity, 27

YHWH (*continued*)
    relationship with Jesus, 107
    as the site of ultimate substance, 9
    as the site at which the concept of an origin is also always already vanquished, 18
    as "the source and author of life" in Judaism, 9n6
    as the unchanging and immovable referent, 10, 79–80

Zeno of Elea, 38–39

www.ingramcontent.com/pod-product-compliance
Lightning Source LLC
Chambersburg PA
CBHW050334230426
43663CB00010B/1855